Asian
America

*Chinese and Japanese
in the United States since 1850*

ASIAN AMERICA

Chinese and Japanese
in the United States since 1850

ROGER DANIELS

UNIVERSITY OF WASHINGTON PRESS

Seattle and London

Library of Congress Cataloging in Publication Data

Daniels, Roger.
   Asian America.

   Bibliography: p.
   Includes index.
   1. Asian Americans—History.   2. Chinese Americans—History.   3. Japanese Americans—History.   I. Title.
   E184.06D36   1988   973'.0495   88-5643
   ISBN 0-295-96669-6

This book was published with the assistance of a grant from the National Endowment for the Humanities

To the memory of
WALTER JOHNSON
(1915–1985)
Friend, Citizen, Scholar

Contents

Illustrations

1st Lt. Howard Y. Miyake being greeted by his sister

President Gerald R. Ford signing Proclamation 4417

The author briefing the Commission on Wartime Relocation and
   Internment of Civilians

Tables

Preface

Some twenty years ago at a meeting of historians, I noted that scholars who wrote about Asian Americans had concentrated on the excluders rather than the excluded. Because I could read no Asian languages, I assumed that I too would write "negative history" about the immigrant generations of Asian Americans: that is, history that recounted what was done to these immigrant peoples rather than what they themselves did. My writing instead has tried to synthesize the Asian American experience, examining and placing into perspective its essential role in American history.

My background and training have focused on United States history in general and immigration history in particular. As the son of immigrants from Britain and Hungary, I began to study the Asian component of our population when the accidents of academic logistics took me to UCLA. There, as a twenty-nine-year-old veteran with eastern and southern roots, I was trained by Theodore Saloutos, one of the pioneers of immigration history and a specialist in Greek American history. In an era that stressed consensus—and the notion of the melting pot is perhaps the arch consensual notion—I was more concerned with conflict and with ethnic and racial relations. In 1957 Theodore Saloutos suggested that I survey the literature dealing with Asian immigration and the reactions it aroused. My subsequent dissertation resulted in my first book, *The Politics of Prejudice*.

In writing about the first generation of Japanese in California, whose principal language was Japanese, I recounted what had been done to them, basing much of my work on the archival remains of their most effective enemies, the California Progressives. Later I wrote about the World War II incarceration of Japanese American people and about the similar treatment of Japanese Canadians. Because English was the principal language of this second or Nisei generation, these later books took account of what this second generation had themselves said and done.

Now, after a quarter of a century of dealing with the Asian American experience, I am attempting a different kind of book. My earlier works are monographic, based largely upon archival evidence. (A text, co-authored with Harry H. L. Kitano, *American Racism* [1970], presents a broad survey of California race relations and is, in a sense, a pedagogical precursor to the present work.) The present book, while it uses much archival evidence, attempts to synthesize the history of Chinese and Japanese in this country and to treat their lives as integral to the American mosaic. Such a synthesis is essential to a clear perspective not only on the ongoing, ever-widening Asian American immigrant experience but on the immigrant experience in general.

The timely and pressing need for such perspective has impelled me to write even though there exists as yet no dense corpus of scholarly books and articles based on expertise in pertinent areas of history, economics, sociology, anthropology, and folklore. This being true, is this book perhaps premature? Obviously I think not. It is important that an attempt be made now to describe and interpret the political and socioeconomic aspects of the Asian American experience, at least of its two oldest and largest segments. What such a broad focus sacrifices in detail, it gains in showing wider patterns and relationships. For example, I would suggest that immigrants from Asia had experiences parallel to those of their contemporaries from Europe. I would also suggest that, despite certain similarities in their circumstances, the Chinese American and Japanese American experiences have differed in significant ways, one from the other. Such perspective is essential to a basic understanding of the recurring tensions within our modern multiracial society.

The title of this book should not be misunderstood. When I speak of "Asian America" or "Chinese America" and "Japanese America," I am not in any way suggesting that the persons who comprised them were "un-American," whatever that means. By such terms I mean self-conscious, residentially concentrated communities of individuals, much of whose daily business was conducted in the language of the homeland and whose chief cultural impulses came from the society the elders had left behind. Many immigrant groups in America have gone through such a stage, but for most European immigrant groups that stage has neither been of as long duration nor has its periodization been so sharp and clear. The crispness of the periodization of both Chinese and Japanese immigration is chiefly owing to the imposition of artificial restraints in the form of immigration restrictions by the American government.

In my discussions of Chinese and Japanese Americans, I have tried to stress the roles of individuals and to show something of the variety of human experience that has existed—and still exists—among Asian Americans. The persons upon whom I focus are not, almost by definition, typical or representative, although I have tried, by use of statistics and tables, to provide representative data. All too often, those who write about "people without history" wind up writing history without people. That, at least, is not the case here.

This book will, I hope, cause historians and others to reconsider the broad patterns of the Asian American experience as they apply to our present and future course as a society. Although the major ethnic divisions in American life are and have been European, and although the major racial stress has been white/black, the Asian element in our history has been more significant than its place in textbooks and general histories would suggest. There is need for further scholarly work, and this book will, I hope, suggest a number of topics to be pursued. Much remains to be said on the role of Chinese Americans. A brilliant monograph by Sucheng Chan, *This Bittersweet Soil: The Chinese in California Agriculture, 1860–1910* (University of California Press, 1986), goes well beyond my remarks on the economics of nineteenth-century Chinese America. More such studies are needed. Also, my description of urban Japanese America before Pearl Harbor looks largely at Seattle and Los Angeles and draws on superior work by Frank Miyamoto and John Modell. More material is needed about the third major urban center of Japanese America—San Francisco—but no comparable study exists as yet for that city.

This book was written, for the most part, between 1975 and 1985. Two ongoing matters—the Vincent Chin case and redress—have been updated, and I have added to the bibliography some titles published as late as 1987.

I hope that specialists in Asian American history and culture will, in general, approve the result here, but this book is not written solely with them in mind. Intended as a catalyst, it is directed as well to historians and other students, professional and lay, of American life. If this book serves its purpose, much of it will be rendered obsolete by new work. This is the natural fate of any synthesis; in the words of Stephen Vincent Benét, I would hope that

> . . . the dry bones littered by the way
> May still point giants to their golden prey.

R.D.
May 1988

Acknowledgments

Since the genesis of this book stretches back to the beginnings of my academic career, an adequate acknowledgment of all the persons who have helped me is obviously impossible. Archivists and librarians at institutions all across the country have given valued aid, almost always cheerfully. There are a few obligations so pressing, however, that they must be noted here.

At the University of Washington Archives, Richard Berner and Karyl Winn not only provided access to their rich and well-ordered collections but also over two extended periods gave me a comfortable working home and provided both counsel and friendship.

At the University of Utah, Sandra C. Taylor, whose scholarly contributions are indicated in the text and notes, arranged for a quarter's stay that she and her colleagues made most profitable.

At the University of Washington Press, Naomi Pascal and her associates always made an author feel welcome, even if he were very late with a manuscript that kept expanding. Julidta Tarver saw the work through the press with good sense and humor. The editor for this book, Gretchen Swanzey, is a wonder who has left her mark on—and improved—almost every page.

Although I utilized libraries in three nations, the brunt of my bibliographic demands fell upon the librarians of my home institution, the University of Cincinnati. Particularly helpful were Daniel Gottlieb and his interlibrary loan staff and, above all, history bibliographer Sally Moffitt. Judith Austin of the Idaho Historical Society knew about and provided the kind of photograph I needed.

Parts of the research were subsidized by grants from the Foundation of the State University of New York, the Charles P. Taft Foundation of the University of Cincinnati and the National Endowment for the Humanities.

Students and colleagues at Cincinnati, and fellow scholars of race, ethnicity, and immigration from all over, patiently listened to papers, lectures, and my ramblings. Often, by question or comment, they helped me to formulate what I wanted to say. One of the latter, my dear friend Sucheng Chan, read it all more than once and provided help in many ways, even though she does not entirely approve of the result.

Finally—and most important—the historian and editor I live with ought properly to be listed on the title page. Judith M. Daniels has modified and clarified my thought in more ways than either of us can recall.

All of these persons, named and unnamed, are partially responsible for the merits of this book and, as the convention properly has it, are blameless for any flaws. I thank them all, and I thank, as well, the much maligned academic enterprise that has given me the training, the tools, and the time to do the job.

R. D.

Asian America

Chinese and Japanese in the United States since 1850

Introduction

The Significance
of the Asian American
Experience

According to the census of 1980 there were 3.5 million Asian Americans in the United States, about 1.5 percent of the total population. This was the first time in history that the Asian American population had amounted to as much as 1 percent of the total. Numerical incidence, however, does not necessarily indicate relative importance. The burden of this book, which treats systematically only the two pioneer Asian American groups, is that the immigration and acculturation of Asians has been much more significant in the history of the United States than their relative numbers would indicate. Examination of the unique experiences of Chinese and Japanese Americans gives a different and instructive perspective to more universal questions concerning the nature of the immigrant experience and the role of race and ethnicity in American life.

To examine the Asian American experience involves, among other things, looking at American history the "wrong way"; that is, from west to east rather than from east to west. Most American history, quite properly, focuses on the Atlantic migration and its consequences; the emphasis here will be on the Pacific. Even the question of the frontier—since the time of Frederick Jackson Turner, a crucial nexus for those concerned with American civilization—assumes an entirely different cast when viewed from a Pacific perspective. The standard approach views the frontier as an internal zone moving relentlessly from the Cumberland Gap to South Pass and beyond. But among westerners, particularly Californians, a defensive rather than expansive frontier psychology often developed. Although Californians dreamed of expansion, territorial and commercial, ever westward toward Japan, China, and India, they often felt that their rocky coastline should serve as a bulwark or dike against the human sea of Asian immigration which seemed to threaten their way of life. This defensive frontier notion—more akin to the attitudes of the Old World than of the New—is perhaps one of the factors that has made the twentieth century West, in many ways, an attitudinal trend setter for much of the rest of the nation. Californians and other westerners modified the fundamental American attitudes toward immigration nearly a half-century before the rest of the nation.

Unfortunately, much of the Asian American experience is what I call "negative history"; that is, for a significant part of their history in this country, Asians have been more celebrated for what has happened to them than for what they have accomplished. At certain times and places in the past, Asians and their children have been a pariah group at the very bottom of the ethnic escalator of American society, holding legal and social status even below that of oppressed American blacks. Today, and for the last few decades, this is demonstrably no longer the case. This remarkable metamorphosis in the image and status of the Asian American since World War II offers dramatic evidence of how rapidly and selectively the supposedly glacial folkways can change.

The treatment of resident Asians has been, in many ways, a barometer of the American social process. Their exclusion, by national and racial proscription, prefigured an even broader national and ethnic proscription of most of those Europeans who wished to emigrate to the United States. Similarly, the removal of the legal stigmatization of Asians during and after World War II prefigured the end of legal discrimination against the most numerous "nonwhite" minority.

When one examines the positive aspects of Asian American history—that is, what these people did rather than what was done to them—other instructive patterns emerge. The historiography of American immigration has been dominated by the symbol of the melting pot, the notion that America, "this great new continent . . . could melt up all race-differences."[1] Yet the persistence or, more precisely, the renaissance of ethnic consciousness, so notable in the 1960s and 1970s, has caused many scholars of immigration to question the entire concept. Past studies have dealt almost exclusively with European immigration.[2] Few scholars have ever supposed that

---

1. Israel Zangwill, *The Melting-Pot*, p. 179.
2. Two recent examples will suffice. Joshua Fishman et al., *Language Loyalty in the United States: The Maintenance and Perpetuation of Non-English Mother Tongues by American Ethnic and Religious Groups*, is an erudite and significant scholarly

race differences, as opposed to ethnic differences, would "melt" in a foreseeable number of generations. But the now widely acknowledged persistence of ethnicity comes as no surprise to the student of Asian Americans.

The various Asian ethnic groups in this country have remained discrete; they have not been affected by what some scholars have called the "triple melting pot," in which ethnic differences have been softened while the larger ethnocultural religious differences—Catholicism, Protestantism and Judaism—have remained.[3] There has been, within the American ethnic experience, no significant assimilation of Asian ethnicity into a pan-Asian bloc. Although Europe-centered scholars of ethnicity may treat "Orientals" as a cohesive group, what Asian American cohesion does exist has been largely imposed from without by discrimination. In terms of intermarriage, perhaps the crucial factor in traditional concepts of "assimilation," the various Asian American groups, until quite recently, have been highly endogamous; when Asian Americans marry outside of their own ethnic groups, the marriages are much more likely to be with non-Asians than with members of another Asian ethnic group.

This calls into question yet another assumption made by most students of American immigration, that immigrants from Asia have been somehow set apart from the tens of millions of other immigrants who have come here. One standard survey of American immigration specifically excludes "Orientals" from its pages because "the study of European immigration should not be complicated for the student by confusing it with the very different problems of Chinese and Japanese immigration."[4] Another treats Asians at some length, but insists that their history has been but "a brief and strange interlude in the general account of the great migrations to America."[5] In general, historians

---

enterprise able to make fine distinctions in terms of European ethnicity yet content to categorize all Asian American newspapers (almost 15% of the foreign-language dailies) as "Far Eastern." Ibid., table 3.1, p. 52. Andrew M. Greeley, *Ethnicity in the United States: A Preliminary Reconnaissance*, contains just two glancing references to an Asian American group in 323 pages of text (only one is indexed); its survey samples of ethnic individuals understate the incidence of Asian Americans (labeled "Orientals") in the population by some 350 percent. Ibid., table 4, pp. 42–43.

3. This notion was first put forth in two articles by Ruby Jo Reeves Kennedy, "Single or Triple Melting Pot? Intermarriage Trends in New Haven, 1870–1940," *American Journal of Sociology* 49 (1944): 331–39, and "Single or Triple Melting Pot? Intermarriage Trends in New Haven, 1870–1950," ibid., 58 (1952): 56–59, and was given wide circulation in Will Herberg, *Protestant-Catholic-Jew*.

4. Edith Abbott, *Immigration: Select Documents*, p. ix.

5. Carl Wittke, *We Who Built America*, p. 458. Thomas Archdeacon, *Becoming American*, makes a serious effort to examine Asian Americans.

and other students of immigration have shown very little sympathy with the excluders—those forces in American life which sought to drive Asians out—but have coupled this with very little understanding of the excluded—the Asian Americans themselves. They have insisted or implied that Asians were somehow outside the canon of immigrant history. Other immigrant groups were celebrated for what they had accomplished; Asians were important for what had been done to them.

This concentration on the excluders rather than the excluded has not been mere eccentricity. Part of the problem has been (and is) the relative paucity of written immigrant materials, such as "America letters" and newspapers. This is coupled with the unfortunate fact that few students of immigration are able to read the East Asian languages. As a result, all but a tiny handful of scholarly works have treated Asian immigrants as faceless, nameless groups, mere pawns in the hands of others or in the blind forces of the economy.

Perhaps even more important has been the facile, not always voiced assumption that Asians are somehow "different." It seems much more reasonable to make the opposite assumption: that immigrants from Asia are, first of all, immigrants. Until incontrovertible evidence to the contrary is offered, the generalizations that apply to most immigrants also apply to Asians. This latter assumption will govern in all that follows.

None of this is to deny that cultural differences have existed between immigrants from Asia and immigrants from Europe. Furthermore, differences have existed between immigrants from various social and economic strata of the same country. It is hard to imagine two more disparate immigrants than a Hakka peasant from Kwangtung and a Shanghai merchant, yet both were viewed as "John Chinaman" by most nineteenth century Californians.

I assume that most Chinese and Japanese were motivated by the same goal that brought the overwhelming majority of immigrants to America: economic betterment. Most came to this country during the period of great industrial and agricultural expansion between the 1850s and the onset of the Great Depression of the 1930s. Most did not have the capital necessary to set up a business or to buy a farm; most did not have the education or training to practice a learned profession or to enter one of the skilled trades. These generalizations would have applied equally to Asian and European immigrants of the period.

There was, apart from race, a major difference in terms of the labor force. Most of the immigrants from Europe stayed in the East, close to the ports at which they debarked. They became unskilled industrial laborers. The Asians, too, stayed largely in the region to which they came, but most of their labor opportunities were in mining and agriculture rather than industry. Within the labor force, then, the chief difference between European and Asian immigrants was that the former started out as industrial proletarians while the latter began as extractive and agricultural proletarians. It must be remembered that this difference was dictated by the nature of the region to which they came rather than by choice.

In diplomatic terms, also, the immigration of Asians to the United States has differed significantly from the immigration of Europeans. Immigration from Asia has involved the United States in disputes with Asian governments about persecutions, legal and extralegal, encountered here by Asian immigrants. The diplomatic aspects of Asian immigration have thus been far more important and complex, and have held far graver consequences, than have the diplomatic aspects of European immigration. Concerning the lengthy and difficult history of diplomatic relations between the United States and Japan prior to World War II, George F. Kennan has written:

> ... Throughout this long and unhappy story we would repeatedly irritate and offend the sensitive Japanese by our immigration policies and our treatment of people of Japanese lineage, and of oriental lineage in general, in specific localities in this country. The federal government was prepared to plead with local authorities in California and elsewhere for a recognition of the element of national interest in these unhappy problems of residence, of land-ownership, of neighborhood treatment; but it was not prepared to force any issues; and the country as a whole remained unwilling to recognize that the actions and attitudes of state and local authorities might constitute an important element in the creation of foreign policy.[6]

This persistent discrimination adversely affected official relations between governments. Even more important, American failure to practice the precepts of ethnic democracy did much to discredit not only American democracy but any form of democracy among the

---

6. George F. Kennan, *American Diplomacy, 1900–1950*, p. 49. Kennan plays down the degree to which anti-Asian discrimination was based on national rather than local policy. For an indication of the importance attached to questions of immigration and discrimination by contemporary students of Asian American relations, see the excellent historiographical survey, Ernest R. May and James C. Thompson, eds., *American-East Asian Relations.* I have commented elsewhere on what I term the "Eurocentric" bias of the *Harvard Encyclopedia of American Ethnic Groups:* see Roger Daniels, "The Melting Pot: A Content Analysis," *Reviews in American History,* 9 (1981): 428–33.

small but crucially important middle classes and intellectuals of Asia. Although, as Kennan indicates, disagreements between the United States and Japan were most prominent, significant disputes also arose with other Asian nations.

But the significance of the Asian American experience transcends its negative history. The United States continues to be a nation of immigrants, a polyethnic experiment unparalleled in human history. In the final analysis, the American experience cannot be understood without trying to understand its constant counterpoint of individual ethnic themes. If what follows is to have more than marginal utility, it must be read as part of a larger entity. The Asian American experience is not just a grace note in the broader American ethnic symphony; it is a minor motif that is essential to an understanding of the whole.

1.

The Coming of the Chinese

The initial period of Chinese immigration to the United States can be defined precisely: although individual Chinese are reported in Pennsylvania as early as 1785, significant migration begins with the California gold rush of 1849 and ends with the passage of the Chinese Exclusion Act on May 6, 1882. During that period, nearly 300,000 Chinese were enumerated as entering the continental United States. A little over 100,000 arrived between 1849 and 1870; another 100,000 between 1870 and 1877; and about 75,000 between 1877 and 1882.[1] Well over 90 percent of these Chinese were adult males.

Although the geographical focus of this work is the United States, any coherent study of immigration must be based, at least in part, on a binational analysis. One must examine both the country of origin and the country of relocation. Students of immigration have developed a few special terms to describe the prevailing forces that seem to shape the myriad personal decisions which, when taken collectively, constitute an identifiable pattern of immigration. The three basic terms are *push, pull,* and *means. Push* refers to the forces in the country of origin which impel the migrants to leave. *Pull* refers to the forces in the country of destination which draw the migrants to it. *Means* refers to those conditions under which the actual migration is accomplished, including the availability of transportation and each country's laws

---

1. Robert L. Brunhouse, "Lascars in Pennsylvania," *Pennsylvania History* 7 (1940): 20–30; for detailed immigration data, see Elmer C. Sandmeyer, *The Anti-Chinese Movement in California,* p. 16.

governing egress and entrance.[2] In addition, one must be aware of the previous and concurrent history of emigration from the area under study to perceive that area's propensity toward migration. It is customary to speak of migration *between* countries, but international migration almost always involves a particular geographical focus in both the country of origin and the country of destination. In the present case, the foci are Kwangtung Province, in southeast China, and California.

The history of emigration from China is long and complex. This work will focus on emigration developments that began at the end of the eighteenth century and that resulted in the creation of the so-called Overseas Chinese, who now number some thirteen millions. About ten million of these live in Southeast Asia, in an area the Chinese call *Nanyang,* or "South Sea."[3] Although mass emigration of Chinese outside of Asia begins only in the 1840s, as early as the 1790s some British imperialist writers were suggesting that, were the slave trade to be abolished, Chinese "servants" could be used since "the Chinese national character [was] favourable to the scheme of substitution." Ten years later a Royal Navy officer suggested the same notion, pointing out that Chinese came from the best cultivated country on earth and were "inured to a hot climate, and habitually industrious, sober, peaceable, and frugal, and eminently skilled in the culture and preparation of every article of tropical produce." In 1806 the first Chinese labor emigrants in the New World were brought to Trinidad, initiating what came to be known as the "Chinese coolie trade." This continued until after World War I.[4] As Hugh Tinker has shown in his

---

2. For a schematic sociological analysis of the factors involved in international migration, see Everett S. Lee, "A Theory of Migration," *Demography* 3 (1966): 47–57.

3. A brief summary of this complex topic is provided in G. William Skinner, "Overseas Chinese in Southeast Asia," *The Annals of the American Academy of Political and Social Science* 321 (1959): 136–47. Recent developments are treated in Stephen Fitzgerald, *China and the Overseas Chinese, 1949–1970,* and in Mary F. Somers Heidhues, *Southeast Asia's Chinese Minorities.*

4. Quotations from B. W. Higman, "The Chinese in Trinidad, 1806–1838," *Caribbean Studies* 12, no. 3 (1972): 21–44 at p. 22. The slave trade, as opposed to slavery, ended in the British Empire in 1807–1808. Persia Crawford Campbell, *Chinese Coolie Emigration to Countries within the British Empire,* is out of date. Although much literature exists, we badly need a full treatment of the coolie trade from China to the New World. Probably the best single work is Robert L. Irick, *Ch'ing Policy toward the Coolie Trade, 1847–1878.* Other recent scholarship includes Elliot Campbell Arensmeyer, "British Merchant Enterprise and the Chinese Coolie Labor Trade: 1850–1874" (Ph.D. diss., University of Hawaii, 1979); Tin-yuke Char and Wai Jane Char, "The First Chinese Contract Laborers in Hawaii, 1852," *Hawaiian Journal of History* 9 (1975): 128–34; M. Foster Farley, "The Chinese Coolie Trade, 1845–1875," *Journal of Asian and African Studies* 3 (1968): 257–70; Eldon Griffin, *Clippers and*

seminal book, *A New System of Slavery*, the use of East Indians as surrogates for Africans was to become much more important than the use of Chinese within the British Empire.[5] What is most significant for this study is to note that by the 1840s the notion was current in the western world that Asians were acceptable substitutes for black labor, and that Asians were actually so employed from Southeast Asia to the Caribbean.

The official Chinese attitude toward overseas expansion in general and emigration in particular was highly negative. This had not always been the case. At the height of the Ming dynasty in the early fifteenth century, vast Chinese fleets probed the Indian Ocean. One 1406 expedition included 62 vessels and a complement of 28,000 men. These voyages of exploration, which antedated those undertaken by the Portuguese Prince Henry the Navigator, were deliberately halted in the 1420s. In the next decade, Chinese were forbidden to go abroad. Had it not been for this change of policy, China might have "discovered" Europe rather than the other way around.[6] Despite imperial edicts, Chinese emigration into Nanyang continued steadily, largely from the southeastern provinces of Kwangtung and Fukien. It increased significantly in the seventeenth century, when opposition to the Manchu dynasty centered in those provinces.[7] The attitude of the imperial government toward émigrées is best indicated in a mid-nineteenth century statement by a Chinese viceroy to an American diplomat: "The Emperor's wealth is beyond computation; why should he care for those of his subjects who have left their home, or for the sands they have scraped together?"[8]

A highly developed ethnocentrism permeated every level of Chinese society. Even the few intellectuals with an orientation to the West viewed emigration in a one-sided manner. One such, writing in the early 1920s, felt that:

Consuls: American Consular and Commercial Relations with Eastern Asia, 1845–1869; Arnold Joseph Meagher, *The Introduction of Chinese Laborers to Latin America: The "Coolie Trade," 1847–1874*; Juan Pérez de la Riva, *El barracón: esclavitud y capitalismo en Cuba*; Marshall K. Powers, "Chinese Coolie Migration to Cuba" (Ph.D. diss., University of Florida, 1953); Alexander Chung Yuan Yang, "O Comercio dos 'Coolie' (1819–1920)," *Revista de História* [Brazil] 56, no. 112 (1977): 419–28; and Juan Jiménez Pastrana, *Los Chinos en la Historia de Cuba, 1847–1930*.

5. Hugh Tinker, *A New System of Slavery: The Export of Indian Labour Overseas, 1830–1920*. See also W. Klosterboer, *Involuntary Labour Since the Abolition of Slavery: A Survey of Compulsory Labour Throughout the World*.

6. Donald D. Lach, *Asia in the Making of Europe*, examines reciprocal influences.

7. G. William Skinner, *Chinese Society in Thailand*, pp. 1–27, describes one aspect of this migration.

8. As cited in Fitzgerald, *China and the Overseas Chinese*, p. 212 n23.

our emigrants have also established some real foundations of economic power. Furthermore, in America, Australia and other places that had no real contact with us before, the question of Chinese immigration has become a world problem. . . . Racial expansion is a matter worth celebrating; and because of this it can be proved that our race is just in its age of youth; it has not yet reached adulthood and is still growing every day.[9]

Those who left China, whether as political refugees or as seekers of economic opportunity, continued to regard themselves as Chinese. The very word for emigrant in Chinese means "sojourner" and carries the distinct implication of eventual return. Evidence clearly suggests that the overwhelming majority of those who became Overseas Chinese had no intention of emigrating permanently.

By the mid-nineteenth century, when statistically significant migration of Chinese to the New World began, much of China's external commerce was under control of western imperialists or "foreign devils," as the Chinese called them. The once mighty empire was approaching its final collapse, which would occur in the early twentieth century. An ever-increasing population, a crumbling internal administration, repeated humiliations at the hands of the western powers, the deterioration of the standard of living—what Arnold Toynbee calls "a time of troubles"—all combined to create classic *push* conditions that encouraged migration.

The *pull* was provided by the West, first by the British Empire, then by other colonial empires, and finally by the United States, or, to be more precise, by California. The *pull* effect of California is reflected in the Chinese ideogram for California, "Golden Mountain." California, which had been wrested from Mexico in the war of 1846–1848, was just starting a spectacular economic boom based on the discovery of gold in 1848. In 1849 perhaps 100,000 immigrants, predominantly male, flocked to California. By 1851 gold production alone was worth $55 million. This boom created a tremendous labor shortage—labor shortages are endemic to frontiers—and the highest wage level in the world. Common labor in San Francisco received $1 an hour; carpenters got $14 a day. Services were not only high, they were virtually unobtainable. Laundry rates ran as high as $20 per dozen items, and some Californians actually had to send their laundry (by sailing vessel!) to Honolulu.[10] It was this economic boom that first drew

9. Liang Ch'i-Ch'ao in 1922, as translated by Ssu-yü Teng and John K. Fairbank, *China's Response to the West: A Documentary Survey, 1839–1923*, p. 269.

10. Frank Soule et al., *The Annals of San Francisco*, pp. 253 and passim for economic data.

Chinese to California and, almost simultaneously, to Australia. Some intrepid Chinese went to both places. A recent historian of the Chinese in Australia reports that "one Chinese in Victoria in the early 1850s, known in the local records as Lee Hong, served as an interpreter and was a veteran of the California gold rush."[11]

The *means* by which Chinese crossed the Pacific was also exclusively western. During most of the nineteenth century, the Nanyang migration had been accomplished largely by Chinese owned and manned junks, but the migrations to the West Indies, South America, and the United States were made aboard western ships, first on sailing vessels and then on steamers. Precisely how the migration to California was financed is not known. Gunther Barth speculates that "the credit ticket system was the dominant mode," but this is not certain. Nor is it clear that the system "became partly a disguised slave trade, managed chiefly by Chinese crimps and compradores who lured artisans, peasants and laborers into barracoons and sold them to ticket agents."[12]

---

11. Kathryn Cronin, *Colonial Casualties: Chinese in Early Victoria*, p. 86. By 1857, Cronin reports, Chinese population was 25,421 men and just three women. Chinese in that year were some 6 percent of Victoria's population and almost 10 percent of its males. Two works specifically compare Chinese emigration to the U.S. and Australia: Charles A. Price, *The Great White Walls Are Built: Restrictive Immigration to North America and Australia, 1836–1888*, (a second volume is promised); and Andrew Markus, *Fear & Hatred: Purifying Australia and California, 1850–1901*. Robert A. Huttenback, *Racism and Empire: White Settlers and Colored Immigrants in the British Self-Governing Colonies, 1830–1910*, treats Australia, New Zealand, Canada, and South Africa. For the logistics of Chinese emigration to Australia, see Sing-wu Wang, *The Organization of Chinese Emigration, 1848–1888*. Anyone interested in Australian racism should begin with A. T. Yarwood and M. J. Knowling, *Race Relations in Australia: A History*.

12. Gunther Barth, *Bitter Strength: A History of the Chinese in the United States, 1850–1870*, p. 67. This echoes the 1922 argument of W. Pember Reeves, a virulently anti-Chinese writer-politician who served as New Zealand's first Minister of Labour. Reeves wrote: "The credit ticket system . . . managed as it was, chiefly by Chinese middlemen, crimps and compradores . . . became largely a veiled slave-trade. Labourers were decoyed into barracoons and virtually sold" (Preface to Campbell, *Chinese Coolie Emigration*, p. xii). Shih-shan Henry Tsai argues, "It is obvious that whether they came with their own money or under credit contract, the Chinese were free agents, as were the European immigrants" (*China and the Overseas Chinese in the United States, 1868–1911*, p. 16). See also June Mei, "Socioeconomic Origins of Emigration: Guangdong to California, 1850–1882," *Modern China* 5 (1979): 463–501; Harry T. Walker, Jr., "Gold Mountain Guests: Chinese Migration to the United States, 1848–1852," (Ph.D. diss., Stanford University, 1976); Kil Young Zo, *Chinese Immigration into the United States, 1850–1880;* idem, "Credit Ticket System for the Chinese Emigration into the United States," *Journal of Nanyang University* 8/9 (1974–75): 129–138; and idem, "Chinese Emigration: The Means of Obtaining Passage to America," *Journal of Asiatic Studies* [South Korea] 18 (1975): 215–30.

Available evidence would suggest that this overstates the case considerably.

As early as the beginning of 1852, Peter Parker, the chief American diplomatic representative in China, reported to Secretary of State Daniel Webster that "the favorable reports of those who have returned to China, having been fortunate at the gold mountain [California], seem to have imparted a new impetus to the tide of emigration." In July of that year, the vice-consul in Hong Kong reported to Webster that, "owing to the opposition contained in the message of the Governor of California and to the increased tax . . . they are somewhat intimidated from Emigrating at present." The reference was to an April 1852 message by Governor John Bigler, and it suggests that prospective emigrants kept close track of developments across the Pacific.[13]

Throughout this period, informed commentators consistently differentiated between voluntary immigration to North America and the Antipodes, and involuntary immigration to plantation areas in the Pacific, the Indian Ocean, and Latin America. This was a distinction that American historians began to forget in the late nineteenth century. An 1860 report of the House of Representatives summed it up nicely by differentiating between

> the "Chinese coolie trade" . . . a servitude in no respect practically different from . . . the . . . African slave trade [and the flow to] California, a Chinese emigration which has been voluntary and profitable to the contracting parties. The discovery of gold in Australia divided the emigration, which has since tended to both places at the option of the immigrants themselves.[14]

Certainly economic exploitation was involved in bringing Chinese to California, exploitation that created profits both for western ship owners and Chinese intermediaries. But similar exploitation has been a factor in most immigration to America. Passage probably averaged about two months and cost as little as $50. This sum was undoubtedly beyond the means of most migrants. Many borrowed money on a credit ticket system that obligated them to pay back a much larger sum. One British official in China in the early 1850s

---

13. Peter Parker to Daniel Webster, Dispatch 24, January 27, 1852; Hong Kong Vice-Consul to Daniel Webster, Letter, July 20, 1852; both printed in Jules Davids, ed., *American Diplomatic and Public Papers: The United States and China*, vol. 17, *The Coolie Trade and Chinese Emigration*, pp. 149, 157.

14. U.S. Congress, House, *Coolie Trade*, 36th Cong., 1st sess., House Executive Document 443 [ser. 1069], p. 3. Similarly, in a "public notification," dated January 10, 1856, Peter Parker wrote of "the 'coolie trade' in contradistinction to voluntary migration of Chinese adventurers," printed in Davids, *Diplomatic Papers* 17:16.

reported that for an advance of $70 ($50 for the passage and $20 for expenses) some emigrants were obligating themselves to repay $200.[15] Others almost certainly used the informal but longstanding rotating credit associations known as *hui* in South China.[16] Still others would have been able to draw upon family resources. What each of these enterprises had in common was the expectation that the individual who received the advance would be able to earn enough to repay it, plus interest, in a relatively short time. The mere fact that these informal credit mechanisms continued to be utilized by both legal and illegal Chinese immigrants well into the twentieth century is presumptive evidence that most creditors were eventually repaid.[17]

In California, Chinese quickly became an integral and vital part of the labor force. Between 1860 and 1880, Chinese were more than 8 percent of California's population; since they were overwhelmingly adult males, they were a considerably larger percent of the labor force.[18] It is impossible to calculate precisely how much Chinese contributed to California's economic growth. The contribution was clearly major, but it remains largely unrecognized in the historical literature. (See chapter 3 for economic aspects of Chinese America.)

While Chinese are relatively well known as miners and as builders of the Central Pacific railroad between Sacramento, California, and Promontory Point, Utah, their contribution to the growth of agriculture and manufacturing is little noted.[19] The wages that Chinese received were significantly lower than those paid to whites but were considerably higher than Chinese could earn at home. That large numbers of them made enough to return to China, presumably with some small savings, is demonstrated by a comparison of the gross immigration figures with the census figures. Although nearly 300,000 Chinese are recorded as having entered the United States before 1880, the census that year enumerates only 100,000. Considerably fewer than 300,000 individuals came, for many Chinese made more than one trip across the Pacific.

---

15. Harry Parkes, as cited in Barth, *Bitter Strength*, p. 68.

16. Ivan H. Light, *Ethnic Enterprise in America: Business and Welfare Among Chinese, Japanese and Blacks*, pp. 23–27.

17. For the persistence of this kind of emigration financing, see Victor G. Nee and Brett de Bary Nee, *Longtime Californ': A Documentary Study of an American Chinatown*, pp. 62–63, and passim.

18. In the censuses of 1860, 1870, and 1880, Chinese comprised 9.2, 8.8, and 8.7 percent of California's population. Of California Chinese, 94.9, 92.8, and 95.5 percent were male. Males were 71.9, 65.1, and 59.9 percent of the total population of California in the same censuses.

19. Sucheng Chan, *This Bittersweet Soil*, is a masterful prize-winning account of Chinese in California agriculture.

It can be safely assumed that the vast majority of all Chinese who came here were sojourners who did not intend to remain. Precisely the same can be said of vast numbers of other immigrants who crossed the Atlantic. The Statue of Liberty mythos of the "huddled masses yearning to be free" has obscured the fact that, from the seventeenth century to the present, a considerable percentage of all who have migrated here have had no intention of staying. Like most Chinese, they have wanted to make some money and go back home. Students of immigration term such migrants "birds of passage."[20] What differentiates the Chinese from most other immigrant groups is not their original intention of sojourning—that was common to many—but the fact that so many actually returned home. For Chinese in the second half of the nineteenth century, this was a majority phenomenon rather than that of a sizable minority, as it was for Italians and other groups.

Part of the problem was that Chinese encountered severe hostility in the United States, but a major factor in the failure of the United States to hold its Chinese population was the extremely unbalanced sex ratio. The development of family ties caused many immigrants to stay rather than to return. This could happen to very few Chinese. Until recently, males have outnumbered females significantly in all migration to the New World, but the prevailing imbalance among Chinese has been more striking than in most other immigrant groups.[21] As late as 1920, seventy years after the migration began, women numbered fewer than 10 percent of the Chinese American population. During the late nineteenth century, women were even less numerous. In 1880, for example, California listed more than 70,000 Chinese men and fewer than 4,000 women. In the rest of the United States, the imbalance was even greater; almost 30,000 men and fewer than 1,000 women.

Large numbers of Chinese women in California were prostitutes, many of them in a condition of semislavery. Women and very young girls were brought from China by brothel keepers and served both Chinese and Caucasian patrons. Prostitutes were a relatively high

---

20. Thomas Archdeacon has constructed a useful if somewhat overprecise table giving what he calls "remigration" rates for twenty-five non-Asian ethnic groups. The rates range from 4.3 percent for "Hebrews" and 8.9 percent for "Irish" to 66.1 percent for "Rumanian" and 87.4 percent for "Bulgarian/Montenegrin/Serbian." The median for his twenty-five groups is 23.5 percent. *Becoming American: An Ethnic History*, p. 139. The pioneer work in the field is Theodore Saloutos, *They Remember America*, which examines Greek return migration. For Italians, see Betty Boyd Caroli, *Italian Repatriation from the United States*.

21. Until after World War II, migration to the United States was heavily male. In the table cited in note 20 above, Archdeacon has computed sex ratios for the same twenty-five groups. The range is from a low of 46.4 percent male for "Irish" to a high of 90.2 percent male for "Bulgarian/Macedonian/Serbian." The median is 65.9 percent.

proportion of all women in gold-rush California, regardless of ethnicity. The traditional ditty certainly exaggerates the matter:

> The miners came in forty-nine,
> The whores in fifty-one.
> They rolled around on the barroom floor,
> Then came the native son.

Still, it must be remembered that in 1850 fewer than one Californian in twelve was female. The difference between the Chinese and the rest of the population was one of degree rather than of kind.

But while the overall sex ratio in California quickly approached the norm, the Chinese community remained predominantly a "bachelor society." After 1882 when Congress forbade the further immigration of Chinese, the demographic shape of the American Chinese community was further distorted. Already disproportionally male and with very few children of either sex, the total Chinese population declined steadily from that time until the 1920s.

While it was shrinking, it was also growing progressively older. The relatively few younger, native-born Chinese were always outnumbered by aging China-born graybeards. The result was that generational conflicts—a recurring theme in the history of American immigrant groups—were largely won by the graybeards. In turn, this reinforced cultural conservatism and certainly retarded the process of Americanization. When we compare the relative stasis of the Chinese American community, three or four decades after the immigration peak, with the flux that occurred in the more demographically balanced Japanese American community, at the same relative point in its development, we shall see some of the communal results of abnormal population distribution.

The Chinese community that developed in the United States in the 1850s and 1860s was both similar to and different from most American immigrant communities. The writings about this community have stressed its uniqueness, so it is important to note the ways in which Chinese American society resembled the kinds of communal living patterns developed by other immigrant groups. Most immigrant groups in the United States have been geographically and occupationally concentrated; the settlement and employment patterns of Irish, German, and Scandinavian immigrants, to name just three mid-nineteenth century groups, are each clear and different and have been delineated by scholars working in several disciplines.[22]

The Chinese concentration in California follows the typical

---

22. See, for example, David Ward, *Cities and Immigrants: A Geography of Change in Nineteenth Century America.*

immigrant group settlement pattern with its development of distinct districts or neighborhoods in which members of one or several ethnic groups predominate to the virtual exclusion of all others. (It has become customary in the past few years to call all such areas "ghettos"; that anachronism will be avoided here.) The reasons for these clusterings were and are both economic and cultural. Most immigrants must live in the cheapest possible residential areas; most have a natural desire to live among "their own kind," where they can use their native language, find foods to which they are accustomed, and recreate familiar, if modified, social organizations. In addition, the pressures of the larger host community usually encourage, and sometimes force, ethnically distinct groups to live in rather strictly defined areas.

From an economic point of view, most immigrants go initially into one of two kinds of occupations. First, the majority will be found holding those unskilled or semiskilled jobs most difficult for the host society to fill because of a combination of factors including physical exertion, minimal remuneration, and low status. In the United States today, such jobs are to be found in agriculture and the service trades: migratory crop workers in California and busboys in the industrial Northeast, to name just two examples, are likely to be unskilled recent immigrants. Second, a significant minority will be found performing services for and within the immigrant community as labor contractors, boardinghouse- and restaurant-keepers, and proprietors of petty retail establishments all catering primarily to members of their own immigrant groups.

The Chinese immigrants in the United States conformed to these patterns; what is distinctive about Chinese immigrants and their descendants in the United States is that the initial patterns persisted for so long. Within the first decade of the Chinese presence in San Francisco, for example, an immigrant community was formed in a shabby urban area that centered on the intersection of Dupont and Stockton Streets. The larger community soon came to call this area "Chinatown"; with a very slight shift in geographical emphasis, San Francisco's Chinatown has persisted to the present day, and similar Chinatowns have come to exist in most urban centers with significant Chinese populations as far away as Boston.[23] Eventually, Chinatowns have become prime tourist attractions, but that has been largely a twentieth century phenomenon. San Francisco's Chinatown and other

---

23. Nee and Nee, *Longtime Californ'*, pp. xxi–xxvii, for San Francisco's China-town today. For Seattle, see Doug Chin and Art Chin, *Uphill: The Settlement and Diffusion of the Chinese in Seattle, Washington.*

nineteenth century Chinatowns were squalid urban slums. Although much of the literature about Chinatowns treats them as uniquely filthy, a shrewd eastern journalist in the early 1870s found San Francisco's Chinatown "nasty . . . [but] not . . . as correspondingly nasty as . . . Five Points," perhaps the worst slum area in New York City.[24]

In the early years of the migration, the largest segment of Chinese workers was engaged in mining. In both 1870 and 1880, Treasury Department figures indicate that about 15,000 Chinese were so employed in California alone, representing about one-third and one-fifth of male Chinese workers, respectively. During the construction of the transcontinental Central Pacific Railroad, up to 10,000 Chinese were employed in construction gangs; almost all were laid off when the road was completed in May 1869. Working from the 1880 Manuscript Census, one scholar has tabulated occupations for almost 75 percent of California's male Chinese. Of this group about one-fifth were miners, one-fifth were common laborers, one-seventh were in agriculture, one-seventh were in various kinds of manufacturing, one-seventh were domestic servants, and one-tenth were engaged in laundering.[25] Since the census was taken in the spring and the greatest demands for agricultural labor were later in the year, this probably understates the importance of agriculture in Chinese employment. Outside of California, where nearly 30,000 male Chinese were reported, employment was less varied and was concentrated in mining, common labor, and the service trades.

Chinese workers soon gained the reputation among employers of being quick and adept learners and, even more important, of being dependable and not prone to strike. In addition, they also worked more cheaply than did white labor. In railroad construction in the later 1860s, for example, white labor rates were at least two-thirds higher than those of Chinese. Except for a few skilled workmen, most Chinese eventually were paid $35 a month by the Central Pacific; since food costs were estimated at $15 to $18 a month and shelter was provided by the railroad, a workman could expect to net close to $20 a month. Thus his original migration indebtedness could soon be paid off.

Early critics of the Chinese charged that they were "servile"

24. Charles Nordhoff, *California, for Health, Pleasure and Residence*, p. 82.

25. These and the labor force data that follow are from Ping Chiu, *Chinese Labor in California, 1850–1880: An Economic Study*. For a discussion of the quality of Chinese labor on the railroad, see the testimony of Charles Crocker in U.S. Congress, Senate, *Report of the Joint Special Committee to Investigate Chinese Immigration, Report 689*, 44th Cong., 2d sess., 1877, pp. 666–88.

laborers; most writers about the Chinese in America, whether hostile or sympathetic, have echoed that early charge. Essentially the modern argument is that they were really "coolies" rather than free laborers. A sympathetic historian, Alexander Saxton, has described the Chinese workers' unique handicaps:

> However the semantics may be deplored, the substance of the matter seems fairly obvious. The Chinese laborer could not escape his Chinese-ness in America. He had knowledge neither of the language nor of the law. In effect, he was at the mercy of the Chinese merchants, the associations, agents, contractors, who had fetched him over from Canton, who arranged for his employment, collected his wages, fed him, "protected" him, and determined when, or if, he would ever return to his homeland. . . . Chinese laborers may have been better off in the Sierra Nevada than their fellows elsewhere; but it is unlikely they were *much* better off.[26]

In reality, the notion that most of these workers were coolies (i.e., bound by illegal indentures) appears overdrawn given their geographic spread, the range of their employments, and their obvious mobility. Since not even the federal government could adequately record and control the entrance and egress of Chinese from western ports, one should not assume that Sino-American mercantile combines could do so.

Differences between the Asian and the European immigrants were of degree rather than of kind. With regard to strictures about the helplessness of ignorant Chinese in an alien environment, the same could be said about most non-English speaking immigrants. Saxton's argument, moreover, seems to imply an essential ineducability that I am sure he would reject. Like other immigrants, Chinese "green-horns" learned "the ropes" with varying effectiveness: some learned quickly, some slowly, and some not at all. It is true that Chinese immigrants wore their "Chinese-ness" on their skins, but millions of European immigrants carried their "German-ness," or their "Italian-ness" or their "Polish-ness" at the tips of their tongues for the rest of their lives.

As to the question of relative economic advantage, the continuation of Chinese immigration to the United States over decades, and the desperate expedients to which many Chinese resorted to effect illegal entry after 1882 make it clear that Chinese continued to envision something to be gained in the United States. A similar

---

26. Alexander Saxton, "The Army of Canton in the High Sierra," *Pacific Historical Review* 35 (1966): 114–52, at p. 151.

argument has been waged over the well-being of Negro slaves in the South, with some even postulating that slaves were economically better off than either free blacks or many white workers.[27] But in no recorded instances did free blacks or whites volunteer for slavery; they did not perceive slavery as an economic blessing, and many in slavery tried desperately to escape. The fact that, over relatively long periods of time, southern blacks wanted to go North and Chinese wanted to come to America should be a persuasive argument. None of this is to deny gross exploitation. Much of America was built by the undercompensated efforts of millions of immigrants, and few in our history have been as exploited as the Chinese worker.

But not all Chinese were laborers, and many who came as laborers did not remain so. From its very beginning, the migration included merchants and other entrepreneurs whose income came from skill and capital investment rather than from physical toil.[28] In addition to being merchants and labor contractors (often one individual played many roles), Chinese entrepreneurs were involved in agriculture as market gardeners and vendors. They were in manufacturing and mining, and they were owner-operators of retail establishments catering both to the growing ethnic community and to white customers. Census returns cited by Ping Chiu indicate that Chinese farmers in California increased from 8 in 1860 to 1,434 in 1880, while those involved in gardening grew from 472 to 1,783 in the same period.

Almost all of these immigrant agriculturists were involved in small operations: perhaps a majority of them paid cash rents to or sharecropped for white landlords. But as early as 1870, one operator in Sacramento County produced a crop worth $9,500, while in the same county ten years later three different Chinese farm operators had as many as eleven laborers in their employ. Similarly, while most of those engaged in manufacturing—largely in textiles, shoe-making, and cigar-making—were "sweated labor" working for a dollar a day or less, a distinct minority were either higher-paid skilled workers or petty industrialists. Census data for Chinese cigar-workers in San Francisco in 1880, for example, show almost 8 percent of them with wage incomes over $400 per year, well above what could be called a "sweat shop" level. This and other available data show that, rather than being an undifferentiated mass of coolies, Chinese immigrants

---

27. Robert W. Fogel and Stanley L. Engerman, *Time on the Cross*.

28. See, for example, Eve Armentrout-Ma, "Big and Medium Businesses of Chinese Immigrants in the United States, 1850–1880: An Outline," *Bulletin of the Chinese Historical Society* 13, no. 7 (1978):1–5, and chapter 3 below.

played varied economic roles in the early decades of their American experience.

Not fully accounted for in the above analysis is the significant percentage of Chinese (20 percent?) who were engaged in economic activities contained within the Chinese community. Some of these activities were legal (e.g., shopkeeping and running a boardinghouse). Others were technically illegal (e.g., prostitution and gambling), but were in fact sanctioned by both American and Chinese American society. It is probably impossible to document precisely the economic impact of intracommunal activities in Chinatowns, legal or illegal. What follows is an impressionistic account based upon both contemporary reports and later scholarship.

The prominence of these activities can be explained by the very nature of the bachelor society that was Chinese America. The immigrant workingmen and petty entrepreneurs wanted recreation that could only be provided within the ethnic community. The most popular entertainment seems to have been gambling—chiefly fan-tan, faro, and lottery, although by the turn of the century poker seems to have had a growing popularity. Opium rather than alcohol seems to have been the favored narcotic, but there is no way of knowing what percentage of Chinese used the drug. In addition, Chinese brothels and, to a lesser degree, opium smoking establishments, were frequented by whites. Just how many of these establishments existed is impossible to say; separate estimates for San Francisco in 1885 speak of 70 brothels and 150 gambling establishments of various kinds.[29] Without accepting these estimates as precise, it is clear that the socioeconomic impact of these establishments was considerable. San Francisco's Chinese population numbered about 25 to 30 thousand, but because the city was the urban focus of Chinese America, it must have regularly attracted many of the thousands of Chinese from the hinterlands.

Since all of these activities were both lucrative and illegal, it seems clear that police and politicians in the white community were involved in sanctioning and profiting from them. It is always difficult to document illegal activities, and the illegal activities of immigrant communities are particularly hard nuts for historians and social scientists to crack. Crime has been, as Daniel Bell points out, one of the traditional ways that urban immigrant groups have "made it" in

---

29. See estimates cited in N. L. Shumsky and L. M. Springer, "San Francisco's Zone of Prostitution, 1880–1934," *Journal of Historical Geography* 7 (1981) 71–94; and Ivan Light, "The Ethnic Vice Industry, 1880–1944," *American Sociological Review* 42 (1977): 464–79.

modern America.[30] As a distinct minority of the Chinese population, Chinese criminal elements were organized into groups known as "tongs." A sociologist recently described their activities during the early part of this century:

> Chinatown vice resorts operated under the authorization of rival syndicates of Chinese criminals. In 1900 a journalist enumerated thirty of these criminal syndicates or tongs in San Francisco's Chinatown. The largest tongs were the Hip Sing, the On Leong, the Bing Kung, and the Suey Sing. The major tongs had branches in every American Chinatown. Each tong operated its own whorehouses, gambling joints, and opium dens—or it sold protection to Chinese specializing in these illegal services. The tongs also claimed territory in which each insisted upon a monopoly of any commercial activities. In New York City's Chinatown, for example, Mott Street was reserved for the On Leongs while the Hip Sings claimed Pell and Doyer Streets. Each tong employed hired gunmen (*boo how doy*) to enforce its claims against rival tongs, to extend armed protection to member businesses, and to intimidate or kill hostile witnesses in criminal proceedings. The tongs also smuggled in women slaves from China to serve as prostitutes in their bordellos. Disputes between tongs often resulted in pitched battles or wars of attrition in which gangs shot up one another's bravos and the premises of local merchants. The last great tong war occurred in 1924–1927 between the On Leong and Hip Sing and their allies. In this war, fought in every major Chinatown, some seventy Chinese were killed.[31]

Over and against this lurid and dramatic account, which might form the basis for yet another sequel to *The Godfather,* the tongs and the tong wars must be seen as merely one aspect of the social organization of Chinese America.[32] Most if not all American ethnic groups have had some kind of organizational focus. For many

---

30. For an insightful comment on the perceived nature of crime, class, and ethnicity in American society, see Daniel Bell, "Crime as an American Way of Life," in his book *The End of Ideology,* pp. 115–36. All of Bell's examples refer to European ethnic groups.

31. Ivan Light, "From Vice District to Tourist Attraction: The Moral Career of American Chinatowns," *Pacific Historical Review* 43 (1974): 367–94, at pp. 372–73.

32. Eve Armentrout-Ma, "Urban Chinese at the Sinitic Frontier: Social Organizations in United States' Chinatowns, 1849–1898," *Modern Asian Studies* 17 (1983): 107–35, is a good introduction to the complexity of the social organization of Chinese America. See also Yung-deh Richard Chu, "Chinese Secret Societies in America: A Historical Survey," *Asian Profile* 1 (1973): 21–38.

European immigrant groups, much of the focus has been provided by ethnic or ethnically oriented churches. Since traditional Chinese religions have tended to be familial rather than societal, religion has not been a unifying community force. This is not true, of course, for the minority of the immigrant generation who were, or who became, Christians. For most immigrant Chinese, the family association or clan (that is, all those who had a common last name and thus a putative common ancestor), was the primary associational focus. In China the clan was a village association based on real rather than hypothetical lineage; the American mutation was necessary because, by his migration, each Chinese had broken the traditional village relationships.

In addition to being a member of a clan, each Chinese was, at least in theory, a member of a district association. These district associations, originally based on regional districts of Kwangtung Province from which almost all of the Chinese immigrants came, were eventually governed by an umbrella organization called the Chinese Consolidated Benevolent Association but popularly known as the "Chinese Six Companies." Headquartered in San Francisco, district associations spread over Chinese America.[33] Their role was essentially dualistic. On the one hand, they had functions similar to the kinds of immigrant mutual protective associations that flourished all over ethnic America. On the other hand, they were also the most important organ of social and economic control within the Chinese community.

In the first capacity, the Six Companies served as community spokesman, playing a role that would have been appropriate for Chinese consular and diplomatic representatives if their government had had much interest in immigrant protective activities. As early as 1853 the heads of the four established companies appeared as representatives of the Chinese community before a committee of the California legislature. During the most virulent phases of the anti-Chinese movement, the Six Companies hired prominent Caucasian attorneys to represent the entire community. In addition the companies performed many genuine protective and benevolent functions within the community: their agents met incoming ships and often arranged for the initial housing and employment of migrants; they organized medical treatment for the sick and performed other welfare functions; they helped to arrange the shipment of the bones of the dead to ancestral burial grounds in China; and they arbitrated disputes between individual members. In an age when government assumed none of the societal responsibilities of what is now called the

---

33. See Nee and Nee, *Longtime Californ'*, pp. 272–77, for detailed charts of communal organizations in San Francisco.

welfare state, other ethnic organizations all over the United States performed similar functions through both secular and religious bodies.

However typical its welfare functions were, the Six Companies came to exercise a degree of control over the lives of Chinese Americans perhaps greater than that achieved by any other immigrant organization, regardless of nationality. Although this control was surely never as total as some writers have alleged, it did affect significantly the life of almost every Chinese in America for more than half a century. Its chief beneficiaries were the merchants who came to dominate Chinese organizational life in America.

In China merchants had little prestige and authority; Chinese government was carried out by a gentry-dominated scholar official-dom whose ideology placed the merchant at the bottom of the social scale. But gentry did not emigrate; some merchants did, and they quickly translated their economic power into social and political power within the Chinese American community.

Although we know virtually nothing about the individuals who became the power elite within the immigrant community, scraps of gossip gleaned from the white press of the period plus community tradition make it clear that some of them acquired great wealth. It can be assumed that many came with capital and had ties with already established mercantile houses in China. While we have little precise data—and are unlikely ever to have much—it may be that there were proportionately more individuals of real affluence within the Chinese American community in the late nineteenth century than in any other contemporary immigrant group.

Merchants' income came from a variety of sources, including normal international trade and the purveying of exotic and indigenous commodities for the Chinese American community. Merchants also profited from the credit ticket system and from services performed as labor contractors. As the leading lights of the district associations, the merchants used the associations to ensure that individuals not only settled their debts but paid their share for the support of the Chinese American welfare system. Every Chinese who returned to China was to be checked at the dock to make sure his debts had been paid. In addition, each returnee was assessed a "tax" to support the welfare functions of the district associations. While there is no reason to suppose that this system of "taxation" was 100 percent effective, its continued functioning suggests that it was more than marginally effective. Since the overwhelming number of Chinese in America were sojourners who wanted to return to China, any system affecting that return was an ideal mechanism for social control.

Parallel to this "establishment" social organization, there developed an "antiestablishment" social organization centered around the tongs. The tongs were secret societies as opposed to the public district associations. In China secret societies had been the traditional way to form an illegal opposition to the establishment since at least the fourteenth century. The district associations were universal; every Chinese immigrant in America, at least in theory, belonged to one. The tongs were particularistic; no one knows how many Chinese Americans belonged. The tongs seem to have been patterned upon—and may have had some direct relations with—the Triad Society, an anti-Manchu, antiforeign secret society that had arisen in Kwangtung. Since, in China, organized political opposition was subversion, the secret societies had both a criminal and a political function, as some revolutionary movements in the West have had. Because Chinese were debarred from a role in American political life, the criminal aspect of the tongs became paramount, although it is also clear that they played an antiestablishment political role within Chinese America.

Eventually some merchants managed to gain membership and influence in some tongs, and some tong leaders gained respectability within the establishment. Also the traditional antiestablishment character of the secret societies was reasserted after 1900 in America, when Sun Yat-sen's revolutionary movement against the Manchu dynasty found its chief support not among the Chinese Americans in the establishment district associations but in the antiestablishment tongs. It also proved more expedient to support a revolutionary movement through a secret organization than through one essentially public.

Although the overwhelming majority of the first generation of Chinese in the United States was part of the socioeconomic nexus just described, from the very outset the lives of a few individuals were shaped by an entirely different pattern. Most of these were Chinese youths who came or were sent to the United States for an education. Recruited at first by missionaries and later by the Chinese government, they were to play an important part in the development of China.[34]

The first and one of the most interesting Chinese graduates of an American college was Yung Wing.[35] Born in Southeast China near

---

34. Y. C. Wang, *Chinese Intellectuals and the West, 1872–1949,* examines in detail Chinese educated in the United States, Japan, and Europe.

35. The account of Yung is drawn chiefly from his autobiography, *My Life in China and America,* and from Edmund H. Worthy, Jr., "Yung Wing in America," *Pacific Historical Review* 39 (1965): 265–87; the quotation below is at p. 283. See also Tsai, *Overseas Chinese,* pp. 38–43, 46–53 and passim. For biographical sketches, see K. S. Latourette in *Dictionary of American Biography* 20:638–39, and Thomas E. LaFargue in Hummel's *Eminent Chinese of the Ching Period,* pp. 402–05. For a contemporary Chinese view, see William Hung, "Huang Tsun-hsien's Poem 'The

Macao in 1828, he attended a missionary school in Hong Kong and arrived in America in 1847. Three years later he entered Yale College and received his degree in 1854. In the meantime he had joined a Christian church, and on October 30, 1852, he became a naturalized citizen of the United States.

After graduation Yung Wing was involved in sizable business transactions in both the United States and China. Between 1863 and 1881 he performed commercial, educational, and diplomatic missions for the Chinese government in America, most notably the celebrated Chinese Educational Mission of 1872–1881 which brought 120 young men to Connecticut. Yung Wing was codirector of this mission. He was also assistant minister to the United States from 1875–1881. In 1875 he married an American woman, Mary L. Kellogg, in a Christian ceremony in Connecticut.

After 1881 Yung Wing was out of favor with the Chinese government and held no more official positions, although he continued to be involved in Sino-American commercial transactions. In 1898, again in China, he applied to the American minister, as an American citizen, for assistance. The upshot of this application was the nullification of his citizenship. Secretary of State John Sherman wrote to the American minister:

> Inasmuch as Yung Wing appears to have been granted his certificate of naturalization previous to the passage of the acts prohibiting Chinese naturalization, a refusal to admit now his right to privileges which he has apparently exercised for many years [Yung had voted regularly in American elections] would on its face seem unjust and without warrant. Nevertheless, in view of the construction placed upon the naturalization laws of the United States by our highest courts, the Department does not feel that it can properly recognize him as a citizen of the United States.

Yung Wing remained in China until 1902, when he returned to the United States. Although his reentry was illegal under American law (one scholar has reported that no record of his arrival appears in immigration records), he lived in Connecticut until his death in 1912. His life would seem to demonstrate that some Chinese, from the very first, did manage to "assimilate" into American life. Arguments about

Closure of the Educational Mission in America,'" Harvard Journal of Asiatic Studies 18 (1955): 50–73. For an account of other early Chinese students in the United States, see Thomas E. LaFargue, China's First Hundred. A contemporary American account is James L. Bowen, "Yung Wing and His Work," Scribner's Monthly Magazine 10 (1875): 106–08.

the "unassimilability," crucial to the Chinese exclusion movement and echoed by many scholars, seem clearly untenable. In Yung Wing's case at least, the failure was not Chinese but American. Although attempts at acculturation were made by only a tiny minority of Chinese, they were made.[36] To understand the reasons for both their relative infrequency and their lack of success, we must turn from an examination of Chinese to an examination of Americans.

---

36. Some of Yung Wing's charges had similar biographies, and this early "brain drain" was one of the causes of the discontinuance of the mission in 1881. According to Wang, "In violation of the mission's regulations, between five and ten students either remained in the United States or returned there soon afterwards. These students violated another regulation by marrying American girls and settling down in the United States." The stated Chinese government objection to intermarriage (1910) was pragmatic rather than racial. "Recently, students in Japan and Western countries have married foreign girls. While there is no good reason to prohibit intermarriages as practiced by ordinary people, in the case of students the disadvantages are very serious. First, with a family burden on him, a student can hardly pay as much attention to his studies. Second, since foreign girls are accustomed to luxuries, a student with large family expenses would have difficulty meeting his tuition fees. Third, a student with a foreign wife tends to become an expatriate, in which case he would not serve China even if he had talent. . . . Hence all students abroad must be prohibited from becoming engaged to or marrying foreign girls" (Wang, *Chinese Intellectuals*, pp. 45, 58).

2.

The Anti-Chinese Movement

R eform movements have been crucial to American life. It is possible, although no longer fashionable, to treat all American history as one grand reform movement. Those who write of reformers and reform movements usually do so in praise rather than criticism, but another spirit persists in which reform is viewed not in celebration but with jaundice. In that mood, three generations ago, John Chamberlain wrote that those who spoke of patriotism as the last resort of every scoundrel had not considered seriously enough the possibilities of reform.[1]

While it is certainly true that many of the goals of American reform or protest movements—such as the abolition of slavery and the extension of suffrage—can be viewed as struggles by the party of humanity, many other American reform movements—such as prohibition and the resistance to Darwinism—have been linked to relatively narrow, obscurantist, and essentially anti-intellectual elements in our society. In practice, of course, the division has been less than polar. Many if not most reformers and reform movements have partaken of both traditions. Nowhere, perhaps, is this ambiguous tendency more apparent than in the movement for immigration restriction, particularly in its first successful crusade, the anti-Chinese movement.

Immigration restriction initially was a movement supported by workers and their organizations and opposed by the employers of labor and the associations that spoke for them. Labor leaders from

---

1. John Chamberlain, *Farewell to Reform.*

Dennis Kearney through Samuel Gompers, and almost all of the leaders of American socialism, insisted that Chinese be kept out, sent home, and denied citizenship. Labor justified its anti-immigrant attitudes chiefly by denying the equal humanity of those it sought to exclude or expel. Some of the most attractive figures in the history of nineteenth century reform, such as Washington Gladden, had a blind spot insofar as the humanity of Chinese was concerned. Intellectuals from Ralph Waldo Emerson to E. A. Ross, politicians from John Quincy Adams to Theodore Roosevelt, all denied to Chinese most of the characteristics and attributes essential to humanity, or at least to white American humanity. Even those Protestant missionary clergy, who were in the late nineteenth century almost the sole public defenders of the Chinese, were distinctly halfhearted in their defense, often speaking of Chinese as a lesser evil to irredeemable, rowdy, and prolific Roman-Catholic Irish.[2]

Few reform movements in American life have triumphed as decisively as did the anti-Chinese movement: few reform movements now seem to contemporaries to be so grounded in absurdity. The movement is thus easy to denigrate and difficult to understand: but to understand the history not only of Chinese America but of all Asian America, it is necessary to understand not only the movement's now-obvious fallacies but also why it triumphed.

Four historians have treated the anti-Chinese movement at length. In 1909 Mary Roberts Coolidge had nothing but contempt for the movement and its leaders. Thirty years later Elmer C. Sandmeyer examined the movement in great detail with the objectivity characteristic of the social sciences between the wars. Thirty years after that in 1969 Stuart C. Miller, in an intellectual history, demonstrated conclusively that anti-Chinese prejudice was a national rather than a regional phenomenon and was linked to the larger racism disfiguring American life. In 1971 Alexander P. Saxton, a historian broadly sympathetic to the aims of labor but repelled by the racism endemic to it, gave us our most comprehensive picture of the movement.[3]

---

2. For a summary of Protestant attitudes, see Robert Seager, "Some Denominational Reactions to Chinese Immigration to California, 1856–1892," *Pacific Historical Review* 28: (1959): 49–66. This topic needs further explication. Seager understates the economic and class bias of most clergy, ignores anti-Chinese Protestant leaders, and magnifies the anti-Chinese role of the Catholic clergy.

3. Mary Roberts Coolidge, *Chinese Immigration;* Elmer C. Sandmeyer, *The Anti-Chinese Movement in California;* Stuart Creighton Miller, *The Unwelcome Immigrant: The American Image of the Chinese, 1785–1882;* and Alexander Saxton, *The Indispensable Enemy: Labor and the Anti-Chinese Movement in California.* I have evaluated all of the above at greater length in "American Historians and East Asian

From the point of view of the present volume, that of Asian America in general and Chinese and Japanese America in particular, none of these studies is entirely satisfactory because none focuses primarily on Asians. All treat the excluders rather than the excluded.[4] From the consciously tendentious point of view of this work, the anti-Chinese movement is particularly significant for two reasons: it shaped decisively the growth of Chinese America, and it provided a prophetic prologue to the anti-Japanese movement of the next century. From the larger point of view of United States history, perhaps its greatest significance is that it provided the first of many examples of overt ethnic discrimination in our immigration statutes.

The America to which Chinese came in 1849 was a nation in which both racism and nativism had become endemic. Two major aspects of the development of American racism involved the dispossession of the American Indian and the importation and enslavement of Africans and their descendants. Although the Declaration of Independence had insisted that "all men are created equal, that they are endowed by their Creator with certain unalienable rights," Jefferson and most of his fellow white Americans assigned somewhat less than human status to Africans and American Indians.

By the 1840s, many Americans were making distinctions within the white race in opposing immigration from Ireland and Germany. Historians have called such discrimination "nativism." John Higham, one of our premier historians, defines nativism as "intense opposition to an internal minority on the grounds of its foreign (i.e., 'un-American') connections."[5] In the eastern United States the nativism of the 1840s and 1850s manifested itself in many ways. Organized and violent anti-Catholicism, which included the burning of an Ursuline convent outside of Boston in 1834 and the destruction of many Catholic churches over the next two decades, was just one of its unsavory features.

On the political level, nativist sentiment in Massachusetts, New York, and other eastern coastal states, prompted the agitation for and passage of state laws that sought to stem the rising tide of European

---

Immigrants," *Pacific Historical Review* 43: (1974)448–72, reprinted in Norris Hundley, Jr., ed., *The Asian American,* and I have commented on Sandmeyer in my Preface to the 1973 reprint edition of *The Anti-Chinese Movement.*

4. For an elaboration of this point, see Roger Daniels, "Westerners from the East: Oriental Immigrants Reappraised," *Pacific Historical Review* 35 (1966): 373–83.

5. The classic statement is John Higham, *Strangers in the Land.* For a recent view that nativism is not merely a phenomenon of the United States, see Howard Palmer, *Patterns of Prejudice: A History of Nativism in Alberta.* For a contrary view, see Lovell C. Clark, "Nativism—or Just Plain Prejudice," *Acadiensis* 10 (1980): 163–71.

immigration. But the Supreme Court of the United States, in a decision that would play a major role in shaping the history of Asian America, ruled in the *Passenger Cases* of 1849 that immigration was, constitutionally, foreign commerce, and therefore could be limited only by act of Congress, since the Constitution assigned to that body exclusive and preemptive power "to regulate commerce with foreign nations."[6] Organized eastern nativism next went through an essentially political phase with the growth of militant anti-Catholic, antiforeign organizations such as the Order of the Star Spangled Banner, from which stemmed the American party (often called the Know Nothing party) of the mid-1850s.

The major stated aim of nativist politicians in the 1850s was to curb foreign influence in American life. They proposed to extend the period required for naturalization to twenty-one years (from seven) and to make American birth a prerequisite for holding most elective and appointive offices at all levels of government. The support for such proposals, while significant, was never broad enough even to force a vote in Congress.[7] During the Civil War, immigrants demonstrated their loyalty by fighting in both the Union and Confederate armies, and nativism as an organized political movement virtually disappeared for a time, although the attitudes that had fueled it remained.

The Americans who poured into California after 1848 brought all of these attitudes with them, but because of the special conditions there, the foci of nativist-racist antagonism were often quite different. Blacks, traditionally the chief target of American racism, were not very numerous in gold-rush California, which entered the Union in 1850 as a "free" state. Yet, as Rudolph Lapp and other researchers have demonstrated, California's blacks had to struggle to gain even a modicum of civil rights.[8] American Indians remained a prime target; in fact California's Indians fared even worse than did most native Americans. Some small tribes, such as the Yahi, were simply exterminated; others were herded into squalid reservations (the "Indian reservation," as opposed to a constantly shrinking "Indian territory" or "Indian nations," was invented for California Indians); many

---

6. 48 *U.S.* 283 (1849).

7. Ray A. Billington, *The Protestant Crusade, 1800–1860*, remains the best study of early nineteenth century American nativism.

8. For the early history of blacks in California, see Rudolph M. Lapp, *Blacks in Gold Rush California*. For a historiographical overview, see Lawrence B. DeGraaf, "Recognition, Racism, and Reflections on the Writing of Western Black History," *Pacific Historical Review* 44 (1975): 22–51.

individuals were arrested for "vagrancy" and were sold into virtual slavery.[9]

In this treatment, the Americans merely followed precedents established by the *Californios,* as the Spanish Mexicans who had settled California called themselves. But the Californios themselves became targets for American nativist discrimination. In theory, under the Treaty of Guadalupe Hidalgo (1848) which settled the Mexican-American War, Californios were entitled to full rights as American citizens, but in fact they soon became outcasts in what had been their own land.[10] Similar mistreatment was experienced by immigrant gold seekers from Latin America, chiefly those from Mexico and Chile.

All of these groups were perceived by most of the Americans in California as being nonwhite. Chinese and other Asians fit nicely into this category. One noteworthy side effect of this preoccupation with color prejudice was that it tended to "promote" the status of all whites. Immigrant Catholics and Jews probably encountered less prejudice in California and other far-western states than they did in the East. Most commentators report that the first Chinese migrants to California were welcomed, but they rarely describe the distinctly patronizing tone of that welcome. In August 1850, for example, Chinese were allowed to participate in civic ceremonies in San Francisco, their colorful costumes making "a fine and pleasing appearance." Their exotic novelty soon wore off, however, and that welcome turned into overt hostility. An 1850 state tax on "foreign miners" had been aimed at Latin Americans, but soon Chinese miners paid the bulk of the tax, which netted the state over $100,000 annually and was a major segment of state income well into the 1860s.

By 1852 American miners in California felt that the presence of large numbers of low-paid Chinese was reducing their wages. Numerous mass meetings in the mining districts passed resolutions of protest against "unfair" competition. The language of these resolutions was a mixture of racial and class antagonism, the hallmark of workingmen's opposition to immigrants:

> It is the duty of the miners to take the matter into their own hands [and] erect such barriers as shall be sufficient to check this asiatic inundation. . . . The Capitalists . . . who are encouraging or engaged in the importation of these burlesques on humanity would crown

---

9. For Indians in California generally, see Robert F. Heiser and M. A. Whipple, eds., *The California Indians: A Source Book;* for the Yahi, see Theodora Kroeber, *Ishi in Two Worlds.*

10. Leonard Pitt, *The Decline of the Californios,* is the standard treatment.

their ships with the long tailed, horned and cloven-hoofed inhabitants of the infernal regions [if they could make a profit on it].[11]

The threat to take matters into their own hands was not just idle talk. Social control in the West was often in the hands of what John Caughey has dubbed "their majesties the mob." Throughout the mining districts of California and eventually throughout the North American West, Chinese were subject to violence, expropriation, and murder.[12]

Whatever chance a Chinese might have had to obtain justice from the courts was still further lessened by the ruling that no Chinese could testify in court against a white man. An 1849 California statute, adapted from southern slave codes, provided that "No Black or Mulatto person, or Indian, shall be allowed to give evidence for or against a white man." In 1854, in an opinion written by Chief Justice Hugh G. Murray, a member of the American party, the California Supreme Court ruled that Chinese were barred from testifying because

> Indian as commonly used refers only to the North American Indian, yet in the days of Columbus all shores washed by Chinese waters were called the Indies. In the second place the word "white" necessarily excludes all other races than Caucasian; and in the third place, even if this were not so, I would decide against the testimony of Chinese on grounds of public policy.[13]

With this sort of "justice" being dispensed from the highest bench in the state, it is understandable that the phrase "a Chinaman's chance" meant no chance at all, as writers from Bret Harte on have testified. Murray's ruling remained in force until the passage of the federal Civil Rights Bill of 1870 made it a dead letter. But even after 1870, when Chinese testimony had to be admitted, it was almost disregarded by white juries. Living in segregated and isolated camps, Chinese miners were largely unused to firearms and rarely carried them until they had become acculturated to the American West. They were thus natural and doubly defenseless victims for bandits, including such Mexican American folk heroes as Joaquin Murietta. Throughout the American West, as John Wunder has shown in a number of studies, Chinese were almost universally discriminated

---

11. Alexander McLeod, *Pigtails and Golddust*, p. 346.

12. John W. Caughey, *Their Majesties the Mob*; see also, W. Eugene Hollon, *Frontier Violence: Another Look*, especially chapter 5, "Not a Chinaman's Chance," pp. 80–105; and Roger Daniels, ed., *Anti-Chinese Violence in North America*, an anthology of eleven articles.

13. *People v. Hall*, 4 Cal. 309 (1854).

against in state courts. They did somewhat better—perhaps less badly would be more precise—in the federal courts.[14]

When the anti-Chinese agitation arose in the mining camps, it quickly found a political response at the highest level of government. In April 1852, when there were perhaps 10,000 Chinese in the state, California Governor John Bigler sent a special message to the legislature insisting that "measures must be adopted to check this tide of Asiatic immigration." He proposed that the state use its power of taxation to stop immigration, and that the legislature ask Congress to prohibit "Coolies" from laboring in the mines. Although the legislature failed to act on either of his proposals, Bigler's message marks the formal political beginning of the anti-Chinese movement. For almost a century, from 1852 until the last year of World War II, California governors and other political leaders would, without exception, give some encouragement to anti-Asian forces. Bigler's two predecessors had welcomed the Chinese; in 1851 Governor John McDougall had called for "further immigration and settlement of Chinese—one of our most worthy classes of newly adopted citizens—to whom the climate and character of our lands are particularly suited."[15]

In 1855 Bigler reiterated his proposals. This time he elicited a positive response. With only one dissenting vote, the legislature passed "An act to discourage the Immigration to this state of persons who cannot become citizens thereof" and placed a tax of fifty dollars on each incoming Asian.[16] The bar to citizenship was based on the 1789 federal statute limiting naturalization to "free white persons," although, as we have seen, some eastern courts were willing to naturalize Chinese. As any good lawyer could have foreseen, this act was quickly voided by

14. John R. Wunder, "Law and the Chinese in Frontier Montana," *Montana* 30, no. 3 (1980): 18–31; ibid., "The Courts and the Chinese in Frontier Idaho," *Idaho Yesterdays* 25, no. 1 (1981): 21–32; ibid., "The Chinese and the Courts in the Pacific Northwest: Justice Denied," *Pacific Historical Review* 52 (1983): 191–211. Charles J. McClain, Jr., "The Chinese Struggle for Civil Rights in Nineteenth Century America: The First Phase, 1850–1870," *California Law Review* 72 (1984): 529–68, is an exciting "first installment of what is intended to be a comprehensive treatment of the Chinese to the development of American law," p. 534 fn. 24. Also see Christian Fritz, "Bitter Strength (*k'u-li*) and the Constitution: The Chinese before the Federal Courts in California," *Historical Reporter* 1 (1980): 2–15; Hudson N. Janisch, "The Chinese, the Courts and the Constitution: A Study of the Legal Issues Raised by Chinese Immigration to the United States, 1850–1902" (J.S.D. diss., University of Chicago, 1971); and Connie Young Yu, "The Chinese in American Courts," *Bulletin of Concerned Asian Scholars* 4 (1972): 22–30.

15. John Bigler, *Governor's Special Message* (April 23, 1852), p. 4; Governor John McDougall as cited in McLeod, *Pigtails and Golddust*, p. 64.

16. Cal. *Statutes*, 1855, pp. 194–95.

the state supreme court, which used the 1849 *Passenger Cases* as precedent. Despite this, the legislature in 1858 passed two bills to "prevent the further immigration of Chinese or Mongolians to this state." These were similarly stricken. The same legislature also passed the first of many California school segregation acts, which barred "Negroes, Mongolians, and Indians" from the public schools.[17]

In 1862 California's first Republican governor, Leland Stanford, used his inaugural message to decry "the presence among us of a degraded and distinct people" and to call for "any constitutional action, having for its object the repression of the immigration of Asiatic races." The legislature quickly translated his suggestion into "An Act to Protect Free White Labor against Competition with Chinese Coolie Labor, and Discourage the Immigration of Chinese into the State of California" by instituting a "Chinese Police Tax" that also failed to survive a court test. Stanford may not have been dismayed by the result, as he displayed a truly Janus-like attitude on the question of Chinese immigration. As governor and later as United States senator, Stanford was consistently anti-Chinese, although his persistence may be questioned. In his private role as gentleman farmer and railroad magnate, he was just as consistently an employer of large numbers of Chinese laborers.

In that same year, 1862, labor politicians in San Francisco began to organize Anti-Coolie Clubs; five years later there was one in every ward of the city. In general, however, while the states and territories of the Far West had little direct involvement in the Civil War, the war-induced prosperity combined with railroad building in the immediate postwar era to keep anti-Chinese agitation below the boiling point, although it never ceased to simmer.[18]

In 1867 the Chinese issue was injected into California politics as a partisan issue. For the next half-century, "anti-Orientalism" was a continuing factor in the politics of California. Three parties were contending for state leadership: the Union party (former Douglas Democrats), the Democrats, and the Union Republicans. Both factions of the Democrats passed resolutions opposing "Oriental" immigration, with the regulars also resolving that it would be

> impracticable to maintain republican institutions based upon the suffrages of negroes, Chinese and Indians, and that the doctrines avowed by the radical leaders of indiscriminate suffrage, regardless of race, color, or qualification, if carried into practice, would end in

---

17. For details, see Carl B. Swisher, *Stephen J. Field*, p. 207; and Lucille Eaves, *History of California Labor Legislation*, p. 121.

18. Details may be found in Sandmeyer, *Anti-Chinese Movement*.

the degradation of the white race and the speedy destruction of the government.

The Chinese issue, which had been almost solely a state and, to a lesser degree, a regional concern, thus became enmeshed with larger national issues. In 1867 the California Republicans, reflecting the leanings of their national party, passed a resolution "in favor of voluntary immigration . . . from whatever nationality it may come." This was a hedge, as Republican politicians could claim that Chinese were not "voluntary" immigrants. But their opponents, and probably many voters, interpreted it as simply "pro-Chinese."

The election that year turned the Republicans out of Sacramento. Before the next gubernatorial race in 1871, the state Grand Old Party went on record as opposing "the presence in our midst of a large number of Chinese" and called on the federal government to halt their coming.[19] This established a pattern that would continue into the twentieth century: on the issue of Asian immigration, western branches of parties would often differ from their parties' national positions. In California, from 1871 on, parties vied with one another in the virulence of their anti-Chinese resolutions (and later, their anti-Japanese resolutions) and in publicly claiming credit for whatever restrictive laws and regulations were put into effect.

By 1871 the anti-Chinese issue began to take on distinct national ramifications. This nationalization of regional prejudice was another pattern to be shared by the anti-Chinese and anti-Japanese movements. Before that pattern became established, the United States Senate, with little opposition, ratified the 1868 Burlingame Treaty with China, which recognized and approved trans-Pacific migration:

> The United States and the Emperor of China cordially recognize the inherent and inalienable right of man to change his home and allegiance and also the mutual advantage of the free migration and emigration of their citizens and subjects respectively, from one country to the other, for the purpose of curiosity, of trade, or as permanent residents . . . but nothing contained herein shall be held to confer naturalization upon the citizens of the United States in China, nor upon the subjects of China in the United States.[20]

The year 1868 was probably the last in which such a treaty could have received the approval of two-thirds of the Senate. The completion of the Union-Central Pacific Railroad in May 1869 resulted in the

---

19. Winfield J. Davis, *History of Political Conventions in California, 1849–1892*, pp. 265, 260, 307–08.

20. William M. Malloy, comp., *Treaties, Conventions . . . 1776–1909*, 1: 234–36.

unemployment of its 10,000 Chinese workmen, who then helped to depress the labor market in San Francisco and elsewhere. In March 1870 the first of the San Francisco "sand lot" meetings of the unemployed were held to protest economic conditions. Although the economic hardship of the 1870s was nationwide and its causes manifold, the working people of California tended to place much of the blame on the nearest tangible factor—the Chinese workman and those who employed him.

By July 1870 a number of anti-Chinese demonstrations and mass meetings had been held in San Francisco with marchers carrying placards and transparencies emblazoned with slogans:

WE WANT NO SLAVES OR ARISTOCRATS

THE COOLIE LABOR SYSTEM LEAVES US NO ALTERNATIVE—STARVATION OR DISGRACE

MARK THE MAN WHO WOULD CRUSH US TO THE LEVEL OF THE MONGOLIAN SLAVE—WE ALL VOTE

WOMEN'S RIGHTS AND NO MORE CHINESE CHAMBERMAIDS

Resolutions were passed demanding an end to Chinese immigration, the halting of federal subsidies to the Pacific steamship companies who profited from and encouraged Chinese immigration, and the abrogation of the Burlingame Treaty with China. The Knights of St. Crispin and other unions "reorganized on an anti-Chinese basis," and a plan of the Mechanics' State Council was adopted to hold an "Anti-Chinese Convention of the State of California." It was resolved that "all partisan politics" should be set aside. Not surprisingly this last goal proved impossible to effect, and the subsequent convention in August 1870 split over the issue of independent political action by labor. The precedent, however, had been set: statewide, labor-based, anti-Asian organizations would remain a factor in California politics until after World War II.[21]

The 1870 agitation did produce results in California: anti-Chinese legislation and ordinances were enacted at the state and municipal levels.[22] The legislature passed an act providing that no persons born "in the Empire of China or in Japan, or in the islands adjacent [thereto]" should be allowed to land without a bond unless they could convince the State Commissioner of Immigration of their "good character." The statute was ostensibly aimed at keeping out prostitutes, and the legislators hoped it would be construed as being

---

21. Ira B. Cross, *History of the Labor Movement in California*, pp. 83–84.
22. For the best contemporary account of these struggles, see Willard B. Farwell, *The Chinese at Home and Abroad*, part 2, pp. 85 ff.

within the police powers of the state. Stephen J. Field, associate justice of the Supreme Court of the United States and a Californian, ruled otherwise. The California statute came before him in his capacity as judge of the circuit court: although definitely anti-Chinese himself, Field ruled that the statute was unconstitutional, since immigration control was a federal function.

The city of San Francisco passed a number of harassing ordinances. Their intent, as stated by the Board of Supervisors, was to "drive [the Chinese] to other states to be their own educators against" further Chinese immigration. These ordinances included the Cubic Air Ordinance and the Laundry Ordinance. The Cubic Air Ordinance, calling for each tenement to have at least 500 cubic feet of air for each inhabitant, was enforced only in Chinatown. City officials arrested not the landlords, most of whom would have been white, but the Chinese tenants. Opponents of this measure pointed out that the city jail, where Chinese offenders were confined, usually provided much less than the statutory 500 cubic feet per prisoner, but this inconsistency did not concern the city fathers. The Laundry Ordinance provided licensing fees on the following scale: $2 every three months for one delivery horse; $4 for two horses; $15 if no horses were used. Since Chinese laundries in San Francisco did not usually deliver, the thrust of the measure was clear.

The Chinese community resisted these and other measures in two ways: its organizations hired prominent white attorneys to fight the measures in the courts; and, foreshadowing the Industrial Workers of the World free speech fights of the early twentieth century and the civil rights movement of the 1960s, Chinese resisted nonviolently and chose to "fill up the jails" rather than pay fines, thus putting the municipality to considerable expense. These ordinances were eventually voided in the courts.

From the 1870s on, discouraged by a chain of court decisions invalidating their anti-Chinese measures, Californians and other westerners began to bombard Congress with petitions and demands for Chinese exclusion. The Chinese issue was essentially a western problem. But before the first congressional committee had delved into it, the Chinese question had already achieved some importance in the East. What was perhaps the opening gun in the eastern anti-Chinese campaign was fired by Henry George on May 1, 1869, in a page-one article in the New York *Tribune*. This may represent the first appearance of what was to become a dominant theme of anti-Asian propaganda—the Yellow Peril: that is, the bogus specter of the invasion of the continental United States by an Asian army. George's argument bore traces of that Social Darwinism usually associated with conservatives:

The 60,000 or 100,000 Mongolians on our Western coast are the thin edge of the wedge which has for its base the 500,000,000 of Eastern Asia. . . . The Chinaman can live where stronger than he would starve. Give him fair play and this quality enables him to drive out stronger races. . . . [Unless Chinese immigration is checked] the youngest home of the nations must in its early manhood follow the path and meet the doom of Babylon, Nineveh and Rome. . . . Here plain to the eye of him who chooses to see are the dragon's teeth [which will] . . . spring up armed men marshalled for civil war. Shall we prohibit their sowing while there is still time, or shall we wait until they are firmly embedded, and then try to pluck them up?[23]

In the summer of that same year some southern businessmen and planters, meeting in Memphis, took a different view of Chinese immigration. Their reasoning conveyed a pious tone:

If God in His providence, has opened up the door for the introduction of the Mongolian race to our fields of labor, instead of repelling this class of heathens and idolators, whose touch is contaminating, should we not exhibit more of the spirit of Christians by falling in with the apparent leanings of Providence, and whilst we avail ourselves of the physical assistance these pagans are capable of affording us, endeavor at the same time to bring to bear upon them the elevating and saving influence of our holy religion, so that when those coming among us shall return to their own country, they may carry back with them and disseminate the good seed which is here sown, and the New World shall thus in a double sense become the regenerator of the old.[24]

Behind this rhetorical facade were secular economic fears. In those uncertain days of radical Reconstruction, many southern planters feared that newly freed blacks would not work for them. These men talked of bringing laborers to the South from China, paying West Coast brokers $100 "per head" and the workers from $8 to $12 per month. Although several hundred Chinese were brought or came to the South and were employed in various endeavors—cotton produc-

---

23. New York *Tribune,* May 1, 1869.
24. As cited in John R. Commons et al., *A Documentary History of American Industrial Society* 9: 81. For Chinese in the South in this era, see Lucy M. Cohen, *Chinese in the Post-Civil War South: A People without a History.* Particularly valuable is chapter 7, "A Mixed Nation," which explores the modes of Chinese assimilation in the South over generations.

tion, sugar refining, and railroad construction were the most important—Asian labor never became a meaningful factor in the economy of the South, which had a surplus of labor and widespread unemployment during the rest of the century. The real significance of this episode is that the project to replace black labor with Chinese labor received a good deal of publicity and helped to make the entire country aware of the Chinese issue.

This awareness was heightened by what seems to be the only physical clash between Chinese and organized labor outside of the Far West. In June 1870 in North Adams, Massachusetts, about seventy-five Chinese were imported to break a strike called by the Knights of St. Crispin in the shoe factory of Calvin T. Sampson. Sampson, an avowed self-made man, found unions and high wages equally obnoxious. He refused to reveal to the Massachusetts Bureau of the Statistics of Labor what he paid the Chinese, but he did admit that it was less than he had paid his unionized operatives *before* they struck for an increase. He saw a great future for Chinese labor: "When this kind of labor becomes general, the consumer will reap the benefit."[25]

The events in Sampson's factory caused a flurry of journalistic comment. "Whoever goes to . . . North Adams," declared the editor of *Harper's Magazine,* "wishes to see the celestial shoemakers." He found the importation ominous. "Labor reduced to the Celestial conditions . . . would be the swift ruin of the country." More typical, however, were comments in the *Nation* and *Scribner's Monthly Magazine,* both of which were vehemently opposed to organized labor and thus tended to be pro-Chinese. The former compared the relatively peaceful Crispins to the notoriously violent Molly Maguires. The latter published five articles between January and September 1871 extolling the benefits to be gained from a widespread use of Chinese labor and arguing that, since there was no American peasantry, "we must look for assistance to the refuse population of older and over-populated countries." The author speculated that, since they had no tradition of unionization, the Chinese might be "the final solution of the labor problem."[26]

---

25. Massachusetts Bureau of Labor Statistics, *Report,* 1871, pp. 98–117. A scholarly account of this episode is Frederick Rudolph, "Chinamen in Yankeedom: Anti-Unionism in Massachusetts in 1870," *American Historical Review* 53 (1947): 1–29.

26. "Editor's Easy Chair," *Harper's Magazine* 42 (1870): 137–39; Frank H. Norton, "Our Labor System and the Chinese," *Scribner's Monthly Magazine* 2 (1871): 61–70. See also *Scribner's* 1 (1871):350–51, 556–59; ibid., 2 (1871): 286–90, 494–99.

A then-obscure Congregational minister of North Adams, Washington Gladden, was an eyewitness to the arrival of the Chinese. In his memoirs almost forty years later, Gladden recalled the vivid scene:

> When the train [bearing the Chinese] arrived, the streets between the railway station and the factory were lined with an excited crowd, but the police were out in force, and no violence was attempted. All kinds of noises and execrations assailed the ears of the slant-eyed Mongolians as they marched to their destination, and the poor creatures were terribly frightened, but they escaped with no injuries. In fact, the curiosity of the crowd was so acute that its brutality was held in check. These pig-tailed, calico-frocked, wooden-shod invaders made a spectacle which nobody wanted to miss even long enough to stoop for a brickbat. . . . The self restraint of the working-people of North Adams, in the presence of this irritating spectacle, was a cause for gratitude.[27]

Apart from that of North Adams, there were at least two other large-scale uses of Chinese labor in the East during the 1870s. Sixty-eight Chinese were employed in a steam laundry near Belleville, New Jersey, and 165 Chinese worked in a cutlery factory in Beaver Falls, Pennsylvania. Some Beaver Falls citizens complained in a petition to Congress that the introduction of Chinese "shows a manifest attempt to revive the institution of slavery." The tariff-conscious Pennsylvanians also charged bad faith, since "the protection of 35 to 50 percent against the importation of foreign cutlery was enacted for the purpose of protecting the American laborer against cheap foreign labor."[28]

These three early instances of labor importation are significant insofar as they alerted the eastern labor movement to the possibility of Chinese being used to break strikes and to lower the wage level. Labor agitation, largely by the Crispins, caused the New York legislature to consider banning the use of Chinese laborers in the state. In the summer of 1870 both the Democratic and Labor Reform parties of

---

27. Washington Gladden, *Recollections*, pp. 171–73. Cf. the unsigned account in the *Nation*, which states "a large and hostile crowd threw stones at them." *Nation* 10 (June 23, 1870): 397. For Gladden generally, see Jacob H. Dorn, *Washington Gladden*, and cf. his remarks at p. 50.

28. U.S. Congress, House, *Misc. Document 81*, 42d Cong., 3d sess., 1873. See also W. F. G. Shanks, "Chinese Skilled Labor," *Scribner's* 2 (1871): 494–99; and U.S. Congress, Senate, *Report of the Joint Special Committee to Investigate Chinese Immigration, Report 689*, 44th Cong., 2d sess., 1877, pp. 550–51 (hereafter cited as Senate, *Report 689*).

Massachusetts passed anti-Chinese resolutions.[29] That same summer for the first time a national labor body went on record as opposing Chinese immigration.

The National Labor Union (NLU), which met in Cincinnati from August 15–22, 1870, took the fateful step. The year before, meeting in Philadelphia with no delegates from California, the NLU had resolved that "voluntary Chinese emigrants ought to enjoy the protection of the laws like other citizens." At the 1870 meeting, however, six Crispin delegates with the North Adams strike fresh in their memories and three California delegates formed an anti-Chinese bloc, overrode the arguments of NLU President Richard Trevellick, and passed the following resolution: "Resolved, that the presence in our country of Chinese laborers in large numbers is an evil entailing want and its consequent train of misery and crime on all other classes of the American people, and should be prevented by legislation." As far as the American labor movement was concerned, this was the Rubicon of the Chinese issue and of its attitude toward all immigrants from Asia.[30] Within a few more years the labor movement would support a general restriction of all immigration, whatever the source.

The first significant congressional debate about the rights of Chinese in the United States also occurred in 1870. The ratification of the Fourteenth Amendment necessitated a change in the naturalization statute. Congress debated whether, in adding "persons of African descent" to "white persons" as being eligible for naturalization, Asians should be included as well. Senator Charles Sumner of Massachusetts, a consistent believer in the rights of man, tried in vain to persuade his colleagues to make the naturalization statutes color blind, arguing that they should apply equally to all. Denying that the naturalization of Chinese would be a peril, Sumner insisted that "the greatest peril to this republic is from disloyalty to its great ideas," such as those of the Declaration of Independence. His view was decisively defeated.[31] The

---

29. Norton, "Our Labor System," p. 69; *Nation* 10 (June 30, 1870): 412–13; U.S. Senate, *Congressional Record,* 1884, p. 3776.

30. Commons, *Documentary History,* 9: 241, 257–67.

31. Sumner's bill was defeated by 30–14, and a motion to reconsider failed by 26–12. An amendment, supported by Sumner, which sought to make "aliens of African nativity and . . . persons of African descent" eligible for naturalization, passed by votes of 21–20 and 20–17. A later attempt by Senator Lyman Trumbull (R-Ill.) to include persons "born in the Chinese Empire" failed by 31–9. For an account of Sumner's efforts for a color-blind naturalization statute, see Charles Sumner, *The Works of Charles Sumner,* 13: 474–98. Curiously, Sumner's modern biographer David Donald omits any mention of this minor crusade, although one would think it pertinent to *Charles Sumner and the Rights of Man.* Frederick Douglass thought it pertinent, writing that Sumner was "in the right place on the Chinese question. As usual you are in the

ruling that Asians were "aliens ineligible to citizenship" would remain the basis for statutory discrimination at both federal and state levels until the naturalization laws were changed in 1952.[32]

In 1874 an American president took first official public notice of the Chinese immigration question. In his annual message, after remarking that relations with China continued "friendly" and after stating our neutrality in disputes between China and Japan, President Ulysses S. Grant suggested his willingness to approve anti-Chinese legislation:

> I call the attention of Congress to a generally conceded fact—that the great proportion of the Chinese immigrants who come to our shores do not come voluntarily, to make their homes with us and their labor productive of general prosperity, but come under contracts with headmen, who own them absolutely. In a worse form does this apply to Chinese women. Hardly a perceptible percentage of them perform any honorable labor, but they are brought for shameful purposes, to the disgrace of communities where settled and to the great demoralization of the youth of those localities. If this evil practice can be legislated against, it will be my pleasure as well as my duty to enforce any regulation to secure so desirable an end.[33]

A year later, realizing that Congress was not yet ready to touch the hot potato of immigration restriction even for Chinese, Grant limited his 1875 recommendation to the problem of Chinese prostitutes. Congress did pass a statute that year making illegal the transport "to or from the United States any subject of China, Japan, or any Oriental country, without their [sic] free and voluntary consent." It also barred both the importation of women from anywhere "for the purposes of prostitution" and the immigration of "persons . . . whose sentence has been remitted on condition of their emigration"; but the act was incapable of enforcement.[34] In the same session Congress appointed a special joint committee to make a thorough investigation of the whole Chinese question.

By that time both national political parties were showing themselves aware of the Chinese question. The Republican platform in

---

van—the country in the rear" (Letter to Sumner, July 6, 1870, as cited by Benjamin Quarles, *Frederick Douglass*, p. 254). I am indebted to my former student Richard A. Reiman for research assistance on this topic.

32. The 1870 act is dated July 14, 1870. Citizenship for Chinese was made possible by the act of December 17, 1943; see below, chapter 6.

33. James D. Richardson, comp., *Messages and Papers of the Presidents*, 7:288.

34. 18 *Stat.* 477.

1876 declared it the "immediate duty of Congress to investigate the effects of the immigration and importation of Mongolians," while the Democrats denounced "the policy . . . which tolerates the revival of the coolie-trade in Mongolian women held for immoral purposes, and Mongolian men to perform servile labor." Four years later both parties were firmly against further Chinese immigration of any kind. In the 1880 election campaign someone thought it worthwhile to forge the Morey letter, which smeared Republican candidate James A. Garfield as a supporter of Chinese labor.[35]

A congressional investigation of 1876 had helped to solidify anti-Chinese sentiment at the national level. But even before the congressional investigating committee could meet, the California senate had set up a committee of its own which held hearings in San Francisco and Sacramento in April, May, and June 1876. Highly partisan in nature, the committee's witnesses were carefully selected and no strong pro-Chinese testimony was given. Its report, together with a curious anthology of anti-Chinese tracts, was ordered printed in "sufficient numbers . . . to furnish copies thereof to the leading newspapers of the United States, five copies to each member of Congress, ten copies to the Governor of each State, and . . . two thousand copies . . . for general distribution."

Altogether sixty witnesses were called, including eighteen Chinese and forty-two whites. Of the Chinese, half a dozen were officers of the Six Chinese Companies; the others were either interpreters and informers for the police or were attached to Christian missions. The representatives of the Six Companies, who were not permitted to make prefatory statements, did everything but take the Fifth Amendment, answering "I don't know" when questioned on matters of common knowledge. The testimony of the other Chinese had obviously been gone over in advance: it stressed the more lurid and seamy details of Chinese life in California.

Of the white witnesses, more than half were local politicians and policemen; there was also a sprinkling of persons who had been in China, usually for short periods of time. Most of the witnesses testified about matters beyond their competence. For example, a Sacramento

---

35. The first national anti-Chinese resolution was in the Labor Reform Party platform of 1872. The Democratic platforms of 1876, 1880, 1888, and 1904 all had anti-Chinese planks, as did the GOP platforms of 1876, 1880, 1888, and 1904. The only pro-Chinese plank was that of the American National Prohibition Party in 1884, which called for extending the "civil equality" of Amendments XIII, XIV, and XV "to Indians and Chinese." See Donald B. Johnson, comp., *National Party Platforms*, passim; Ted C. Hinckley, "The Politics of Sinophobia: Garfield, the Morey letter and the Presidential Election of 1880," *Ohio History* 89 (1980): 381–99.

policeman, obviously not well educated, gave testimony on the theory and practice of Buddhism.

As an investigation, the proceedings were a farce. The report, however, was an effective if crude propaganda device, and material drawn from it surfaced in the national press for years afterward. Attached to the report was a memorial to Congress, setting forth a summary of the committee's "findings" and asking that California and the West be provided with legislative relief.[36]

The congressional investigation was another matter. The committee was composed of three senators and three representatives, one of whom did not serve. Republican Senator Aaron A. Sargent and Democratic Representative William A. Piper were both, at the time of the investigation, honorary vice-presidents of the Anti-Coolie Union of San Francisco. Democratic Senator Henry Cooper of Tennessee and Democratic Representative Edwin R. Meade of New York followed their lead. The powerful chairman of the committee, Senator Oliver P. Morton of Indiana, had different views, however, as well as some interesting notions of how an investigation should be conducted. During a Senate debate he had proposed that a committee should visit the Pacific Coast to discover "the character, extent, and effect of Chinese immigration to this country." And this is precisely what his committee did, setting up shop in the opulent Palace Hotel in San Francisco from 18 October to 18 November 1876, with an eleven-day recess for electioneering.

Although no formal statement of procedure is included in the report, it is easily reconstructed from the records. The committee attached to itself representatives of both pro- and anti-Chinese forces in California; these groups, not the committee, arranged for witnesses. Each group was given the right to cross-examine the witnesses of the other. Frank M. Pixley, attorney and politician, led the anti-Chinese forces; two San Francisco corporation lawyers, Colonel F. A. Bee, official spokesman for the Six Chinese Companies and sometime Chinese consul in San Francisco, and Benjamin S. Brooks, represented the pro-Chinese forces. Each of these three asked more questions than any committee member. Thus, as in a court of law and except for a few officials who merely recited statistics, each witness was first conducted through his testimony by a friendly interrogator and then was subjected to a hostile cross-examination. In all, 128 witnesses, none of whom was Chinese, appeared before the committee; about one-fourth were favorable to the Chinese.

---

36. Special Committee on Chinese Immigration, *Chinese Immigration: Its Social, Moral and Political Effect,* pp. 7, 61–65 and passim.

The anti-Chinese forces made the usual allegations. They claimed that the Asians lowered wages and thereby lowered the standard of living. They claimed that they were unassimilable and that their "heathen" customs were disgusting and tended to debauch and degrade those around them. The lawyers for the Chinese sought to demonstrate that without Chinese labor the development of California would not continue. They also denied the special immorality of the Chinese and sought to demonstrate that the rest of the population, or much of it, was less industrious than were the Asians.

The Irish, the largest immigrant group in California, were blamed as fomenters of the racial unrest. Not all the Irish but "the prejudiced Irish, the same class that burned the hospitals in New York; . . . [and] who filled the Molly Maguire societies in Pennsylvania . . . [and who have been] the rabid anti-Coolies here," were stigmatized by Brooks as the troublemakers. The testimony, over a thousand printed pages, was almost all of it prejudicial and most of it contradictory. Nowhere in the whole report was there anything even remotely resembling a balanced picture.[37]

Not surprisingly one of the best contemporary evocations of the volatile and paradoxical California attitude toward the Chinese comes from the pen of eastern journalist Charles Nordhoff. Visiting San Francisco in 1873, Nordhoff took sardonic note of all he heard regarding the character of the Chinese:

> He is patient, docile, persevering, quick to learn, no eyeservant, the best cook or waiter you ever saw.
> Last week he stole $600 out of my drawer, and is now in State Prison.
> He is sober.
> Last night you saw him smoking opium in the most horrible of dens.
> He saves his money.
> And takes it out of the State to spend in China.
> He is indispensable.
> But he is a curse to the community.
> He will make a useful citizen.
> His whole race is vicious and degraded.[38]

Whether fiction or reportage, Nordhoff's satire sums up the whole contradictory plethora of pamphlets, speeches, and testimony

---

37. Senate, *Report 689*, pp. 1–7. The witness list is at pp. 1255–57; Brooks quotes from ibid., p. 56. William D. Foulke, in *The Life of Oliver P. Morton*, describes the hearings inaccurately at 2: 238–41.

38. Charles Nordhoff, *California, for Health, Pleasure and Residence*, pp. 84–85.

on the subject. But more must be said. Opposition to or approval of the Chinese was not merely a parlor debate over abstract questions of morality, taste, prejudice, or ideology. Money and power were often the bottom line, and decisions depended on the tangible factors of economic and political advantage, real or imagined.

The employers of labor on a large scale welcomed the Chinese worker as cheaper, more dependable, and sometimes even more productive than his white competitor. Charles Crocker was one of California's "Big Four" and the man responsible for the introduction of large numbers of Chinese workers into railroad construction (the Chinese were often called "Crocker's Pets"). Crocker testified that although he had been initially skeptical about the ability of Asians to do heavy construction work, "today if I had a big job of work to do that I wanted to get through quick with, and had a limited time to do it in, I should take Chinese labor . . . because of its greater reliability and steadiness, and their aptitude and capacity for hard work." In answer to a standard question about the "social, moral and financial effect upon this coast" of Chinese, Crocker read a prepared statement:

> I think that the presence of Chinese as laborers among us goes very far toward the material interest of the country. . . . I believe that the effect of Chinese labor upon white labor has an elevating instead of a degrading tendency. . . . I believe, today, if the Chinese labor was driven out of this State, if there are 75,000 Chinese laborers here today, there are 75,000 white laborers who would have to come down from the elevated classes of labor they are now engaged in and take the place of these Chinamen, and therefore it would degrade white labor instead of elevating it. . . . There is a certain class of white laborers in this country, as in every country, . . . who are not capable of elevation; they will not elevate themselves . . . [and] the more money they get for their labor the less labor they will do.[39]

Industrial entrepreneurs were not alone in speaking for the Chinese. As early as November 1848 agricultural interests in California had been looking toward Asia for a solution to their labor problems. The *Californian* of that date commented that "if white labor is too high for agriculture, laborers on contract may be brought from China, or elsewhere, who if well treated will work faithfully at low wages." The same tack was taken by all of the large-scale farmers and ranchers who testified at the 1876 congressional hearings. Wil-

---

39. Senate, *Report 689*, pp. 666–88, for Crocker's testimony.

liam W. Hollister, a Santa Barbara rancher who grazed some 50,000 sheep on 75,000 acres, is typical in his attitude as an employer of labor: "As to the character of the labor in this country my experience in this State makes me put Chinamen entirely above others. . . . I think that the [future] labor of this country will be due to the advent of cheap labor."[40]

Additional vocal support for the Chinese came from certain religious groups, especially those engaged in missionary activity among the Chinese on both sides of the Pacific: in California, Congregationalists, Baptists, Methodists, and Presbyterians were the most active.[41] Some missionaries, testifying for the Chinese, sounded very much like the employers. Asked about the possible effects of driving the Chinese out of the state, the Reverend Augustus W. Loomis, a Presbyterian, testified:

> As soon as the Chinese were driven fairly away, the artisans, employees, and servants [would ask for higher wages]. . . . Let the Chinese be driven away and all the manufacturing interests would be seriously affected, if not stopped. They are now only able to sustain themselves in the face of the Eastern and foreign competition by means of . . . the Chinese.[42]

Later, under cross-examination, Loomis revealed certain biases, and in this he seems representative of most of the pro-Chinese opinion in California:

Q. You would restrict [Chinese] from the ballot? You would not allow them to become citizens?

A. Certainly. I would restrict them in that respect.

Q. Is it desirable to introduce into a free republic a class of people . . . who are not citizens and who cannot become citizens?

A. I think we have gone too fast in admitting so many foreigners without proper qualifications. . . .

Q. Do you think Chinese immigration is less dangerous to our institutions than Roman Catholics?

A. I think so; decidedly less.

Q. Suppose . . . Chinese would become Catholics, then they would be dangerous?

A. I think so.

---

40. Ibid., pp. 766–95, for Hollister's testimony. See also Paul S. Taylor, "Foundations of California's Rural Society," *California Historical Society Quarterly* 24 (1945): 193–228.

41. Senate, *Report 689*, pp. 1172–73, for a table of converts by denomination.

42. Ibid., pp. 444–84, for Loomis's testimony.

Perhaps Loomis was more extreme in some of his prejudices than most of his brethren. Perhaps he was simply more candid. At any rate, he was not atypical. The large majority of the Protestant clergy in California seems to have been pro-Chinese up to this time.[43]

At least one Roman Catholic priest was virulently anti-Chinese: On February 25, 1873, Father James Chrysostom Bouchard, S.J., delivered a public lecture in San Francisco entitled, "Chinaman or White Man, Which?" In rolling periods, Father Bouchard delivered a diatribe:

> The man or woman who would dismiss a faithful, virtuous servant because the wages were so much higher, to receive into the family one of these immoral creatures, because he will work at a lower rate—that would expose the children to be contaminated and ruined by such a wretch, scarcely deserves the name of a human being. . . . [The Chinese] are an idolatrous, vicious, corrupt and pusillanimous race. . . . It is the white race we want. . . . The only race that has ever proved itself capable of self-government or really progressive civilization.

Ironically, although his auditors did not know it, Father Bouchard was himself of an "inferior race," being partly of American Indian ancestry. Bouchard's explicit racism made him an exception among the Roman Catholic clergy of the time, and although the hierarchy gave him no public rebuke on this issue, at least one Chinese Roman Catholic priest was deliberately brought into the diocese. Nonetheless, no Roman Catholic priest in California publicly espoused the cause of the Chinese.[44]

But of all the divines working among the Chinese in California (and to one who has waded through the literature of the period, it sometimes seems as if the missionaries were as numerous as the

---

43. The Congregationalists, on October 9, 1877, were the first large Protestant body to go on record against the Chinese. See the resolution of the General Association of the Congressional Churches and Ministers in California as printed in the Special Committee on Chinese Immigration, *Chinese Immigration*, p. 240.

44. John B. McGloin, *Eloquent Indian*, is an excellent biography. The name is sometimes spelled Burchard or Buchard. Sandmeyer, *Anti-Chinese Movement*, p. 36, and many who follow him with and without attribution, speak of "Roman Catholic priests" as being anti-Chinese, but no evidence is cited. Otis Gibson, a Methodist missionary to the Chinese who attacked Bouchard (see note 45 below), was decidedly anti-Catholic, but in *The Chinese in America* he mentions no other anti-Chinese priest. Gibson also states that after he had attacked Bouchard about his anti-Chinese sentiments, "that crafty priest omitted the 'Chinaman' altogether from his catalogue of lectures," ibid., p. 281. For a Chinese priest, see Henry L. Walsh, *Hallowed Were the Gold Dust Trails*, p. 476 n31.

Chinese), one stands out: the Reverend Otis Gibson. A Methodist, Otis Gibson was clearly the paladin of the pro-Chinese forces; his arguments, from a modern point of view at least, seem closer to being "Christian" than those of his colleagues. His position can best be seen in his reply to Father Bouchard's lecture. Basing himself on the "traditional policy of the United States," Gibson declared that "it is the God-taught principle that *all men are born free and equal*." Although his economic views were typical of the upper-middle classes and were indistinguishable from those of Loomis, Gibson's discussion of the alleged inferiority of China and the Chinese demonstrates that he was remarkably free of that Anglo-Saxonism then so rampant. Noting that China had once been "in advance of the civilization of our ancestors," Gibson pointed out that "the inferior civilization of any people, at any certain point of the world's history, is no gauge of the possibilities of that people in progressive development, under favorable circumstances."

Gibson was not, of course, without prejudices. He ran a shelter for reformed Chinese prostitutes and reported that one of them had been married "to a white man"; but he immediately added "of course, not to an American citizen." He was strongly anti-Catholic; his philippics against the Church of Rome are only slightly less virulent than those of Loomis. But at his best, Gibson sounded more like the twentieth century than the nineteenth. He concluded his polemic against Bouchard with a noble restatement of the American ideal:

> The doors of our country are open equally. . . . We have room for all. Ours is "the land of the free, and the home of the brave." The oppressed and down-trodden from all nations may alike find shelter here, and under the benign influences of our free institutions, and of our exalted faith, with the blessing of Almighty God, these different nationalities and varying civilizations shall, in time, blend into one harmonious whole, illustrating to a wondering world the common Fatherhood of God, and the universal brotherhood of man.[45]

To summarize, the pro-Chinese forces were generally "the rich, the good and the wise": merchants interested in trade with the Far East; manufacturers, ranchers, and farmers interested in keeping the wage level as low as possible; those groups interested in a cheap and docile solution to the servant problem, which seemed important in

---

45. Gibson, *Chinese in America*, pp. 248–81. For Gibson's testimony, see Senate, *Report 689*, pp. 145–46, 396–436, 496–504, 512.

Gilded Age America; and a majority of the Protestant clergy. I suspect, but cannot demonstrate, that the attitudes of nonmissionary clergy were greatly influenced by whether their congregations included large working-class elements, which most did not.

Who then comprised the anti-Chinese forces? In general, they included working people, the politicians who depended on their votes, and the newspapers that catered to popular interests. It is significant that the only San Francisco newspaper, apart from the religious weeklies and monthlies, that took a pro-Chinese position was the *Commercial Herald and Market Review*.[46] The anti-Chinese forces recognized and proclaimed the economic bias of their opponents. One of their witnesses, Los Angeles journalist John Arroup, gave succinct testimony:

> I never found a strong advocate of Chinese immigration who was not actuated by fanaticism or selfishness. . . . I have seen men, American born, who certainly would, if I may use a strong expression, employ devils from hell if the devils would work for 25 cents less than a white man, even though the white man may be an American citizen who had gone through all the rebellion.

The burden of much anti-Chinese propaganda can be reduced to a short phrase: "the Chinese worked cheap and smelled bad." Much of the testimony stressed the filthy living conditions of Chinatown and indicated that these were owing to the singularly foul personal habits of the Chinese. Conditions there were certainly deplorable but were probably no worse than similar conditions produced elsewhere in the western world by nineteenth century industrialization and urbanization. If the reader merely reflects about the conditions described by Charles Dickens, Victor Hugo, or Stephen Crane, it will be clear that Chinatown was not uniquely sordid.

Perhaps it will suffice to quote one more anti-Chinese diatribe from a small Bay Area paper, the *Marin Journal*, in early 1876. The Chinese immigrant was denounced in a litany of abuse:

> [That he] is a slave, reduced to the lowest terms of beggarly economy, and is not a fit competitor for an American freeman. That he herds in scores, in small dens, where a white man and wife could hardly breathe and has none of the wants of a civilized white man. That he has neither wife nor child, nor expects to have any. That his sister is a prostitute from instinct, from religion, education and interest, and degrading to all around her. . . . That the health, wealth,

---

46. See the editorials reprinted in Senate, *Report 689*, pp. 1184–89.

prosperity and happiness of our State demand their expulsion from our shores.[47]

All the evidence available to us, including political behavior, testimony taken before the congressional committee, opinions expressed in newspapers, magazines, and surviving literary materials of all kinds, suggests that an overwhelming majority of Californians shared these sentiments. This being the case, it is not surprising that the Joint Special Committee of Congress's report supported the California position. Written by California Senator Aaron A. Sargent, the report concluded that the very survival of America was at stake:

> The Pacific coast must in time become either American or Mongolian. There is a vast hive from which Chinese immigrants may swarm. . . . To compete with them and expel them the American must come down to their level, or below them. . . . The deduction from the testimony . . . would seem to be that there is not sufficient brain capacity in the Chinese race to furnish motive power for self-government. Upon the point of morals there is no Aryan or European race which is not far superior to the Chinese. . . . Chinese do not come to make their home in this country, . . . do not desire to become citizens, . . . do not desire the ballot. . . . The tide of Chinese immigration is gradually tending eastward and before a quarter of a century will probably have to be met upon the banks of the Mississippi, and perhaps on the Ohio and the Hudson. . . . The committee recommends that measures be taken by the Executive toward a modification of the existing treaty with China, confining it to strictly commercial purposes; and that Congress legislate to restrain the great influx of Asiatics to this country.[48]

The chairman of the committee, Senator Oliver P. Morton of Indiana, issued a minority report attributing much of the economic growth of California to Chinese labor. Senator Morton recommended no action by either the executive branch or Congress, and he insisted that

> if the Chinese in California were white people, being in all other respects what they are, I do not believe that the complaints and warfare made against them would have existed to any considerable extent. Their difference in color, dress, manners, and religion have,

---

47. *Marin Journal*, March 30, 1876, as cited in Sandmeyer, *Anti-Chinese Movement*, p. 25.
48. Senate, *Report 689*, pp. iii–viii.

in my judgment, more to do with this hostility than their alleged vices or any actual injury to the white people of California.[49]

The report was presented to Congress in February 1877 when the contested election of 1876 was being settled, so immediate action was impossible. The Democratic House of Representatives had already passed two resolutions calling for modification of the Burlingame Treaty, but the Republican Senate had taken no action. In 1878 after West Coast senators and representatives had met in a special anti-Chinese caucus to plan strategy, the whole Congress did invite the attention of the president to the desirability of treaty modification.

In the lame-duck session of the Forty-fifth Congress, the so-called Fifteen Passenger Bill was sent to the president. Although Rutherford B. Hayes vetoed this measure and the veto was upheld, and even though it would have had little effect on Chinese America, Elmer Sandmeyer has correctly argued that the Fifteen Passenger Bill marked a "turn in the road" of American immigration policy because it indicated that passage of some kind of restriction was only a matter of time.[50] The bill sought to provide that only fifteen Chinese per ship could enter the United States. It also instructed the president to notify the Chinese government that parts of the Burlingame Treaty pertaining to immigration were abrogated. Rutherford B. Hayes's veto had as much to do with protecting the powers of the executive and maintaining the international commitments of the nation as it did with immigration. President Hayes made it clear that the matter could be adjusted by diplomatic rather than congressional action.[51]

Principled political opposition to the anti-Chinese movement at the national level was all but nonexistent. Not only were the racial biases of the movement consistent with the post-Reconstruction climate of opinion but the even balance between the parties during this period also contributed to near unanimity on the subject. The presidential election of 1880 in California was decided by fewer than one hundred votes in a canvass of 164,000, and in no national election from 1876 through 1896 did the winning candidate have a margin of more than 13,000 votes in California. Senator George Frisbie Hoar, a Massachusetts Republican, was one of the few national figures to oppose anti-Chinese measures. According to his biographer, Hoar believed that "Chinese exclusion represented nothing less than the legalization of racial discrimination." This made Hoar a target for western scorn: he was burned in effigy in Nevada, and a California

---

49. U.S. Congress, Senate, *Misc. Document 20*, 45th Cong., 2d sess., 1879, p. 4.
50. Sandmeyer, *Anti-Chinese Movement*, p. 91.
51. Richardson, *Messages and Papers*, 7: 514–20.

paper sneered that "the great chair of Webster is held, but not filled, by a dwarf."[52]

For a brief time the anti-Chinese issue helped transform California politics. The anti-Chinese forces evolved into the Workingman's party with a broad platform that read like a prelude to populism. The greatest nineteenth century success of labor parties in California came in the elections to the state constitutional convention of 1878–1879, when labor elected 50 of the 153 delegates. This bloc inserted an entire anti-Chinese article into the new constitution, much of which was patently unconstitutional. After an initial section, which attempted to evade the question of constitutionality by invocation of the police power, the rest of the article forbade California corporations from employing "in any capacity, any Chinese or Mongolian," barred Chinese from state, county, or municipal employment, and empowered the cities and towns of the state to enact ordinances segregating Chinese into "prescribed portions" of municipalities. Also included were instructions to the legislature to "provide the necessary legislation to prohibit the introduction into this State of Chinese after the adoption of this Constitution," an instruction easier to formulate than to execute.[53]

By the end of 1880 a new treaty had been agreed to after five weeks of negotiation in Peking. It gave the United States, unilaterally, the right to "regulate, limit or suspend" the "coming or residence" of Chinese laborers, but it allowed Chinese subjects "proceeding to the United States as teachers, students, merchants or from curiosity, together with their body and household servants, and Chinese laborers now in the United States to go and come of their own free will and accord."

The treaty was quickly ratified and was proclaimed in October 1881.[54] The following spring both houses of Congress passed an act that suspended the immigration of Chinese laborers for twenty years and, consonant with the treaty, exempted those already here or who might arrive within ninety days of the approval of the act. It also reconfirmed the inadmissibility of Chinese to citizenship. President Chester A. Arthur vetoed this bill. His message made it clear that he was opposed because he felt that the twenty-year suspension was too long:

---

52. Richard E. Welch, Jr., *George Frisbie Hoar and the Half-Breed Republicans*, pp. 193–94. San Francisco *Daily Alta California*, March 3, 1882, as cited in Sandmeyer, *Anti-Chinese Movement*, p. 93.

53. Sandmeyer, *Anti-Chinese Movement*, pp. 66–72.

54. Malloy, *Treaties*, 1: 237–39.

It may be that the great and paramount interest of protecting our labor from Asiatic competition may justify us in a permanent adoption of this policy; but it is wiser in the first place to make a shorter experiment, with a view hereafter of maintaining only such features as time and experience may commend.[55]

Despite complaints from the Democrats, the veto was upheld. Congress quickly wrote and enacted a new bill, which Arthur signed on May 6, 1882, just two days more than a month after his veto message.

That bill, although entitled "Chinese Exclusion Act," in fact only suspended immigration for ten years. The law exempted Chinese already in the United States or who might come within ninety days after the approval of the act, and it provided that Chinese leaving the country should get a certificate from American officials as evidence of their "right to come and go." Official representatives of the Chinese government and others exempt from the act were to be furnished certificates, and the bar against naturalization was restated.[56]

Soon, and probably with good reason, many complaints arose about the fraudulent nature and use of documents supplied by each government. In addition other loopholes appeared which had not been foreseen. Federal courts soon ruled that the law affected only Chinese who were domiciled in China, declaring that Chinese coming to the United States from some other place, say Cuba or Canada, did not need to have a certificate. An 1884 act closed this loophole and sought to make foolproof the regulations concerning certificates.[57] Amid continuing anti-Chinese agitation and increasing anti-Chinese violence throughout the West, the United States and China negotiated a new treaty in early 1888. The treaty draft extended the bar against Chinese laborers for twenty years, with a clause continuing it for a further twenty years—that is, until 1928—if neither party denounced the treaty. The Senate, however, inserted several provisions, including one that would have barred even the return of Chinese who were out of the United States *with* a certificate entitling them to reentry. These provisions were unacceptable to the Chinese government, and the treaty was never ratified.[58]

When Congress learned that Peking would not ratify the treaty, it passed a bill (the Scott Act), introduced into the House by William L. Scott of Pennsylvania, who was also President Cleveland's campaign manager. This bill's chief provision canceled all outstanding American

---

55. Richardson, *Messages and Papers*, 8: 112–18.
56. 22 *Stat.* 58.
57. 23 *Stat.* 115.
58. Sandmeyer, *Anti-Chinese Movement*, pp. 99–101.

certificates that had allowed reentry of Chinese who had left the United States.[59] President Cleveland signed this unjust measure. By his so doing, the United States openly broke its promise to thousands of individuals who had left the country with official government documents saying that they could return. In a message reeking of election-year politics, Cleveland made his racist position clear by declaring the "experiment of blending the social habits and mutual race idiosyncra-cies of the Chinese laboring classes with those of the great body of the people of the United States . . . proved by the experience of twenty years . . . in every sense unwise, impolitic, and injurious to both nations." The president ignored the cancellation of the certificates and argued that any Chinese who had money owed to him could collect it in the courts where, he insisted, "it cannot be alleged that there exists the slightest discrimination against Chinese subjects." In addition, he added, many provisions of the Scott Act had been previously agreed to by the Chinese government. The mere existence of President Cleve-land's unusual message justifying the *signing* should be taken as evidence of the president's uneasy feelings about the obvious injustices the bill contained.[60] Those who portray the Bourbon Democrat as a fearless and courageous leader usually ignore his treatment of the Chinese.

The Scott Act was quickly challenged in federal court because it was in violation of the still valid treaty of 1881, which allowed Chinese laborers already in the United States "to go and come" freely. Nonetheless, the judicial rulings all the way to the Supreme Court were universally favorable to the 1888 statute; the courts held that acts of Congress and treaties were equally the law of the land, and that whichever came later should prevail.[61]

The confused, hurried, and sometimes overlapping legislation of 1888 left the duration of exclusion in doubt. Some authorities thought it had been made permanent; others felt that the ten-year limit of the statute of 1882 still applied. That being the case, another restriction act in 1892 was a foregone conclusion: the only question was how strict the new legislation would be and for how long it would run. More than a dozen measures were introduced and debated that year.

The result was the Geary Act of 1892, which extended exclusion for another ten years and made further restrictive changes in the

---

59. 25 *Stat.* 504. Before learning that China would not ratify the treaty, Congress passed a strongly anti-Chinese statute, which, however, was less strict than its successor. See 25 *Stat.* 476.

60. Richardson, *Messages and Papers*, 8: 630–35.

61. 130 *U.S.* 581.

administrative provisions of exclusion. The most significant of these changes placed upon each individual Chinese the burden of proof that his presence in the country was legal; if he could not prove this, he could be deported. Bail was denied to Chinese aliens in habeas corpus proceedings and all Chinese in the United States, upon pain of deportation, were required to get a certificate of residence, a kind of internal passport.[62]

For a time not only did most Chinese Americans refuse to register but the Geary Act was challenged in the courts. The Six Companies of San Francisco hired expensive constitutional lawyers but to no avail. The Supreme Court in effect denied most of the civil rights of prospective entrants, holding that the right to exclude or expel aliens was an "inherent and inalienable" attribute of sovereignty, and that the registration system set up by the Geary Act was valid.[63] Although only around 13,000 Chinese registered in the period prescribed by law, no mass arrests or expulsions followed as there were no funds for enforcement. After the Supreme Court decision, Congress extended the time for registration by six months and the boycott of registration ceased.[64] By May 1894 about 105,000 Chinese had registered. In an 1894 treaty the Chinese government accepted the terms of the legislation. In a face-saving measure, the United States agreed to allow the Chinese government to require American laborers in China to register there, promising to furnish the Chinese government a list of all Americans in China, save for officials and their servants.[65]

The legislative history of the anti-Chinese movement cannot be fully understood without taking into account the violence that punctuated it. The late nineteenth century American West was a violent region; with the exception of the American Indians, no group there suffered as much from violence as did the Chinese. No one can ever know how many Chinese were murdered and brutalized, but some of

---

62. 27 *Stat.* 25.

63. 149 *U.S.* 698. Chief Justice Fuller and Justices Field and Brewer dissented. For a discussion of the legal and constitutional issues involved in this and other Chinese immigration cases, see Milton R. Konvitz, *The Alien and the Asiatic in American Law.*

64. 28 *Stat.* 7. The language and terms of all these Chinese immigration statutes were insulting. The following, from the statute cited above, is representative: "When an application is made by a Chinaman for entrance into the United States on the ground that he was formerly engaged in this country as a merchant, he shall establish by the testimony of two credible witnesses other than Chinese the fact that he conducted such business as hereinbefore defined for at least one year before his departure from the United States, and that during such year he was not engaged in the performance of any manual labor, except such as was necessary in the conduct of his business as such merchant, and in default of such proof shall be refused landing."

65. Malloy, *Treaties,* 1: 241–43.

the worst outrages can at least be catalogued here.[66] In the earliest urban anti-Chinese riot, which took place in 1871 in the sleepy city of Los Angeles (1870 population: 5,728), twenty-one Chinese were shot, hanged, or burned to death by white mobs that must have involved a sizable percentage of the non-Chinese male population.[67] Many, many more were killed singly or in small groups in isolated mining regions throughout the West. One recent historian has claimed that over one hundred Chinese were killed in Idaho in 1866–1867. A decade later, in 1879, Indians killed five Chinese in Idaho, setting off the so-called Sheepeater War.[68] Most of the early violence was in California: Elmer Sandmeyer lists thirty-one urban centers, from Los Angeles in the South to Red Bluff in the North, that underwent burnings of Chinese stores and residences and expulsions of Chinese residents.[69] But the worst and most widespread anti-Chinese rioting took place outside of California after the passage of the 1882 Chinese Exclusion Act.

In the 1880s the most serious violence shifted to the Pacific Northwest and the Mountain states. The highest incidence of Chinese ever shown for any American state or territory was in Idaho in 1870. The 1870 census for the territory recorded 4,274 Chinese who represented 27 percent of the total population. Chinese were also statistically significant in Montana, Oregon, and Washington (see table 2.1), and major anti-Chinese disorders occurred in each of these areas.

There were major anti-Chinese riots in Denver, Colorado, in 1880 and in Rock Springs, Wyoming, in 1885. A whole series of related riots and "deportations" followed in Seattle and Tacoma,

---

66. Historians have ignored much of the anti-Chinese and anti-Asian violence. Richard Maxwell Brown, "Historiography of Violence in the American West," in Michael P. Malone, ed., *Historians in the American West*, pp. 234–69, can find room for only two sketchy paragraphs on anti-Chinese violence (at pp. 250–51). Brown relegates anti-Filipino violence to a footnote dealing with "Hispanic violence," and he totally ignores violence directed at Japanese and South Asians. See also works cited in note 12, this chapter.

67. William R. Locklear, "The Celestials and the Angels: A Study of the Anti-Chinese Movement in Los Angeles to 1882," *Historical Society of Southern California Quarterly* 42 (1960): 239–56.

68. F. Ross Peterson, *Idaho*, pp. 60–61, 85–86.

69. Sandmeyer, *Anti-Chinese Movement*, pp. 48, 97–98. For a detailed account of what happened to Chinese in one nonmetropolitan California county, see two articles by Lynwood Carranco: "Chinese Expulsion from Humboldt County," *Pacific Historical Review*, 30 (1961): 329–37; and "Chinese in Humboldt County, California: A Study in Prejudice," *Journal of the West* 12 (1973): 139–62. For interesting but one-sided material about how Chinese fared in a pair of small California mining towns in the latter nineteenth century, see Roger D. McGrath, *Gunfighters, Highwaymen and Vigilantes*, especially chapter 7, "Violence and the Minorities."

Table 2.1
Chinese Americans in Washington, Oregon, Idaho, and Montana,
1870–1910

	Chinese Population					Chinese as Percentage of State Population				
Year	1870	1880	1890	1900	1910	1870	1880	1890	1900	1910
Washington	234	3,186	3,260	3,629	2,709	1.0	4.2	.9	.7	.2
Oregon	3,330	9,510	9,540	10,397	7,363	3.6	5.5	3.0	2.5	1.1
Idaho	4,274	3,379	2,007	1,467	859	27.0	10.4	2.4	.9	.03
Montana	1,949	1,765	2,532	1,739	1,285	9.4	4.5	1.9	.7	.03

SOURCE: U.S. Census.

Washington, and in the vicinity of Portland, Oregon, throughout 1885–1886. All of these outbreaks have been attributed, in part at least, to the depressed regional economic conditions, particularly in the Pacific Northwest, that followed the completion of northern transcontinental railroads. All could claim at least some support from most segments of the communities involved; although labor clearly took the lead in the anti-Chinese movement and supplied much of the "muscle," the growing national consensus about the supposed inferiority and perpetual alienness of the Chinese was a vital contributing factor.

In Denver just before the election of 1880, the *Rocky Mountain News* fanned the Chinese presence and the forged Morey letter into chief campaign issues. Day after day at the end of October, the *News* stressed the menace of what it called the "Pest of the Pacific Coast" and, on October 28, even incited to violence: "There has been considerable talk about town the past few days about running out the Chinese. The flock is increasing every week and they are not wanted."

The 1880 census showed 612 Chinese in Colorado, with 238 living in Denver. After the October 31 riot, the Chinese consul from San Francisco, F. A. Bee, estimated that the Chinese population in Denver had grown to perhaps 450, most of whom ran laundries or wash houses, in a city of some 40,000. On the afternoon of October 31 a mob shouting death threats to the Chinese and crying "Garfield's a Chinaman!" overwhelmed the eight police on duty as well as the firemen, whom the mayor had ordered to turn their hoses on the rioters. The mob destroyed most of the buildings in the Denver Chinatown and managed to get their hands on one hapless Chinese, a laundryman named Sing Lee. They put a rope around his neck, dragged him through the streets, and kicked and beat him to death. Some persons were indicted and tried for Sing Lee's murder, but a jury found them not guilty in February 1881.

In the riot's aftermath, the *Rocky Mountain News* blamed the "alleged riot" on "the outrageous throwing of water." The Fort Collins *Express*, a Republican newspaper, insisted that only "the party that hung Negroes to lamp posts and burned colored orphans in New York would torture . . . Chinamen in Denver." A more appropriate comment came from one Wong Chin Foo, whose Chicago lecture was reported in a Denver newspaper. Wong pointed out that if anything like the Denver riot had happened to Americans in China, 100,000 "missionaries" would have been sent to "civilize the heathen."[70]

Another incident, usually termed the Rock Springs Massacre, was more cause specific than most of the anti-Asian racial violence. Rock Springs, Wyoming Territory, was a division point on the Union Pacific railroad and also a coal-mining center. Chinese had been brought there in 1875 by the Union Pacific Railroad to serve as strike-breakers in a mining strike.[71] The railroad had, of course, employed thousands of Chinese in its construction, and it continued to employ Chinese in its many enterprises throughout the century.

In the fall of 1885 there seem to have been 331 Chinese and 150 Caucasians employed by the Union Pacific in mining in Rock Springs. A dispute on the morning of September 2, 1885, over who had the right to work a particularly desirable "room" in the mine—miners were paid by the ton so that where one worked in the mine was significant—led to an exchange in which two Chinese were badly beaten by white miners. The white miners, most of whom were members of the Knights of Labor, then walked out.

The men gathered in saloons waiting for a 6:00 P.M. meeting "to settle the Chinese question." Around 2:00 P.M. all the groceries and saloons were persuaded to close—almost certainly by a Union Pacific official—and perhaps 150 men, about half of them armed with "Winchester rifles," headed for the Chinese quarter. Shots were fired; many Chinese ran. As one eyewitness later described it, "the China-men were fleeing like a herd of hunted antelopes, making no resistance. Volley upon volley was fired after the fugitives. In a few minutes

---

70. Roy T. Wortman, "Denver's Anti-Chinese Riot, 1880," *The Colorado Magazine* 42 (1965): 275–91.

71. The following account of Rock Springs is drawn from Paul Crane and Alfred Larson, "The Chinese Massacre," *Annals of Wyoming* 12 (1940): 47–55, 153–60. Only the first portion was reprinted in Daniels, *Anti-Chinese Violence*, owing to a publisher's error.

the hill east of the town was literally blue with hunted Chinamen." Others, as the coroner's jury later reported, "came to their death from exposure to fire" as much of the Chinese quarter was burned to the ground by the mob.

The official toll was 28 Chinese dead and 15 wounded; property damage was officially assessed at $147,000. The total Chinese population of Rock Springs, which Larson and Crane estimate at between six and seven hundred, was driven away. A deposition collected by the Chinese government in mid-September and signed by 559 former Chinese residents of the town reported that: "while they knew that the white men entertained ill feelings toward them the Chinese did not take any precautions . . . inasmuch as at no time in the past had there been . . . fighting between the races."

Although hundreds of persons must have known who was guilty, the miners had the kind of community consent that lynch mobs often enjoyed. The grand jury of Sweetwater County, clearly speaking for the white majority, indicted no one, claiming no cause for legal action:

> We have diligently inquired into the occurrence at Rock Springs . . .
> and though we have examined a large number of witnesses, no one
> has been able to testify to a single criminal act committed by any
> known white person that day. . . . We have also inquired into the
> causes. . . . While we find no excuse for the crimes committed, there
> appears to be no doubt of abuses existing that should have been
> promptly adjusted by the railroad company and its officers. If this
> had been done, the fair name of our Territory would not have been
> stained by the terrible events of the 2d of September.

The sixteen whites who had been arrested for riot participation had to be released. The Coal Department of the Union Pacific apparently knew more than the grand jury; it discharged forty-five miners for participation in the riot. United States Army troops, requested by territorial Governor Francis E. Warren, escorted some Chinese back to Rock Springs on September 9, and the Union Pacific continued to employ some of them there until well into the twentieth century. Sentiment in the towns along the Union Pacific mainline in southern Wyoming, where most of the territory's 50,000 people lived, was virulently anti-Chinese according to the historians of the massacre. The Laramie *Boomerang*, although it "regretted" the riot, found extenuating circumstances, as did the Cheyenne *Tribune*: the Rock Springs *Independent* denounced the railroad's alleged intention of making a "Chinatown" out of Rock Springs and called for a rebellion against both the railroad and law and order: "Let the demand go up from one end of the Union Pacific to the other, THE CHINESE MUST GO."

The week after the Rock Springs massacre, a Seattle newspaper insisted that "the civilization of the Pacific Coast cannot exist half Caucasian and half Mongolian."[72] Four days earlier three Chinese had been shot to death and three others wounded in a midnight ambush of thirty-seven hop pickers in western Washington. Seven persons—five whites and two American Indians—were actually indicted but could not be convicted. Later that month Chinese miners were violently expelled from at least three western Washington coal mines, and similar anti-Chinese expulsions took place around Portland, Oregon. Even worse, five Chinese were lynched near Pierce City, Idaho.

The most persistent anti-Chinese movements were entrenched in the Puget Sound communities of Tacoma and Seattle. Again, much of the pressure came from the Knights of Labor. A representative of the Knights told a Seattle gathering on September 21, 1885, that if Chinese were not removed from Tacoma and Seattle, "there will be riot and bloodshed [and a] proceeding similar to that which lately happened in Wyoming territory." Fortunately casualties were few in the mass expulsions from Tacoma, Seattle, and other communities in the Puget Sound region. The disturbances involved more property loss than loss of life. Chinese were given deadlines to leave; those who did not were "escorted" to steamers, which took them elsewhere. Often their shops were looted; their stores and homes were burned. In Tacoma the mayor, two councilmen, a probate judge, and twenty-three other whites were indicted for conspiracy and insurrection but, as it was almost always impossible to convict "respectable" whites of crimes against persons of color, none were found guilty.

To avoid similar disorder, 350 federal troops were brought to Seattle, where they patrolled for less than two weeks, administering random beatings to Chinese in the process. Although many Chinese left Seattle in November in the aftermath of the Tacoma expulsions, some remained and apparently some returned. About dawn on February 7, 1886, nearly five months later, groups of whites went to

---

72. The materials on the Pacific Northwest are drawn from Jules Alexander Karlin's fine essays: "The Anti-Chinese Outbreaks in Seattle, 1885–1886," *Pacific Northwest Quarterly* 39 (1948): 103–29; and "The Anti-Chinese Outbreak in Tacoma, 1885," *Pacific Historical Review* 23 (1964): 271–83; and from Robert E. Wynne, *Reaction to the Chinese in the Pacific Northwest and British Columbia, 1850–1910.* See also James A. Halseth and Bruce A. Glasrud, eds., *The Northwest Mosaic: Minority Conflicts in the Pacific Northwest;* Kenneth Owens, "Pierce City Incident," *Idaho Yesterdays* 3 (1959): 8–13, which describes lynching of five Chinese; Larry D. Quinn, "Chink, Chink, Chinaman: The Beginnings of Nativism in Montana," *Pacific Northwest Quarterly* 58 (1967): 82–89; and Margaret Willson and Jeffrey L. MacDonald, "Racial Tension at Port Townsend and Bellingham Bay, 1870–1886," *Annals of the Chinese Historical Society of the Pacific Northwest* 1 (1983): 1–15.

Chinatown to inform all Chinese that they must leave on a steamer at one o'clock that afternoon. Almost 200 Chinese did leave on the steamer, but a number remained. Gunfire broke out between rioters and the "Home Guard," which was escorting back to their homes those Chinese who did not leave. Five white persons were killed. The governor declared martial law, and, for the second time, federal troops came, arriving on February 10 and remaining until February 22. In the meantime most of the remaining Chinese left. Six anti-Chinese leaders were arrested and indicted but were acquitted by a jury. Although the violence was sparked by labor, it is again clear that the majority of the white community wanted the Chinese to go: the only real dispute was about the method of their going.

The last major bloody event of the decade in the region was the Snake River Massacre of 1887, described by David Stratton as "one of the worst, yet least known, instances of violence against Chinese" in America. Thirty-one Chinese miners were robbed, murdered, and mutilated by a white gang in the isolated Hell's Canyon gorge in Oregon. Although eventually the names of the murderers were learned—one turned state's evidence, and three were actually brought to trial—none was convicted. As Stratton points out, although this seemed different from other kinds of anti-Chinese violence in the region, it was cut from the same cloth and stemmed from the same kind of racism.

> . . . The killers might have robbed a small group of white miners, and might presumably have shot some of them, but would they have casually slaughtered thirty-one of their fellow Caucasians? Probably not. As a contemporary white rancher commented about the acquittal of the three gang members who stood trial, "I guess if they had killed 31 white men something would have been done about it, but none of the jury knew the Chinamen or knew much about it, so they turned the men loose.[73]

Northwesterners had the same kind of regional paranoia that consumed Californians. The editor of one small-town Puget Sound newspaper put it nicely, writing two months before the September 1885 wave of violence began, and three years after the Chinese Exclusion Act:

---

73. David H. Stratton, "The Snake River Massacre of Chinese Miners, 1887," in Duane A. Smith, ed., *A Taste of the West: Essays in Honor of Robert G. Athearn*, at pp. 124–25. Stratton's careful reconstruction includes such details as "a Chinese skull fashioned into a sugar bowl graced the kitchen table of one ranch home for many years" ibid., p. 119.

The chicken hearted Puritans of the east who for years have refused to aid the Pacific Coast in its efforts to check Chinese hordes from swarming into this country should be given a dose of their own medicine. Let us do everything to encourage the Chinese to leave for the eastern states and a few years will bring about a revolution that will retire the 'man and brother' element from eastern politics.[74]

As noted, most of this regional violence took place after the passage of the 1882 Chinese Exclusion Act. While exacerbated by the economic stringency of the mid-1880s, the regional behavior pattern cannot be accounted for merely by economic factors. The national climate of opinion, pervaded by racism and a burgeoning feeling of ethnic superiority or what Barbara Miller Solomon has called the "Anglo-Saxon complex," certainly contributed not just to the violence but also to the virtual unanimity with which the white majority put its seal of approval on anti-Chinese ends if not means.[75] John R. Wunder's description of what happened to Chinese in Montana's courts describes essentially what was happening in almost every sphere of human endeavor throughout the region:

> At first the legal institutions in Montana faced their tasks squarely and blunted the force of anti-Chinese public opinion. From the late 1860s until the first passage of a federal statute limiting Chinese immigration in 1882, Montana's courts listened to Chinese complaints, recognized their seriousness, and judged them equitably. But it was not too long before their judicial monitoring broke down and the Chinese lost in the courts. After the mid-1880s, Montana's justices seemed to reflect popular attitudes toward the Chinese. The court became anti-Chinese too.[76]

Another factor was probably psychological. The national anti-Chinese campaign was not just a crusade for the halting of immigration. In terms of rhetoric, at least, it was a campaign to get rid of Chinese. But in the Northwest it was clear that the Chinese did not go: in many northwestern towns and cities the end of the regional railroad boom after 1883 brought a greater number of Chinese, absolutely and relatively, than had been there before. Adding this influx to the regional feelings of inferiority and resentment toward the East, feelings typical of the attitude of a frontier toward a metropolis, did much to fuel the disgraceful and largely irrational events of the middle eighties. The fact that similar anti-Chinese activities were taking place

---

74. Halseth and Glasrud, *Northwest Mosaic*, p. 117.
75. Barbara Miller Solomon, *Ancestors and Immigrants*.
76. Wunder, "Law and the Chinese," p. 31.

just north of the border in British Columbia and as far away as Juneau, Alaska, during the decade lends credence to the notion of a kind of regional reflex action.[77]

However they might be driven from this or that community, or be deprived of employment, or suffer destruction of their property, the Chinese did not go. Their numbers diminished for half a century, but they remained—as William Faulkner might have put it, they endured. The nature of that endurance is what makes the story of Chinese America unique.

77. For a perceptive and provocative hypothesis about transnational regional relationships, see Carlos A. Schwantes, *Radical Heritage: Labor, Socialism, and Reform in Washington and British Columbia, 1885–1917*. Ted C. Hinckley, "Prospectors, Profits and Prejudice," *The American West* 2, no. 2 (1965): 59–65, describes the 1886 expulsion of Chinese from Juneau.

3.

Chinese America, 1880–1941

While some scholars tend to treat ethnic groups in the way that politician Spiro Agnew treated slums—"If you've seen one, you've seen them all"—the fact remains that each and every ethnic group expresses its ethnicity in a unique way. Asian ethnic groups are no exception. As this book will try to demonstrate, significant differences continue to exist between the experiences of Chinese Americans and Japanese Americans. Furthermore, although there will be no attempt to tell their stories here, real differences remain between the experiences of Korean Americans, Filipino Americans, Asian Indian Americans, and each of the other groups that have come to comprise Asian America.

From a legal and legislative point of view, of course, Asian Americans have shared a common status: all were "aliens ineligible to citizenship." Starting with the Chinese in 1882, all suffered from invidious treatment by American immigration law until 1965. Until recently, therefore, immigrants from Asia were in a special category: they were the first to be singled out for discriminatory treatment by our immigration laws, and they were the only ethnic groups ever to be totally excluded.

Looking just at the Chinese experience, several factors stand out, including geographic distribution and patterns of employment. The critical factor, however, that differentiates the Chinese American experience from a more generalized Asian American experience, is the demography of Chinese America. For four decades, from the early 1880s until sometime in the 1920s, the number of Chinese Americans shrank. From an intercensal peak of perhaps 125,000 in 1882, the numbers dropped to a census low of just over 60,000 in 1920 and then rose to almost 80,000 in 1940. That long period of decline, in and of itself, is unprecedented in the history of American ethnic groups.

Raw Chinese American population figures can be misleading: the extremely skewed sex and age patterns in the community must also be taken into account. In all ethnic groups, from the time of Jamestown until the end of World War II, immigration to America had been predominantly male, that sex accounting for perhaps two-thirds of all entries to the United States. Among the Chinese, however, and later among some other Asian groups, the sex ratios were much higher. A predominantly bachelor society prevailed in Chinese America until after World War II. In 1860 there were more than 18 Chinese men to every Chinese woman; by 1940 (see table 3.1), the ratio had dropped to 2.9 to 1. But for foreign-born adult males, the available partners were much scarcer than the overall community sex ratios would indicate. In 1900, for example, when the general sex ratio was almost 19 to 1, the sex ratio for foreign born was nearly twice that, more than 36 to 1. Since the overwhelming number of citizen females were small children, the larger figure was the more meaningful one. For 1920, when we have age-specific data (see table 3.2), we can be more precise. The median age of the male Chinese population that year was 42; that is, half the men were older and half younger. For women the median age was 19. If we subtract all Chinese, male and female, under age 10 that year, we find that for Chinese age 10 and over, there were almost 10 males to every female (9.84 to be precise).

We can also see from table 3.2 that Chinese America was a community dominated by old men, as the median age of 42 suggests. The largest single five-year cohort comprised men of ages 50 to 54. Foreign-born males outnumbered citizen males into the World War II era; citizens had been in the majority among females since before the turn of the century. If one were trying to create a population model likely to resist acculturation, one could choose the reality of Chinese America. Add to this a heavily male-dominated culture, a history of brutal discrimination, extreme residential segregation, and a high degree of cultural differentiation between Chinese and most other Americans, and one can begin to understand the relatively slow acculturation of the Chinese American community.

This is not to suggest, as some authorities have, that Chinese America was a static sojourner society between 1880 and 1941. Those years saw great and continual changes, with geographic changes being only the most easily noticeable. Chinese became, like certain other immigrant groups, predominantly not only urban but large-city urban. Unlike most other urban-centered ethnic groups, however, Chinese moved to large cities after having been primarily rural and small town.

Table 3.1
Chinese American Population, Sex, Citizenship, and Sex Ratio,
1860–1940

Year	Male	Female	Total	Ratio Males:Females
1860	33,149	1,784	34,933	18.6:1
1870	58,633	4,566	63,199	12.8:1
1880	100,686	4,779	105,465	21.1:1
1890	103,620	3,868	107,488	26.8:1
1900	85,341	4,522	89,863	18.9:1
Foreign born	78,684	2,169	80,853	36.3:1
Citizen	6,657	2,353	9,010	2.8:1
1910	66,858	4,675	71,531	14.3:1
Foreign born	54,935	1,661	56,596	33.1:1
Citizen	11,921	3,014	14,935	4.0:1
1920	53,891	7,748	61,639	7.0:1
Foreign born	40,573	2,534	43,107	16.0:1
Citizen	13,318	5,214	18,532	2.6:1
1930	59,802	15,152	74,954	3.9:1
Foreign born	39,109	4,977	44,086	7.9:1
Citizen	20,693	10,175	30,868	2.0:1
1940	57,389	20,115	77,504	2.9:1
Foreign born	31,687	5,555	37,242	5.7:1
Citizen	25,702	14,560	40,262	1.8:1

SOURCE: U.S. Census.

In 1880, for example, only 21.7 percent of Chinese lived in cities of over 100,000. This percentage increased with every census. By 1910 almost half (48.5 percent) of Chinese Americans lived in such cities. By 1940 the figure had risen to 71 percent.

Initially, large city meant San Francisco, which Chinese called *dai fou* or "big city." By 1940, however, only 17,782 of 55,030 large-city Chinese Americans (32.3 percent) lived in San Francisco, with an additional 3,201 (5.8 percent) across the bay in Oakland. Seven other cities had more than 1,000 Chinese in 1940; there were 12,302 in New York, nearly 5,000 in Los Angeles, and just over 2,000 in Chicago. Seattle, Portland (Oregon), Sacramento, and Boston each had between 1,000 and 2,000 Chinese.[1]

It is customary today simply to write off such ethnic enclaves as "ghettos." While Chinatowns certainly had many of the worst characteristics of ghettos, for many of the Chinese immigrants and Chinese Americans of later generations, a positive aspect obtained. And there was a positive aspect of ethnic enclaves generally. As one Chinatown resident remarked in the mid-1920s:

> Most of us can live a warmer, freer and a more human life among our relatives and friends than among strangers. . . . Chinese relations with the population outside Chinatown are likely to be cold, formal, and commercial. It is only in Chinatown that a Chinese immigrant has society, friends and relatives who share his dreams and hopes, his hardships, and adventures. Here he can tell a joke and make everybody laugh with him; here he may hear folktales told which create the illusion that Chinatown is really China.[2]

The shift to larger cities was accompanied by a distinct reduction of the percentage of Chinese found in California and the West, although the Golden State contained an absolute majority of Chinese Americans in every census of the period except that of 1920. Within California the incidence of Chinese in the total population sank slowly and steadily throughout the nineteenth century: in 1860 Chinese had comprised 9.2 percent of the population; in 1880, 8.7 percent; in 1900, 3.1 percent. By 1940 Chinese represented only .6 of 1 percent. Put another way, in 1860 about one Californian in eleven was

---

1. We know very little about Chinatowns in this era apart from those in San Francisco and New York. Three essays by geographers give capsule histories of those of Oakland, Chicago, and Los Angeles in *The China Geographer* 4 (1976): 1–42. See also Loren B. Chan, "The Chinese in Nevada: An Historical Survey," *Nevada Historical Society Quarterly* 25 (1982): 266–314; Art Chin, *Golden Tassels: A History of the Chinese in Washington, 1857–1977;* Willard T. Chow, *The Reemergence of an Inner City: The Pivot of Chinese Settlement in the East Bay Region of the San Francisco Bay Area;* Nelson C. Ho, *Portland's Chinatown;* Rhoads Murphey, "Boston's Chinatown," *Economic Geography* 28 (1952): 245–55; and Edward J. M. Rhoades, "The Chinese in Texas," *Southwestern Historical Quarterly* 81 (1977): 1–36. David M. Deal, "Chinese Labor in Walla Walla," *Chinese Historical Society of America, Bulletin* 12, no. 10 (1977): 2–6 is an account of the Chinese in a small western city.
2. Ching-Chao Wu, "Chinatowns: A Study in Symbiosis and Assimilation" (Ph.D. diss., University of Chicago, 1928), p. 158.

Chinese; in 1940 about one in two hundred was Chinese. Table 3.3 demonstrates the nature of this population change.[3]

In Idaho, Montana, and Nevada, the precipitate decline in the number of Chinese represents their elimination from the mining industry, or, in some instances, the decline of that industry. For a time, however, the incidence of Chinese in the population of certain western states and territories was relatively high, with a peak of 28.5 percent in Idaho in 1870. Other high incidences were 9.5 percent of Montana's population in the 1870 census and 8.7 percent of Nevada's population ten years later.

These Chinese pioneers have largely been written out of the histories of those states; if they have appeared at all, it has been as exotic curiosities or victims. Their pioneering role as developers of the economy of the West has simply been ignored.[4] Much of the history of Chinese America remains to be written, particularly that part of it

---

3. The following table indicates the 1890 distribution.

City	Chinese Population	% of Population
San Francisco	21,745	9
Oakland	1,974	6
Sacramento	1,781	8
Portland	1,668	9
Stockton	687	7
San Jose	634	5
Los Angeles	605	5
Virginia City	519	5

SOURCE: Lawrence H. Larsen, *The Urban West at the End of the Frontier*, p. 26.

4. Part of the problem is the Eurocentricity of most scholars of American immigration. For example, Frederick C. Luebke, author of path-breaking studies of German immigrants, in his historiographical essay devoted to "Ethnic Minorities in the American West," chooses to exclude the large literature about Asian Americans, acknowledging that "no attempt is made here to survey the many contributions to Asian American history." In my view, the ethnic history of the American West is unique owing to the presence there, since the mid-19th century, of statistically significant numbers of Asians, and, since the 18th century, of Mexican Americans. Luebke finds the experience of "Non-Europeans . . . fundamentally different." I, of course, strongly disagree. In addition, I would argue that the experience of European ethnics in the West cannot be understood without noting the effect on their status of the presence of "nonwhites." In a nutshell, the presence of large numbers of such persons raised the status of all "whites." Luebke's essay is in Michael P. Malone, ed., *Historians and the American West*, pp. 387–413; quotations at pp. 401–02.

Table 3.2
Chinese Americans 1920
Age and Sex Distribution

Age Cohort	Male	% in cohort	Female	% in cohort
75 +	522	1.0	23	0.3
70–74	1188	2.2	29	0.4
65–69	2261	4.2	42	0.5
60–64	4416	8.2	88	1.1
55–59	5476	10.2	118	1.5
50–54	5850	10.9	195	2.5
45–49	5242	9.7	285	3.7
40–44	4913	9.1	432	5.6
35–39	4789	8.9	530	6.8
30–34	4093	7.6	589	7.6
25–29	4543	8.4	736	9.5
20–24	4122	7.6	723	9.3
15–19	2161	4.0	599	7.7
10–14	1223	2.3	782	10.1
5–9	1370	2.5	1141	14.7
0–4	1480	2.7	1418	18.3
age unknown	242	0.4	18	0.2
Total	53,891		7,748	
Median Age	Males 42 years		Females 19 years	

SOURCE: United States Department of Commerce. Bureau of the Census. *1920 Census of Population* 1, tables 4, 5, and 10, pp. 157, 166–67.

which existed outside of California. In one of the few available studies, a 1947 doctoral dissertation at the University of Chicago, sociologist Rose Hum Lee examined her own hometown, the China-town of Butte, Montana. I will use Butte as surrogate for the dozens of "lost" Chinatowns, which either no longer exist or exist as mere shadows of what they once were. Since few of these Chinatowns have been studied, it is impossible to know if Butte was representative, but I suspect that it was not.

Butte, of course, is one of the most famous mining towns in

Table 3.3

Chinese American Population in California and Other Western States, 1870–1940

Year	1870	1880	1890	1900	1910	1920	1930	1940
United States	63,199	105,465	107,488	89,863	71,531	61,639	74,954	77,504
California	49,277	75,132	72,472	45,753	36,248	28,812	37,361	39,556
% in California	78.0	71.2	67.4	51.5	50.7	46.7	50.1	51.0
Oregon	3,330	9,510	9,540	10,397	7,363	3,090	2,075	2,086
Washington	234	3,186	3,260	3,629	2,709	2,363	2,195	2,345
Idaho	4,274	3,379	2,007	1,467	859	585	335	208
Montana	1,949	1,765	2,532	1,739	1,285	872	486	258
Wyoming	143	914	465	461	246	252	130	102
Colorado	7	612	1,398	599	373	291	233	216
Utah	445	501	806	572	371	342	342	228
Nevada	3,152	5,416	2,833	1,352	927	689	483	286
Arizona	20	1,630	1,170	1,419	1,305	1,137	1,110	1,449
New Mexico	…	57	361	341	248	171	133	106
Total in West	62,831	102,102	96,844	67,729	51,934	38,604	44,883	46,840
% in West	99.4	96.8	90.1	75.4	72.6	62.6	59.9	60.4

SOURCE: U.S. Census.

western America, where gold, then silver, and finally copper mining dominated all economic activity. As is usually true for frontier towns, Butte was predominantly male, with more than two males for every female as late as 1890. In the early days of Butte, Chinese were a significant proportion of the population—710 out of 3,363 or 21.1 percent in 1880. But Butte grew, and the Chinese population shrank; by 1910 the 281 Chinese in Butte were less than 1 percent of the city's 39,000, and by 1940 the 88 Chinese were just over .2 of 1 percent of Butte's population.

Although originally attracted to Montana by mining, Chinese mining entrepreneurs were deprived of their claims by the Montana Territorial Supreme Court's ruling in 1883, which declared void all mining claims held by aliens ineligible to citizenship.[5] Other Chinese entrepreneurs, particularly laundrymen, were harrassed first by boycotts and later by special taxes that discriminated against them in the California manner. As early as 1866 a group of Helena laundrymen felt constrained to place the following advocacy advertisement in the Montana *Radiator* in response to a boycott:

GOOD CHINAMEN

This is to certify that we, the undersigned, are good Chinamen and have lived in California and other parts of the United States, and that we have at all times been willing to abide by the laws of the United States, and the States and Territories in which we have lived. And are now willing to deport ourselves as good law abiding citizens of Montana Territory, and ask but that protection that the liberal and good government of this country permits us to enjoy. We pay all our taxes and assessments, and only ask that the good people of Montana may let us earn an honest living by the sweat of our brow.

YE SING
HOB HEE
YE HOB and others[6]

In Butte, particularly after they had been driven from mining, Chinese established laundries and restaurants catering to the general population. Others entered into domestic service in private homes, hotels, and rooming houses. Still others engaged in tailoring and produce-peddling. That many of these occupations were regarded as "women's work" is not accidental. In Butte, as elsewhere in the West, the unbalanced sex ratio in the general population encouraged Chinese to enter this sphere after they had been driven from mining and after primary railroad construction had been finished.

---

5. For a recent account of Chinese mining, see Randall E. Rohe, "After the Gold Rush: Chinese Mining in the Far West, 1850–1890," *Montana* 32 (1982): 2–19.

6. Montana *Radiator*, January 24, 1866, as cited by John R. Wunder, "Law and the Chinese in Frontier Montana," *Montana* 30, no. 3 (1980): 20.

The worst of the anti-Chinese movement in Butte was between 1895 and 1906, a period in which Butte was adversely affected by the so-called War of the Copper Kings, a struggle for control of the town's mineral riches. During that time the labor unions, often abetted by the local chamber of commerce, organized a citywide boycott of Chinese establishments—laundries, restaurants, and noodle parlors—while also campaigning against white businesses that employed Chinese labor. Union members caught patronizing Chinese establishments were fined. This period also witnessed anti-Chinese state laws and city ordinances as well as random but persistent violence against Chinese persons and property.

What makes the Butte story distinctive is that the town's Chinese had some success in resisting the boycott. They employed a prominent white lawyer, Colonel Wilbur Fisk Sanders (1834–1905), a former United States Senator from Montana and a Grand Master Mason. An old Chinese resident recounted the story to Rose Hum Lee in the winter of 1943–1944:

When the unions became strong, they tried to boycott the Chinese businesses and to put the Chinese out of work. H. F[aye], then one of the leading men in the community, together with three others [Dear Vick, H. Tong and Huie Pock] started a lawsuit. Each man put up $20, and with a thousand people, we had a big sum to fight with. When this amount was not enough, we subscribed more. Two of the leaders went to San Francisco and reported the matter to the Six Companies. They said out there, "You are crazy to go against labor unions and the American law." But we hired Sanders from Helena; he came here several times to see us and get our evidence. We went ahead with the lawsuit even though we knew we may not win it. If we lose, then every Chinese would have to leave town; we would have no room to stand. Fortunately, we won, else no Chinese would be in Butte today.

The Unions had men stationed in front of H. F[aye]'s place, which was then uptown on West Park and Montana Street. Later, he moved back to Chinatown; he bought a piece of property. The way the pickets were caught was when Sanders and several officials of Butte decided to go to the noodle parlor just to see what the pickets would do. They were not allowed to enter; immediately Sanders and the officials held the pickets, called the police and had them arrested. Then he brought suit against the unions for the Chinese.

We won the lawsuit after many hearings. When the Six Companies in San Francisco heard of the decision, they said, "The Butte Chinese are the smartest anywhere in the United States." We had no idea we would win either, but if we had not, none of us would be here today.[7]

But even as discrimination and hostility continued, some Chinese businessmen prospered. The Montana tax rolls show a steady increase in the value of Chinese real estate. As late as 1889 only one Chinese owned real estate, which had an assessed value of $200. Ten years later eleven Chinese owned real estate valued at $26,200. By 1909 the number of owners was down to six and the value up slightly to $33,720. By 1919 ten Chinese owned real estate assessed at $213,875; $71,733 of the total was the property of one merchant. The 1920s saw a slowing of growth; on the eve of the Depression eleven Chinese held property assessed at $262,060. For a community that totaled only 148 persons, this was a significant amount of property. We have no information about other assets, but they must have been considerable. After 1930 property data reflects the impact of the Depression and a declining population. At least ten parcels of Chinese-owned real estate with an assessed valuation of $116,140 were deeded to the county in lieu of taxes. As of 1944 ten Chinese owned property whose total value was down to $91,915.[8]

In its heyday Butte's Chinatown catered to a large non-Chinese clientele as well as to the local Chinese community (and, beginning in the early twentieth century, to smaller communities of Japanese, Koreans, and Filipinos). It also served as the economic and cultural center for the Chinese of Montana, Wyoming, and Idaho. Rose Hum Lee's data about the growth of the Chinese business community in Butte shows how over time Chinese became predominantly mercantile. In 1890, with nearly 600 Chinese in Butte, there were 13 Chinese-owned businesses. Twenty years later, when population had shrunk to just over 300, there were 69 businesses or 1 for every 4.6 persons. By 1930, when the wealth of the Chinese community measured in taxable real estate was highest, a population of only 148 operated 40 businesses or 1 for each 4.1 Chinese persons. Businesses catered increasingly to non-Asian clientele: in 1890 about half of the Butte businesses did; by 1910, 60 of 69 did. By 1945, when the Butte Chinatown was almost a ghost town, only 1 of 14 businesses catered primarily to Asians.[9]

7. Rose Hum Lee, *The Growth and Decline of Chinese Communities in the Rocky Mountain Region*, p. x. This is a photographic reprint of Lee's 1947 doctoral dissertation in sociology at the University of Chicago. For a brief assessment of her career, see Stanford M. Lyman, "In Memoriam: Rose Hum Lee (1904–1964)," in his *The Asian in North America*, pp. 259–60. For Wilbur Fisk Sanders, see *Biographical Directory of the American Congress*.

8. Lee, *Chinese Communities*, pp. 155–69.

9. Ibid., pp. 190–91.

Butte and other smaller Chinatowns had a higher degree of entrepreneurship per capita than did the larger urban centers. Many other American cities had one or two Chinese families and one or two Chinese businesses. The resultant high incidence of petty entrepreneurship among Asian Americans, long noted by observers, has often been misunderstood. For example, Gunnar Myrdal, in his massive 1945 study of black America, noted of Asian Americans that "in 1929 they owned one-and-a-half times as many businesses per 1,000 population as other residents of the United States.[10] But Myrdal did not suggest the underlying reasons for this. First, "new" ethnic groups tend to have a relatively high degree of ethnic businesses simply because of the special needs of the group: not only would one's ethnic grocer import and stock the articles with which one was familiar but also one could shop in one's own language. But how to explain the exceptional growth in "outpost" Chinatowns like Butte of businesses that catered largely to non-Chinese customers? Here a number of factors obviously interacted: Chinese men were driven from some of their earliest occupations, such as placer mining; the relative scarcity of women in the American West pushed these men into "women's work"; they came from a culture in which business and business dealings were highly developed; the law itself both barred them from many professions and gave special preference to what were called "treaty merchants." The Chinese American could exploit the labor of other Chinese, sometimes his kinsmen and usually his fellow clansmen, who had fewer employment options than other American workers. Furthermore, the Chinese employer often had a special hold on his workers—many of them were "illegals" whom he could turn in.

Sociologist Ivan Light correctly points out another factor, the existence of rotating credit associations among Chinese and Japanese immigrants which enabled these Asian Americans to raise money.[11] These kinds of informal pre-banking arrangements, however, are ethnically widespread and so do not in themselves account for the singular success rate of Asian American enterprises. Other factors would seem to be much more important. If one compares, for example, the business success of post-1945 Puerto Rican and Cuban migrants to the United States, one must conclude that the chief advantage of most of the Cubans—at least until the Mariel exodus in

---

10. Gunnar Myrdal, *An American Dilemma*, 1:310.

11. Ivan H. Light, *Ethnic Enterprise in America*. See my review in *International Migration Review* 6 (1972): 455–56; Light's reply in ibid., 7 (1973): 219–20; and review essays by R. Takaki, W. E. Perkins, and L. Wang, in *Journal of Ethnic Studies* 1, no. 4 (1974): 69–88.

the Carter administration—was that they were from a culture and of a class in which business enterprise prevailed. Thus ensued the differences between Spanish Harlem and Little Havana.

The Chinese American economy began to shift away from catering to Chinese American customers, who were declining in numbers while the number of Chinese American businesses was increasing. This happened in Butte as well as in the nation. In another of Rose Hum Lee's mid-1940s interviews, the oldest Chinese woman in Butte reminisced with great charm about the late nineteenth and early twentieth centuries:

> I made all my pin money sewing dozens upon dozens of [loose-fitting Chinese-style] suits for the merchandise stores. I was always busy. The suits even went to men outside of Butte; they would send in their orders. As soon as I made a dozen, I would start on another. Practically all of the women of the community sewed like I did, or mended. We had all we could do.
>
> I made two kinds of suits; washable ones for every day and woolen ones for special occasions. I never saw the men but my husband took orders at our store. He wrote down the measurements; I made the garments and sent them back through my husband. I saved several thousand dollars doing this until the Revolution [1911, not 1949!]. Then all the men cut their queues and changed over to American clothes. I was caught with some extra suits; I still have them. No one wants them now.[12]

This interview also illustrates an important and often unnoticed factor in Asian American economic success: that is, the contribution made by Asian American married women at a time when most married women in this country were not in the labor force.

One aspect of Butte's Chinatown seems unique: the predominance of the noodle parlor as opposed to the Chinese restaurant. By the mid-nineties noodle parlors had been established in Butte and were a great success. These wet noodles, *yatcamein,* could be found on Chinese menus elsewhere, but only in Montana were they a specialty. The noodles were cooked in clear chicken or meat broth and served with sliced hard-boiled eggs and slices of roast pork, duck, or chicken.[13] Operating somewhat like the modern fast-food franchise, the noodle parlors did a large takeout business. In those days of cheap labor before the auto, the orders were delivered to customers by Western Union messenger boys, with the city divided into zones for

---

12. Lee, *Chinese Communities,* pp. 193–94.
13. Ibid., pp. 187–89.

delivery charges. A Montana state publication described "seven noodle parlors . . . with a steady string of messenger boys carrying covered trays from noodle parlors to rooms of gamblers, West side homes and the cribs."[14]

Most numerous among the business enterprises of Butte's Chinese was the laundry; this business came to symbolize Chinese American enterprise. The laundry business was ideal for Chinese. It required relatively little capital or education and could be easily learned by working in a laundry run by a clansman.[15] The Butte laundry business, during much of the period under consideration, differed from the national pattern in that Chinese laundries in Butte were an absolute majority of all laundries; few operations were as big as the ones described below, and very few Chinese laundries in other cities delivered. Selections from several of Rose Hum Lee's interviews vividly describe the situation:

> When I first came to Butte (1905) laundries were plentiful. There were about thirty-two of them. They were located all over the city. Everything had to be done by hand. Each laundry had at least two washers, one main washer and one assistant washer. There were at least two "outdoor men"; they collected clothes and delivered the finished work in baskets which they carried over their shoulders. There were four ironers—maybe a starcher, and one man to do the odds and ends, like tying tickets and boiling water. . . .
>
> As customers lived on the West Side, the "outdoor men" had a long way to walk with their baskets of clothes. It was not until 1926 that automobiles were used: Hung Sing was the first to buy one. Then other laundries followed. Machinery was put into laundries about this time; we put in gas mangles and ironers for collars. This helped with the work but reduced the number of men. We had to do it because the immigration law restricted "students" from coming. Laundries were short of help. It used to be that young boys ten, twelve or older could come, go to school a few years, learn some English, and help their relatives. . . . The automobile saved time; clothes could be delivered one day a week and collected the same day. [This could have been done earlier with horses; the earliest laundry proprietors would not have had the capital for them, but,

---

14. WPA Writers Program, Montana, *Copper Camp*, p. 116.

15. For Chinese laundries generally, see Paul C. P. Siu, "The Chinese Laundryman: A Study in Social Isolation" (Ph.D. diss., University of Chicago, 1954); and Paul Ong, "An Ethnic Trade: The Chinese Laundries in Early California," *Journal of Ethnic Studies* 8 (1981): 95–113.

even when they did, it was more profitable to use manpower until it began to run out.]

A good wage was considered $30 to $40 a month when I was a newcomer. This did not include food, a place to sleep, and sometimes a suit of work clothes provided by the bosses. If the business is a partnership, the profits were pooled after deducting expenses. . . .

Today things are different. Even the occasional worker [hired by the day] gets $3.50 to $4.00 a day. They work or not as they please. For instance "G" works two days a week at one laundry and two days at another. The rest of the week he loafs or washes dishes in a restaurant. [Clearly, Social Darwinistic notions about workers are not entertained only by the middle and upper classes. Although not specified here, in the good old days Chinese laundries often worked seven days a week.] Today if a laundryman becomes ill, he either has to work while ill or close his door. It wasn't like that when I was a newcomer. Others in the laundry would help out, or I'd hire a substitute and pay him myself. Or if I wanted to take time off, I'd hire someone to come in. [Obviously, there was Chinese underemployment in Butte, and, clearly, there was for decades, a large, floating male Chinese population that may never have been included in the census.] I used to have to do this often because I was a washer. My hands used to get red, rough and sore from constant soaking in lye and hot water. I also had to wring all the clothes by hand. I'd have to take days off to give my hands time to heal from the sores.

After a while I gave up working in a laundry. My uncle put up some money for me so I ran my own laundry. . . . I bought this from a man who wanted to go away; he couldn't get along with his partner. I went into partnership with a clan cousin; I couldn't get along with him so I sold my share and opened another laundry half a block away. I finally sold that and went to work in a herb store. Then I went to work in a merchandise store.

Laundries were so plentiful when I came that they were constantly changing hands. When a laundry was put up for sale, the owner would put up a red paper notice in Chinatown. He'd state the price for "po aye" (goodwill and equipment), give a general description of the location, amount of business done each month, and what equipment he had. . . . When a deal was closed, another red paper notice giving the name of the buyer, price of sale, date of sale, was posted so all could read. In case of a quarrel later, those who saw and read the red paper notices would know who is right and who is wrong.[16]

---

16. Lee, *Chinese Communities*, pp. 198–99.

There were further advantages to the laundry business for most Chinese: for one, it was an easy business to get in and out of. Since many if not most Chinese men returned to China relatively often considering the rigors and expense of the trip, this was an important consideration. Chinese men, particularly those with wives in China, tended to regard a return visit every three, five, ten, or fifteen years, as a "release from oppression," and a laundry business was easy to sell. It was usually not difficult to find a kinsman or clansman who was willing to operate the laundry for a fixed period of time as a way of gaining both capital and experience for his own move from the ranks of labor to those of management. As another advantage, it was a business that could provide employment to newly arrived kinsmen and clansmen.

Complicating the life of Chinese Americans was the transfer of the clan and family association from the Old World. Originally village oriented, the clan system among Overseas Chinese was adapted to fit conditions wherever Chinese traveled. Outside of the *dai fou,* San Francisco, one clan tended to dominate the smaller Chinatowns. For example, in Pittsburgh, the Yee clan predominated; in Chicago, the Moy clan; and, in Denver, the Chin clan. If an individual were in a Chinatown in which his clan did not predominate, he might attach himself to a clan from the distaff side. A Moy in Pittsburgh whose mother or wife had been a Yee, for example, could affiliate himself with and expect support from that city's powerful Yee clan. In cities where no one family name predominated, use was made of an ancient adaptation of the system: the four-clan association. In Butte two such associations arose: one included members of the To'om, Tom, Huie, and Chieh clans; the other was formed by members of the Lau, Kwan, Chang, and Chew clans.

The functions of these associations resembled, in some ways, those of protective and benevolent societies of other immigrant groups: they rendered protection and mutual aid to members. In other ways, however, they went far beyond such societies insofar as the four-clan associations were considered to be extended family groups. For example, a wife was considered a member of her husband's clan. If he predeceased her, however, she would often be financially assisted by her own clan, as her husband's clan might regard her and her children as not being entitled to the clan's scarce resources. This happened often, because marriages were discouraged within one's own four-clan association. In Butte, the two four-clan associations were bitterly at odds, so cross-marriage between the two four-clan associations was also strongly discouraged. According to Rose Hum Lee, because of the special tensions there, not one of the ninety-nine members of the Chinese American community born in

Butte had married a fellow resident of Butte as late as the mid-1940s.[17]

The lives of the women of Chinese America are even less understood than those of the men. Much of what little has been written is about prostitutes. Although her experience may not have been typical, the oldest woman in Butte's Chinatown provides insight into what life was like for some of the wives of the mercantile classes:

> When I came to America as a bride, I never knew I would be coming to a prison. Until the [1911] Revolution, I was allowed out of the house but once a year. That was during New Years when families exchanged . . . calls and feasts. We would dress in our long-plaited, brocaded, hand-embroidered skirts. These were a part of our wedding dowry brought from China. Over these we wore long-sleeved, short satin or damask jackets. We wore all of our jewelry, and we put jeweled ornaments in our hair. The father of my children hired a closed carriage to take me and the children calling. Of course, he did not go in with us, as this was against the custom practiced in China. The carriage waited until we were ready to leave, which would be hours later, for the women saw each other so seldom that we talked and reviewed all that went on since we saw each other. Before we went out of the house, we sent the children to see if the streets were clear of men. It was considered impolite to meet them. If we did have to walk out when men were on the streets, we hid our faces behind our silk fans and hurried by. Word always spread around that so-and-so's mother was going out and the men would watch for us to come out of the house. They were anxious to see us dressed in our finest and would discuss our finery among themselves. What was said always came back to us because the women's husbands told their wives and their wives told us. So we knew how we stood with the men of Chinatown.
>
> The women were always glad to see each other; we exchanged news of our families and friends in China. We admired each other's clothes and jewels. As we ate separately from the men, we talked about things that concerned women. When the New Year festivals were over, we would put away our clothes and take them out when another feast was held. Sometimes, we went to a feast when a baby born into a family association was a month old. Otherwise we seldom visited each other; it was considered immodest to be seen too many times during the year.

---

17. Ibid., pp. 234–60.

After the Revolution in China, I heard that women there were free to go out. When the father of my children cut his queue he adopted new habits; I discarded my Chinese clothes and began to wear American clothes. By that time my children were going to American schools, could speak English, and they helped me buy what I needed. Gradually the other women followed my example. We began to go out more frequently and since then I go out all the time.[18]

Other women rebelled by breaking up the family. A notorious incident in Butte involved an American-born Chinese woman from Portland who was married to a Butte man at her parents' insistence. She deserted her husband and returned to Portland. She then went off to China with another man and was believed to be living happily in Shanghai. Thirty years later the episode was still much discussed in Butte. The husband, who apparently never remarried, was particularly affected because the mother of his child took their son with her when she left. The community regarded this as much more shocking behavior than the desertion, because when the husband died—he was probably much older than his wife—he would have no son to perform the proper filial rituals. In such a case his association would have taken charge.

The associations also served as dispute-settling organizations, both within the four-clan association and between neighboring four-clan associations. White Americans often complained about the "invisible government" among Chinese Americans: actually, the dispute-settling mechanisms, when they worked, contributed to law and order and should have been approbated rather than denigrated. Another of Rose Hum Lee's informants described how the system worked in Butte. It must be noted in the interview that "not friendly" was an extreme understatement. According to Lee, children of the rival associations did not speak to one another and the women exchanged no visits:

---

18. Ibid., pp. 252–53. Much, probably too much, of what has been written about Chinese American women in the nineteenth century deals with prostitution. That very large numbers of Chinese American women were prostitutes was clearly true, but much of the source material, most of it generated by Caucasians, is dubious at best. For examples of recent scholarship see Lucie C. Hirata, "Free, Indentured, Enslaved: Chinese Prostitutes in 19th Century America," *Signs* 5 (1979): 3–29; and Raymond Lou, "The Chinese American Community of Los Angeles, 1870–1900: A Case of Resistance, Organization, and Participation" (Ph.D. diss., University of California, Irvine, 1982). For the best work on 19th-century prostitution, see Judith Walkowitz, *Prostitution and Victorian Society*.

When I first came to Butte [in the 1890s] there were about thirty-two laundries in the city. About twenty belonged to our clan cousins, while the others belonged to members of the opposite four-clan association. . . . The members [of the rival four-clan associations] were not friendly toward each other.

In case of a dispute within our own association, it would be settled here. The elders—business men and those men who have lived in Butte longest—would hear the facts from the parties in the dispute. The council of elders would decide who was right and who was wrong.

When we needed to call a meeting, a ticket . . . would be circulated. On the ticket was stated the time, place and date of the meeting. Every member of the association was notified. One member of the association—say, some unemployed one at the time—would pass these tickets around to all our association members. For this work he was paid $2.50. The man who petitions the elders to call a meeting to settle a dispute would pay for this expense as well as for brewing tea and buying cigars. These were passed around to all who came in response to the ticket.[19]

Clearly the Chinese American system of justice, like the American, although supposedly impartial, actually favored the well-to-do. In the system described above, the judges were upper class and a poor man would have the same kinds of difficulties paying the expenses of a meeting as he would have in paying for the services of a lawyer. The interview continues:

The accused is expected to come and state his side of the case. If he is afraid to come, knowing he is in the wrong, the meeting goes on without him. But he is told the verdict after the public meeting has discussed the facts and the elders have decided the dispute . . . [The loser] can appeal . . . to the four-clan association headquarters in San Francisco. A letter would be sent by our association secretary stating the facts . . . After the case is heard in San Francisco . . . the decision given there is final. In the case of disputes between the two four-clan associations in Butte, the meeting would be held at the temple. . . . Here the elders and members of both four-clan associations meet and settle the matter. . . . When both clan associations cannot come to an agreement, the matter is referred to the Chinese Six Companies in San Francisco.

19. Lee, *Chinese Communities*, p. 229.

In any society, the mechanisms of law and order will occasionally break down. One such breakdown, originating in Butte's Chinatown, had consequences for all of Chinese America. As noted earlier, only a small minority of Chinese Americans belonged to tongs, and very few of these were engaged in their strong-arm and assassination squads. But the squads did exist. In Butte, the first tong, the Hip Sing, was not established until 1917. Most of its activities apparently involved narcotics and liquor. In 1922, violating a long-standing agreement that no other tong should operate there, the Bing Kung decided to move in from its West Coast bases of operation.

There had already been a good deal of bloodshed nationally between Hip Sings and Bing Kungs. The previous year a murderous quarrel between tong members in San Francisco spread not only to other northern California Chinatowns but even into Nevada. Loren Chan has described the murder of Tom Quong Kee, a seventy-four-year-old laundry proprietor and nominal member of the Bing Kung. On the night of August 27, 1921, the old man responded in pajamas to a knock at his door in tiny Mina, Nevada. He was shot to death with a Colt .38 by Gee Jon, a twenty-nine-year-old Cantonese "hit man" from San Francisco who had come to the United States in 1907 or 1908. The "finger man" was Hughie Sing, nineteen years old and perhaps born in the United States. Sing had been educated in the Nevada public schools and knew the victim well, having been apprenticed to him for two years. Since the perpetrators were arrested and convicted—which did not usually happen in tong killings—we know something of the details.[20]

The only good descriptions of what happened in Butte is in Ching Chao Wu's 1928 University of Chicago doctoral dissertation. The Hip Sings tried to stop the Bing Kungs from organizing. On the evening of the crucial organizing meeting, four men were elected, in succession, as president of the new tong chapter. As soon as each went out into the street, he was assassinated. All of this happened between seven and eleven o'clock. Clearly, as Wu surmises, the Hip Sings had a spy in the Bing Kung election meeting. Telephone calls to the Seattle headquarters of the two tongs alerted each to what had happened in Butte. With the retaliatory shooting down of three Hip Sings in Seattle, the war spread to every Chinatown in America and was not settled for three years.[21] Who "won" in Butte and nationwide is not at all clear. Many tong "soldiers" were killed; others were deported. By the mid-1940s, only the interloper Bing Kung tong remained in Butte.

---

20. Loren B. Chan, "Example for the Nation: Nevada's Execution of Gee Jon," *Nevada Historical Society Quarterly* 18 (1975): 90–106.

21. Wu, "Chinatowns," pp. 213–14, 232.

During interviews in Butte, many people spoke to Rose Hum Lee of how terrible and divisive the tong war had been. Children were sent to school under guard; the American superintendent of the Baptist mission to the Butte Chinese said that for two years he saw his flock only during home visits.[22] While it is clear that some of the tong soldiers had been imported from urban centers on the West Coast, it is also probable that there had been overlapping membership in the tongs and in the four-clan associations. It is tempting to speculate that, because there were two tongs and two four-clan associations, there may have been a tie between pairs of each, but I know of no evidence to support that possibility.

The four-clan associations provided welfare both for the living and for the dead. These welfare functions, in many ways similar to those provided by benevolent societies of other immigrant groups, were unique in the way they helped to maintain communications between the immigrants and sojourners in America and their home villages in China. All immigrants and immigrant groups have had some kind of continuing tie to the "old country," even those chiefly impelled to migrate by dissatisfaction with conditions in the homeland.

For many of the early Chinese, the tie with the homeland—really the home village—was very strong.[23] Many, as we have seen, returned or tried to return for a visit every few years. Large numbers had wives, children, and other family members there. Many sent money home. We know almost nothing about the scale of these remittances from Butte and elsewhere in the continental United States. One figure sometimes cited, from the Chinese consulate in Honolulu, is that Hawaiian Chinese in 1930 sent almost $4 million back to China, some of which may have been for investment. The leading student of Hawaii's Chinese, Clarence Glick, points out that, with about 5,300 foreign-born male Chinese employed in Hawaii in 1930, the per capita remittance would have been about $750. Many not listed as "foreign born" might have sent remittances, however, and the Hawaiian Chinese had, by then, more assets per capita than did Chinese Americans. And, of course, one or two large investments by a wealthy businessman or banker could skew those figures badly.

What remains clear is that the remittances did exist and that the tie to China was very important. One of Glick's Hawaiian informants

---

22. Lee, *Chinese Communities*, pp. 173–74.
23. For an extreme example of continuing connections in the post-World War II era, see James L. Watson, *Emigration and the Chinese Lineage: The Mans in Hong Kong and London*.

in the early 1930s has described the relationship between remittances and home ties, explaining how letters and remittances got from Honolulu to China. The options in Butte would have been much fewer, and the letters would almost certainly have been funneled through San Francisco. The Chinatown store, therefore, became both the post office and the secretarial pool for the immigrants:

> Take Wing Song Wo store on Hotel Street, for example. You go in there any day and you will find a great many letters stuck into a wire rack which stands in the back of the store. These letters are for Chinese who communicate with their folks at home through this store. Suppose a man in Honolulu wishes to send some money to his mother in See Dai Doo. . . . He will be likely to go to Wing Sing Wo rather than to some other firm because it has a sub-branch store in Hachak Hee, the market town in See Dai Doo nearest the village of Ngai How. If he was from another district he would go to some store in Chinatown run by people from that district. The Ngai How man goes to Wing Sing Wo and says he wants them to write a letter for him. He tells the writer of the letter what he wants said. . . . Sometimes the letter is written as the man dictates; sometimes the writer listens and then writes it later. These writers know what the proper things are to say and what this man's folks will like to hear. Most of the men who could write Chinese, especially in the old days, were the bookkeepers in the stores. . . . One used to get twenty-five to fifty cents for writing one . . . for there were many Chinese who could not write a letter or did not want to do it themselves. . . . A few days after a boat arrives from China, the stores usually put in the paper a list of names of people who have [letters waiting for them].

Glick notes the difficulty and expense of such communications. He suggests that most men wrote only when they were sending money. Often the connection between mail and remittance became so strong that immigrants who were unable to send money simply stopped writing.[24]

The four-clan associations, in ideal situations, were responsible for the welfare of all their members; working members contributed to funds for widows, orphans, old age, and burial. Passage money could be made available to the indigent aged or ill who wished to return to China. A widow might be given money to join her nearest kin, in America or China.

---

24. Clarence E. Glick, *Sojourners and Settlers: Chinese Migrants in Hawaii*, pp. 102–03, 137–39.

But perhaps even more important than the services to the living were those performed for the dead: as an old saying put it, it was a "greater service to give a kin a decent burial when dead than to keep him alive with food and clothing." If a deceased member had enough savings to finance his own funeral, the association was responsible for overseeing both the local ceremony and the shipping of the remains to China for burial in the appropriate village cemetery. If the decedent's estate was not able to bear this expense, he was buried locally. The association assumed the biannual grave visitation rituals as well as the responsibility for eventually transferring a small portion of the remains for burial in China. Traditionally, this occurred eight years after death and was arranged through the Six Companies in San Francisco.[25]

The declining and aging population obviously put a severe strain on the whole internal welfare system of Chinese America, and the Great Depression of the 1930s caused it to break down badly. Although some writers have made the claim that "Orientals" never or rarely used welfare facilities, that is certainly not the case as far as Chinese Americans were concerned, although it is certainly true that, for a variety of reasons, including ignorance, fear of the authorities, prejudice, and statutory discrimination against aliens, Chinese Americans underutilized available governmental relief during the Depression. Lee gives heartrending case histories from Butte—whole families without significant heat during a Montana winter. She reports that thirty different applications for relief were made by Chinese individuals from the 1930s to the mid-1940s in Silver Bow County. Since Chinese populations in those years ranged from 165 in 1930 to 52 in 1945, this was a sizable portion of the total community.[26]

On the national level, federal data indicate that statistically significant numbers of Chinese Americans were on relief as early as February 1933. In San Francisco, where federal relief was dispensed through the Chinese Six Companies for the first two years of the New Deal, one scholar has calculated that 13.3 percent of the Chinese population was on relief in October 1933, as opposed to 11.0 percent of the white population. Conversely, where no ethnic umbrella agency served as intermediary, only a very small percentage of the Chinese population received federal relief: 1.2 percent in New York and 4.3 percent in Chicago.[27] This is not to say that the traditional forms of

---

25. Lee, *Chinese Communities,* pp. 230–31, 245–46.

26. Ibid., pp. 288–305.

27. U.S., Federal Emergency Relief Administration, *Unemployment Relief Census: October, 1933. United States Summary,* p. 78. Light, *Ethnic Enterprise,* pp. 87–88, uses

mutual aid completely disappeared. Rather, the aging of the community plus the extreme economic dislocation of the national economy created problems with which the traditional system could no longer deal, although often it tried. Some San Francisco family associations, for example, placed large barrels of rice in the lobbies of their headquarters so that members could simply take from them as needed, without having to make formal application or otherwise ask for help.

The Butte experience—and the experience of the other outposts of Chinese America for which it stands as a surrogate—was, in the years before World War II, largely an experience of adaptation, partial acculturation, and little, very little, assimilation. Some assimilation did occur, however, even in Montana. One such instance involves a Chinese immigrant who became a Montana farmer, married a Caucasian woman, raised a family, and won the respect of his neighbors.

He was born Sing On somewhere in China about the year of Lincoln's first election. In 1873 he arrived somehow in Montana Territory, living first in Helena, where he supported himself and attended public school. He then moved, first to Chouteau and then to Teton County, where he farmed 480 acres. In 1879 the Montana Territorial Assembly passed an act changing his name to George Taylor, which he later embellished to George Washington Taylor. In 1890 he married Lena Bloom, a Swedish immigrant, and their union was blessed by four boys and three girls. In early 1917 their eldest son, Albert Henry Taylor, was a sergeant of Company D, 2d Montana Regiment, serving on the Mexican border. The Taylors can be found, like flies in amber, embedded in a petition of the Montana Legislature asking Congress to grant citizenship to the father, who was certified as an "honorable . . . and upright man . . . opposed to anarchy and polygamy." The sixty-fifth Congress did not act on that petition, and I have found nothing more in the legislative record about the Taylor family.[28]

Butte represents one largely ignored aspect of Chinese America. Its great metropolis, San Francisco, must also be considered. San Francisco's population, absolute and relative, as shown in table 3.4, was no real indication of its importance for Chinese all over the United States.

Around the turn of the century, as one of Victor and Brett Nee's

---

this same data to conclude that "the percentage of Chinese receiving unemployment relief in 1933 was generally much lower than the figures for Negroes and whites." The percentage calculations are his.

28. Roger Daniels, "Westerners from the East: Oriental Immigrants Reappraised," *Pacific Historical Review* 35 (1966): 383.

Table 3.4
Chinese American Population of San Francisco, Absolute and Relative, 1880–1940

Year	Chinese in San Francisco	Chinese in United States	Percentage of United States Chinese in San Francisco
1880	21,475	105,465	20.4
1890	25,833	107,620	24.0
1900	13,954	89,863	15.5
1910	10,582	71,531	14.8
1920	7,744	61,639	12.6
1930	16,303	74,954	21.8
1940	17,782	77,504	22.9

SOURCE: U.S. Census

informants remembered about his father's experience, employment opportunities were scarce for Chinese in San Francisco. Despite this difficulty, San Francisco's Chinatown was still "home base," the "safest place."

> In the summer he went out to Watsonville and picked fruit. In November he was cutting sardines in Monterey. He went up to Alaska to the salmon canneries . . . and then he got back to the valley again to harvest the asparagus in the spring.[29]

But, always, he would return to San Francisco's Chinatown.

San Francisco was the cultural, economic, and administrative hub of Chinese America, the entrepôt through which most of the Chinese goods and services were distributed, the communications center through which information and people passed back and forth between the Old World and the New. Headquarters for the Six Companies, the family associations, and the tongs, San Francisco also became one of the political centers for the Overseas Chinese, whose financial and moral support was crucial to the success of Sun Yat-sen and his Kuomintang. The support of Chinese America for Sun was not nearly as important for him as was the support he drew from the Overseas Chinese of Nanyang, but it was significant.

A meaningful reconstruction of the life of late nineteenth century

---

29. Victor G. Nee and Brett de Bary Nee, *Longtime Californ'*, p. 22. For a history of Chinese schooling in San Francisco, see Victor Low, *The Unimpressible Race.*

Chinese San Francisco is still quite difficult, chiefly because we know very little about the merchants who were at the top of its steep pyramidal society. In the California metropolis, as elsewhere in Chinese America, individual Chinese merchants amassed great wealth. They dealt on terms of equality, or near equality, with the commercial and industrial leaders of America. We get occasional glimpses of these entrepreneurs through their correspondence in the archives of firms that used Chinese labor. For instance, Seattle entrepreneur Wa Chong complained to a lumber mill owner about treatment meted out to laborers he had supplied:

> The Chinamen in your employ complain bitterly of the usage they receive from the hands of some of your men, more particularly at the hands of the mate of [your] steamer "Blakely." We have had during the past year [1878] over 50 men at Port Gamble and have had no complaints whatever. We write to you in person about this trouble, feeling that you are not aware of the abuse our men are receiving at the hand of these other workmen. . . . Chinamen have feelings and know when they are properly used. . . . The men sent to wood up the Blakely last evening took their coats off on the steamer and could not find them afterwards. No doubt they were hidden or thrown overboard by the white men—please see about this matter.[30]

Merchants like Wa Chong not only had economic power but they were also specially favored by the immigration legislation. The Chinese Exclusion Act of 1882 had been directed against Chinese laborers; special provisions had been made favoring travelers, students, and, most significant, merchants and their wives and families. This favored status was reemphasized in Sino-American treaties, hence the term "treaty merchant." There was great concern about such merchants and about who did and who did not qualify. An 1893 United States statute specified the crucial, and insulting, requirement that the status of any Chinese merchant had to be attested to "by the testimony of two credible witnesses other than Chinese."[31] Naturally there were fraudulent claims, and most immigration personnel came to believe that all Chinese were born liars. Elaborate methods and questionings were devised to examine those who claimed entry rights. Up until 1910 incoming Chinese in San Francisco were examined and

---

30. Port Blakely Mill Company Mss., University of Washington Archives, letter, Wa Chong to Captain William Benton, November 22, 1878. Richard C. Berner called my attention to this letter.

31. 28 *Stat.* 7. See chapter 2, above.

held, often for months, in a facility known as "The Shed" on the San Francisco waterfront. One interested observer, the Reverend Ira M. Condit, a missionary to and spokesman for Chinese Americans, described in 1900 how incoming Chinese were treated:

> When they do arrive, merchants, laborers are all alike penned up, like a flock of sheep, in a wharf shed, for many days and often weeks at their own expense and are denied all communication with their own people, while the investigation of their cases moves its slow length along. The right of bail is denied. A man is imprisoned as a criminal who has committed no crime, but has merely failed to find a white man to prove his right to be here.[32]

Even after being admitted to this country, the Chinese could never feel completely safe because a nativist immigration service, convinced that ten thousand or more Chinese had been smuggled into the United States, staged raids in Chinatowns all across the country in the early years of this century. The distinguished American lawyer and diplomat John W. Foster, grandfather to John Foster Dulles, described one such raid and mass arrest which took place in Boston on October 11, 1903. According to Foster, immigration officials swooped down on Chinatown on a Sunday night, entering restaurants and private homes without warrants. More than two hundred Chinese were arrested and hustled down to the federal building. Residence certificates were demanded; those who did not have them on their persons were kept in two small rooms, so closely packed that all had to stand until late Monday afternoon. Eventually, fifty persons were deported as a result of the raid; the majority presumably had been harassed for no good reason. Even Commissioner General of Immigration Frank P. Sargent felt that his officials had been overzealous in this instance.

Bona fide students, whose admission was guaranteed under both the Chinese Exclusion Act and the Sino-American treaties, were often detained for long periods of time. Even one of the famous Soong sisters, Ai-ling, later married to Chiang Kai-shek's finance minister, was subjected to over two weeks' confinement on board ship when she arrived to attend Wesleyan College in Georgia. This took place even though Soong Ai-ling was traveling with two white American missionaries, and intercessions on her behalf were made by a number of influential people, including a United States senator.[33] This kind of

---

32. Ira M. Condit, *The Chinaman as We See Him*, pp. 86–87.
33. John W. Foster, "The Chinese Boycott," *Atlantic Monthly* 97 (1906): 118–27. For an account of Foster's labors on behalf of China, see Michael J. Devine, *John W. Foster*.

needless affront to upper-class persons infuriated not only Chinese Americans but Chinese officials in America, who had little sympathy for working-class Chinese. The redoubtable Wu Ting-fang, Chinese minister to Washington from 1897–1902 and the most articulate in English of the early Chinese officials to serve here, fully understood the reasons for the maltreatment of Chinese and the abuse that they received in the press. "'Why can't you be fair?' Wu demanded of New York reporters in 1901. 'Would you talk like that if mine was not a weak nation? Would you say it if the Chinese had votes?'"[34]

After 1910 a special immigration facility was set up on Angel Island in San Francisco Bay. Although some have called it the "Ellis Island of the West," the analogy is a poor one. Ellis Island and Angel Island were very different kinds of places. For most of the millions who came in via Ellis Island, the immigration facility was a mere way station, a fleeting stop at which only a very few—mostly those who could not pass the physical examination—met with disappointment. For most of the thousands who came in via Angel Island, the place seemed a prison in which they were pent up for weeks and months, examined and reexamined, humiliated time and again before being allowed to cross the few hundred yards of water that separated them from the center of Chinese America. The isolation facility at Angel Island was abandoned by the government in 1940, since applicants for admission from China had been cut to a handful by the Sino-Japanese War. In recent years Chinese American scholars and activists have explored the old buildings and have discovered a number of poems carved into their wooden walls in Chinese calligraphy. One of them from Building 317, the Chinese Detention Barracks, has been translated:

> There are tens of thousands of poems composed on these walls,
> They are all cries of complaint and sadness.
> The day I am rid of this prison and attain success,
> I must remember that this prison once existed.
> In my daily needs I must be frugal.
> Needless extravagance leads youth to ruin.
>
> All my compatriots please be mindful.
> Once you have some small gains, return home early.
>
> By one from Xiangshan.[35]

---

34. New York *Tribune*, November 28, 1901, as cited by Delber L. McKee, *Chinese Exclusion versus the Open Door Policy, 1900–1906*, p. 51. Wu published an interesting account of the U.S., in *America through the Spectacles of an Oriental Diplomat*. For an account of his career, see Linda P. Shin, "China in Transition: The Role of Wu T'ing-fang (1842–1922)" (Ph.D. diss., University of California, Los Angeles, 1970).

35. Him Mark Lai et al., *Island: Poetry and History of Chinese Immigrants on*

From 1882 on there had been a certain amount of illegal entry by Chinese, but a natural disaster created special opportunities for chicanery. The San Francisco earthquake and fire of April 1906 destroyed most of the city's vital-statistics records. It became possible thereby for a significant number of Chinese fraudulently to claim American birth. If a Chinese were a citizen, he could not only come and go as he pleased but any children he fathered abroad could also claim derivative citizenship under American laws. Such children, or putative children, were almost always sons. They could *not* be accompanied by their mothers, who were usually inadmissible under American law, so the maleness of the bachelor society was accentuated. In addition, wives and children of treaty merchants could enter. There developed a regular commerce in documents allowing some Chinese to come in as other men's sons. These illegals were known in Chinatown as "paper sons," a phenomenon best described by Victor and Brett de Bary Nee in their brilliant book, *Longtime Californ'* (required reading for anyone who wants to understand life as it was lived in San Francisco's Chinatown in the twentieth century). One of the subjects recounts his experience as a paper son:

> In the beginning my father came in as a laborer. But the 1906 earthquake came along and destroyed all those immigration things. So that was a big chance for a lot of Chinese. They forged themselves certificates saying that they were born in this country, and when the time came they could go back to China and bring back four or five sons just like that! They might make a little money off it, not much, but the main thing was to bring a son or a nephew or a cousin in.
>
> Now my father thought he was even smarter than that. When he came in the second time he didn't use that native-born certificate he had. He got a certificate saying he was a student. But that didn't make sense at all. He thought he was so smart being a student, but then, if you came in as a student, how could you bring a son into this country? If he had used his birth certificate, I could have come in as a native son. Instead, we had to go back to the same old thing,

---

Angel Island, 1910–1940, p. 66. Other works on the island include: Mary Bamford, *Angel Island: The Ellis Island of the West*; L. Ling-Chi Wang, "The Yee Version of Poems from the Chinese Immigration Station," *Asian American Review* (1976): 117–26; Judy Yung, "A Bowlful of Tears: Chinese Women Immigrants on Angel Island," *Frontiers* 2 (1977): 52–55; and Him Mark Lai, "Island of Immortals: Chinese Immigrants and the Angel Island Immigration Station," *California History* 57 (1978): 88–103. For excellent sequences on Angel Island, see the film by Loni Ding, "How We Got Here."

"paper son." They had to send me over not as my own father's son, but as the son of another cousin from our village.[36]

Paper son Jim Quock (in a 1979 interview with Diane Mark and Ginger Chih) provides more detail:

> [I came to America] because my grandfather was here during the Gold Rush times, the 1860s. Somebody robbed him and he got killed and they never found the body or anything. My grandmother told us that grandpa had a lot of gold, made quite a bit of money, you know. So that's what got in my mind, "Oh, this is a fortune. I'm going over to America to make money." Only fifteen at the time. So the only way I could come is to buy a paper, buy a citizen paper. I paid quite a bit of money, too. I paid $102 gold! That's quite a bit of money at that time in China.[37]

Immigration officials soon became all too aware of the paper son gambit. They subjected those who claimed citizenship or entry because of treaty merchant, student, or traveler status to detailed and drawn-out interrogation sessions in an effort to find flaws or inconsistencies in the prospective entrants' stories. Ironically, some of the first Chinese Americans to get federal jobs were employed to help break the cover of the illegals. The would-be immigrants, or at least the successful ones, devised countermeasures, as Jim Quock has related:

> They give you a book of about 200 pages to study—all your life, your family, your brother's name, the whole village, almost. They ask you all kinds of questions when you get to the United States, the immigration (station) at Angel Island. . . . I was there for three weeks. They ask you questions like how many steps in your house? Your house had a clock? Questions like that. You got to remember all this. They asked me, "Where do you sleep at your house?" I said, "I sleep with my grandmother and my brother." They say, "Okay, which position do you sleep?" All kinds of questions, you got to think. But, I'm pretty smart. I said, "Tonight I sleep over here, tomorrow I sleep over there, it doesn't matter."

Crib sheets have survived, describing in detail some Chinese village and obviously intended for the use of paper sons. Clearly, successful paper sons were not dull witted; to have used such relatively

---

36. Nee and Nee, *Longtime Californ'*, p. 63.

37. Diane Mei Lin Mark and Ginger Chih, *A Place Called Chinese America*, pp. 47–48. This is a good popular history with excellent illustrations, including one of a crib sheet.

sophisticated devices effectively they would also have had to be more than marginally literate.

The immigration service and the federal courts were often capricious, depending on the proclivities of the inspectors and the judges. Perhaps the most bizarre case involved one Mock Kee Song, who had made at least five round trips between the United States and China based on his claim of American citizenship. He had brought five children, all sons, into the United States. On his sixth trip, however, the immigration service held that he was not a citizen. In 1938 a federal court upheld his deportation to China.[38]

There is no way of ascertaining how many paper sons and other illegal Chinese immigrants gained entry. United States immigration records show almost 95,000 individual entries of Chinese "immigrants" between 1883 and the end of Chinese exclusion in December 1943, for an average of about 1,500 per year. Many of these entries were of former residents returning from China, and many individuals came several times. One must assume there were also ship jumpers, border crossers from the North and the South, and persons smuggled from Cuba and elsewhere in the Caribbean who were never recorded by the immigration service.

Admissions of Chinese were quite uneven; in the 1890s, about 15,000 came; in the next decade, almost 20,000; in the 1910s, nearly 21,000; in the 1920s, over 30,000; and in the 1930s, fewer than 6,000. The decade averages conceal the effects of the 1924 immigration law; in the four years prior to the law's taking effect, more than 20,000 Chinese entries were recorded; from that time until after World II there were never as many as 2,000 Chinese entries in any one year. These figures demonstrate that Chinese exclusion was never total. What must be kept in mind is the steady decline in total Chinese population in the United States.

The 1924 immigration law, which imposed the national origins system on all nonwestern hemisphere immigrants, also made it impossible for United States citizens of Chinese ancestry to bring in alien Chinese wives. From 1906 to 1924 an average of about 150 such women per year had been legally admitted; from 1924 to 1930 none were. A 1930 act relaxed this ban: it provided for the entry of such wives as long as the marriage had taken place before May 26, 1924,

38. *Mock Kee Song. v. Cahill*, 94 F.2d 975 (1938), as cited by David R. Chan in "The Tragedy and Trauma of the Chinese Exclusion Laws," in Chinese Historical Society of America, *The Life, Influence and the Role of Chinese in the United States, 1776–1976*, p. 201.

the date that the 1924 law had been enacted.[39] Under this provision about 60 Chinese women per year were admitted between 1931 and 1941. Thus both Chinese practice and American immigration law combined to reinforce the existing sexual imbalance.

As the discussion of paper sons indicates, large numbers of Chinese men in the United States had wives in China. The census of 1930, for example, showed four times as many married men as married women. These separated families—termed "mutilated families" by sociologist Charles Frederick Marsden—far outnumbered "normal," united families in Chinese America until well after the end of World War II. A similar condition prevailed in Canada. Peter S. Li has studied the pattern of Chinese marriages in Canada more thoroughly than has anyone for this side of the forty-ninth parallel. In 1941 (Canada's census is taken in years ending in -1), Li estimates that there were 1,177 intact conjugal families of Chinese Canadians, 1,459 broken families, in which one or both partners were widowed or divorced, and 20,141 mutilated families that were separated with the wife outside of Canada. Just over 88 percent of Chinese Canadian families were mutilated, and it is likely the data for the United States in 1940 were similar.[40]

Because of this pattern of family life, the acculturation of many Chinese Americans was retarded; many immigrant bachelors spent most of their lives in American Chinatowns without learning more than a handful of English language phrases. Even some of those Chinese born here to united families had their aspirations turned toward China, both by family tradition and by the frustrations of Chinese life in America. In this context, Ng Poon Chew (1866–1931), an early Chinese American editor and a literary paladin of the Chinese Americans, could surmise toward the end of his life that "perhaps . . . our American born Chinese will have to look to China for their life work. In this there is much hope China will open thousands of lines for ambitious modernized young men to utilize their learnings to help develop the country's resources."[41]

Similarly, the distinguished ceramicist and autobiographer Jade Snow Wong remembers that her father, one of the minority who had a united family in San Francisco and who was a Christian, still oriented his children toward China. He thought, not surprisingly, that

---

39. The 1930 law is 46 *Stat.* 581.

40. Peter S. Li, "Immigration Laws and Family Patterns: Some Demographic Changes Among Chinese Families in Canada, 1885–1971," *Canadian Ethnic Studies* 12, no. 1 (1980): 58–73.

41. As cited by Stanford L. Lyman in *The Asian in North America*, p. 23.

only in China could Chinese realize their full potential. In planning her older brother's career, "Father and son agreed that the study of medicine in China would prepare Older Brother for his career. Knowing the Chinese language, he could establish himself where medical personnel was greatly needed, and he could strengthen his ancestral ties by visits to Daddy's native village and relatives."[42]

These dreams of China remained, however, for most Chinese Americans, only dreams. The worldwide depression of the 1930s, the Sino-Japanese War, the increasing acculturation of native-born Chinese Americans, the tightening of American immigration policy all combined to turn the main thrust of most Chinese American lives increasingly away from China and toward America in a pattern that resonates, with variations, to the whole American immigrant experience. The change is depicted, Hollywood-style, in the Charlie Chan movies, one of the most annoying Chinese American cultural stereotypes and rightly resented by most Chinese Americans today. But even stereotypes have their value. The contrast between the wise, inscrutable Chinese American detective—always played by Caucasian actors—and his wisecracking, shallow number-one and number-two sons—played by such skilled Chinese American actors as Keye Luke and Victor Sen Yung—is not unrelated to the reality of generational conflict in Chinese America. The literary evidence for this is considerable, most notably in the autobiographies of Jade Snow Wong, *Fifth Chinese Daughter* (1950) and *No Chinese Stranger* (1975), and Pardee Lowe, *Father and Glorious Descendant* (1943). Perhaps in these instances the degree of acculturation, as shown by the mastery of literary style, is higher than that of most of their peers.

By the 1940s one phase in the history of Chinese in the United States would have been coming to an end in any event. But America's involvement in World War II changed dramatically not only the position of Chinese in American society but that of all ethnic and minority groups. Sometime in the 1940s Chinese America, a world in which the major focus was still on what happened in Asia, was replaced by Chinese American society, a world in which the major focus was on what happened in the United States.

The change, of course, was not and is not total or polar. On the one hand, there are still sojourners who long to return to China; and some actually do. On the other hand, as early as 1895, some Chinese Americans in California were motivated to form their own American organization, the Native Sons of the Golden State, a name mimetic of

---

42. Jade Snow Wong, *Fifth Chinese Daughter*, p. 95. See also idem, *No Chinese Stranger*; and Pardee Lowe, *Father and Glorious Descendant*.

the nativist Native Sons of the Golden West.[43] Despite such exceptions, the center of gravity prior to the forties, in thought if not in fact, had remained in China. From the earliest days of Chinese America, this center had been shifting ever so slowly toward the New World.

Perhaps what happened in the years after 1940 represents the belated recognition of a long, drawn-out process, a gradual change of consciousness rather than a dramatic change of condition. In any event, the changes that took place during and immediately after the war years are so great that they cannot be ignored by the historian. Before looking at this war period and beyond, however, it is necessary to explore the somewhat parallel experiences of the other major group of Asian immigrants and ethnics in the United States, the Japanese Americans.

---

43. Sue Fawn Chung, "The Chinese American Citizens' Alliance: An Effort in Assimilation" (Honors Thesis, University of California, Los Angeles, 1965), in my possession. The Chinese American Citizens' Alliance evolved from the NSGS in 1915. The Americanizing thrust of the organization can be seen in this clause from its first constitution: "It is imperative that no members shall have sectional, clannish, Tong or party prejudices against each other or to use such influences to oppress fellow members. Whoever violates this provision shall be expelled."

4.

The Coming of the Japanese and the Anti-Japanese Movement

Although a few Japanese came to North America in the middle decades of the nineteenth century—shipwrecked seamen, diplomats, students, and even one or two small colonies of refugees—meaningful immigration began only in the 1880s.[1] Unlike the Chinese, who had a long tradition of overseas dispersal, very few Japanese had traveled outside of their home islands before the closing years of the nineteenth century. As Hilary Conroy has shown, one group of Japanese—141 men, 6 women, and 1 child—was brought to Hawaii to work on sugar plantations as early as 1869. These pioneers, known as *Gannen Mono* or "first-year people," had no successors for a decade and a half. Large-scale contract immigration of Japanese to Hawaii began in 1884, and in the next decade some 30,000 came.[2]

The Hawaiian story is important for four reasons. First, as the initial large-scale emigration from Japan, it set an important precedent that would eventually take substantial numbers of Japanese across the Pacific to the United States, Canada, Brazil, Peru, Bolivia, and other New World nations.[3] Second, for many Japanese, Hawaii served as an important staging point in the migration to the North American mainland, just as in the years after World War II, southern cities in the

---

1. Roger Daniels, *The Politics of Prejudice*, pp. 2–3.
2. F. Hilary Conroy, *The Japanese Frontier in Hawaii, 1868–1898*.
3. James Tigner, "Japanese Immigration into Latin America: A Survey," *Journal of Inter-American Studies and World Affairs* 23 (1981): 457–82, is excellent. For Canada, see Roger Daniels, *Concentration Camps, North America*, pp. 171–78.

United States would serve as staging points for rural blacks who eventually moved North and West.[4] Third, Japanese were brought to Hawaii not only for their labor but also to serve as a counterweight to the relatively large number of Chinese in the islands. In 1884 perhaps 18,000 Chinese comprised between one-fourth and one-fifth of the Hawaiian population. The white American sugar-planter-merchant-missionary oligarchy had begun to regard them as troublesome elements in a multiracial plantation society.[5] Thus began a contrapuntal relationship in the minds of men, white and yellow, between Chinese and Japanese and among the images of Chinese, Japanese, and whites that has continued into the present.[6] Fourth, after Hawaiian statehood in 1959, the presence of Asian American legislators in Washington—most of them Japanese Americans—began to have a truly national impact.[7]

Although the Hawaiian Japanese story will not be told in detail here, some of the differences between the situation in Hawaii and that on the mainland must be noted.[8] In Hawaii, Japanese first arrived as a result of a conscious decision made by the white power structure, but the migration to North America evolved largely without direction. In Hawaii, both as a kingdom and then as an American territory, there was considerably less democracy than on the mainland. And finally, the numerical incidence was different: in Hawaii, whites were always a minority, and Japanese quickly became the largest single ethnic group. On the mainland, Japanese were never more than a tiny fragment of the population, although they did dominate some small enclaves and certain specialized types of agriculture and agriculturally related trades.

The Japan that trans-Pacific migrants left in the quarter-century after 1880 was a nation very different from the dissension-wracked, victimized China. It was a nation undergoing, by the will of its own

---

4. For a fine analysis of how some aspects of black migration occurred, see the forthcoming University of Chicago Press book by James Grossman on the migration to Chicago in the era of World War I.

5. Clarence E. Glick, *Sojourners and Settlers*, is the best account of Chinese in Hawaii.

6. For one such episode, see John E. Reinecke, *Feigned Necessity: Hawaii's Attempt to Obtain Chinese Contract Labor, 1921–23*.

7. See chapter 7, below.

8. Gavin Daws, *Shoal of Time*, is perhaps the best general history of the state. No full English-language history of the Japanese in Hawaii exists, but for two useful compilations, see Dennis Ogawa, *Jen Ken Po: The World of Hawaii's Japanese*, and idem, *Kodomo No Tame Ni: For the Sake of the Children*. The most detailed treatment of Japanese migration to Hawaii in English is Alan Takeo Moriyama, *Imingaisha: Japanese Emigration Companies and Hawaii*.

leaders, one of the most remarkable modernizations known to history, a modernization that brought Japan, technologically at least, from the later middle ages to the industrial era in decades rather than centuries. This rapid modernization, of course, produced great social dislocations, particularly of rural Japanese. It was from rural Japan that the bulk of the trans-Pacific migrants came. Gross immigration data show fewer than 400,000 persons departing from Japan for Hawaii and North America in the quarter-century after 1880. The pre-1900 data are impressionistic rather than precise, more attention having been paid on this side of the Pacific to those arriving than to those leaving. Many individuals made more than one round trip. In the Pacific Northwest significant numbers of Japanese went back and forth between Vancouver and Seattle and were sometimes counted by both Canada and the United States.

The memoirs of a pioneer immigrant to the Pacific Northwest are illuminating. Kihachi Hirakawa remembered, many years later, his initial trip to North America. A rate war between Yokohama ticket agencies in the summer of 1890 cut fares from fifty to twenty-five yen, giving the twenty-six-year-old bachelor a long-awaited "chance to go to a foreign country." He found out about it just three days before departure, which did not leave him enough time to get a passport. As Hirakawa relates it, a ship's officer said that "a passport was not necessary, and if I paid my fare I would be accepted. Then I asked if I could land without a passport at Vancouver, B. C., and the officer replied, 'Maybe you can land at Vancouver, but, I am not sure.'"9

Hirakawa, gambling that he would get in, borrowed forty yen, bought the ticket and a secondhand suit, and changed his remaining ten yen into $8.10 American money. After a fifteen-day journey, during which he was so seasick that he could eat only on the first two days, his ship, the British steamer *Abyssinia* (3,250 tons), arrived in Vancouver. Still concerned about the lack of a passport and so sick that he had to be helped down the gangplank, Hirakawa encountered no problems in entering Canada. After resting two days in a hotel, he began the last leg of his trip to Seattle on August 11, 1890. "A few customs house officials boarded our boat from a small boat to examine our baggage. Again I was concerned about the lack of a passport [but] they merely made a brief inspection. . . . The next morning our boat docked at the port of Seattle. Thus I easily entered the United States." The experience was not unusual for those early

---

9. Kihachi Hirakawa Mss., University of Washington Archives (hereafter UWA), "Autobiography," pp. 13–16. I hope soon to publish Hirakawa's autobiography.

years. Hirakawa would make four more Pacific crossings before settling for good on Bainbridge Island, just off Seattle.

During the 1890s small Japanese American communities developed along the Pacific Coast from Vancouver to San Diego. Turn-of-the-century censuses found almost 4,600 Japanese in British Columbia and nearly 25,000 in the United States. As this population grew, the Japanese government began to show concern centered on the problems that its emigrants might create for the image-conscious policy makers in Tokyo.

From the beginning of trans-Pacific migration, the Japanese government had evinced great interest in the way its subjects were treated abroad. Its motivation was not humanitarian. Japanese policy makers in the late nineteenth century, like most of their counterparts in the western nations that they emulated, cared little for the poor and middling ranks of society. As early as 1887 at least two Tokyo newspapers had "encouraged the Japanese government to rid the nation of undesirables by sending them abroad."[10] But most of the Japanese elite viewed the matter differently. Japan's "ever jealous watch against discriminatory treatment" of her emigrants abroad was chiefly motivated by the desire to protect "her own prestige as a nation."[11] Even before significant numbers of Japanese had emigrated anywhere, some Japanese bureaucrats became aware of the ways in which Chinese and other Asians had been shipped to all parts of the world as semifree labor and exploited in what Hugh Tinker has rightly called a "new system of slavery." They concluded that allowing Japanese laborers to suffer such degradation would be incompatible with Japan's aspirations to great power status.[12]

As early as 1888, as Donald Hata has demonstrated, Japanese diplomatic representatives on the West Coast were sending danger signals to the foreign ministry in Tokyo.[13] In June of that year a new Japanese minister to the United States, Munemitsu Mutsu, stopped off in San Francisco on his way to Washington. He had instructions from the foreign minister, Shigenobu Okuma, to investigate conditions among the local Japanese. He arrived already convinced that the "shameless activities of . . . undesirable Japanese will no doubt impair

---

10. Donald T. Hata, Jr., *"Undesirables": Early Immigrants and the Anti-Japanese Movement in San Francisco, 1892–1893*, p. 65 n 24.

11. Conroy, *Japanese Frontier*, p. 140.

12. Hugh Tinker, *A New System of Slavery: The Export of Indian Labour Overseas, 1830–1920*, is a seminal work for anyone concerned with the Asian diaspora of the nineteenth and twentieth centuries.

13. Hata, *"Undesirables,"* p. 49. In earlier work I dated these anxieties only to 1891.

Japan's national honor and dignity." A short stay in San Francisco and a briefing by the local consul enabled him to find what he was seeking. Although there were some respectable and industrious elements, Mutsu focused on the *shosei*, persons whom Hata terms "pseudo-students" and whom Californians and eventually Japanese Americans themselves termed "schoolboys." Most schoolboys had no real connection with higher education but came to learn English and "the ropes." An early historian of U.S.-Japanese relations, Inazo Nitobe, always anxious to put a good face on matters, described these schoolboys positively as "youths with scanty means, but with abundance of ambition, who cross the ocean thoughtlessly and with wild hopes of 'making their way' or who with earnestness, and in patience perseverance, acquire knowledge, defying the harsh obstacles set by 'chill penury.'"[14]

Mutsu, however, took a negative view of these strivers, some of whom were political radicals. The local consul and some pillars of the Japanese commercial community in San Francisco, who were perhaps the source of his concern, warned that these "knavish" undesirables would not only bring "disgrace" on local Japanese and damage "Japan's national honor" but might even bring down upon the local Japanese "the same ill fortune as has fallen upon the Chinese residents of this country."[15] The "truth" about the schoolboys and other early Japanese is probably somewhere between these two extremes.

Three years later in 1891 a new Japanese consul in San Francisco, Sutemi Chinda, made similar findings and drew similar conclusions. He was particularly upset about Japanese prostitutes and their pimps. The "ignominious conduct" of these people, Chinda felt, could be used "as a pretext for attacking the Japanese residents by those who openly advocate the exclusion of the Oriental race from the country." The Chinese in America, he told Tokyo, "are now detested and discriminated against wherever they migrate simply because they

---

14. Inazo Nitobe, *The Intercourse between the United States and Japan*, pp. 165–73, for a general discussion of real students. According to Japanese statistics cited by Nitobe, as of December 31, 1887, there were 1,275 Japanese men and 77 Japanese women in the United States. Of these, 686 of the men and 13 of the women were listed as students, mostly in eastern institutions. There were 108 men and four women listed "in mercantile vocation." Nitobe also felt that "a large number have crossed the Pacific solely to evade" conscription (ibid., pp. 167–68). Most of the "shosei" were on the West Coast. An analyst of Japanese foreign students in the U.S. has calculated that only about 900 Japanese studied at American institutions of higher education between 1867–1902, using some 14% of the 6,395 passports issued for study in the U.S. during those years. See James T. Conte, "Overseas Study in the Meiji Period: Japanese Students in America, 1867–1902" (Ph.D. diss., Princeton University, 1977).

15. Hata, *"Undesirables,"* pp. 54–59.

failed to grasp the seriousness of the situation at the outset. Their failure must be a lesson to us Japanese." He urged his government "to adopt appropriate measures so as to prevent the departure of these undesirable Japanese to this country in the future."[16]

Later that year Chinda sent Yoshiro Fujita, secretary of the San Francisco consulate, to the Pacific Northwest to investigate local conditions prevailing among Japanese. Fujita knew what his chief had already reported to Tokyo, so the impartiality of his investigation is questionable. Fujita discovered widely varying circumstances. In Seattle he found all but 10 of the 250 Japanese residents deeply involved in illegal (but tolerated) prostitution and gambling. In nearby Tacoma, however, he was happy to report that all of the 50 Japanese inhabitants were "enterprising young men" following legitimate occupations. In Spokane, in eastern Washington, Fujita found a smaller-scale repeat of the Seattle situation: among 59 Japanese, 12 worked in two restaurants, 17 were prostitutes, and 30 were pimps or gamblers.

How seriously is one to take Fujita's report? Its class bias is clear, and its sources of information are sometimes suspect. In Seattle, for example, his information came from "a few sober and earnest ones" concerned that Japanese not be expelled en masse as Chinese had been from Tacoma just six years before.[17] When he visited a large lumbering operation at Port Blakely, he complained that only ten of the eighty Japanese day laborers there "worked thirty days a month regularly." Only in Portland, Oregon, during the last major stop of his three-week tour did Fujita speak to a whole spectrum of a local community. His report on Portland is qualitatively different.

In Portland, Fujita found about one-hundred thirty Japanese and heard about an unspecified number of others working at a sawmill there. Seven restaurants employed sixty Japanese, while the remainder were "prostitutes, their employers, gamblers, or sailors." The restaurants catered to a workingman's clientele serving fifteen-cent meals.

---

16. Report, Sutemi Chinda to Shuzo Aoki, Foreign Minister, March 10, 1891, with enclosures. These documents, along with that cited in note 25 below, were translated for Robert Wilson by Yasuo Sakata from copies in the Japanese American Research Project Archives, UCLA. I am indebted to both of them for permission to use the fruits of their research. For an uncritical use of these and other Japanese documents, see Yasuo Wakatsuki, "Japanese Emigration to the United States, 1866–1924: A Monograph," *Perspectives in American History* 12 (1979): 387–516, which ignores American and Hawaiian sources.

17. For the Tacoma riots, see Jules A. Karlin, "The Anti-Chinese Outbreak in Tacoma, 1885," *Pacific Historical Review* 23 (1954): 271–83. Curiously, Fujita's informants seem not to have mentioned the concurrent Seattle riots. See Karlin, "The Anti-Chinese Outbreaks in Seattle, 1885–1886," *Pacific Northwest Quarterly* 39 (1948): 103–29. See also chapter 3 above.

Fujita claimed that only one or two were owned by "respectable Japanese and operated with sufficient capital," that two or three were run by *shosei,* and that the rest were "owned or financed by the proprietors of houses of pleasure and gamblers." Fujita wondered why so many engaged in this occupation, which, according to him, was regarded by Americans as being peculiarly Japanese, like Chinese in the laundry business or "Negroes in the tonsorial art." It was explained to him that a restaurant could be opened for only four or five-hundred dollars and that small profits could be made quickly. Most of the Portland restaurants had been financed by a number of Japanese pooling their money and forming a partnership. He also noted that the three grocery stores carrying Asian staples were run by Chinese. Regarding Japanese prostitution in Portland, Fujita evidenced no real understanding of the business: he thought there were about twenty prostitutes and about forty pimps. He claimed to have talked to "most" of the prostitutes but noted that "most Japanese men . . . tried to avoid seeing me or having a conversation with me."

The whole question of the role of prostitution in American immigrant communities is only now being investigated by scholars, and we do not know nearly enough about Japanese prostitutes in America or what became of them. As Mikiso Hane has demonstrated, the exploitation of very young Japanese girls and women in brothels was widespread in Japan and all around the Pacific Rim. In countries like Canada and the United States, where prostitution was not governmentally sanctioned, girls and women were sometimes hidden in barrels and boxes to get past the often cursory customs examinations. In 1893 a pimp was caught in Vancouver trying to bring in seven prospective prostitutes in this manner. One Japanese prostitute in America later became well known. Wada Yamada, a renowned Japanese feminist, has told of being tricked as a young girl by a man in Japan into believing that he was recruiting her for a respectable job in California, but she wound up in a brothel. A 1910 Japanese survey of overseas Japanese prostitutes reported 913 in Honolulu and 371 in San Francisco.[18]

---

18. Mikiso Hane, *Peasants, Rebels and Outcasts,* pp. 219–20 n 46, 287. Yuji Ichioka, *"Ameyuki-san:* Japanese Prostitutes in Nineteenth-Century America," *Amerasia Journal* 4, no. 1 (1977): 1–22, is the best treatment of Asian prostitutes in America. See also his *"Amerika Nadeshiko:* Japanese Immigrant Women in the United States," *Pacific Historical Review* 49 (1980): 339–57. The best study I know of Asian prostitutes in a "white" country is D. C. S. Sissons, *"Karayuki-san:* Japanese Prostitutes in Australia, 1887–1916," *Historical Studies* 17 (1977): 323–41, 474–88. The term "karayuki" meant, originally, a person bound for China (*Kara*) but came to mean an overseas prostitute. See also the works cited in chapter 3, note 18 above.

Fujita's report is valuable and gives us a snapshot, however blurred or distorted, of some early Japanese American communities. They were communities characterized by a great deal of petty entrepreneurship. One suspects that many of their members came, like Hirakawa, from urban backgrounds. Hirakawa's account of the Seattle community at about the same time is significantly different. He writes of earnest and sometimes cultured small businessmen: a fruit-and-cigar stand proprietor, a tailor, and a restaurateur. Hirakawa went to work at the same Port Blakely lumber mill that Fujita had visited, reporting that most Japanese there worked "10 hours every day but Sunday, but every night were gambling until midnight or two or three in the morning." He was paid a dollar per day and was given three meals, so he was able to send a ten dollar monthly remittance to his family in Japan.[19]

Similar urban communities existed in California. In Los Angeles, for example, two scholars have estimated that in 1896, when there were perhaps one hundred Japanese in the city, there were at least sixteen Japanese-owned restaurants. These, like those in Portland, specialized in serving ten- and fifteen-cent American-style meals to workingmen. One of the larger establishments was George Y. Horio's Yokohama Restaurant, which employed four waiters, two cooks, and a dishwasher. They all lived in one house. One of Horio's cooks, Frank K. Miyakawa, eventually owned two restaurants of his own. Nearly all of the one-hundred fifty Japanese in Los Angeles at the turn of the century were the owners of small businesses or were employed therein. Few were employed by non-Japanese.[20]

By the mid-1890s, however, the urban locus of the nascent Japanese American community began to be displaced by a rural one, although the West Coast cities would continue to be the cultural centers of Japanese America. Starting with a trickle of laborers who had completed their contracts in Hawaii, lower-class rural Japanese— the same group that had made up the bulk of the Hawaiian immigration—began to filter into the United States. The Hawaiian authorities reported as of the end of 1894 that 771 Japanese former laborers had "left for America," where there was no effective immigration legislation to keep them out.[21] Chinese were barred—the 1882 Exclusion Act had been extended in 1892—as were prostitutes and contract laborers, but the contract labor laws were almost impossible to enforce. A provision of the 1891 statute, known as "the l.p.c. clause,"

19. Hirakawa Mss., UWA, "Autobiography," pp. 17–19.
20. William M. Mason and John A. McKinstry, *The Japanese of Los Angeles.*
21. Conroy, *Japanese Frontier*, p. 154.

barred the entry of any "paupers or persons likely to become a public charge," but until administrative changes were made in the interpretation of this clause during Herbert Hoover's presidency, this was of little significance in keeping out immigrants.

Agriculture in the Far West would continue to experience endemic labor shortages, given prevailing wages and working conditions. Dating from the earliest attempts at western agriculture by the Spanish mission fathers in the eighteenth century, a semiservile labor force has been sought by the proprietors of large tracts of farmland. American Indians, Chinese, Japanese, Mexicans, refugees from the Dust Bowl in the 1930s, all, at one time or another, have been utilized by what Carey McWilliams has called "Factories in the Fields," today usually described as "agribusiness."

To meet the need for recruiting large numbers of transient workers, individuals and agencies known as "labor contractors" came into being. With a multiplicity of employers needing labor at varying times in different localities for discrete crops no single employer interest group existed—such as the Hawaiian Sugar Planters' Association, which had sponsored immigration to the islands—that could offer year-round employment or anything like it. The labor contractors were usually enterprising negotiators of the same ethnicity as the laborers being recruited.

Among the first western labor contractors were Chinese firms supplying large numbers of laborers to railroad builders such as Leland Stanford. After the end of the railroad building boom of the 1880s, these same Chinese labor contractors serviced other kinds of enterprises, largely industrial. Railroads continued to use immigrant labor for maintenance and construction through World War II, and a significant number of Japanese found such employment. The bulk of contractor-supplied Japanese labor was, however, for agriculture.[22]

The earliest evidence I have found of large-scale Japanese labor gangs dates from the mid-1890s and probably represents small groups recruited from Hawaii by enterprising Issei skilled enough to negotiate with individual growers. Often these entrepreneurs had connections

---

22. For railroad labor in the Pacific Northwest, see Yuji Ichioka, "Japanese Immigrant Labor Contractors and the Great Northern Railroad Companies, 1898–1907," *Labor History* 21 (1980): 325–50; Thomas E. White, "A History of Railroad Workers in the Pacific Northwest, 1883–1934" (Ph.D. diss., University of Washington, 1981); and Yuzo Murayama, "The Economic History of Japanese Immigration to the Pacific Northwest, 1890–1920" (Ph.D. diss., University of Washington, 1982). For a more skilled group, see John J. Culley, "World War II and a Western Town: The Internment of the Japanese Railroad Workers of Clovis, New Mexico," *Western Historical Quarterly* 13 (1982): 43–61.

with the restaurants, boardinghouses, and hotels in the urban ethnic enclaves. Initially Japanese labor gangs competed with and even undercut Chinese labor gangs. Levi Varden Fuller reports that in 1894, in Santa Clara County, California, Japanese worked for 50 cents per day; the going rate for Chinese was $1.00. Two years later the Japanese labor gangs reduced the piece-work rate from $1.20 to 70 cents per ton of sugar beets.

This ethnic competition was shortlived, however. Chinese were declining in number, were aging, and were becoming more and more urbanized with every passing year. Although Japanese were at first welcomed by California growers, from about 1903 on, their demands for higher wages began to meet resistance. One grower went so far as to complain about the "saucy, debonair Jap" who wanted to be able to work "in a white starched shirt." Many growers remembered that the Chinese had been more docile and reliable. The United States Immigration Commission shrewdly noted, in 1909, that such opinions were voiced only after most Chinese had left the industry. The commission suggested that the reputation of the Chinese had risen "with their scarcity and at the expense of the races at present employed." In any event, the Japanese quickly became an important factor in the ethnic equation on the agrarian Pacific Coast. They would remain so until their uprooting in 1942.[23]

The city, however, remained the cultural focus of Japanese America, and in the early years of the twentieth century San Francisco was its metropolis. San Francisco was where most Japanese entered America, where the most important *Nihonmachi* or "Japan town" developed, where the Japanese consul general had his headquarters, and where the anti-Japanese movement had its birth during the 1890s.

While one can encounter derogatory and racist comments about Japanese in America from the 1860s on, nothing that can be called an anti-Japanese movement existed until the 1890s. Yamato Ichihashi notes the first recorded acts of violence against Japanese shoemakers in San Francisco in 1890, and Donald T. Hata has chronicled the brief but significant anti-Japanese flurry in San Francisco in 1891–1893.[24] That flurry was triggered by depressed economic conditions combined with the arrival of a few hundred rather ragged immigrants from Japan proper. Sutemi Chinda, the new consul general, reported that

---

23. Levi Varden Fuller, "The Supply of Agricultural Labor as a Factor in the Evolution of Farm Organization in California," in *Hearings before a Subcommittee of the Committee on Education and Labor . . . pursuant to S. res. 266 74th Congress* (76th Cong., 1st sess., 1940), Part 54, p. 19778. See also *California Fruit Grower* 28 (1903): 2. See also U.S. Immigration Commission, *Reports*, vol. 23, p. 108.

24. Yamoto Ichihashi, *Japanese in the United States*, p. 229.

these laborers, many of them "indeed illiterate" and unable to "write their own names even in Japanese," usually traveled in "groups of five or ten persons from the same village or prefecture." Many of them came from the agricultural prefectures of Wakayama, Hiroshima, and Yamaguchi, all in southwest Honshu, from which most of the early contract laborers to Hawaii were recruited. The area, like Kwangtung in China, had a tradition of emigration.

Chinda was told that many of these migrant laborers had sold their possessions to get enough money to pay their fares, and he reported that he "could not but feel pity for them." Concerned about Japanese honor, the consulate managed to find jobs for the first nine migrants whom the authorities threatened to bar under the l.p.c. clause, but he told Tokyo that he and his staff could not continue to do this. Chinda advised his superiors that any passenger without fifteen dollars in his possession would likely be rejected. Labor contractors quickly learned of this and, if necessary, provided immigrants with that much "show money," which the latter returned after they landed.[25] In any event, the l.p.c. clause while annoying was not crucial. Of the more than 80,000 immigrants who arrived from Japan from mid-1892 to 1910, nearly 5,600 (7 percent) were denied admission. (More than one-third of these denials occurred in 1907–1908.) Fewer than 1,500 were kept out because they had no show money, while more than 2,500 were rejected because of tuberculosis, trachoma, or other diseases.[26]

Chinda was alarmed because the press took notice of the new labor immigration. In 1891 a San Francisco paper commented on the "filthy state" of the immigrants who came out of the "dark, dank hold" of the tramp steamer *Remus* from Nagasaki. Many had apparently tried to dress for success with pitiful results. "Their clothes," the reporter commented, "a fearful and wonderful mixture of male and female attire—would have made even a dress reform advocate blush." He continued his story, perhaps coining the stereotype of the imitative Japanese: "With the irrepressible mimicry of his race, one Japanese was arrayed in an American necktie tied around a

---

25. Report, Satemi Chinda to Shuzo Aoki, April 25, 1891.

26. U.S. Immigration Commission, *Reports*, vol. 23, p. 20. Other causes for exclusion included: 805 as contract laborers; 83 as assisted aliens; 51 anarchists; 36 prostitutes or pimps; 24 because of a surgeon's certificate that they could not earn a living; 8 criminals or convicts; 4 mental defectives; and 1 polygamist. After 1905, 368 Japanese were barred for having no passport. In addition, 1,119 were deported. In the same period, only 130,726 persons of all nationalities were debarred or deported, so Japanese were over-represented. See also, *Annual Report of the U.S. Commissioner-General of Immigration* (1924): 128–29.

Japanese skin free of any shirt. Over his bare skin was an old vest several sizes too large for him. He was the 'dude' of the consignment."[27] After Chinda had alerted Tokyo to this and other stories, officials in Japanese ports were instructed to warn prospective emigrants against calling attention to themselves by their shabby or outlandish appearance.

Headlines in another San Francisco newspaper, the pro-labor *Bulletin,* put the new immigrants in a nativist perspective: UNDESIRABLES; ANOTHER PHASE IN THE IMMIGRATION FROM ASIA; JAPANESE TAKING THE PLACE OF THE CHINESE; IMPORTATION OF CONTRACT LABORERS AND WOMEN. According to the *Bulletin,* Japanese were becoming common in at least two San Francisco neighborhoods. The newspaper warned that, "like the Chinese they come in contact with our white girls in the lighter occupations, and many a family that would disdain to employ a Chinaman now sees nothing wrong in hiring Japanese as cooks, chambermaids and housemaids." The paper also noted that some were employed as laborers on the "fruit farms and ranches of the interior."[28]

A few politicians tried to make political capital out of the Japanese issue, and the old anti-Chinese agitator Dennis Kearney amended his slogan to "The Japs Must Go." But despite the negative press coverage and a few speeches by Kearney and other demagogues, only the school board took brief issue with the Japanese. On June 10, 1893, the San Francisco Board of Education passed a resolution ordering all persons of the Japanese race to attend the Chinese school. Sutemi Chinda, rather than any group of Japanese Americans, opposed this resolution. In a letter to the press, the consul general pointed out that there were only between forty and fifty Japanese students in the school system. All of them were young men characterized as "respectable and well behaved." Chinda ended with an appeal to the "liberal spirit" of San Francisco, and he accompanied his letter with petitions from white students, clergymen, educators, and businessmen, all of whom he had marshaled in support.

California law gave discretion to school boards by allowing them to set up "separate schools for children of Chinese or Mongolian descent," but when such schools did exist, Chinese or Mongolian children could not be admitted to other schools. Since San Francisco did have a Chinese school, the only question to be decided was whether Japanese were "Chinese or Mongolian." By a vote of seven to two, the school board reversed its action after Board President F. A. Hyde said

27. As cited by Hata, *"Undesirables,"* p. 122.
28. May 4, 1891, as cited in ibid., pp. 125–26.

that "to exclude [Japanese] from the public schools was an unjustifiable and unwarranted insult of the Japanese race." Despite some complaints from the anti-Japanese press, the issue soon subsided.[29]

The reasons for the failure of "Japanophobia" to catch on in the early 1890s are probably complex, but surely the very small number of Japanese immigrants was a chief factor. The 1890 census had found only 1,147 Japanese in all of California and fewer than another 1,000 in the remainder of the country. In addition, Japan had yet to play a significant role on the world's stage. When these conditions changed in the next decade, a more robust anti-Japanese movement, backed by politicians with real power, would become decidedly successful.

At the turn of the century, another outbreak of anti-Japanese activity occurred, demonstrating the ripple effect of prejudice against one Asian group extending to another. In 1900 westerners began a campaign for further extension of the Chinese Exclusion Act, due to expire in 1902. Their success was crowned when Theodore Roosevelt made exclusion "permanent" by signing the renewed act on April 29, 1902.[30] Some of those involved in that campaign wanted to keep out all Asians. The first large anti-Japanese meetings took place in the spring of 1900, on April 19 in Seattle and on May 7 in San Francisco. No available evidence links the two meetings, but the arguments advanced at each were similar. Some of the San Francisco speakers were or became nationally prominent. The meeting was organized by local American Federation of Labor leaders. The chief political representative was James D. Phelan, a progressive Democrat who was then mayor of San Francisco. Sociology professor E. A. Ross of Stanford University spoke for the intellectuals.

Phelan insisted that the struggles against Chinese and Japanese were the same: "The Japanese are starting the same tide of immigration which we thought we had checked twenty years ago. . . . Chinese and Japanese . . . are not the stuff of which American citizens can be made."[31] Ross's anti-Japanese arguments were couched solely in economic terms. Throughout his long career the progressive and controversial academic would insist that his views were not racially motivated, a contention that most scholars have not accepted. Ross likened immigration restriction to the tariff: "We keep out pauper-made goods but let in the pauper."[32]

---

29. Ibid., pp. 140–53.
30. 32 *Stat.* 176.
31. San Francisco *Examiner*, May 8, 1900. For Phelan, see Robert Hennings, *James D. Phelan and the Wilson Progressives of California.*
32. San Francisco *Chronicle*, May 8, 1900. For Ross, see Julius Weinberg, *Edward Alsworth Ross and the Sociology of Progressivism.*

The meeting had little immediate effect. Chinese exclusion was still the chief item on the restrictionist agenda, and it had a broad national consensus: in 1900 all three national parties called for immigration restriction. The Republicans were vague but supportive; the Democrats called for an extension of Chinese exclusion and "its application to the same classes of all Asiatic races." One wing of the dying Populist party called for the exclusion of "mongolian and Malayan immigrants" and a halt to the "importation of Japanese and other laborers under contract." Just after the election, the national convention of the American Federation of Labor, insisting that "the Pacific coast and inter-mountain states" were being injured by "Chinese and Japanese cheap coolie labor," asked Congress to renew the Chinese Exclusion Act and to include "all Mongolian labor" in its provisions.

The California campaign for renewal of the exclusion law climaxed with a statewide Chinese Exclusion Convention in San Francisco in November 1901, just prior to the new session of Congress. Predictably, some of the speakers called for the inclusion of Japanese and other Asians in the ban. A few Japanese immigrants passed out leaflets in a novel counterdemonstration protesting any restriction of Japanese immigration. An Issei editor even made a speech condoning the exclusion of Chinese but insisting that Japanese were the equal of Americans. Thus, while their opponents sought to lump them together, spokesmen for Asian groups in this country often attempted to keep their images discrete and were not above denigrating, or at least approving the denigration of, other Asian groups. There would be no meaningful pan-Asian movement among Asian American ethnics until the late 1960s.[33]

Following the Chinese Exclusion Convention in 1901, an awareness of Japanese immigration began to impinge on the consciousness of educated Americans. Also, by the middle of the decade, the international image of Japan had changed significantly, directly affecting the Japanese American image. To understand the nuances of the latter, the former cannot be ignored. Overseas communities, whether they like it or not, are affected by what happens at home. The Issei generation and most of their children—until 1941—continued to identify with and take pride in Japanese as opposed to Japanese American achievements.

There were, of course, exceptions. Some of the earliest immigrants were Socialists, including Sen Katayama, who, after returning to the Old World, became the leading Japanese member of the

---

33. Daniels, *Politics of Prejudice*, pp. 21–23.

Communist International.[34] But most of Japanese America—or over-seas Japanese anywhere—were supporters of the new Japan. The emperor's birthday was an important holiday; visiting Japanese officials were lionized; Japanese consular officials were, until perhaps the 1920s, the chief spokesmen and leaders of the community. As the historian of the Seattle Japanese American community put it: "The Japanese consul was accorded more respect than any member of the local community. He was certain to be the central figure at any community affair which he chose to attend."[35]

The reasons for this are varied and should be analyzed, since the relations between Japanese in America and the Japanese Empire, real and imagined, would be closely linked with the destiny of Japanese America. First, as has been indicated, the Japanese government perceived that its own aspirations to great power status, to be a colonizer rather than the colonized, depended upon getting at least equal treatment for its subjects. Although other nations were some-times concerned about the treatment their overseas nationals received, as with China's concern over the coolie trade, for Japan that concern was more central. A more telling analogy would be Victorian En-gland's insistence upon respect for its subjects abroad. Many of the leaders of Japan took Britain as a model, and Japan's participation with western powers in suppression of the Boxer Rebellion in 1900 symbolizes the way Japan wished to be perceived. The signing in 1902 of the Anglo-Japanese Alliance was, for the Japanese, another mile-stone on the road to great power status.

But economic and population pressures drove Japanese to emi-grate not only to the Asian mainland—Korea and China—but also to Hawaii, the United States, Canada, Peru, Bolivia, and Brazil. These latter emigrants were mostly following patterns established by Chi-nese. Tokyo was sensitive to the implications of such resemblances and was willing to do almost anything—whether it was in the interest of its overseas subjects or not—to get differential treatment. This concern was heightened as a result of the Russo-Japanese War (February 1904 to September 1905), which saw Japan defeat a white colonial power. On the one hand, the war made it clear that Japan was a force with

---

34. For Katayama, see Hyman Kublin, *Asian Revolutionary: The Life of Sen Katayama*. Other early Japanese radicals are examined in Yuji Ichioka, "A Buried Past: Early Issei Socialists and the Japanese Community," *Amerasia Journal* 1, no. 2 (1971): 1–25.

35. S. Frank Miyamoto, "An Immigrant Community in America," in Hilary Conroy and T. Scott Miyakawa, eds., *East Across the Pacific: Historical and Sociolog-ical Studies of Japanese Immigration and Assimilation*, p. 236. See also S. Frank Miyamoto, *Social Solidarity Among the Japanese in Seattle*, pp. 112–13.

Table 4.1
Japanese Americans in the Contiguous United States, 1900–1940

Years	Japanese in United States	Japanese (percentage of total)	Japanese on Pacific Coast	Japanese (percentage of total)	Japanese in California	Japanese (percentage of total)
1900	24,326	.03	18,269	.7	10,151	.6
1910	72,157	.08	57,703	1.4	41,356	1.7
1920	111,010	.1	94,490	1.7	71,952	2.1
1930	138,834	.11	119,892	1.5	97,456	1.7
1940	126,948	.09	112,353	1.2	93,717	1.4

SOURCE: U.S. Census.

which to be reckoned, and it did much for Japanese pride—the anniversary of Admiral Togo's victory in the Tushima Straits was celebrated annually in Japanese America. On the other hand, it also created postwar economic stresses that greatly increased emigration.

Since much has been written—and is still written—about waves and floods of Japanese immigrants to America, it is important to understand, in both absolute and relative terms, the numerical significance of Japanese immigration. More Italians entered the United States (283,000) in the one year from July 1, 1913 to June 30, 1914, than Japanese entered (ca. 275,000) in the whole period of emigration through 1924. In 1907, the heaviest year of immigration from Japan, 30,842 Japanese were recorded as entering the United States, just 2.4 percent of the 1,285,349 who came from all countries that year. Table 4.1 shows numbers of Japanese counted by each census, 1900–1940, and indicates what percentage of the population persons of Japanese ethnicity comprised for the continental United States, for the Pacific Coast (California, Oregon, and Washington), and for California alone. The data demonstrate that, at the time of their highest incidence (1920), about one Californian in fifty was Japanese and about one American in a thousand either came from Japan or was a child of Japanese immigrants.

In the middle of the first decade of this century, with about 50,000 Japanese in the whole United States, the Japanese immigration issue exploded into national and international prominence and stayed there for two decades. Organized anti-Japanese agitation began in San Francisco. The focus on San Francisco was more cultural than demographic. There were significantly more Japanese in Seattle (King County) than in San Francisco County: 3,212 versus 1,781 in 1900;

7,497 versus 4,518 in 1910. But the press and the relatively powerful local labor movement fomented such rapid agitation that in just two years it required the intervention of the White House.

The proximate cause was a campaign begun on Feburary 23, 1905, by the most important paper in San Francisco, the *Chronicle*, which was not usually supportive of labor's demands. The reasons for the *Chronicle*'s crusade are not at all clear, but the episode is a clear example of irresponsible journalism. The Russo-Japanese War was still going on and, as a result, Japanese immigration was actually on the wane: 20,000 had come in 1903; 14,000 in 1904; and only 11,000 would arrive in 1905. But no reader of the *Chronicle* would have gained that impression.

The crusade began with a page-one streamer: THE JAPANESE INVASION, THE PROBLEM OF THE HOUR. The story warned that, "once the war with Russia is over, the brown stream of Japanese immigration" would become a "raging torrent." There were, the paper claimed, at least 100,000 Japanese here already, and they were "no more assimilable than the Chinese." The campaign continued for months with one scare headline following another:

JAPANESE A MENACE TO AMERICAN WOMEN
THE YELLOW PERIL—HOW JAPANESE CROWD OUT THE WHITE RACE
BROWN MEN AN EVIL IN THE PUBLIC SCHOOLS
BROWN ARTISANS STEAL BRAINS OF WHITES
CRIME AND POVERTY GO HAND IN HAND WITH ASIATIC LABOR[36]

Five years earlier Fresno newspaper editor Chester Harvey Rowell, who would become an important member of the Progressive movement both in California and nationally, had put together a calmer but equally racist anti-Japanese rationale:

Japanese who come to this country [are no more objectionable] than the immigrants from Southern Europe [except that] they do not belong to the white race, but the country is hardly ready to enact the principle "this is a white man's country" into laws. . . .

Japanese coolie immigration is of the most undesirable class possible, and we are quite right in objecting to it and demanding that something be done about it. The only question is what we can get done, and in this we must reckon with the cowardice and apathy of the rest of the country. Nothing is going to be done that is worth doing in regard to Japanese immigration unless the country can be

---

36. San Francisco *Chronicle*, February 13–March 13, 1905, passim. The campaign continued for more than a year.

aroused to the necessity of doing something in regard to immigration in general. . . .

But, when all is done, there will still remain more Japanese than we want [who are] neither paupers nor contract laborers . . . and in regard to these there is simply nothing to do but accept the inevitable, until we can arouse the sentiment of the East, not on the Japanese question alone, but on the whole menace of unfit immigration.[37]

Rowell, who wrote this when there were fewer than 25,000 Japanese in America, honed his anti-Japanese views carefully. By the next decade he had made some subtle changes in his argument, if not his position. The following statements are gleaned from his numerous published remarks:

'[Racial discrimination] is blind and uncontrollable prejudice . . . yet social separateness seems to be imposed by the very law of nature.' 'Race . . . counts more than anything else in the world. It is the mark God placed on those whom he put asunder. It is grounded in the instincts of man, and is not amenable to reason.'

'[An educated Japanese] would not be a welcomed suitor for the hand of any American's daughter [but] an Italian of the commonest standing and qualities would be a more welcomed suitor than the finest gentleman of Japan. So the line is biological, and we draw it at the biological point—at the propagation of the species.' '[Intermarriage between a Japanese and a white would be] a sort of international adultery. . . . The instinct of self-preservation of our race demands that its future members shall be members of our race. . . . Personally, I think that this instinct is wise and beneficial.' 'If we deal with this race question now, our descendants will have no race question to deal with. If Californians do not deal with it now, they, like ante-bellum South Carolinians, will leave a race question which their descendants will have to deal with, and against which they will be helpless.'

'The only time to solve a race problem is before it begins.' 'It is for the white peoples to resolve and the brown peoples to accept the permanent physical separation of the races. But as to those who are already over the border, it is for Californians to treat them

37. Fresno *Republican*, April 28, 1900; Chester H. Rowell Mss., Berkeley, Bancroft Library. The most detailed treatment of Rowell is in Miles C. Everett, "Chester Harvey Rowell, Pragmatic Humanist and California Progressive" (Ph.D. diss., University of California, Berkeley, 1966). Everett tends to be apologetic about Rowell's racism.

justly, and for Easterners to be sympathetic and Japanese forebearing if they occasionally fail to do so.'[38]

What needs to be stressed for the modern reader, who may be stunned by the naked racial arrogance of Chester Harvey Rowell's considered remarks, is that the California editor was for his time and place a racial moderate. Many who were more conservative than he—historian Hubert Howe Bancroft, for example—saw no reason why those whom they considered racial inferiors—Chinese, Japanese, and Mexicans—should not be allowed in to do the dirty work of society and then sent back to where they came from when there was no more economic use for them.

It is important to note the differences between the sophisticated views of a middle-class Progressive such as Rowell, with his emphasis on noneconomic factors, which came to characterize the anti-Japanese movement, and the earlier anti-Chinese movement, in which arguments and stresses were almost all on easily predictable economic lines. There was, to be sure, some of this kind of economic argument in the anti-Japanese movement, especially among the trade unionists for whom anti-Asianism was a culturally conditioned reflex, but more and more as the century wore on, the middle-class racial and cultural concerns predominated.

The press agitation, begun by the San Francisco *Chronicle* and echoed elsewhere in the state and in the region, received an almost instant endorsement from the California legislature. In March 1905 the legislature adopted a detailed anti-Japanese memorial to Congress without a dissenting vote. Two months later the anti-Japanese movement gained an organizational center with the creation of the Asiatic Exclusion League (née the Japanese and Korean Exclusion League). This organization soon developed branches in other Pacific Coast states, Nevada, Colorado, and the Canadian province of British Columbia, and gave birth to a short-lived Asiatic Exclusion League of North America, which held a "First [and last] International Convention" in Seattle in 1908.

The league was largely a paper organizational offshoot of San Francisco building trades unions. It thus represented the most conservative wing of the labor movement. More radical segments of the trade union movement were at least equally anti-Japanese and anti-Asian. In 1907 the national executive committee of the Socialist party unanimously opposed all Asian immigration: some of the Socialists justified their stand on purely economic grounds, but others were as

---

38. For the varied sources of these quotations, see Daniels, *Politics of Prejudice*, pp. 131–32 n 15.

openly racist as Progressive Chester Harvey Rowell. One Socialist insisted that "our feelings of brotherhood toward the Japanese" had to be shelved "until we no longer have reason to look at them as an inflowing horde of Alien scabs." Morris Hillquit, a leading theoretician, wanted to restrict immigration from "all backward races," while his colleague Victor Berger expressed fears that the United States might become a "black-and-yellow country within a few generations." Jack London probably spoke for most American Socialists when he declared that, "I am first of all a white man and only then a Socialist." Opposition to Asian immigration—and to a lesser degree all immigration—thoroughly permeated the American labor movement and its political supporters. Only the Industrial Workers of the World and a few affiliated unions were able to resist the racism and nativism that was endemic to American life.[39]

The primary importance of the Exclusion League was not its influence on the labor movement but rather its existence as the first anti-Japanese pressure group. From the time of its formation until after World War II, at least one such group was always functioning on the Pacific Coast. These pressure groups could be counted on to keep the pot of prejudice simmering: when opportune exiguous events occurred, it was relatively easy to bring it to a boil. The history of Japanese America—and of Asian America—in the twentieth century has been structured by a series of external crises, of which the attack on Pearl Harbor was only the most drastic. The San Francisco School Board crisis of 1906, which seemed on the surface to be a simple reaction to the immigration of Japanese, was, in fact, affected by the changed international position of Japan.

As we have seen, even before the end of the Russo-Japanese War (the peace treaty was signed at Portsmouth, New Hampshire, on September 5, 1905) a postwar increase in immigration had been predicted. That increase did eventually occur but only *after* the school board affair had begun. The relationship of the war to that crisis, I believe, was to make Japan seem more threatening to the average American and to give the federal government a motive for intervening. The political situation in San Francisco also contributed: a violent teamsters' strike in 1901 had discredited the reform administration of James D. Phelan. This was replaced by a Union Labor party government, sponsored by the same trade unionists who had created the Exclusion League. The Union Labor administration, dominated by its college-educated young boss Abraham Ruef, was spectacularly cor-

---

39. For details of labor and labor-oriented opposition to Japanese, see ibid., pp. 16–30 and passim.

rupt. (It should be noted that, whatever their other differences, the San Francisco reformers and laborites were equally anti-Japanese.) Then, on April 16, 1906, San Francisco suffered the earthquake by which all subsequent urban American earthquakes have been measured. Rightly or wrongly, most contemporary observers felt that the earthquake somehow contributed to an atmosphere in which a large number of extralegal attacks on Japanese and other Asians occurred. (After the great Kanto earthquake of 1923, Japanese mobs lynched resident Koreans, who were somehow felt to have caused it.)

Almost a year before the earthquake, the local school board, also dominated by Union Labor, had again resolved to send Japanese pupils to the Chinese school. Caucasian children would thereby not have to associate "with pupils of the Mongolian race," thus reversing the determination of the previous decade that Japanese were not "Mongolian." But no action was taken on this May 1905 resolution until after the earthquake. On October 11, 1906, the board formally ordered all Japanese pupils to attend the Chinese school. A little over a week later, garbled versions of what had happened were published in Tokyo newspapers. These reports were picked up by the American press. Thus local discrimination was transformed into an international incident.

Washington had long been aware of possible problems with Tokyo about discrimination. From his personal correspondence, we now know that President Theodore Roosevelt reacted to events in California as early as May 1905, when he wrote privately about the "idiots" of the California legislature. Roosevelt actually agreed with the substance of the exclusionist argument: he felt that the "very frugality, abstemiousness and clannishness [of Japanese laborers] make them formidable to our laboring class"; he indicated that he would not oppose a move to bar them, although he did object to the "foolish offensiveness" of the legislature's language.[40] In the summer of 1905, he informed Japan through his minister to Tokyo that "the American Goverment and the American people at large have not the slightest sympathy with the outrageous agitation against the Japanese. . . . While I am President the Japanese will be treated just exactly like . . . other civilized peoples."[41]

The first public statement from Roosevelt came in his December 1905 State of the Union message. It should be noted that Roosevelt's messages were prolix and, as was the custom until Wilson's day, were read to the Congress by clerks. Thus they did not command the

40. Elting E. Morison, ed., *The Letters of Theodore Roosevelt*, 4: 1168–69.
41. Ibid., pp. 1274–75.

attention that such messages do today. The passages below were ignored by the California press. Roosevelt tailored one short section of his message for Tokyo's consumption: he made a sharp distinction between Chinese and Japanese. "The entire Chinese coolie class," he insisted, were "undesirable immigrants . . . because of their numbers, the low wages for which they work, and their low standard of living." This followed a passage in which the president had at least implied that he favored extending naturalization to Japanese.

> It is unwise [the president wrote] to depart from the old American tradition and to discriminate for or against any man who desires to come here as a citizen, save on the ground of that man's fitness for citizenship. . . . We cannot afford to consider whether he is Catholic or Protestant, Jew or Gentile; whether he is Englishman or Irishman, Frenchman or German, Japanese, Italian, Scandinavian, Slav or Magyar.[42]

This public distinction between Japanese and Chinese—at variance with his private classification of Japanese laborers as "undesirable immigrants"—is understandable only in light of Roosevelt's awareness that Japan had become a first-class power. He took no further action then and apparently did not expect action from Congress. When, almost a year later, the San Francisco School Board affair became an international incident, Roosevelt acted quickly. Before the end of October he had sent the only Californian in his cabinet, Secretary of Commerce Victor H. Metcalf, to San Francisco with instructions to investigate and issue a report. Privately, he assured the Japanese ambassador of his regrets. Formally, he authorized the "use of the armed forces . . . to protect Japanese . . . if they are menaced by mobs."[43] Publicly, in his December 1906 annual message, he made an important and controversial statement about the Japanese question in the United States.

After a platitudinous passage stressing the necessity of treating all nations and immigrants fairly (no mention of Chinese here), Roosevelt denounced the "sporadic" hostility toward Japanese which he claimed was "limited to a very few places." He called this "discreditable" and noted that "it might be filled with the gravest consequences to the nation." Should anyone not understand what those consequences might be, the president pointedly hailed Japanese military achieve-

---

42. James D. Richardson, comp., *Messages and Papers of the Presidents,* 10: 7388–89.
43. Letters to Elihu Root and Victor Metcalf in Morison, *Roosevelt Letters,* 5: 484, 510–11.

ments, which he genuinely admired. He condemned, in advance of his formal receipt of Metcalf's report, the action of the San Francisco School Board. Apparently misunderstanding what the board had ordered, Roosevelt called "shutting them out of . . . the public schools . . . a wicked absurdity." He attributed the hostility to Japanese to fears about their "efficiency as workers." He recommended that Congress pass a law "specifically providing for the naturalization of Japanese who come here intending to become American citizens." He then returned to reasons of state, asking Congress to enable the president to protect the rights of alien residents. He warned that, because of the preposterous situation, "the mob of a single city [might] at any time perform acts of lawless violence which would plunge us into war. . . . It is unthinkable that we should continue a policy under which a given locality may be allowed to commit a crime against a friendly nation."[44]

Roosevelt's strong statement was denounced by almost the entire western press and by numerous western politicians. But words are not always what they seem. No evidence suggests that Roosevelt really wanted naturalization privileges for Japanese: no bill to that effect was ever introduced in Congress. Less than two months later the secretary of state informed our minister in Tokyo that the subject of naturalization should not be discussed with the Japanese, because "no statute could be passed or treaty ratified" which would grant it. Even Roosevelt's language—"Japanese who come here intending to become American citizens"—is curiously hedged and convoluted. Roosevelt's words and deeds would suggest that he was deliberately taking an advanced position from which he could make a planned retreat. Roosevelt, like the overwhelming majority of his fellow white Americans, clearly thought his own race superior to all others. But Roosevelt, perhaps unlike most of his contemporaries, could have sincere admiration for successful individuals of all races.[45] Without in any way excusing the president's actions and attitudes, it must be noted that he was more tolerant than most of his fellow citizens.

While the sound and fury about Roosevelt's message was still raging, Metcalf's report was made public (mid-December 1906). Very few Japanese pupils were in the San Francisco school system: ninety-

---

44. Richardson, *Messages and Papers.* 10: 7433–36.

45. That Roosevelt was a racist is clear. But those who would place him in a racist triumvirate with Hitler and Verwoerd of South Africa, simply ignore time and place. See Pierre L. van den Berghe, *Race and Racism,* pp. 13, 16, 87, 94. The most detailed examination of Roosevelt's racial views is in Thomas G. Dyer, *Theodore Roosevelt and the Politics of Race.* Dyer argues that, for TR, "race remained prime, the indivisible factor of human experience" (p. 169).

three Japanese students spread among the twenty-three public schools in the city. Twenty-five students were native-born American citizens; the others were aliens. The press had complained that young men were in the primary grades (San Francisco had no system of public adult education), and Metcalf demonstrated that this was true. Twenty-seven alien teenagers were well above the age limits for their grades, the worst example being two nineteen-year-olds in the fourth grade. But there were also two bright Nisei seven-year-olds in the third grade, forerunners of thousands of Asian American children who would excel in public education. Metcalf suggested that the school board set age and grade limits to eliminate that problem, but he recommended that the rest of the students be allowed to return to school. He gave as his chief reason "fifty years of more or less close friendship with the Empire of Japan." He made no mention of Chinese students; China was not a world power.[46] Public opinion split on regional lines: the Far West and the South supported California; the rest of the nation supported Metcalf and the president.

This generally favorable public reaction, however, did nothing for the weak legal position of the federal government. Both custom and law supported segregation: *Plessy* v. *Ferguson* (1896), with its "separate but equal" doctrine, would govern until 1954. The federal government, with Secretary of State Elihu Root directing strategy, decided that it could do nothing for the twenty-five pupils who were American citizens. After getting agreement from the local Japanese consul that the twenty-seven overage students need not be considered, the government filed suits in both state and federal courts to force the reinstatement of the forty-one alien students who were in the normal grade for their age. Their protection was not the Constitution—as then interpreted it was useless—but a portion of the 1894 treaty between the United States and Japan which guaranteed reciprocal "most favored nation" rights of residence to the nationals of each country.

These suits never came to trial because Roosevelt and his advisors preferred a political settlement that would placate both the Japanese government and public opinion in California. Roosevelt made it clear to the Japanese ambassador that stopping "all immigration of Japanese laboring men" was "the only way to prevent constant friction" between the two countries, a position the Japanese government did not resist. Its chief concern was that any restriction be self-imposed. The last thing the Japanese policy makers wanted was a Japanese

---

46. For Metcalf's report, see U.S. Congress, Senate, *Japanese in the City of San Francisco, Cal., Document 147*, 59th Cong., 2d sess., 1907.

version of the Chinese Exclusion Act or of the Sino-American treaties that recognized it. Roosevelt had three separate interests to placate: California public opinion and political leadership; Congress; and, least troublesome, the Japanese government.

Four intermediate steps had to be taken before some kind of agreement with Japan could be made: the San Francisco segregation order had to be revoked; the California government had to be stopped from further anti-Japanese action; Congress had to be prevented from taking action of its own; and, eventually, Congress had to be persuaded to enact legislation to enforce whatever agreement Washington might work out with Tokyo.

The California problem was solved first. Outgoing Governor George C. Pardee, a moderately progressive Republican, criticized Roosevelt, blaming his wrongheadedness on the fact that "in common with . . . people of the Eastern states," he just didn't understand the Japanese question. Pardee reaffirmed the right of California school boards to segregate Asians in conformity with state law until the courts should rule otherwise. Sentiment in the legislature was overwhelmingly anti-Japanese, and most observers were certain that some of the anti-Japanese bills and resolutions that had been introduced at the beginning of the session would pass.

Today, in such a situation, the president would probably ask the governor to Washington for a conference, but cross-country journeys before the air age were not taken casually. Roosevelt called the California congressional delegation to the White House instead. After a meeting on January 30, 1907, the delegation wired the following message to the new governor, James N. Gillette, a conservative Republican:

> Delegation has just had important conference with President and Secretary of State. At their request we have wired Superintendent of Schools and President of Board of Education of San Francisco to come here immediately for conference. Entire delegation joins in request that you send for leaders in both houses in Legislature, and ask that all legislative action concerning Japanese matters be deferred for some time. We consider this most important.

The governor and the legislature agreed to cooperate and did so. The San Francisco officials were not so easy to corral. San Francisco's public school system was controlled by the local political machine, and its two leaders, boss Abe Ruef and his henchman Mayor Eugene E. Schmitz, were both under indictment, mostly for stealing public funds. Mayor Schmitz persuaded his education officials (their ties with the politicians were quite close: the president of the board of education was Ruef's brother-in-law, and the superintendent of schools had been a trombonist in Schmitz's orchestra before they had entered politics together) to insist on Schmitz's going to Washington, too. This must have upset Roosevelt—on both moral and ideological grounds, Schmitz was anathema to him—but he eventually agreed. When the local officials arrived in the nation's capital in early February, a week of parlaying produced the desired result. The board revoked the segregation order, and the federal government promised to do something to stop immigration. Eugene E. Schmitz, for the one statesmanlike act of his life, caught what one observer called "unshirted hell" from his constituents, and his political career, not previously affected even by indictment, went into permanent eclipse.

The city officials having been placated, Sacramento still remained potentially troublesome. Roosevelt wrote directly to the governor saying that any legislation would interfere with direct negotiations with Japan about the immigration question. Governor Gillette prevailed on the legislature to pass no such legislation. It should be noted that as long as the White House and the state house were controlled by the same party—the Republicans—no harmful anti-Japanese legislation was passed.

With the Californians mollified, Roosevelt now turned to Congress. Legislation was drafted to enable the president by executive order to prevent persons (really Japanese) in American insular possessions (really Hawaii) with passports valid for those places, from coming to the United States. When passed and executed this would stop the secondary migration of Japanese from Hawaii while enabling Japanese laborers to continue to go where they were wanted by sugar planters. There still remained the growing immigration from Japan itself. This was stopped by the so-called Gentlemen's Agreement, actually six notes exchanged between the United States and Japan in late 1907 and early 1908, which climaxed more than a year and a half of negotiations. As this was an executive agreement, it required no congressional ratification, and, although its terms were generally known, the notes themselves were not published until 1939. The Japanese agreed not to issue passports valid for the continental United States to laborers, skilled or unskilled. Laborers who had already been to America might return, however, and passports might be issued to the "parents, wives and children of laborers already resident there."[47]

Although it was a triumph of diplomacy, a model of reasonableness and mutual accommodation, the Gentlemen's Agreement was a

---

47. U.S. Department of State, *Foreign Relations of the United States, 1924* (Washington, D.C., 1939), pp. 339–69. For further details, see Daniels, *Politics of Prejudice,* pp. 31–45.

disaster for international relations. In the long run, it exacerbated rather than eased tensions between the two Pacific powers. From the point of view of Japanese America, however, the Gentlemen's Agreement meant that there would be a viable and burgeoning Japanese American community. Neither the failure nor the success was foreseen on either side of the Pacific. The failure is easier to explain.

The Gentlemen's Agreement was "sold" to Californians as tantamount to exclusion. It was not. Under its terms Japanese American population would more than double in less than twenty years. What the American negotiators, and perhaps even their Japanese counterparts, did not realize was that, under the terms of the agreement, thousands of Japanese men resident in the United States would marry and bring their wives here. Many of these marriages were by proxy, but they were legal under Japanese law, and they were usually resolemnized once the women had arrived in the United States. The steady advent of these "picture brides" added to the already existing cultural paranoia of Californians, who always felt that people back East didn't understand "their Asian question," just as southerners insisted that Yankees didn't understand "their colored people."

The Gentlemen's Agreement changed drastically the nature of the Japanese American population in the United States. Female immigrants began to predominate. As a result, the sex ratio among Japanese in America began to change from one that was overwhelmingly male to one that by 1924 was beginning to approach a balance. Table 4.2 indicates the population and sex ratios for Japanese in California, the other forty-seven states, and the Territory of Hawaii from 1900 through 1940.

If immigration had been totally cut off in Theodore Roosevelt's time, when the Japanese population was about 90 percent male, most of the Nisei generation simply would not have been born. In addition, one must assume that many of the Issei already here would have returned to Japan or migrated elsewhere. Given these assumptions, some of the conventional wisdom about Japanese population in the United States needs to be reconsidered. In both the United States and Hawaii, the Japanese American community calls the years right after the Gentlemen's Agreement the *yobiyose-jidai*, "the period of summoning families," and that is clearly what happened. The data show, however, that family formation was beginning even before the Gentlemen's Agreement. In 1900, eight years before the agreement, the female Japanese population of Hawaii was already above 22 percent. As table 4.2 demonstrates, from 1900 to 1920 the sex ratios in Hawaii roughly "predict" the mainland sex ratios ten to fifteen years later. This is at least suggestive of the process beginning on the mainland. The children, alien and native born, who were the focus of the school

Table 4.2
Sex Ratio of Japanese Americans in the Contiguous United States and Hawaii, 1900–1940

Year	California			Other 47 States			Hawaii		
	Numbers (Male)	Numbers (Female)	Percentage (Female)	Numbers (Male)	Numbers (Female)	Percentage (Female)	Numbers (Male)	Numbers (Female)	Percentage (Female)
1900	9,598	553	5.4	13,716	405	2.9	47,503	13,608	22.3
1910	35,116	6,240	15.1	27,954	2,847	9.2	54,784	24,891	31.2
1920	45,414	26,538	36.9	27,293	11,765	30.1	62,643	46,625	42.7
1930	56,440	41,016	42.1	25,331	16,047	38.9	75,008	64,623	46.3
1940	52,550	41,167	43.9	19,417	13,813	41.6	82,820	75,085	47.5

SOURCE: U.S. Census

board dispute in San Francisco demonstrate the family formation taking place before 1908. It is not possible to determine how many Japanese children attended public schools in California because the state's school census figures list only "Mongolians," but most of the increase between 1900 and 1910, from 2,818 to 4,048, was surely owing to Japanese rather than Chinese children. Similarly the immigration data show a steady rise in female entries before 1908. After 1908 female entries predominate.

The Gentlemen's Agreement also changed the relationship between the Japanese government and Japanese immigrants in America. As we have seen, Japan had been concerned from the outset about the larger implications of emigration to the United States, but the Gentlemen's Agreement placed special responsibilities on the Japanese government for determining the socioeconomic status of Japanese residents in the United States. Some method was needed for comprehensive registration and control of Japanese Americans.

In February 1909 the Japanese consulate general in San Francisco caused the founding of the Japanese Association of America. In theory, all Japanese residents in the United States would belong to this organization through local chapters to be established in every part of the country with significant numbers of Japanese residents. In practice, of course, not all Japanese belonged to the association. Some undoubtedly stayed out as a matter of principle; others, particularly those living away from the major centers of Japanese American population, stayed out because of indifference or inconvenience; a third group, perhaps the most numerous, stayed out because it cost money to join. In the beginning, annual membership fees ranged from one to three dollars per year.

Both for its own bureaucratic convenience and to apply pressure on individual Japanese to join the appropriate local organization, the Japanese government gave the Japanese associations an official role. They were made the intermediaries through which a Japanese resident had to work if he wished to retain official connection with the Japanese government. Both Japanese law and the Gentlemen's Agreement required that the Japanese consular service issue certain documents to resident Japanese. The responsibility for these certificates was delegated to the Japanese associations, which, in turn, were empowered to collect fees for their issuance.

Certificates required by the Gentlemen's Agreement related largely to Issei traveling outside the country with the right to return and the ability to bring wives, parents, and other relatives into the United States. Thus, any Japanese who wished to keep or establish family ties across the Pacific was forced to do so through a Japanese association. In addition, Japanese law required that men of military age who had not fulfilled their service obligations must register every year that they resided abroad. Certificates were required to register marriages, divorces, births, inheritances, and other vital statistics.

The true role of the Japanese associations has been much debated. Exclusionists such as V. S. McClatchy of the Sacramento *Bee* insisted, on the one hand, that the associations were a sinister "invisible government," part of the Japanese plan to take over America. This charge reechoed throughout anti-Japanese propaganda and was repeated as late as the 1940s by the Committee on Un-American Activities of the United States House of Representatives. The Japanese government and its apologists, on the other hand, insisted that the associations were self-help and protection groups analogous to organizations established by other immigrant communities.[48] In October 1920 the Japanese ambassador to Washington, Baron Kijuro Shidehara, sought to clarify the role of the associations during formal negotiations with the United States:

> Turning to the question of Japanese Associations in the United States it was, in the opinion of Ambassador Shidehara, entirely erroneous to regard them as organs of Japanese propaganda. These Associations were evidently intended to promote general welfare of Japanese residents in their respective localities, but not, by any means, to carry on activities disregardful of American institutions. They had, on the contrary, directed their attention and labor for educational work among their own nationals with a view to familiarizing Japanese settlers with American manners and customs. They were largely responsible for the improvement which had recently manifested itself in the relations of personal intercourse between Japanese settlers and their American neighbors in many rural districts of California. It was true that Japanese residents had made use of these Associations in an attempt to seek relaxation of harsh discriminatory treatment imposed against them by local legislation or otherwise, and to guard themselves against further anti-Japanese measures. But these movements were to be explained in the light of human nature of self-defense and were not influenced

---

48. For the associations, see Valentine Stuart McClatchy, *The Germany of Asia;* M. Fujita, "The Japanese Associations of America," *Sociology and Social Research* 14 (1929): 211–17; Ichihashi, *Japanese in the United States,* pp. 224–26; Miyamoto, *Japanese in Seattle,* pp. 113–17; Roger Daniels, "The Japanese," in John Higham, ed., *Ethnic Leadership in America,* pp. 41–46; and, superior to all previous treatments, Yuji Ichioka, "Japanese Associations and the Japanese Government: A Special Relationship, 1909–1926," *Pacific Historical Review* 46 (1977): 409–37. As Ichioka points out (at p. 411) local associations of one kind or another had been organized under the aegis of Japanese consular officials as early as 1891.

by design of interfering in American political situation. It would certainly be too much to expect that they could be induced to remain inactive and tolerant in the face of any anti-Japanese agitations which might threaten their security and their means of livelihood. These agitations had indeed compelled them to organize themselves to avert their common danger. The Japanese Associations were requested, in many cases, by the Japanese Consulates to serve as sureties for their nationals making applications to the Consular authorities for various forms of certificates. It was practically impossible for a limited number of Japanese Consular staff to conduct personal examination of each of these numerous applications, and they naturally sought, for this purpose, the assistance of the Japanese Associations which might be deemed reliable.[49]

Despite the equivocations of the Japanese ambassador, the associations were, in fact, semiofficial organs of the imperial government. Their functions were essentially bureaucratic and not at all sinister. Many of these functions were dictated not by imperial ambition but rather by Japanese governmental attempts to comply with an executive agreement entered into with the United States government. Contemporary documents indicate that the United States government at times pressed the Japanese to exercise an even greater degree of control over the immigrant Issei than the imperial government either desired or was able to accomplish.

The special relationship between the associations and the Japanese government meant that leadership in the Japanese community devolved upon individuals who were far from independent. At the apex of the Japanese associations stood Japanese consular officials. Much of the income of the associations depended upon their ability to charge fees for certificates and other official documents which most immigrants would need at one time or another. This "right" could be withdrawn from a local association at any time, and in some instances it was. The leaders of recognized associations thus had to be persons who were acceptable to the Japanese consular bureaucracy. These leaders were almost always economically well-established individuals. Businessmen, editors of Japanese-language newspapers, and successful agricultural entrepreneurs were typical "establishment types" who headed local associations.

The leaders of the national associations were cut from the same

---

49. U.S. Department of State, *Report of the Honorable Ronald S. Morris on Japanese Immigration and Alleged Discriminatory Legislation against Japanese Residents in the United States*, p. 46.

pattern. The first president of the national Japanese Association of America, founded in 1909, was George Shima (born Kinji Ushijima), a spectacularly successful agricultural entrepreneur who was called the "Potato King" by the California press and was probably the first Issei millionaire. Many of the association leaders were officials of banks and other corporations headquartered in Japan, and virtually all of them had come to the United States as adults.

Of all the certificates under association control, the one most crucial gave the right to bring one's wife, proxy or otherwise, to the United States. From the point of view of the Japanese government, which tried to abide by the terms of the Gentlemen's Agreement, the problem was how to determine who was eligible to have a wife join him. Under the Gentlemen's Agreement, Japan had agreed to "undertake a system of registration" of Japanese residents in the United States and not to issue passports to laborers or their families. Eventually a rule of thumb was established, after much discussion between consular officials and Japanese American community leaders, that anyone who could show an established bank account or other liquid assets of $800 or more would be eligible to have his wife and other admissible relatives join him. Once a local association certified to the consulate that a resident was eligible, the consulate would arrange for the issuance of the necessary passport and travel documents. The amount of potential power that this placed in the hands of petty association officials is obvious. The abrogation of the Gentlemen's Agreement in 1924 deprived association officials of this power and "greatly reduced the day to day relationships between Japanese consular officials and the associations."

Interviews with surviving Issei and others knowledgeable about the community make it clear that the regulations were not hard to circumvent. Even for the hardworking and frugal Issei, $800 was a sizable nest egg to accumulate. In 1910, for example, the average annual earnings of American railroad workers, who were among the highest paid blue-collar workers in the country, was only $677. Therefore, in many instances, groups of men pooled their assets into "show money." Over a period of time, the same $800 could provide travel documents for a number of wives, picture brides, and other relatives.

Not surprisingly, conflicts often developed between local associations and the central body that met periodically in San Francisco and was subject to direct pressure and control by the consuls general. A number of local associations, for example, had protested futilely that $800 was too high a figure and that perhaps half that would be more reasonable. The most bitter—and revealing—controversy came in 1919. The Japanese government, hoping to blunt the growing postwar anti-Japanese movement led by then-Senator James D. Phelan (D-Cal.), decided to stop issuing passports to picture brides. The imperial government persuaded the national Japanese association to endorse this step. For those eligible immigrants who had the time and money, it was still possible to return to Japan and get married. Some leaders, such as W. K. Abiko, publisher of the San Francisco *Nichibei Shimbun*, one of the largest and most influential of the Japanese-language newspapers in the country, and several associations protested in vain what they rightly characterized as abandonment of their rights and privileges for reasons of state by the imperial government and its agents, the Japanese associations. This was one of the rare instances in which Japanese community leaders publicly challenged an action of the imperial government.

Apart from their role as agents of the Japanese government, the associations and the central association performed two other major functions. Not only did they serve as protective agents when the rights of individual Japanese were attacked but they were deliberate agents of acculturation. Through the associations and other channels such as the immigrant press, the Issei and their children were exhorted to dress in the western fashion, to attend schools and to excel academically, not to carouse in public, and, in general, to keep as low a social profile as possible.

For many immigrants, this indoctrination had started back in Japan. At least some of the many immigration companies had coached prospective emigrants to America how to behave and, more important, how to get through the immigration procedure. Before the Gentlemen's Agreement, one emigrant, for example, gave United States officials an affidavit describing a coaching session allegedly run in Yokohama by an employee of the Consolidated Immigration Companies of Japan. The emigrant was described as about fifty years old and wearing American clothes. He was undoubtedly a returnee from America or Hawaii. According to his affidavit, the coach had advised them that "the only reason for anybody being deported [i.e., refused admission] is a contagious disease, and if you have brains enough to remember what I say you will not be deported."[50]

Advice from such a source was likely to be followed. Advice from the associations, which had real powers of social control, was even more suasive. It was also well understood that anyone who brought disgrace upon the Japanese image might have trouble getting certain certificates. The Japanese government itself had protested when the San Francisco School Board had tried to force their children to attend

---

50. Affidavit quoted in ibid., p. 88.

schools with Chinese, and the government had been able to involve the president of the United States in that successful struggle. This was clear evidence, understood by all Issei parents, of the value that their home government placed upon education. And, since the Issei could never hope to become American citizens, that home government was the only one they had.

This official emphasis upon proper behavior and education may well have been one of the causal agents for the importance the Japanese American community put upon schooling. At a time when most American immigrant groups were, at best, indifferent to anything more than a rudimentary education for most of their children, the commitment of the leadership of the Japanese American community to a maximization of schooling for as many young Nisei and Issei as possible is remarkable. It would lead within a generation to native-born Japanese Americans having considerably more education than the average American.

Approximately contemporaneous with the political furor about the Gentlemen's Agreement, an important socioeconomic change was taking place in the young Japanese American community: its center of gravity was moving from the city to the country. While community tradition attributes the move, at least in part, to the great San Francisco earthquake, the phenomenon is far too widespread for that factor to have been responsible. Not just in California but throughout the West, Japanese were moving from the ranks of farm laborers to becoming farm operators.

In Idaho, Colorado, and Utah, for example, Japanese labor was crucial in the establishment of sugar beets as an important cash crop. In Idaho by 1913 Japanese farmers accounted for nearly 8,000 acres of sugar beets, perhaps one-third of the crop, and they farmed another 10,000 acres producing other products. In Utah by 1914 Japanese growers controlled nearly 4,500 acres of sugar beets, or about one-tenth of the crop. In Colorado, in the same year, they had over 12,500 acres in sugar beets and about that much devoted to other crops.

According to figures provided by the Japanese association of Colorado, less than 500 of those acres were owned by Japanese in 1914; nearly 9,000 were leased for cash, while more than 16,000 were leased on shares. A similar pattern of land tenure would develop, as we shall see, on the Pacific Coast. Because land ownership was a goal of Issei farmers, the proportion of land owned would increase steadily. One interesting difference can be noted between Rocky Mountain and Pacific Coast Japanese American agriculture. On the coast, the relatively large pool of Japanese labor meant that most Japanese agriculture there was contained within the ethnic community: that is, when Japanese farmers needed seasonal labor, that labor was almost always Japanese. In the Rocky Mountain region, by contrast, the entrepreneurial element was a much higher proportion of the population. Almost from the beginning, farm laborers of other ethnicity were hired by Japanese farmers. As early as 1914, according to Harry Millis, Japanese farmers in northern Colorado were hiring "other races . . . especially the lower-priced Mexicans."

The coastal pattern prevailed in the Pacific Northwest, although the crops were different. By 1910, according to the census, Japanese in Washington controlled almost 9,500 acres; by 1914, this had grown to more than 16,000 acres. All of this acreage was leased, because Washington had a law, dating from the Populist era, that prevented landownership by aliens who had not formally declared their intention to become United States citizens. Nearly all of the Japanese agriculture was labor intensive rather than resource intensive: it specialized in berry and vegetable farming. By 1914 Japanese in Seattle dominated the public market, operating some three hundred of the four hundred stalls and stores. In both Washington and California, and particularly in Seattle and Los Angeles, Japanese agriculture quickly developed a vertical ethnic structure in which Japanese vendors, peddlers, stall holders, and retail merchants marketed Japanese-produced fruits and vegetables. Rocky Mountain farmers, by contrast, sold their chief crop to white-owned beet sugar concerns, some of which became large corporations.[51]

Most Issei enterprises were quite small, but there were exceptions. The most spectacular of these was run by the Issei millionaire, George Shima (1863–1926). Late in life, Shima recounted that he had come to America from Fukuoka Prefecture in 1889 with less than a thousand dollars in capital. But this, of course, was a significant sum at that time. He had started as a common laborer but soon had become a labor contractor. Some time before the turn of the century, he had begun to lease land, often with other Issei as partners. By the time he was made president of the Japanese Association of America in 1909, Shima had already become a pioneer in applying corporate managerial techniques to agriculture and in using the latest developments in agricultural science.

Shima and his associates created an agricultural empire on the virgin "drowned islands" of the San Joaquin delta, and they were among the first to raise potatoes successfully for the market in California. In 1920 a Caucasian newspaper claimed that Shima controlled 85 percent of the potato crop with a total value of more

---

51. H. A. Millis, *The Japanese Problem in the United States*, pp. 79–102; quotation at p. 87.

than $18 million. In 1913 a University of California graduate student wrote a research thesis on Shima's operations. In that year Shima controlled 28,800 acres actually in production and, by means of marketing agreements almost entirely within the ethnic community, disposed of the produce grown on many thousands more. His work force numbered more than 500 and included agronomists, engineers, and boat captains (the islands were then accessible only by water) as well as foremen and common laborers. Although most of Shima's employees were Japanese, they also included South Asians and Caucasians, both native and foreign born. When George Shima died in 1926, his pallbearers included David Starr Jordan, the chancellor of Stanford University, and James Rolph, Jr., the mayor of San Francisco. The "Potato King's" success was different only in scale from that of most Issei farmers.[52]

Nowhere did these farmers make such an impact as in California. Their role in the expanding California economy, particularly in the decades after 1900, made California the heart of Japanese America. At the turn of the century only four Japanese Americans in ten lived in California; by 1910 the number was almost six in ten, and by 1920 the number was up to seven in ten. By 1910 Los Angeles had become the metropolis of Japanese America, and it has remained so, except for the years of the wartime evacuation. From a population of about 1,000 in 1900, Japanese in Los Angeles County numbered almost 9,000 in 1910, nearly 20,000 at the next census, and just over 35,000 in 1930. Even in the decade from 1930 to 1940, when the national Japanese American population dipped by almost 9 percent, the ethnic Japanese population of Los Angeles County increased just over 4 percent.

Although a major urban ethnic enclave developed in downtown Los Angeles—the "Little Tokyo" area centering on a few blocks around East First Street—the economy of Japanese Los Angeles was predominately agricultural.[53] The historian of Japanese Los Angeles, John Modell, has described the area's economic development:

---

52. Hiram W. Johnson, III, Mss., Bancroft Library, letter, George Shima to Hiram Johnson, February 11, 1911. See also Kaizo Naka, "Social and Economic Conditions Among Japanese Farmers in California" (M.A. thesis, University of California, 1913), pp. 55–60. See also George Shima, *An Appeal to Justice*; K. K. Kawakami, *The Real Japanese Question*, pp. 44–47; Dorothy Swaine Thomas, *The Salvage*, pp. 181 ff., see also San Francisco *Chronicle*, March 8, 1909; January 6, April 7, December 15, 1910; January 21, September 1, 16, 1911; June 25, 1912; January 19, 26, 1917; November 20, 1919; March 27–30, April 18, 1926; July 19, 1927; and April 26, 1952; San Francisco *Examiner*, February 23, 1917.

53. Mason and McKinstry, *Japanese of Los Angeles*, has an excellent series of maps showing Japanese residences and businesses, 1898–1907, at pp. 42–43.

Agriculture [provided] the backbone for an ethnic economy that sustained the Los Angeles Japanese-American community until World War II [although] it was not agriculture alone that permitted the Japanese-American economy to grow alongside that of the whites. . . . Japanese-American economic enterprise followed the traditional pattern of minority enterprise in this country; it started out by exploiting the fringes of Caucasian economic enterprise, where initiative, hard work, and the ability to put up with a great deal of discomfort can make a substantial difference. Los Angeles had many "fringes", as Japanese Americans discovered. . . . But . . . a ghetto is still a ghetto, even in the absence of poverty, and the Japanese Americans were in the larger sense ghettoized. The peculiar characteristics of Los Angeles—its growth, its climate and the way of life associated with it, the comfort and prosperity so openly displayed—affected the resident Japanese. The size, economic security, and group aspirations of the Japanese community contributed to a large and communally vibrant ghetto. The phenomenon tells us a great deal about "separate but equal"—or, more precisely, somewhat separate and in some ways equal.[54]

The patterns of life in Japanese Los Angeles prevailed, to a greater or lesser degree, for most of Japanese California. By 1920 when the population pattern was fairly well established, 28 percent of California's Japanese lived in Los Angeles County; another 50 percent lived in Sacramento, Fresno, San Francisco, Alameda, and San Joaquin Counties; the rest were scattered in thirty-four counties, and in eight counties census enumerators failed to find any Japanese at all. In almost all parts of California and, for that matter, the Pacific Coast, Japanese lived in ethnic enclaves, worshipped in ethnic churches, but attended integrated schools. Their incidence was never large in any county; even in Los Angeles County at the time of highest census incidence (1920), they comprised just over 2 percent of the population.

There were a few small farming communities where incidence was much higher. Four such communities in Sacramento County— Courtland, Isleton, Walnut Grove, and Florin—were so heavily Japanese that Japanese pupils made up a majority of the public school students. In these four school districts—which in 1929 had a total of just 575 Japanese students—separate "oriental schools" were estab-

---

54. John Modell, *The Economics and Politics of Racial Accommodation: The Japanese of Los Angeles, 1900–1942*, pp. 26–27.

lished and maintained.[55] Yamoto Ichihashi has quoted one Florin resident as admitting that the reason was simply "race prejudice. It got so my daughters went mostly with Japanese girls. The principal was letting Japs crowd our boys off the grammar school team just because they could play better baseball. The towns around us began to razz our kids because of that. Well, we couldn't stand for it any longer, so we separated our schools."[56]

But these Sacramento County pupils were the only Japanese of the approximately 30,000 of school age in the state at the time who attended segregated schools. If schools were largely integrated, other public facilities were not. Municipal swimming pools, for example, were closed to "orientals" and, in many instances, only the balconies of moving-picture theaters were open to them.

The shift of the economic center of gravity of Japanese America from the city to the country, from a dependence on labor to entrepreneurship, was not immediately perceived by the white power structure. As late as 1905, when the movement to the country had already begun, the California legislature had included in its bill of particulars against the Japanese the complaint that "Japanese laborers . . . are mere transients [who] do not buy land [or] build or buy houses. . . . They contribute nothing to the growth of the State. They add nothing to its wealth, and they are a blight on the prosperity of it and a great and impending danger to its welfare."[57] The legislators, however, soon learned of their error, and the second diplomatic crisis between Japan and the United States was set off by California's attempts to inhibit the growth of agricultural entrepreneurship by Japanese Americans.

All of the available evidence indicates that the California politicians represented the prejudices of their constituents. White Californians and, in fact, white westerners were vehemently opposed to Japanese immigration and economic growth. Whenever the matter was discussed in Congress, westerners received almost total support for their views from southerners, with scattered but increasing support from the Middle West and the Northeast. What continued to complicate the matter—and to prolong the controversy—was the fact that Japan had become a major power. In practice, the national

---

55. Two detailed accounts of California school segregation are in Irving G. Hendrick, *Public Policy Toward the Education of Non-White Minority Group Children in California, 1849–1970;* and Charles M. Wollenberg, *All Deliberate Speed: Segregation and Exclusion in California Schools, 1855–1957.*

56. Ichihashi, *Japanese in the United States,* pp. 351–352.

57. *Journal of the Senate of the State of California,* Sacramento, 1905, pp. 1164–65.

leaders of the party in power tried to allay the agitation, while the state politicians of the party out of power nationally used the Japanese issue in an attempt to win votes. Thus, through 1912, with Republican presidents in Washington and Republican governors in Sacramento, there was at least a degree of cooperation.

Although his anti-Japanese credentials were, in the final analysis, as good as anyone's, Hiram W. Johnson, who became governor of California as a progressive Republican in January 1911, "sat upon the lid," as he put it, and prevented the 1911 legislature from passing any significant anti-Japanese measures. In this, he followed his conservative Republican predecessors.[58] (Johnson remained governor until 1917, when he entered the United States Senate. He stayed there until his death in 1945.)

The Democrats used Johnson's position to their advantage, not only in state but national elections. In 1908 western Democrats had labeled William Jennings Bryan as "Labor's Choice" and William Howard Taft as the "Japs' Choice." Four years later, Hiram Johnson himself was the vice-presidential nominee with Theodore Roosevelt on the Progressive party ticket. Democrats distributed hundreds of thousands of cards contrasting anti-Japanese statements by the Democratic candidate, Woodrow Wilson (and drafted by Democratic Japanophobe James D. Phelan) with some of Roosevelt's most advanced pro-Japanese statements from the San Francisco School Board and Gentlemen's Agreement crises, including his momentary advocacy of naturalization for Japanese. Hiram Johnson was convinced that "at least ten thousand votes were lost in this state upon this issue." Since he and Roosevelt lost California by only 174 votes in a total of more than 700,000, the issue had obviously been crucial. In addition, the state Democratic party platform had contained a plank calling for an alien land act to "prevent any alien not eligible to citizenship from owning land in the State of California."[59]

President Woodrow Wilson found a bitter and implacable foe in the California governor's mansion. Wilson and Secretary of State William Jennings Bryan each had not only made distinct and specific anti-Japanese statements but also had espoused white supremacy and state's rights. From the very first days of Wilson's administration, which began on March 4, 1913, the Democrats found their ideological

---

58. Daniels, *Politics of Prejudice*, pp. 46–50.
59. For Hiram Johnson's reaction to all of this, see his letter to Theodore Roosevelt, June 21, 1913, printed in Daniels, *Politics of Prejudice*, pp. 112–17.

preconceptions in conflict with the practical realities of foreign policy.[60]

By the time Wilson was inaugurated, two different kinds of anti-Japanese land bills had been introduced in the California legislature. The first was a simple anti-alien bill, similar to the one on the books in Washington, a number of other states, and the District of Columbia. This barred all aliens from owning land, although it treated persons who had formally declared their intention to become citizens as if they were citizens.[61] For most Californians, such a bill had the drawback of barring investment in land by foreign corporations. In fact, foreign corporations rather than individuals had been the real targets of most of the earlier acts passed in the 1880s and 1890s.

The second kind of bill forbade land ownership only by "aliens ineligible to citizenship." The phrase referred not to any constitutional bar but to the naturalization statute passed in 1870. It replaced a statute passed in 1790 which had restricted naturalization to "free white persons." The end of slavery and the passage of the Fourteenth Amendment, which gave blacks citizenship, made that phrasing inappropriate. The resultant new statute made "white persons and persons of African descent" eligible for naturalization, deliberately omitting Chinese, as the congressional debates show, and providing yet another link between anti-Chinese and anti-Japanese behavior. Although the precise meaning of "white persons" would not be definitively established until Supreme Court rulings in 1922, it was generally assumed that all Asians were barred from naturalization. But, it should be remembered, the Fourteenth Amendment also provided that "all persons born . . . in the United States . . . are citizens of the United States and of the State wherein they reside." This provision, designed to protect the rights of newly freed blacks, became absolutely vital in protecting the economic rights of Japanese America.

On the second day of Wilson's presidency, Japanese Ambassador Sutemi Chinda called to discuss the California problem. The ambassador reported to the Japanese Foreign Office that Wilson had told him that "the Constitution did not allow the Federal Government to intervene in matters relating to the rights of individual states," but both he and Secretary of State Bryan gave assurances that they would attempt to use their influence to prevent anti-Japanese legislation.

---

60. The 1913 Alien Land Act crisis is treated at length in Daniels, *Politics of Prejudice*, pp. 46–64.

61. For an account of Alien Land Laws generally, see Douglas W. Nelson, "The Alien Land Law Movement of the Late Nineteenth Century," *Journal of the West* 9 (1970): 46–59.

Wilson also apparently told Chinda that, because of Hiram Johnson's "emotional character," it would be useless to appeal to him directly. Indirect pressure from Washington was applied throughout March and early April. During the same period the state's anti-Japanese forces were also applying pressure on the legislature. Johnson arranged a large public hearing in the assembly chamber which was attended not only by business and church groups that wished to keep relations with Japan undisturbed but also by various anti-Japanese spokesmen. The anti-Japanese forces clearly carried the day, with the most flamboyant and publicized testimony raising the irrelevant issue of racial intermarriage. (The issue was irrelevant because it was statistically insignificant. Interracial marriage was unlawful in California, but such marriages performed elsewhere were valid.) One agitator, a former Congregational minister named Ralph Newman, inveighed against his Japanese neighbor: "Near my home is an eighty-acre tract of as fine land as there is in California. On that tract lives a Japanese. With the Japanese lives a white woman. In that woman's arms is a baby. What is that baby? It isn't Japanese. It isn't white. It is a germ of the mightiest problem that ever faced this state; a problem that will make the black problem of the South look white" (Daniels, *Politics of Prejudice*, p. 59). Throughout this period Governor Johnson had made no overt moves, but in mid-March he had privately described the whole complicated situation as "one out of which we can get a good deal of satisfaction."

In early April Governor Johnson received telegrams from William Kent, a Progressive congressman from California who was cooperating with the administration, asking, "on highest authority," that any bill passed be a general anti-alien measure rather than one that discriminated only against aliens ineligible to citizenship. The governor replied to the congressman that if the president had anything to communicate to him, he should do so directly, as previous administrations had done. The point of this was, as one of Johnson's advisors put it, to "smoke out" Wilson into saying publicly what he was saying privately. Secretary of State Bryan then wired Johnson asking that no land bill be signed until the federal government could present arguments to justify a veto. Johnson replied that any arguments should be made before, not after, the vote of the legislature. While the long distance sparring was going on, public concern, both in California and Japan, began to heighten. In California the Progressive majority, by mid-April, swung to a bill which barred only aliens ineligible to citizenship, and affected corporations only if the majority of the stock were held by such persons. This, Johnson admitted privately, "points the bill."

Meanwhile the international aspects of the proposed anti-

Japanese legislation became more complex. On April 12 Ambassador Chinda, obviously worried, voluntarily offered Bryan a concession that further demonstrates how little the Japanese government really cared for the human rights of its overseas citizens: he suggested that Japan might be willing to curb the coming of picture brides.[62] Bryan, who may not even have known what picture brides were, ignored the offer. Chinda, following the pattern of the school board settlement, was offering Washington something concrete it could trade to Sacramento in exchange for cooperation. On April 17, a Tokyo crowd estimated at 20,000 "cheered wildly" as one of the less responsible members of the Japanese parliament called for gunboat diplomacy by insisting that the Japanese fleet be sent to California to protect the rights of Japanese subjects and to make the natives behave.

Finally, on April 22 after more than a month of watchful waiting and behind the scenes maneuvering, the president moved publicly. In identical telegrams to Governor Johnson and the legislature, Wilson requested that, if they thought an alien land bill necessary, they exclude "all aliens who have not declared their intention to become citizens" from owning land. The bill under consideration, Wilson claimed, would violate the treaty rights of Japanese as well as "national honor and national policy." The treaty to which Wilson referred had been signed in 1911. Its pertinent provisions provided that the citizens of each nation be able to

> enter, travel and reside in the territories to carry on trade, wholesale and retail, to own or lease and occupy houses, manufactories, warehouses, and shops, to employ agents of their choice, to lease land for residential and commercial purposes, and generally to do anything incidental to or necessary for trade upon the same terms as native citizens or subjects, submitting themselves to the laws and regulations there established.

Johnson replied almost immediately to Wilson that the pending bill did not violate the treaty, which said nothing about agricultural land; the governor then had California Attorney General U. S. Webb and Progressive lawyer Francis J. Heney draft a bill explicitly protecting the treaty rights of Japanese. After passage of the 1913 Alien Land Act (sometimes called the Webb-Heney Law), the State Department took the same position, in negotiations with the Japanese, that the governor had earlier taken: the California statute violated no treaty provisions. Before the fact, however, Washington had made no such

---

62. Teruko Okada Kachi, *The Treaty of 1911 and the Immigration and Alien Land Law Issue between the United States and Japan, 1911–1913*, pp. 233–34.

admissions. Wilson's response to Johnson, in a telegram sent the same day, was to request that the governor receive Secretary of State Bryan, who would go to California "for the purpose of consulting . . . and cooperating . . . in the framing of a law which would meet the views of the people of the State and yet leave untouched the international obligations of the United States." Johnson agreed to this request and Bryan almost immediately boarded a train for the four-day trip to California.

Bryan came, conferred with, and addressed the legislature at some length—the transcripts of his two executive sessions with the California legislature run to 113 typewritten pages—but he had absolutely nothing to propose. If Hiram Johnson's acerbic comment is hyperbolic—"Mr. Bryan presented nothing that could not have been transmitted within the limits of a night letter, without using all of the words"—Bryan himself told the legislature that "I came here with no program. I came simply to confer." The whole performance, which by the standards of today's shuttle diplomacy may seem petty, was unprecedented. It must have been intended to impress the Japanese, who presumably did not know what went on in the executive sessions and private meetings. The bill passed the legislature overwhelmingly—35 to 2 in the senate, 72 to 3 in the assembly—and Johnson signed it into law. The governor justified his actions in a long letter to Bryan:

> By the law adopted we offer no offense; we make no discrimination. The offense and discrimination are contained, it is claimed, in the use of the words "eligible to citizenship." . . . We do not mention the Japanese or any other race. . . . If invidious discriminations ever were made in this regard, the United States made [them] when [it] declared who were and were not eligible for citizenship. . . . If discrimination it is discrimination against California. We insist that justly no offense can be taken by any nation to this law. . . . We of California . . . have violated absolutely no treaty rights; we have shown no shadow of discrimination; we have given no nation the right to be justified in taking offense.

Johnson's claim that no discrimination was intended was simply nonsense dressed up in a lawyerlike argument. The apparent intent of the law was to stop further ownership of land by Japanese. Johnson was correct in noting that it was the racist nature of the federal naturalization statute that made it possible for California to discriminate between Asians and non-Asians in the matter of agricultural land ownership. The California law actually did very little, as we shall see, and Johnson and some of his closest advisors knew in advance that this would be the case, although it is not clear that the hundred-odd legislators and other anti-Japanese leaders in the state understood the real situation. From my own study of James D. Phelan's personal papers, for example, I am convinced that he was ignorant of the real effect of the act, although one might expect a leading politician to be better informed.

The psychic effects of the 1913 Alien Land Act were disturbing to Japanese Americans. The whole agitation merely underlined their alienness and encouraged other kinds of discrimination and unpleasantness. Nonetheless, the law did not significantly inhibit Japanese control of agricultural land. Just as population continued to grow after the immigration of laborers was stopped, Japanese land tenure continued to expand after the passage of the 1913 Alien Land Act. There were two reasons for this.

First, much of the land that Japanese tilled was leased rather than rented. The 1913 act merely limited the terms of agricultural land leases to Japanese to three years, which was actually longer than almost all such leases. To have outlawed leasing would have been seriously to disrupt certain sectors of California's agricultural economy—the lessors were, after all, almost always white entrepreneurs. The elimination of Japanese lessees would have lowered significantly the cost of renting agricultural land in California.

But second, and even more important, really large operators, such as George Shima, could get around the law in one of two ways. One of Johnson's most trusted advisors had pointed this out to the governor before the act was put into final form. "It will be perfectly easy," wrote Chester Harvey Rowell, for corporations "to evade the law by transferring to . . . local representatives enough stock to make fifty-one per cent of it ostensibly held by American citizens." The other and even simpler way was for alien Japanese to transfer ownership to their native-born children, who were, under the Constitution, citizens of the United States.

The statistics of Japanese agricultural land tenure in California clearly show a steady growth (see table 4.3). Unfortunately we have no good figures for 1914, but there is very reason to believe that they lay roughly midway between those of 1909 and 1919. Not only did total acreage nearly triple in the decade from 1909 to 1919, but the percentage of agricultural land owned grew from 10.6 to 16.3. In 1919 the Japanese controlled acreage amounted to about 1 percent of California's land used in agriculture, but this is a misleading figure because much of that land was used for grazing and was then of little value. Most of the Japanese-held land, however, was quite fertile—or had been made so by their improvements—and was farmed intensively in crops that usually entailed much hand labor. More indicative of the significance of Japanese in California

Table 4.3
Japanese-controlled Agricultural Land, California, 1900–1919
(in acres)

Year	Owned	Leased/Shared Crop	Total
1900			4,698
1904	2,422.0	54,831.0	57,253
1909	16,449.5	139,233.5	155,683
1919	74,769.0	383,387.0	458,156

SOURCE: Data for 1900, 1904, 1909 in *Reports of the Immigration Commission*, 23:79; for 1919 in California State Board of Control, *California and the Oriental*, Sacramento, 1922, p. 48.

agriculture was the fact that in 1919 the gross income from their crops was computed at more than $67 million, or about 10 percent of the total value of all California agricultural production that year.

Claims were always being made that Japanese farmers were driving out whites. That may have been true insofar as certain specialized crops were concerned or in a few very small geographical areas, such as the Florin vicinity. The fact is, however, that California agriculture and just about everything else in the state was expanding. Considered in sectoral terms, Japanese agriculture in California—and elsewhere in the West—did not displace existing farmers. Often Issei farmers opened up new lands and introduced new crops with the labor-intensive, high-yield style of agriculture they brought with them as opposed to the resource-intensive, relatively low-yield style of agriculture characteristic of American farming. The Japanese farmers supplemented rather than competed with other western producers. It is clear that the Japanese did not, as James D. Phelan and other exclusionists claimed, "spurn the hand that [fed] them," but rather, to reverse the metaphor, they fed the hand that slapped them. To be sure, this was out of economic interest rather than altruism.

The startling rate of continued growth in Japanese American agriculture produced the almost inevitable political reaction from the Japanophobes: outrage that they had again been "betrayed," and a push for another, more effective alien land law. Hiram Johnson had misjudged. Just after the passage of the 1913 act he had assured Theodore Roosevelt that "never again in California can the Japanese question be a political question, except as we shall want it to be." Nonetheless, seven years later the Japanese question reasserted itself politically in California. This time it was exploited largely by Democrat James D. Phelan.[63]

The drive for a new law was sponsored by a broad anti-Japanese coalition including representatives of labor, farmers, and middle-class patriotic and fraternal organizations who formed the Japanese Exclusion League. The league laid down an anti-Japanese program calling for five national objectives:

1. Cancellation of the "Gentlemen's Agreement"
2. Exclusion of "Picture Brides"
3. Rigorous exclusion of Japanese as immigrants
4. Confirmation of the policy that Asiatics shall be forever barred from American citizenship
5. Amendment of the Federal Constitution providing that no child born in the United States shall be given the rights of an American citizen unless both parents are of a race eligible to citizenship

But a new alien land law was first on the agenda. Rather than trust the politicians, exclusionists drafted a new, tougher law and submitted it to the voters as an initiative after a petition drive in which members of three middle-class organizations, the Native Sons of the Golden West, its distaff counterpart the Native Daughters, and the American Legion had gathered most of the signatures. The initiative measure was designed to plug loopholes in the 1913 law. It had four major provisions: (1) prohibition of any transfer of land to Japanese nationals; (2) barring of any leasing of land to Japanese nationals; (3) barring of acquisition, by lease or purchase, of land by any corporation in which Japanese held a majority of the stock; and (4) prohibition of noncitizens from acting as guardians for citizens in matters of land tenure.

The proposition was overwhelmingly popular in California, passing by a vote of 668,483 to 222,086, almost exactly three to one. From March to November 1920 an intensive, high-powered campaign was waged for the proposition. The state government, whom the original progressive proponents of the initiative procedure had presumed would be neutral in such matters, was an unabashed proponent of the measure, as were both political parties. So perhaps the fact that a fourth of the voters opposed the measure is the statistic to be particularly noted. The campaign was not just directed at landholding, although only that was affected by the initiative. It also capitalized on the postwar unpopularity of Japan for its demands on China. For the

---

63. For the 1920 Alien Land Act and the campaign to enact it, see Daniels, *Politics of Prejudice*, pp. 79–91.

first time the Nisei, the native-born American citizen Japanese, became a focal point of hostility.

According to Governor William D. Stephens, a progressive Republican successor to Hiram Johnson, "the fecundity of the Japanese race far exceeds that of any other people." A state report made it appear that the Japanese birthrate was three times that of whites. In the most recent year, the 15,211 Issei married women in the state had produced 4,378 children, while the 313,281 white married women in the state had produced only 30,893. The inappropriateness of the comparison should be apparent; at that time almost all of the Issei women were not only in their prime childbearing years but also were in the first years of their marriages. The white women ranged from ages 15 to 45 and had been married for a varying number of years. But the governor was relatively restrained; California's leading anti-Japanese propagandist V. S. McClatchy concocted what he called "indisputable facts and figures" to show that, if even a few Japanese were let in every year, Japanese population in the United States would pyramid to 318,000 in 1923; 542,000 in 1933; 875,000 in 1943; 2,000,000 in 1963; 10,000,000 in 2003; and 100,000,000 in 2063. Although no demographer has yet computed the net reproductive rate for Issei women—that would be the total number of daughters that they produced—it seems to have been only slightly above that of the "native white" birthrate at the time and significantly below that for certain contemporary European immigrant groups. This is perhaps in part because of the lack of any serious inhibition against birth control in Japanese culture.

Although the passage of the new land law was much feared—as early as March 23 the Japanese government had claimed that it would "deprive Japanese settled agriculturists . . . of their principal means of livelihood"—it was a classic case, from the exclusionist's point of view, of locking the barn after the horse had been stolen. Had the terms of the 1920 initiative been enacted in 1913, as they could have been, the growth of Japanese American agriculture would have been seriously inhibited. But now, given the large number of native-born Japanese Americans in whose name land could be leased or owned, the law was more of a nuisance than an inhibition. Japanese agriculture, to be sure, shrank in number and size of farms in the 1920s. But at the same time, as John Modell has shown in his study of the Japanese of Los Angeles, the value of Japanese-controlled farmland and improvements increased fourfold.[64] I suspect that parallel studies would produce similar results for other major agricultural regions of Japa-

---

64. Modell, *Economics and Politics*, p. 99.

nese America, like the state of Washington, where a similar act was passed in 1921. In addition to placing land deeds or leases in the name of their children, Washington's Japanese, working through the Japanese association, formed a corporation under the trusteeship of Caucasian attorneys. The corporation bought some eight-hundred acres of land and redistributed it to Japanese farmers who had lost their land and apparently had no citizen children in whom to vest title.

All of this, however, ignores the psychic shock which the renewed agitation must have had for Japanese. S. Frank Miyamoto, in his pioneering study of the Seattle community, cites a poll taken in Seattle in 1925 showing that not one Japanese family of 2,000 interviewed (given community standards, this was surely a poll of Issei males only) was willing to say that "they definitely will not go back to Japan."[65] But this highly improbable result surely is owing to the fact that the poll was taken under the auspices of the Japanese association. Respondents knew that the results and perhaps the names would be made available to the Japanese government. More significant is the fact that, at a time when community morale must have been at a pre-World War II low, almost two-thirds of the family heads were "undecided," which I read as meaning "no." Conversely, almost one-fourth of the family heads said that they would return, and one-eighth reported that they would like to. In the event, many fewer than that did return. But in most American immigrant groups at any given time in our history, more people say, perhaps honestly, that they intend to return than ever do so.

As the anti-Japanese movement picked up steam in 1920, Tokyo initiated a new series of diplomatic conversations with the United States. The imperial government was correctly concerned that the agitation would eventually result in the abrogation of the Gentlemen's Agreement and would cause both loss of prestige abroad and political disturbance at home. In a last effort to accommodate American prejudice, the imperial government announced at the end of February 1921 that it would no longer issue passports to picture brides. This, as we have seen, caused consternation in the Japanese American community. The results of both this change and the changed climate of opinion can be seen in the immigration figures. The excess of Japanese immigrants over emigrants, as counted by American immigration officials, averaged about 8,000 per year from 1913 through 1919, and a little less than 4,000 per year after that. Despite this slackening, the agitation grew stronger. The talks between Japan and the United States made the exclusionists nervous—almost to a man they dis-

---

65. Miyamoto, *Social Solidarity*, pp. 85–86.

trusted Washington and the "East" in general and the State Department and professional diplomats in particular. Had they known what chief American negotiator Ambassador Roland S. Morris really thought, they would have been even more distrustful.

Ambassador Morris, in a secret January 1921 report, recommended both the cessation of immigration *and* a removal of the bar to Asian naturalization. His reasons are worth quoting at length:

> The Japanese Government is prepared to cooperate in effectually prohibiting further immigration. If this is accomplished and if as a result no more Japanese immigrants are permitted to enter or settle in the United States the problem is narrowed to the limited number of those Japanese aliens who are already here and who are not eligible to American citizenship. In one generation this entire class will have disappeared and there will remain only persons of Japanese blood born in the United States who will be American citizens under provisions of our Constitution. It seems, therefore, unnecessarily harsh and short sighted to deprive this generation of Japanese aliens of rights which their children will possess and which are enjoyed by other aliens. There is a further consideration: if we wish to assimilate into our national life the Japanese born here, we can do nothing that would more effectively defeat that purpose than to discriminate unfairly against aliens of that race.[66]

If Congress were to prove unwilling to change our naturalization statutes, Morris and Japanese Ambassador Kijuro Shidehara had worked out a plan under which Japan and the United States, by amending the Gentlemen's Agreement, would all but end Japanese immigration of any kind. By means of a new treaty, which they had drafted, each government would grant reciprocal rights to nationals to hold, lease, and otherwise transmit property on a most favored nation basis, which would have voided, as far as Japanese were concerned, state alien land laws that discriminated on the basis of ineligibility to citizenship. However conservative and rational, this approach, as Hiram Johnson and other senators made clear to the State Department, was unacceptable to Congress:

> No class of citizens within our borders should be made citizens who do not in reality become American citizens. It is an inconvertible fact that the Japanese continue ever Japanese, that their allegiance is always to Tokyo, and even in the event of naturalization, they

---

66. U.S. Department of State, *Morris Report*, p. 13.

would continue alien and their loyalty would ever be, not to the United States but to Japan.[67]

Johnson supported his friend V. S. McClatchy and rejected all temporizing proposals because he felt that "the only way to deal with Japan is to [do] what we have the jurisdiction and the right to do." Johnson endorsed the five national objectives of the California anti-Japanese movement and organized a small steering committee of western congressmen to help them through.[68]

But Congress was not amenable to special anti-Japanese measures. Restriction of Japanese immigration, when it came, was merely part of a general movement for immigration restriction which was crowned by the passage of the Immigration Act of 1924. That statute crystallized the quota system which, in one form or another, prevailed until 1965. Although most of those opposed to Japanese immigration had assumed that restriction would take a form similar to that of the Chinese Exclusion Acts, there never was a Japanese Exclusion Act. Nonetheless, one can find literally dozens of references to such an act, and a scholarly encyclopedia once asked me to write an article on "the Japanese Exclusion Act of 1924."

A brief recapitulation of the evolution of American immigration law is necessary for an understanding of how Japanese exclusion came about. As we have noted in chapter 2, apart from the inhibition of the slave trade in 1809, no restrictive federal immigration legislation existed until after the Civil War. At the time of heavy Irish and German immigration in the 1840s, some eastern states passed restrictive immigration laws. In 1849, however, the Supreme Court ruled in the *Passenger Cases* that immigration was "foreign commerce" which only Congress could regulate, although states could impose health and safety regulations as part of their police power. In the late nineteenth and early twentieth centuries, Congress did pass a number of laws restricting immigration, the most significant of which were the several Chinese Exclusion Acts. A 1917 law banned all other Asian immigrants, except Japanese and Filipinos, by means of a so-called barred zone, described by degrees of latitude and longitude. (The Japanese, of course, were exempt because of the Gentlemen's Agreement; the Filipinos were American nationals.) The other exclusions were non-

---

67. Johnson Mss., Bancroft Library, letter, Hiram Johnson to Roland Morris, January 21, 1921. Morris's report was dated four days later. Johnson had been told by Morris that he was "inclining personally" to recommend naturalization early in January. I have seen no evidence to suggest that Johnson ever saw Morris's report. See Johnson Mss., telegram, Hiram Johnson to V. S. McClatchy, January 3, 1921.

68. For the struggle for exclusion, see Daniels, *Politics of Prejudice*, pp. 92–105.

ethnic: criminals, persons with various diseases, paupers or persons likely to become a public charge, illiterates, prostitutes, pimps, polygamists, certain radicals, and persons who failed to meet certain moral standards had all been denied admission by act of Congress.

Beginning in the 1890s, a national movement for a general restriction worked to limit immigration into the United States. Immigration had increased enormously since the Civil War. Fewer than 3 million had come during the 1870s, but more than 5 million came in during the next decade. The economically depressed 1890s saw immigration drop to "only" 3.6 million, but it soared to 8.8 million during the first decade of the twentieth century. Until the outbreak of World War I in 1914, it had been running at more than one million each year.

The war checked migration only temporarily. Its postwar rise encountered the heightened nationalism promoted by the war, the disillusionment of many Americans with Europe and with Wilson internationalism in the postwar period, and the tensions caused by the sharp postwar economic slump in the United States. All contributed to a climate of opinion characterized by John Higham as the "tribal twenties." Passage of some kind of major immigration restriction was a foregone conclusion.[69]

In 1921 Congress passed a short-term "emergency" immigration measure which it later extended to mid-1924. This act introduced the quota system while retaining all previous restrictions. This further limited the number of immigrants allowed into the country in any one year to a finite number. It further divided that number into national quotas based on a small percentage of the number of persons from that country who had presumably been in the United States at some previous date.

The technical problems with the quota system need not concern us here: what should be kept in mind is that for Japan and the Japanese, one of two results could have ensued. Japan might have been given a quota as other countries were: since the base year from which quotas were determined eventually became 1890, the Japanese would have received the minimum quota of 100 persons per year. Or the Gentlemen's Agreement, as modified, might have been kept in effect. For the Japanese, the first possibility was preferable: under the quota system they would have been treated as well as the nations of Europe

---

69. The best account of American nativism generally is John Higham, *Strangers in the Land*. For a brief account of immigration restriction, see Roger Daniels, *Racism and Immigration Restriction;* and Roger Daniels, "Changes in Immigration Law and Nativism since 1924," *American Jewish History*, 76 (1986): 159–80.

and better than other independent Asian nations, which were still under the barred zone prohibition.

But neither of these rational courses was to be followed. Spear-headed by Hiram Johnson's band of western Japanophobes and aided by a theatrical and unscrupulous performance by Senator Henry Cabot Lodge of Massachusetts (who apparently convinced most of the United States Senate that the words "grave consequences" in a friendly diplomatic note from Japanese Ambassador Masano Hanihara to Secretary of State Charles Evans Hughes constituted a "veiled threat"), a special anti-Japanese provision was inserted into the bill. Using precisely the same language as the 1913 Alien Land Act, the federal statute barred from entry as an immigrant any person who was "ineligible to citizenship." Thus, although not named, Japanese were excluded. "I am repaid for all my efforts," James D. Phelan gloated. "The Japs are routed."

Congress could safely use this formula in 1924 because the meaning of the original 1870 naturalization statute had finally been judicially determined two years previously. In a case that had begun in Honolulu's Federal District Court in 1914, the court ruled in 1922 on the application for naturalization of Tadeo Ozawa, who had been deliberately chosen as a test case. Although born in Japan, Ozawa had lived almost all of his life in the United States or Hawaii. He was a graduate of Berkeley High School and had attended the University of California. He was a Christian, and English was spoken in his home. The court decided that white meant "Caucasian" and that Ozawa, although "well qualified by character and education for citizenship," was not a Caucasian. He was therefore ineligible under terms of the naturalization statute.[70]

The Immigration Act of 1924 represented a triumph for the forces of American nativisim in general and for the western anti-Japanese movement in particular. It represented a disaster for Japanese America. Immigration was cut off, apparently forever. No longer could the Issei element of the community grow: the whole community, in fact, shrank for a time as many Issei left for Japan, some taking minor Nisei with them. But since there was no special exclusion act, Japanese aliens who had established residence in the United States could continue to come and go. And, it must be noted, the triumph of the exclusionists was only partial. Congress never considered a constitutional amendment making the status of "aliens ineligible to citizenship" hereditary. Revocation of United States citizenship for persons of Japanese ancestry was not discussed until after the attack on Pearl

---

70. *Ozawa* v. *U.S.*, 260 U.S. 189 (1922).

Harbor, when the United States treated the Nisei as if they were not citizens.

The 1924 act thus cut off one element of Japanese American growth and froze the Issei community for almost thirty years. Had the act come even ten years earlier, its consequences for Japanese America would have been much graver than they were. By 1924 the predominantly female immigration of the years since the Gentlemen's Agreement had produced a viable, self-sustaining demographic foundation for a "permanent" Japanese America, as the census of 1920 demonstrates.

In 1920, as can be seen from an examination of table 4:4, there were just over 111,000 Japanese Americans in the contiguous forty-eight states. The tendency to cluster was more pronounced with each census in the century, both in the Pacific Coast region and in California. The percentage of all Japanese on the Pacific Coast grew from 75.1 percent to 83.3 percent between 1900 and 1920, and the California percentage grew in the same period from 41.7 percent to 64.8 percent. Conversely, this meant a decrease in relative percentages in the state of Washington from almost 25 percent to just over 15 percent, and a drop in the Mountain states from just over 20 percent to less than 10 percent, with practically no population growth from 1910 to 1920. The only region other than the Pacific Coast (really California) to show a percentage gain was the Middle Atlantic States, from 1.8 percent to 2.9 percent. These figures mainly reflected a New York City population of 2,312 in 1920.

More significant than mere numbers, however, was the changing sexual ratio, which is illustrated by table 4.5 and table 4.6. By 1920 males comprised fewer than two-thirds of the Japanese American population. Even more important was the fact that more than one-fourth of the Japanese American population was native-born, 26.6 percent. (In California, where family formation was most pronounced, the figure was slightly higher, 28.9 percent native-born.) Table 4.6 shows the surge of Nisei births which began about 1910 and would continue for the next twenty years. The differential bulges for male and female young adults, show that, on the average, Issei wives tended to be about a decade younger than their husbands. Table 4.5 shows that Issei males outnumbered Issei females by ca. two to one. Since the female immigration from 1920 through 1924 was not high enough to redress the balance completely, this meant that tens of thousands of Issei men were either consigned to bachelor status or forced to go elsewhere if they wished to marry. A few, of course, married older Nisei: marriage outside the Japanese ethnic community was all but unknown.

By the time of the passage of the 1924 immigration law perhaps

Table 4.4
Japanese Americans in the Contiguous United States, 1900–1920
(with percentage where meaningful)

Region or State	1900 Number	1900 Percentage	1910 Number	1910 Percentage	1920 Number	1920 Percentage
United States	24,326	...	72,157	...	111,010	...
New England	89	...	272	...	347	...
Middle Atlantic	446	1.8	1,639	2.8	3,266	2.9
E.N. Central	126	...	482	...	927	...
W.N. Central	223	...	1,000	...	1,215	...
S. Atlantic	29	...	156	...	360	...
E.S. Central	7	...	26	...	35	...
W.S. Central	30	...	428	...	578	...
Mountain	5,107	20.9	10,447	14.5	10,792	9.7
Pacific	18,269	75.1	57,703	80.0	93,490	83.3
Washington	5,617	23.1	12,929	17.9	17,387	15.7
Oregon	2,501	10.3	3,418	4.8	4,151	3.7
California	10,151	41.7	41,356	57.3	71,952	64.8

SOURCE: U.S. Census.

Table 4.5
Sex and Nativity of Japanese American Population,
Contiguous United States, 1920

Nativity	Male Numbers	Male Percentage	Female Numbers	Female Percentage	Combined Total Numbers	Combined Total Percentage
Foreign born	57,304	78.8	24,198	63.3	81,502	73.4
Native born	15,403	21.2	14,105	36.8	29,508	26.6
Total	72,707	65.5	38,303	34.5	111,010	

SOURCE: United States Bureau of the Census, *1920 Census of Population* 2, passim.
Minor discrepancies in the census data have not been resolved. For example, tables at pp. 694, 695, and 699 give the foreign-born Japanese population at 81,502, which, by subtraction (111,010 minus 81,502) would make native-born 29,508. But a chart at p. 804 gives native-born Japanese as 29,672. I have used the first figure.

Table 4.6
Japanese Americans 1920
Age and Sex Distribution

Age Cohort	Male	% in cohort	Female	% in cohort
75+	13	*	6	*
70–74	26	*	5	*
65–69	134	0.2	17	*
60–64	443	0.6	46	0.1
55–59	1094	1.5	120	0.3
50–54	3129	4.3	386	1.0
45–49	6184	8.5	997	2.6
40–44	10670	14.7	2092	5.5
35–39	12396	17.0	3025	7.9
30–34	10819	14.9	4434	11.6
25–29	4600	6.3	6670	17.4
20–24	4535	6.2	5101	13.3
15–19	3081	4.2	1261	3.3
10–14	1379	1.9	1190	3.1
5–9	4048	5.6	3695	9.6
0–4	9853	13.6	9176	24.0
age unknown	330	0.5	82	0.2
Total	72,707		38,303	
Median Age	Males 34 years		Females 24 years	

* less than 0.1 of 1%

SOURCE: United States Department of Commerce. Bureau of the Census. *1920 Census of Population* 1, tables 4, 5, and 10, pp. 157, 166–67.

another fifteen thousand Japanese had entered the United States, but never again would the census record so many alien Japanese (80,000). Unwittingly the forces of diplomacy had created a new Japanese America whose continuity would depend not on Japan and continued immigration but on the native Nisei generation. This native generation, 30,000 strong in 1920, soon outnumbered the generation of its parents. The latter generation shrank with unnatural speed as discouraged Issei returned to Japan in growing numbers after exclusion was substantively achieved.

5.

Japanese America,

1920–1941

While there were clear similarities between the immigrant experiences of Chinese America and Japanese America, there were even more important differences. Geographic distribution and patterns of employment were decidedly divergent, and the demographic history of the two groups was markedly distinct. The time span of the Chinese American immigrant experience covered six decades; that of the Japanese American covered two. The Japanese immigrant group was later arriving, but Japanese women came sooner and in much greater numbers than did Chinese women. The unbalanced sex ratio among Japanese Americans was therefore much less pronounced, and the prolonged rule of old, unacculturated men did not occur among their group. And, finally, the Issei came from a nation emerging rapidly into modernity.

The Japanese American population experienced a very brief period of shrinkage in the 1930s, owing largely to the return of some bachelors and Issei families to Japan. As table 5.1 shows, the native-born Japanese American population almost equaled the foreign-born by 1930.

The citizen Japanese or Nisei predominated by early in the 1930s. The overwhelming majority were children. Before the end of the decade, these children would greatly outnumber their parents' Issei generation. In a typical first generation Japanese American family, children were born in the years 1918–1922 to a thirty-five-year-old father and a twenty-five-year-old mother. This meant that the largest group of Nisei came of legal age between 1939 and 1943. One could reasonably have projected a serious change in the lives of many if not most Japanese Americans in the 1940s, even if the great Pacific War

Table 5.1

Year	Total Population	Foreign Born	Native Born	Native Born (Percentage)
1920	111,055	81,383	29,672	26.7
1930	138,834	70,477	68,357	49.2
1940	126,947	47,305	79,642	62.7

SOURCE: U.S. Census.

had not intervened. Japanese America was thus a creation of one generation; under any likely set of circumstances, it would not have prevailed beyond the period of that generation's prime.

Geographically, Japanese America remained highly concentrated on the West Coast and increasingly within the state of California. Just over two out of five Japanese Americans lived in the Golden State at the turn of the century; by 1920 this number had risen to almost two out of three. By 1940 almost three out of four of the residents of Japanese America lived in California. Since an additional 15 percent lived in Washington and Oregon, 14,500 and 4,000 respectively, only one Japanese American in nine did *not* live on the Pacific Coast in 1940. Of those 14,000 who lived elsewhere in the country, nearly 10,000 lived west of the Mississippi. Of these, over 6,000 lived in the Rocky Mountain states of Colorado, Utah, and Idaho. In the East, the only sizable Japanese American community was in New York, where some 2,500 lived.

Within California, by 1910, Los Angeles County alone contained more Japanese than did any other state. By 1940 Los Angeles County had become the undisputed population center of Japanese America, containing 36,866 members of the ethnic group, or nearly two out of every five in the state and almost 30 percent of the national total. Of the county's Japanese population, almost two-thirds or 23,321 lived in the city of Los Angeles.

San Francisco had just over 5,000 Japanese in 1940. Nonetheless, because of its original cultural primacy and the large Japanese American population in adjoining counties (over 5,000 across the bay in Alameda and another 1,000 plus in San Mateo down the peninsula), San Francisco continued to have a cultural importance far beyond its numbers. San Francisco's *Nihonmachi* or Japantown was one of the liveliest, and the national organizations of each generation—the Japanese associations and the Japanese American Citizens League—maintained their headquarters there.

The real second city of Japanese America was Seattle, which had almost 7,000 with another 2,700 in surrounding King County and 2,000 more in adjacent Pierce County. Only six other cities (Sacramento, Oakland, Berkeley, and Stockton in California, Portland in Oregon, and New York City) had as many as 1,000 ethnic Japanese.

But urban population data say much less about Japanese America than they do of Chinese America. In 1940, when more than nine out of ten Chinese Americans were city dwellers, only a little more than half of Japanese Americans were, 54.9 percent to be precise. Even this figure overstates the urbanization of Japanese America, as in a number of western counties, particularly in Los Angeles, annexation in the 1920s placed much farm land within city boundaries. Slightly more than half (51.4 percent) of all the Japanese males employed in 1940 in the three West Coast states were employed in agriculture, forestry, and fishing, as were about one in three (33.4 percent) of working Japanese women. (More than 60 percent of the latter were what the census called "unpaid family workers.")

The second major occupational classification for Japanese Americans was wholesale and retail trade, in which almost one in four (23.6 percent) of all working Japanese were employed. The third major area of employment was personal service, in which more than one in six (17.1 percent) worked. These three sectors, thus, employed seven in eight working Japanese, or 42,621 of 48,691 (87.5 percent).

If we compare this data with that for all employed persons in the same three states, we see how the economy of Japanese America varied from that of its host states. In California, Oregon, and Washington, agriculture employed only one worker in eight (12.3 percent); wholesale and retail trade employed just over one in five (21 percent); while personal service occupied just under one in eleven (8.9 percent). These three sectors employed just over two of five working persons, or 1,490,063 of 3,522,751 (42.3 percent).

The different economic position of women in Japanese America is suggested by the fact that, although their proportion of the population was significantly smaller in the Pacific states than that of their white sisters (females made up nearly 44.1 percent of the Japanese American population as opposed to 49.1 percent in the white population), Japanese women comprised a higher percentage of Japanese workers than white women did of white workers: 26.2 percent to 24.1 percent. Also, a higher percentage of Japanese women than white women were employed: 25.7 percent to 18.5 percent.

Described negatively, relatively few Japanese Americans were involved in manufacturing, transportation, communications, the professions, or government service. A significant proportion of their retail and wholesale employment was in Japanese-owned businesses. A very large proportion of this work was an extension of Japanese agriculture, as a large percentage of Japanese-grown crops was marketed by Japanese wholesalers and retailers. John Modell's conclusion about the Los Angeles Japanese, that "agriculture was the foundation of much of the enterprise and prosperity" of the whole ethnic economy, can be applied to almost all of Japanese America from San Diego to Seattle.[1] He has described how Japanese came eventually to dominate the production and marketing of most of the fresh green vegetables consumed within the Los Angeles area, while organized white wholesalers kept almost exclusive control of produce marketing for shipment outside of the area. In the highly structured central market, the City Market of Los Angeles, most Japanese businesses in the 1930s were still mere stall operations, although a few of the larger Japanese produce houses grossed over $1 million annually. Total annual wholesale produce volume for all Japanese firms has been estimated at $25 million.

Most Japanese in the Los Angeles produce industry were organized into what were de facto ethnic entrepreneurial associations; by the late 1930s, there were daily market sheets published in Japanese as well as regular Japanese-language radio broadcasts of wholesale market prices. There were ethnic organizations not only in sectors where Japanese enterprise either dominated or had a significant share of the total market, such as fruits, vegetables, flowers, fishing, and contract gardening, but also in fields where the Japanese presence was marginal. Thus there was a Japanese Jewelers Association and a (Southern California) Japanese Physicians and Surgeons' Association, which each had fewer than fifteen members.

Although early in the century almost all labor on Japanese owned and operated farms had been Japanese, by the middle of the 1920s there were more Mexicans and Mexican Americans (Chicanos) in the Los Angeles farm labor force than there were Japanese. Although much of the Japanese-grown produce was still picked by Japanese hands, either hired or provided by unpaid or underpaid family members, many of the larger Japanese agricultural entrepreneurs became employers of Chicano laborers.

In June 1933, encouraged by the New Deal, unionism was spreading even in Los Angeles, a bastion of the open shop. Mexican workers went on strike in and around the Los Angeles suburban town of El Monte, a berry-growing area dominated by Japanese growers. The strike chiefly protested a wage scale of six to fifteen cents an hour,

---

1. John Modell, *The Economics and Politics of Racial Accommodation: The Japanese of Los Angeles, 1900–1942*, p. 94.

wages characterized by strike leaders as "inhuman, oppressive, un-American." An estimated 1,500 of the striking Chicano pickers worked for Japanese growers. A few Japanese workers joined the strike, but neither ethnic group paid much attention to them. The Japanese community, as a whole, was pro-employer.

Japanese growers were assisted in defeating the strike by the sheriff's office and the Los Angeles Police Department, including the latter's notorious "Red Squad." The Los Angeles chapter of the Japanese American Citizens League (JACL) was able to convince some area high-school principals to release Nisei children to work in the fields as strike breakers. Later that year the Japanese Chamber of Commerce, working with its white counterparts, proposed that "Mexican farm labor strikers . . . be deprived of further county relief aid if found participating in any labor agitation. . . . Deportation of foreigners implicated in such action is further recommended." In 1933, of course, the overwhelming majority of the members of the Japanese chamber would have been "foreigners."

During a series of agricultural strikes in Southern California in 1936, the Japanese Farm Laborers Association became too conspicuous to be ignored. The Japanese American establishment used the same weapons against its own radicals as did the white power structure. Insisting, possibly correctly, that most of the Japanese involved in radical activities had Communist connections, the elders called for cutting off all of their credit, encouraged raids by white law officers, and apparently alerted federal immigration officials. Modell finds these antiradical activities unusual but "entirely characteristic." Speaking of the Issei establishment, he writes:

> The Japanese community . . . perceived with great clarity its economic underpinning and moved with concern and purpose to preserve it, whether against outside attacks or from dissident elements within. Much of the unified face it presented to the rest of society, and much of the hierarchical order which characterized its internal structure expressed [its] conscious economic motive.[2]

Certain variations in the economic pattern of urban Japanese America may be seen if one looks at its second city, Seattle. Here, agriculture was almost entirely outside the city, and Japanese Americans were not as concentrated in produce operations. S. Frank Miyamoto's pioneering 1939 study of Japanese Seattle is based in part on two community-sponsored censuses, one of businesses in 1930 and

---

2. Ibid., pp. 122–26. For the El Monte strike, see also Cletus E. Daniel, *Bitter Harvest: A History of California Farmworkers, 1870–1941*, pp. 146–49.

one of employment in 1935. Miyamoto's book still provides the most detailed collection of discrete data about prewar ethnic enterprise. This was a period of declining Japanese American population: Seattle's Japanese population shrank from almost 8,500 to perhaps 7,500 in the five-year period; during that time, probably from 6,000 to 5,000 Japanese lived in the immediate surrounding area.

The 1930 listing showed 905 businesses with a total income of just over $24 million, giving an average income of almost $26,600. These businesses employed 5,973 persons, but this figure is misleading because two railroad contractors and five cannery contractors (Seattle was the hiring center for Alaska canneries) accounted for 61 percent of the employees listed. Of those hired for the canneries, 1,520 were Issei men, 891 were Filipino and Mexican men, 115 were white American women, 97 were Nisei men, 85 were American Indian women, and 20 were white American men. Average monthly wages ranged from $125 for white American men to $65 for Filipino and Mexican men. Issei men averaged $80 and Nisei men $71.50. (No racial wage differential is reported between white and Indian women. The $96 wage seems relatively high. No explanation is offered. Perhaps all were skilled packers.) Of the 1,141, all males, hired for the railroads, 605 were Filipino and Mexican, 514 were Issei, 15 were Nisei, and 7 were Chinese, who were probably cooks, judging from their monthly pay of $115. The remaining 2,304 employees of Japanese businesses were overwhelmingly from within the ethnic community, 84 percent. Of these, 38 percent were members of the proprietors' families.

The 1935 survey, as summarized by Miyamoto, indicates the ten most numerous types of businesses run by Japanese in 1935. Table 5.2 provides the details. The idiosyncratic business for Seattle Japanese was a hotel trade catering largely to working-class white men. (A good description of life in one of these hotels may be found in Monica Sone's charming memoir of a Nisei girlhood in Seattle, *Nisei Daughter*.) The hotel men and twenty-one other groups of Japanese businessmen had organized trade associations by the mid-1930s.

According to the 1935 survey, only 11 workers or 3.7 percent of the 2,867 ethnic Japanese labor force were employed in agriculture, forestry, and fishing. Another 886 or 30.9 percent, were in domestic and personal service, most of them in hotels. The largest single group, 1,292 or 45.1 percent, worked in various small businesses. One unusual group was the 69 Japanese men employed in transportation and communication, most of whom were redcaps at Seattle's railroad terminals.[3]

---

3. Frank Miyamoto, *Social Solidarity Among the Japanese in Seattle*, pp. 70–82.

Table 5.2
Ten Leading Trades among Japanese in Seattle, 1935

Trades	Numbers
Hotels	183
Groceries	148
Dye Works	94
Public-Market Stands	64
Produce Houses	57
Gardeners	42
Restaurants	36*
Barber Shops	36
Laundries	31
Peddlers (produce)	24

SOURCE: Miyamoto, *Social Solidarity*, p. 72.
*The 1930 census listed 39 American restaurants and 24 Japanese restaurants.

Similar variations occurred in the other urban centers of Japanese America: in San Francisco a large number of Japanese were employed in curio stores and other tourist-oriented attractions, even to the extent of "moving in" on Chinatown and establishing commercial operations there or on its fringes, which created resentment among many Chinese Americans. In addition, in each of the three major centers of West Coast Japanese population, a significant and growing number of white-collar jobs was being provided by American branches of Japanese trading companies and banks. These Japanese-based firms were known as *kaisha* or "headquarters," a term used in many of the firms' formal titles. In Seattle in 1930, the Japanese association census showed 167 persons employed by twelve such foreign-based firms, including 56 Issei, all male, and 9 Nisei, 5 males and 4 females. No wage data were available.

A 1980 study based on company records seized just after Pearl Harbor (1941) gives us an inside look at one of the largest of the Japanese-based firms, the Mitsubishi trading company, *Mitsubishi Shoji Kaisha*. Nobuo Kawabe's study (doctoral dissertation, Ohio State University), does not give us detailed employment data, but it

---

See also idem, "An Immigrant Community in America," in Hilary Conroy and T. Scott Miyakawa, eds., *East Across the Pacific*, pp. 217–43.

does provide a unique look at company policy. Mitsubishi made a basic distinction between its employees hired in Japan and those taken on in America, regardless of whether the latter were Japanese or Caucasian, Japanese-born or American-born. They even used a different descriptive term: those who had been employed in Japan were *seiin* or "formal employees," persons to whom the firm had a presumably lifetime commitment; those who had been employed in America were *yoin* or "hired employees," persons to whom no permanent commitment had been made.

As members of the Nisei generation came of age, the various kaisha began to employ more and more of them. As one Mitsubishi executive put it, not only was it a "practical policy" but it was a policy "to brighten their lives by showing sympathy to them to ease their difficulty to find jobs." But the home office refused to allow any employees hired overseas to enter even the bottom ranks of top management. Kawabe gives details of one case in which the San Francisco office wanted a *Kibei* (a Japanese-educated Nisei) with particularly good language skills to be sent to Japan for training after four years of service in San Francisco. The home office said no.

Although not directly involved with the business of the American branches, Mitsubishi and presumably the other Japanese businesses in this country were accustomed to recruiting American-trained Nisei engineers for employment in Japan. Kawabe quotes one undated memorandum from San Francisco to Tokyo which was apparently written in the late 1930s or early 1940s:

> Recently there is a trend that Japanese companies look for and employ eminent *Nisei* Japanese-American engineers. Therefore, we keep the close relationship with them and make an effort to recommend eminent persons to Mitsubishi related companies. Please let us know if you have any requirement[s] and condition[s].

Kawabe adds, without further elucidation, that "American born and trained engineers began to serve the Japanese war effort in air craft design and other areas of heavy industry." Certainly, as we shall see, employment opportunities outside of the ethnic community for educated Japanese Americans were even worse than for other educated Americans during the Great Depression. And, of course, their race and their ethnicity were a real detriment to their hiring in the defense-related employment that began to open up after the fall of France in June 1940.[4]

---

4. Nobuo Kawabe, "Japanese Businesses in the United States before World War

In one area, that of civil service, Nisei were beginning to make some progress. The state of California had 314 classified Japanese American civil service employees, all citizens, by early 1942. Others worked for subordinate branches of government. There were in Los Angeles, for example, 95 city and county Japanese employees. Although a relatively large number of Nisei were trained as teachers, not one ethnic Japanese teacher had been hired by any school board in Los Angeles before World War II, although a few had been hired in Seattle.

The major economic concentration of Japanese America was, of course, in agriculture. Although many of the older Nisei, some quite reluctantly, followed their parents into agriculture and agriculturally related enterprises, the agricultural achievement was largely the accomplishment of the Issei generation. These Issei were pioneers in a pioneering region. Their eventual achievement was archetypically American, paradoxical as that may seem in view of their reputed alienation from the mainstream of the American tradition.

When one examines the Issei agricultural achievement, it relates directly to the American dream, if that nebulous entity can be defined as hard work, modest aspirations, and upward social mobility. Most of the Issei, as we have seen, came to America in straitened circumstances if not actually penniless. Although some Issei bachelors and others remained below or near the poverty line, by the eve of Pearl Harbor most Issei families were at least mildly prosperous members of the lower-middle class. These families owned real property—farms and businesses—to a much greater degree than did the general population. Their industry was proverbial to their admirers, to their detractors, and to their overworked and underpaid offspring.

By 1940 in the three Pacific Coast states, over 6,000 farms were operated by Japanese, comprising a total of more than 250,000 acres and valued at $72.6 million. The average farm was just over 40 acres, more than three-fourths of it in harvested cropland as opposed to pasturage or fallow. The average value of these farms was slightly higher than the value of all farms in those states ($11,867 to $11,717). Most of the Japanese-run farms were small family enterprises concentrating on intertilled vegetables, fruit, and specialty crops.

The Issei farmers generally did not replace whites, despite such allegations by anti-Japanese propaganda. As noted in chapter 4, they opened up new lands with their labor-intensive, high-yield style of agriculture as opposed to the resource-intensive, low-yield agriculture characteristic of American farming. A syndicate of Issei farmers in Los

---

II: The Case of Mitsubishi Shoji Kaisha, the San Francisco and Seattle Branches" (Ph.D. diss., Ohio State University, 1980), pp. 130, 185–87.

Angeles County even leased lands below high-tension wires from Pacific Gas and Electric and grew crops there. (Later this enterprise was used unfairly against them. When California Attorney General Earl Warren appeared before the Tolan Committee in February 1942, he brought with him specially prepared maps showing, in red, Japanese controlled farm land and its relation to major defense plants. On these maps the leased land under the power lines seemed like intrusive red arrows aimed at such major aircraft factories as the North American Aviation plant, which were, of course, large consumers of electricity.)

A detailed accounting of the Japanese contribution to the California vegetable industry was made by two Department of Agriculture economists as part of the statistical analysis of the effects of the 1942 relocation. This showed that Japanese farmers produced half or more of the artichokes, snap beans, cauliflower, celery, cucumbers, garlic, and certain types of onions. In addition, they produced a quarter or more of the asparagus, lima beans, cabbage, cantaloupe, carrots, and lettuce. Other crops in which Japanese were major producers, in California and elsewhere, included strawberries, apples, peaches, sugar beets, nursery stock, and a dominant share of the southern California business in cut flowers.[5]

Considered as a sector of West Coast agriculture, the Japanese farmers supplemented rather than competed with other West Coast producers. It was, in part, the food production of Japanese America that made possible the dramatic growth of West Coast population, from 2.4 million in 1900 to 9.7 million in 1940. Earnings from the shipments of their produce out of the region clearly made a significant contribution to regional economic growth.

Upon this economic base the Issei, like many immigrant generations before and since, tried to recreate a world similar to the one they remembered, a Japanese society in America. But the image of Japan that most of them held was static. They remembered, as immigrants usually do, the homeland of their youth, not the emerging industrialized Japan of the twenties and thirties. Since the United States, both by statute and custom, deliberately tried to keep them separate, the Issei were probably more insulated against Americanization than were most contemporary immigrant groups.

All the institutions of the first generation—the Japanese associa-

---

5. Lloyd H. Fisher and Ralph L. Nielsen, "The Japanese in California Agriculture" in U.S. Congress, House, Select Committee Investigating National Defense Migration, *Hearings*, 77th Cong., 2d. sess., 1942, Part 31, pp. 11822 ff. (hereafter cited as Tolan Committee, *Hearings*). Earl Warren's testimony is at pp. 10973–11023.

tions, the associational groups based on place of birth in Japan, the business and professional associations of the Little Tokyos and the Little Osakas, the press, the churches—were centered on Japan and the Japanese language. Denied the right of naturalization, the Issei could not become voters. Most trade unions and trade associations of the larger society barred them from membership. If they went to a Buddhist temple, the priest was subsidized by the Japanese government; if they adopted a western religion, as a growing number did, it was likely to be in a segregated congregation—a domestic mission church—with a pastor who was either a former missionary or a convert from Japan.

The major organization of the immigrant generation—the Japanese associations—declined steadily in importance after 1924 for a number of reasons. First, the abrogation of the Gentlemen's Agreement by the American government in 1924 eliminated the most important practical function of the associations: no wives or other relatives could be brought over. There were no Japanese treaty merchants, and both the time of entry into the United States and the demographic structure of the Japanese American community made any kind of paper sons arrangement all but impossible. Added to the association's loss of function and the estrangement from it of some leaders of the Issei generation, as noted earlier, was the changing structure of the community, in which the citizen Nisei generation assumed more and more importance every year.

S. Frank Miyamoto, in his study of Seattle, gently notes and documents the association's decline. In 1936–1937, for example, the Seattle association had three sources of income: dues and contributions of $3,186.50; a donation "from the Emperor of Japan" of nearly $1,000; and $3,647.99 from the Community Chest. The grant from the Community Chest was less than the Japanese community had contributed to that organization, and the fact remains that by the mid-1930s Japanese Americans in Seattle chose to give more financial support to an umbrella organization of the larger community than to its own. Membership in the association had always been perfunctory. As one Seattleite put it: "When I first came to this country . . . the only thing I did join was the *Nihonjinkai* (Japanese Association) but that was because everybody in the store was a member and they urged me to become one also. It only meant that I paid my dues, but I never went to any of the meetings."[6]

This indifference was not atypical; John Modell notes that in Los Angeles only about 20 percent of the members usually voted, and that

---

6. Miyamoto, *Social Solidarity*, pp. 115–16.

even the bitterest controversy would only produce a 40 percent turnout.[7] But some reactions went beyond indifference: particularly after the association gave up the picture bride option, many community members became hostile. One former member justified his defection aggressively: "What good is the Japanese Association anyway? I used to pay one dollar a month to them, but I tell you that an organization like that can't do any work on a little bit of money. . . . All those fellows do down there is get together and talk about each other. They never do anything useful for the community." Miyamoto predicted in 1939 that the association would "gradually pass into senility" unless some crisis should revive it.[8] The crisis, of course, came just two years later, but instead of reviving the associations it completely destroyed them.

The other major secular organizations of Japanese America were the prefectural associations or *ken-jin*, literally, "prefectural person." *Ken* groups were more important in Japanese America than in Japan, because the prefecture—there were forty-six in Japan proper—was much too large and diffuse for any kind of primary association: in Japan the village and neighborhood associations were more important. Unlike the Chinese who came chiefly from a small part of Kwangtung, Japanese immigrants came from widely scattered parts of Japan. In Japanese America, therefore, given the natural human urge for association, ken-groupings made sense.

The ken-jin had economic as well as social functions. As a Seattle Issei explained it:

> There was a tendency towards the concentration of people from the same prefectures in Japan at the same places, and in the same lines of work. For example, the barbers in Seattle, at least in the old days, all tended to be people from the Yamaguchi-*ken*, for Mr. I. came first and established himself in that line, and then helped his friends from Japan to get started. . . . Homes like those of Mr. I. were places of congregation for the young men who were eager to learn things and discuss them, and in the course of their association learned such things as their friends knew.[9]

"Learning things," of course, often took the form of unpaid or low-paid apprenticeships. In addition, the ken-jin functioned as mutual aid societies, giving financial help to members who were in need.

---

7. Modell, *Japanese of Los Angeles*, p. 82.
8. Miyamoto, *Social Solidarity*, p. 118.
9. Ibid., pp. 74–75, 117–19.

The social aspects of the ken-jin were stressed by one of their early students. Describing their influence in Los Angeles in 1927, Fumiko Fukuoka wrote that "the Japanese who comes to America, a strange land, is exceedingly happy to meet other Japanese, and more so when they are from the same *ken*. They feel an intimacy which they did not know when they were in their home land."[10] The ken group within a community in Japanese America became the primary association group larger than the family. Since there was, at least in the larger communities, a tendency for most of the older generation friendships to be among ken-jin, a disproportionate number of marriages were within the ken group. The ken-jin also sponsored purely social events, occasional gatherings to honor a distinguished visitor from the prefecture, frequent dinners, and memorable annual picnics. In Los Angeles, where by 1940 there were forty separate ken-jin, these annual picnics were lavish and competitive. (Midwestern non-Japanese migrants to Los Angeles in the interwar years did much the same kind of thing: from the time of H. L. Mencken, the annual "Ioway" picnics in Long Beach have been a subject of humor and scorn. Japanese, feeling far more alien than Iowans, needed the *ken* organizations for many different kinds of functions, as has been noted, but the basic impulse is the same.)

Another institution which served as a unifying force in Japanese America was the immigrant press. Robert E. Park noted more than half a century ago how important the foreign-language press could be. It could serve, in some instances, as an umbilical cord to the culture and politics of the motherland or, conversely, as a focal point of resistance to the political and cultural aspirations of the homeland.[11] Most of the Japanese-language press in America, and all of its well-established papers, were in the former category. For most of the older generation, the Japanese newspaper was the only source of access to the news of the world. Thus, in many Issei households, otherwise Americanized children grew up hearing only the Japanese side of things, as radio news was almost nonexistent before World War II. This was particularly important in the 1930s, when Japanese America almost totally accepted the official imperial Japanese version of the "China incident" through the medium of its own community newspapers. Gordon K. Hirabayashi, for example, remembers that it never occurred to him until after he came to Seattle to attend the

---

10. Fumiko Fukuoka, "Mutual Life and Aid Among the Japanese in Southern California with Special Reference to Los Angeles" (M.A. thesis, University of Southern California, 1939), p. 16.
11. Robert E. Park, *The Immigrant Press and Its Control.*

University of Washington that there was another side to the "China incident."[12] S. Frank Miyamoto commented on this acutely in 1939:

> No better illustration of the kind of influence which the Japanese newspapers have in making for the solidarity of the community is to be had than in the type of news which these two papers have published over the recent Sino-Japanese conflict. Since the beginning of warfare in July, 1937, the papers have covered with unabated avidity all the important news to be had about the Oriental crisis, and there has not been a day since that time when the war news was not the most important item on the front page. Not alone on the fact that they give so much space to this event do we have the significance of this news in furthering the solidarity of the people, but rather in their consistent and vigorous defense of the Japanese cause in this war do we see the peculiar influence which it was. That their news is weighted heavily in that direction is not surprising when we consider that all their news items from Japan are direct transcripts of daily wireless dispatches taken through their own receiving stations directly from Japan, and when we note that this news is censored by the Japanese government before it leaves the nation.
>
> The powerful effect of this publicity is apparent in the solid attitude of the community in support of the program to which the Japanese government has committed itself in China, and the vigorous and bitter attacks that the people make against the American newspapers which, they claim, deliberately falsify their reports in favor of China.

It must be remembered in addition that the Japanese American community, which had been steadily reviled by these same newspapers, had little reason to believe in the objectivity of the American press. Such apologetic behavior was also typical in the 1930s of both German American and Italian American newspapers. Although there was a distinctly anti-Nazi German-language press in the United States, largely staffed by exiles from the Hitler regime, the established papers of both communities, right up to Pearl Harbor, tended to be pro-motherland.

In all of these communities, there was understandable concern that the American-born generation would not be sympathetic to the problems of the mother country. In Seattle, as Miyamoto noted, the newspapers in conjunction with the consulate of Japan were particu-

---

12. UWA, interview with Gordon K. Hirabayashi by Roger Daniels, February 1981.

larly concerned to get the message about Japan's mission in East Asia into the hearts and minds of the younger generation. "Thus," he wrote, "in their news and editorial columns, one finds admonitions to parents to interpret the Japanese newspapers to their English-speaking sons and daughters so that the latter may correctly state the case to the larger American public."[13]

This understandable pro-Japanese bias was evident even in English-language materials published in Japanese America. There were pamphlets directed at the larger American public, such as the 1931 attempt by the Japanese Chamber of Commerce of Los Angeles, which complained of "China's oppressive policy toward the Japanese." Similar attitudes prevailed in the one or two English-language pages that began to appear in vernacular newspapers in the late 1920s and 1930s and in English-language newspapers aimed at the Nisei generation. In 1937, for example, Los Angeles Nisei journalist Togo Tanaka warned his English readers in the *Rafu Shimpo* about "Chinese propaganda" and urged them to act as "instrument[s] for preserving the peace and neutrality of this country." Throughout the decade, Seattle Nisei editor James Y. (Jimmy) Sakamoto, an energetic Americanizer, pushed the line of the imperial government in his all-English weekly.[14]

Religion in Japanese America was much more centrally organized than in Chinese America, and it was more complex and plastic than among many immigrant groups. Unlike Korean Americans, many if not most of whom were Christians before they emigrated, relatively few Japanese emigrants were adherents of western religions before they came. But certainly Christians were a larger percentage of Japanese emigrants than they were of all other Japanese. It also should be noted that Japanese immigrants have had a strong and striking propensity to adopt the religion of the local majority in their diaspora to the New World. Thus, in Brazil a majority of Japanese immigrants and their descendants has become Roman Catholic; in Utah and adjoining states a significant minority of Japanese has become Mormon; in most of the United States, not surprisingly, large numbers of Japanese Americans have become Protestants of one denomination or another, while a small minority has become Roman Catholic.

---

13. Miyamoto, *Social Solidarity*, pp. 119–20.

14. Togo Tanaka, as quoted in Modell, *Japanese of Los Angeles*, p. 176. Modell's comment, "in mid-1939 Nisei newspapers began to contradict rather than support Japanese policy," is based on an account by Togo Tanaka. The validity of Modell's generalization has not been demonstrated. My comments on James Y. Sakamoto are based on my reading of his manuscripts in the University of Washington Archives and a file of his newspaper, the *Japanese American Courier*, in the Suzzallo Library there.

The numbers game among religious groups tends to magnify size, and no prudent person would attempt to be precise. S. Frank Miyamoto estimated that, in 1936, of perhaps 6,000 Japanese American Seattleites, 1,200 were members of Christian churches and 980 belonged to Buddhist or other eastern religious establishments. He warned that, although the Christian figures represented "actual members," those of the eastern denominations were quite inflated. As an example, he felt that the Shinshu Buddhist sect, which represented 650 of the number listed above, probably had only 250 real members.

John Modell's discussion of religion in Los Angeles eschews numbers altogether. The United States Army estimated, on the basis of behavior in assembly centers in the spring of 1942, that perhaps one-tenth of the immigrant generation and one-half of the Nisei were Protestants, and that a majority of the older generation and some of the younger generation belonged to the Buddhist faith.[15] Clearly, whatever the numbers really were, Christianity had made significant inroads among the immigrants from Japan and their children. Those inroads were fully consistent with the overall pattern of enthusiastic adaptation that has been characteristic of Japanese emigrants outside of Asia.

Many, both inside and outside of the ethnic community, have interpreted the adoption of Christianity as a hallmark of successful adaptation. One Japanese Christian lay group in Los Angeles went farther than most when it formally resolved that "Americanization can only be realized through Christianity" and insisted, as part of its proselytization, that "we who are in the United States are to be, first of all, loyal to our land of adoption."[16] The implication here, that Buddhism represented loyalty to Japanese rather than to American ideals, would find resonance in United States government policy after Pearl Harbor when Buddhist priests were separated from their congregations and interned.

In most parts of Japanese America, rivalries between Buddhists and Christians seem to have been distinctly low-key, particularly when contrasted with the hostility that existed in Hawaii. There a relatively large and militant Buddhist establishment, partially subsidized as it was on the mainland by the imperial government, was seen as a threat by both secular and clerical exponents of Americanization. One Christian minister insisted that "Buddha has been the light of Asia . . .

15. Miyamoto, *Social Solidarity*, pp. 99–104; Modell, *Japanese of Los Angeles*, pp. 76–79; U.S. War Department, *Final Report: Japanese Evacuation from the West Coast, 1942*, p. 211.

16. Modell, *Japanese of Los Angeles*, p. 79.

Christ is the Light of the World." Others such as Sidney J. Gulick argued that no alien could be transformed into a "whole hearted American citizen" unless he accepted "the Christian ideals of personal responsibility, of duty to God and to fellow men." Hostility to Buddhism even brought about a sort of ecumenism among Christian clerics. At one celebrated Honolulu confrontation in 1929, a Catholic and an Anglican priest united in refusing even to shake hands with one of their Buddhist opposite numbers, with the Catholic bishop proclaiming: "I love Protestants but I hate Buddhists."[17]

Although identified with things alien and seen as the opposite of acculturation, Buddhism in America was itself Americanized, at least in part, by its losing struggle with American Christianity, which was always eager to count coup in converts. Some Buddhist countermeasures included Buddhist Sunday schools from which could occasionally be heard such non-Asian melodies as "Buddha loves me, this I know."

Many Japanese immigrants took an attitude toward religion similar to that attributed to President Eisenhower: it was a good thing and it didn't make too much difference in what size or shape it came. Since attending religious services was seen as a positive form of acculturation, even the most Japan-oriented organizations and institutions of Japanese America, such as the Japanese associations, encouraged some kind of attendance, in much the same way as a modern corporation will encourage its executives to participate in some kind of community activity. As one Seattle Issei put it: "I told my children that it didn't matter whether they went to a Christian church or a Buddhist church, but that they should go to some kind of a church. Since their friends were going to the Methodist Church, they went there, but after I joined the Congregational Church, I transferred them to the latter."[18]

If religion didn't matter much to some of the inhabitants of Japanese America, it did matter tremendously to the various clergy who tried to convert them and minister unto them. As had been true for the Chinese, many of the first, strongest, and stoutest defenders of Japanese immigrants in America were ministers or priests of mission churches, which were subsidized by most of the major Protestant denominations and by the Catholic Maryknoll fathers. Those Japanese Americans who attended Christian churches did so in an almost

---

17. Louise H. Hunter, *Buddhism in Hawaii*, pp. 156–57 (1st and 3d quotations); Sidney L. Gulick, *Hawaii's American-Japanese Problem*, pp. 23–24. The best account of Buddhism among Japanese Americans is Tetsuden Kashima, *Buddhism in America*.

18. Miyamoto, *Social Solidarity*, p. 102.

totally segregated environment: for yellow people in America, as well as for blacks, Sunday morning was as much or even more segregated than the rest of the week, except that for Japanese most of the pastors were Caucasians. In many instances, the pastors were returned missionaries or those with a missionary vocation who had been unable to obtain posts in Asia.

All of the community institutions contributed to the acculturation of Japanese America, but surely the most dynamic and dramatic force for change was created by the community itself: the young people of the Nisei generation. A special combination of circumstances made the Nisei impact greater than that of other young immigrant generations and telescoped tremendously the temporal period of that impact. The constraints imposed on migration from Japan, first by international agreement and then by national law, stopped significant migration of males after 1908 and of all Japanese after 1924.

Different conditions prevailed among other groups. Among the Chinese Americans, for example, both the relatively small number of American-born Chinese and the continued migration, legal and illegal, of unacculturated Chinese youths and men, diluted the impact of the American born and retarded the pace of acculturation in the community. In contemporary Euro-American communities, the continued migration of individuals and family units diluted the impact of the American-born generation. In those communities with a more "normal" demographic structure, the conflict between the generations was more attenuated and less dramatic. In fact, intergenerational conflict has been one of the leit motifs of American immigration history. One of the founding fathers of American immigration history, Norwegian American historian Marcus Lee Hansen, pointed out long ago that the second generation of all immigrant groups tend to reject many if not most of the values of the first, and that the third generation tends to find more merit in those values.[19] (Those with a Freudian bent can maintain the same thing in a different way.) Perhaps in no American immigrant community was "Hansen's Law" more pronounced than among Japanese Americans, even *before* the great Pacific War had made the native land of the first generation enemy territory in law as well as in belief.

The self-consciousness of the Nisei generation existed in the late 1920s and early 1930s when there were few adults. One cannot read the Nisei newspapers and periodical literature without being struck by the almost obsessional concern with what John Modell has called

---

19. Marcus Lee Hansen, *The Problem of the Third Generation Immigrant*, reprinted in *Commentary*, November 1952.

"The Nisei Dilemma."[20] Even more striking, I believe, is the degree to which the older, Issei generation—or much of it—was aware of the changes that were sure to come. I am convinced that the awareness of different generational roles existed among the first generation of Japanese Americans to a much greater degree than among other first-generation immigrant groups, although such a hypothesis is difficult to demonstrate. It seems to me, however, that two factors are probably paramount: first, the insistence by most of the authority figures in Japanese America—starting with the men at the top, the Japanese consular officials—that the immigrants, and particularly their children, not only acculturate but excel in that acculturation; second, the fact that, after the passage of the various state alien land laws, the legal status of the children was obviously superior to that of the parents. This meant, in many instances, that the family livelihood was vested in the names of small children, a circumstance that undoubtedly had a great and ongoing impact. Yet, like most immigrant generations, the Issei also wanted to perpetuate, at least in part, the institutions and customs that they cherished from the Japan that they remembered. These conflicting desires created what might be called "the Issei Dilemma." Nowhere were the patent contradictions of that dilemma more apparent than in the efforts of the parents to educate their children.

From almost the very beginning of the Japanese American experience, the Japanese associations and other organizations of the older generation placed great stress on acculturation, not only for the older generation but also for the children. Not just attending public schools but excelling in them was seen as a community goal. The size of the Japanese American population meant that most of the schools the Japanese American students attended were predominantly white, although there were a few public primary schools, such as the Bailey Gatzert School in downtown Seattle, which became predominantly Japanese. Although California statutes specifically provided permission to segregate Japanese students, legal segregation, as previously noted, occurred only in four small Sacramento County school districts—Courtland, Isleton, Walnut Grove, and Florin. In each of those districts, Japanese students were an absolute majority of all school children. Some of the schools established there were also attended by Chinese pupils.

In the public schools, Japanese students were notable for their

---

20. Modell, *Japanese of Los Angeles*, pp. 127–72. Modell finds the salient characteristics of that dilemma in chapters entitled "A Place in the World" and "Defining a Generation."

good behavior and better-than-average grades. The most detailed studies, done by Stanford educational psychologists and sociologists in the late 1920s and early 1930s, show that both in achievement and in attitude, Nisei pupils were well above the norm.[21] Their behavior, in particular, was exemplary; a study of truancy in Los Angeles in 1933 reported that only one case in ten thousand involved a Japanese American student. Although Japanese students received higher marks overall, studies by Reginald Bell and his associates showed that, starting in the seventh grade, the marks of these students began to decline toward the median and that in the senior year of high school the grades of Japanese students were slightly below average. While some have interpreted this as somehow a function of social control, it should be noted that by 1940 a significantly higher percentage of Nisei than whites were completing high school. (In Los Angeles the figures were 61 percent as opposed to less than 50 percent.)[22] The overall grade drop *might* well be the result of academically unmotivated Nisei students being pressured to stay in school, while their white counterparts could drop out.

If one looks only at excellence, it is clear that Japanese American students did very well. As Frank Miyamoto has shown, Japanese high school students in Seattle won academic honors "out of all proportion to their numbers in school." In 1937, for example, three Nisei were valedictorians and two were salutatorians at the nine high schools there. These students were made much of in the local communities. The comment of the San Pedro fisherman to his son "If you graduate from college, I will proudly meet our ancestors in Heaven" is probably extreme but it is not atypical. That father's further admonition "Continue with American higher education . . . show the Americans your ability . . . that is your duty to your parents" nicely epitomizes the attitude of the whole community. As early as 1920 the Seattle Japanese American community offered to contribute $10,000 toward construction of a new primary school in its neighborhood.[23]

---

21. Reginald Bell, *Public School Education of Second-Generation Japanese in California,* and work there cited. The research had the support of the Carnegie Corporation and the Laura Spelman Rockefeller Foundation.

22. Modell, *Japanese of Los Angeles,* pp. 157–58; Bell, *Public School Education,* pp. 52–60. For a brief account of Japanese public school experience in Canada, see Jorgen Dahlie, "The Japanese Challenge to Public Schools in Society in British Columbia," *Journal of Ethnic Studies* 3 (1974): 10–24.

23. Miyamoto, *Social Solidarity,* p. 108; Kanichi Kawasaki, "The Japanese Community of East San Pedro, Terminal Island, California" (M.A. thesis, University of Southern California, 1931), pp. 109–10. That minorities as well as majorities can use educational data for racist purposes is demonstrated by the following from the *North American Times,* a Japanese American newspaper in Seattle, commenting on the fact

Asian immigrants arriving Angel Island, ca. 1911. U.S. Public Health Service photo courtesy National Archives #90-G-2038.

Wedding portrait of well-to-do Chinese American woman. Although this portrait of Greta Fong of Boise, Idaho, dates from 1927, the costume would be similar to those described by the oldest Chinese woman in Butte. Photo by Ansgar Johnson, Sr., courtesy Idaho Historical Society.

Los Angeles' Chinatown celebrates the New Year, January 1928.
Courtesy National Archives #306-NT-164999c.

Chinese Americans, mostly students, demonstrating against Japan's aggression in China near Columbia University, February 1932. Courtesy National Archives #306-NT-963E-8.

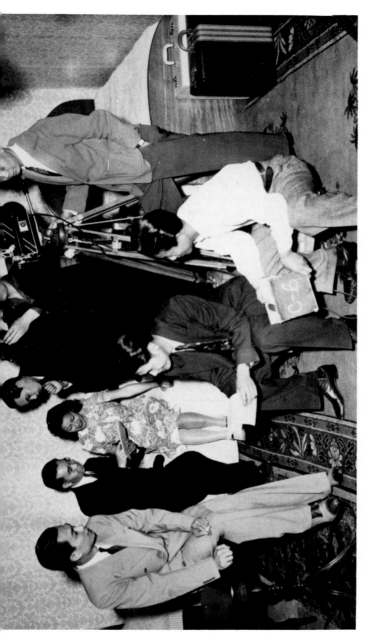

Chinese American film crew, San Francisco, ca. 1935. Members of the Grandview Film Company, the only company producing Chinese motion pictures in the United States. Most of these people held other jobs. Left to right, leading man Wong Cheu Mo, producer Jue Shee Sunn, leading lady Joe Quan-ling, actor Wong Hock Sing, sound engineer Wong Sheong, cameraman Jue Mon Liang. Seated, front are dialogue director Chiang Kay and "prop" man Chinn Chun Wah. Courtesy National Archives #208-LU-28K-1.

Soldier posting Exclusion Order No. 1, Bainbridge Island, Washington, March 1942. Courtesy National Archives #220-WR-176.

Two Nisei MISLS graduates (seated, facing camera) interrogate a captured Japanese machine gunner, Southwest Pacific Theater. U.S. Army photo.

Col. Kai E. Rasmussen, commandant, Military Intelligence Specialists Language School, pins major's leaves on John F. Aiso. U.S. Army photo.

The first and only group of Nisei WACS to be graduated from the Fort Snelling, Minnesota, language school, about to fly to occupied Japan, late 1945. U.S. Army photo.

1st Lt. Howard Miyake being greeted by his sister, Mrs. Duayne M. Kimball, Denver, January 29, 1945. The original photo service captioned this "PATRIOTS OF JAP DESCENT," and noted that Mrs. Kimball had been sent to a relocation center (Heart Mountain) in 1942. The U.S. Office of War Information used the picture, changed the caption to "AMERICAN VETERAN OF JAPANESE DESCENT RETURNS TO U.S." and suppressed the fact that Mrs. Kimball had been incarcerated. Both captions noted that Miyake had been wounded in Italy and awarded the Silver Star, and that Kimball had just enlisted in the Women's Army Corps. World Wide Photo courtesy National Archives #208-N-37540.

President Gerald R. Ford signing the Proclamation 4417, "An American Promise," rescinding Executive Order 9066, in the Cabinet Room, the White House, February 19, 1976. Standing immediately behind the president are the Asian American Congresspersons then in office. Left to right, Sen. Daniel K. Inouye, Reps. Patsy T. Mink, Norman Y. Mineta, and Spark M. Matsunaga, and Sen. Hiram L. Fong. Courtesy Gerald R. Ford Library.

The author briefing the Commission on Wartime Relocation and Internment of Civilians, Washington, D.C., June 23, 1981. The two visible commission members, with backs to camera, are, left to right, Hugh B. Mitchell and Arthur S. Fleming. Courtesy National Archives #220-WR-20.

But while most Issei parents were insisting on an American education for their children, they were simultaneously trying to give their children a Japanese education. They did this in two ways: by establishing a whole series of Japanese language schools or *Gakuen* throughout Japanese America, and by sending a significant number of their children, chiefly males, to Japan for a considerable portion of their education.

The language schools, in part subsidized directly and indirectly by the imperial government, functioned as after-school schools. In California just before Pearl Harbor, the United States Army claimed that there were "over 248 schools with an aggregate faculty of 454 and a student body of 17,800." This would mean that the average school had fewer than two teachers and just over seventy pupils. In Seattle, according to Miyamoto, there were 1,250 students in the mid-thirties and attendance was declining, a phenomenon Modell also notes in prewar Los Angeles.[24]

Opponents of the Japanese delighted in citing the language schools as evidence of the "un-Americanness" of the Nisei generation. V. S. McClatchy, for example, insisted that "the real purpose of the [language] schools is to teach Japanese ideals and loyalty and to make dependable Japanese citizens for whom are claimed, by birth, all rights of American citizenship."[25] The California legislature attempted to regulate the schools with a 1921 law establishing qualifications for teachers and instructional materials. In 1923 it passed an act abolishing the schools altogether, but Governor Friend W. Richardson vetoed the measure. A 1927 United States Supreme Court decision, involving a Hawaiian statute, struck down most such regulations.[26] Apologists for the language schools, not to be outdone, sometimes went so far as to argue that "the Japanese always desire that their children will become good American citizens and also make distinct contributions

---

that three high school valedictorians and two salutatorians that year were Nisei: "That they [the second generation] are, in general, by heredity, of a superior quality, we must recognize. This is equivalent to saying the Japanese people are of a superior biological quality; but the way in which they have surpassed the white students . . . almost makes them out to be of an entirely different class" (cited in Miyamoto, *Social Solidarity*, p. 110).

24. U.S. War Department, *Final Report*, p. 13; Miyamoto, *Social Solidarity*, p. 111; Modell, *Japanese of Los Angeles*, pp. 159–63.

25. V. S. McClatchy, *California's Language Schools*, p. 2. See also idem, "America and Japan," reprinted in V. S. McClatchy, ed., *Four Anti-Japanese Pamphlets*, pp. 11–12.

26. Charles Wollenberg, *All Deliberate Speed: Segregation and Exclusion in California Schools, 1855–1975*, p. 72.

by means of the finer qualities of their parentage." The Gakuen, they asserted, were merely a means to that end.[27]

More rational explanations exist for the language schools. First, many if not most Issei parents and certainly all Japanese American cultural institutions of the immigrant generation wanted to perpetuate at least the rudiments of formal Japanese culture in the second generation. In addition, as Miyamoto has argued, it was felt that there were economic advantages in knowing Japanese. It was assumed that much Nisei employment would be in the ethnic economy, with the branch offices of Japanese firms, or would involve employment in or travel to and trade with Japan.[28]

In any event, few of the students acquired significant proficiency in Japanese, as United States Army intelligence recruiters discovered to their sorrow when they tried to find Nisei with real language skills. The reasons for this are many, including the fact that few of the language-school teachers were trained or skilled teachers of language. They tended to be persons highly unacculturated to American life, and they enjoyed little prestige within the ethnic community. It is hard to imagine, for example, a Japanese American community sending a Gakuen teacher on an all-expense tour of Japan and seeing him off with a lavish reception, as Seattleites did for Ada Mahon, longtime principal of the Bailey Gatzert School.[29]

The whole question of education is complicated by the existence of *Kibei:* Nisei who had been sent back to Japan for a significant part of their education. There are no good statistics for Kibei; Alexander Leighton estimates that about 15 percent of the American-born Japanese sent to the relocation center at Poston during World War II were Kibei. If similar proportions prevailed throughout Japanese America, there would have been perhaps 11,000 Kibei; since parents were more likely to send sons than daughters to Japan, the proportion of Kibei among male Nisei may have been 20 percent or higher.

Much that has been written about Kibei is little more than stereotypical. The assumption is usually made that Kibei, because of their presumed indoctrination in militaristic Japan in the later 1920s and 1930s, were more likely to be pro-Japanese than were Nisei. Also, because they had missed some or all of the Americanizing experience

27. Statement by Kiichi Kanzaki, General Secretary, Japanese Association of America, as printed in, U.S. Congress, House, Committee on Immigration and Naturalization, *Japanese Immigration, Hearings,* 66th Cong., 2d sess., 1921, p. 679. A garbled version of this statement is printed in Bell, *Public School Education,* p. 21.

28. Miyamoto, *Social Solidarity,* p. 111.

29. Ibid., p. 107. A similar trip was later provided for a Mr. Sears, the principal of another Seattle school.

of the United States public school system, Kibei were assumed likely to be less acculturated than Nisei who stayed home. Alexander Leighton suggests a more balanced characterization, pointing to the existence of "another sort of Kibei, little mentioned, but of considerable importance. . . . These persons seem to stress the advantages of their marginal position between two cultures. . . . Their tendency seems to be toward living peacefully with all types and if they become active at all, it is to promote understanding and the expansion of common ground."[30] The one incontrovertible fact about Kibei is that, unlike other Nisei, most of them had significant fluency in spoken and written Japanese.

But the mere existence of a numerically significant Kibei group speaks volumes about the attitude toward America of some Issei parents. Certainly some Kibei melted into the population of Japan, and evidence, largely anecdotal, indicates that many Kibei eventually felt uncomfortable in both cultures. The Pacific War, as we shall see, brought the Kibei question to the fore in a way that never would have occurred in peacetime, but perhaps their chief significance is as an indicator of at least one horn of the Issei dilemma. In many Issei families only some children were sent to Japan. How and why these choices were made we simply do not know, but they must have been agonizing decisions. It may well be that sending some children to the mother country was a kind of insurance: no matter what happened the parents would have children who could cope in either culture. But regardless of the reasons, the whole question is just one more indication of the pervasive ambiguity that prevailed in Japanese America.

The children of 1940 Japanese America had lived their lives in this ambiguity and almost everything we know about them is flavored by it. Some of these Nisei were in fact adults by 1940 with children of their own—perhaps 4 percent of Japanese America, some 5,000 persons, were third generation or *Sansei*. Although the Nisei had done very well in school, and had charmed a whole generation of West Coast school teachers in the process, their marginal position began to become clear to most of them as they approached or reached adolescence. Physically too small for most athletic competition, their sports participation was usually confined to Nisei leagues. Interracial dating was frowned upon by elders of both communities and apparently was relatively rare. After-school activities were also circumscribed by race: Nisei children were likely to spend many afternoons

---

30. Alexander Leighton, *The Governing of Men: General Principles and Recommendations Based on Experience at a Japanese Relocation Camp*, p. 80.

a week in Gakuen—which most of them despised—and organized social activities were within the ethnic community. Even at most West Coast institutions of higher learning, the Nisei students made up their own groupings, often joined by exchange students from Japan.

Once school was completed, the Nisei encountered a society that rejected or ignored them regardless of their formal accomplishments. Throughout the 1930s, all but a few of the second-generation adults were confined, economically and socially, within Japanese America. Fully credentialed education majors were virtually unemployable in the very schools in which they had excelled. The first Japanese American to be graduated from the University of Oregon Law School could find professional employment only with a consulate of Japan. John Modell has accurately described the prewar Nisei dilemma: "[The Nisei] had inherited from his parents a remarkable desire to succeed in the face of hardship, but had also learned the American definition of success, by which standard the accommodation made by his parents could not be considered satisfactory."

One young Los Angeles Nisei essayist described his situation in 1937: "I am a fruitstand worker. It is not a very attractive or distinguished occupation. . . . I would much rather it were a doctor or lawyer . . . but my aspiration of developing into such [was] frustrated long ago. . . . I am only what I am, a professional carrot washer."[31] The realistic zenith of his aspirations, he said, was to save money and get a business of his own, which would probably be a fruit or vegetable market. Others got jobs—apparently much more success-fully than most young American workers in the 1930s—elsewhere in the ethnic economy but found them equally unsatisfactory. However satisfactory the ethnic economy might have been to the older Issei generation, it did not fit within what Modell has called the "American definition of success" accepted by most Nisei.

Some young Nisei professionals did manage to break out, but they were exceptions in more ways than one. John Aiso, born in Los Angeles in 1909, became controversial at age thirteen when he was elected student body president of Le Conte Junior High School in predominantly white Hollywood by a margin of 600 votes. Under pressure from outraged white parents, local newspaper publicity, and an anti-Asian student petition ("We students . . . stand for America

---

31. Taishi Matsumoto, "The Protest of a Professional Carrot Washer," Kashu Mainichi, April 4, 1937, as cited in John Modell, "Class or Ethnic Solidarity: The Japanese American Company Union," Pacific Historical Review 38 (1969): 192–206. See also Roger Daniels, "Japanese America, 1930–1941: An Ethnic Community in the Great Depression," Journal of the West 24, no. 4 (1985): 35–50.

and want no other but an American as our student body president."),
the principal suspended student government until Aiso graduated.

At Hollywood High School three years later, John Aiso won an
oratorical contest sponsored by the American Legion, but a Caucasian
classmate was sent to the national finals in Washington, D.C., and,
incidentally, won the prize. The subject of the contest was "The
American Constitution"! Aiso did get a consolation trip to Washington, where he met the Japanese ambassador, who suggested that he
attend an eastern university "to get a taste of New England life." The
ambassador introduced him to Brown University President W. H.
Faunce, who assured him of a scholarship. After a year of studies in
Tokyo—he was thus technically a Kibei but hardly fitted the stereotype—Aiso entered Brown at seventeen, graduated *cum laude,* and
was chosen valedictorian. He went on to Harvard Law School and
joined the New York firm of Patterson, Eagle, Greenough and Day.

While nothing in John Aiso's career, then or later, could be called
typical, it was easier for an occasional Nisei to break out of the
economic enclave away from the Pacific Coast in a place like New
York, where Japanese of any kind were few, just as it was easier for
blacks in those years to achieve success outside of the South. But the
pull of Japanese America was strong, and Aiso returned to Los
Angeles to practice law in 1939.[32]

Most Nisei professionals—lawyers, physicians, dentists and
nurses—never left, and their professional as well as their cultural
interests remained centered in the ethnic community. These older
Nisei professionals were instrumental in establishing what became the
Japanese American Citizens League (JACL), the key organization of
the second generation, although some of the same kinds of energies
went into the formation of such groups as the Japanese American
Young Republicans and Young Democrats. The JACL, founded in
1930, was the outgrowth of several regional organizations, some of
which we know little about. The most significant was the American
Loyalty League, founded by a young dentist, Tomatsu Yatabe, who
had been one of the pupils involved in the San Francisco School Board
controversy in 1906. A special meeting at a San Francisco YMCA in
November 1924 was attended by thirty-three delegates from five
Northern California chapters (San Francisco, San Jose, Florin, Salinas,

---

32. Bill Hosokawa, *Nisei: The Quiet Americans,* pp. 167–68, 394. See also
Masamori Kojima, "Judge John F. Aiso," *Chicago Scene,* August 1954, pp. 11–12.
Ironically, the classmate who went to Washington, Herbert Wenig, helped to write the
briefs for California and other states supporting the incarceration of Japanese Americans during World War II. For Wenig's role, see Peter Irons, *Justice at War: The Story
of the Japanese Internment Cases,* pp. 121, 180–81, 212–18.

and Fresno) and two fraternal delegates from the like-minded Progressive Voters League of Seattle.[33]

At that meeting, President Yatabe, who had set up a dental practice in Fresno, sounded some of the themes that would recur time and again in Nisei rhetoric, themes, I think, that are typical of self-conscious second generation groups of any ethnicity:

> We American-born Japanese have depended too much upon our parents in the work which must be performed by ourselves. We are gradually coming to the age where we must be independent in whatever work we do. The people of this country, as well as the people beyond the seas are waiting to see what we, the members of the second generation, are able to accomplish. Self-reliance must be cultivated. Instead of depending on the first generation, let us become strong enough to lead the older generation through thick and thin. In order to achieve this end we must first put forth our utmost effort to make the A.L.L. a stronger and more influential organization.

In 1930 the groups listed above and representatives from other parts of Japanese America united to form the JACL, which still exists as *the* Japanese American organization. Despite the fact that some Issei had encouraged the formation of Nisei organizations (according to Bill Hosokawa, the second generation groups had even received small subventions from the Japanese association headquarters in San Francisco), the citizen group was on a collision course with the organizations of the older generation.

Since the JACL was an organization for citizens, it effectively barred Issei from membership. Since it stressed Americanization and the exercise of civil rights, the Issei could not hope to gain except vicariously from its successes. While some of the original organizational goals of the predecessor groups had stressed the "study of Japanese culture," cultural ties with Japan were increasingly minimized as the "China incident" and imperial Japanese aggression expanded in the 1930s. Thus certain of the JACL goals became

---

33. American Loyalty League, Mss., UWA, Minutes of the Special Meeting of the American Loyalty League, Sutter Street Branch, YMCA, San Francisco, November 28–29, 1924. These were donated by Minoru Masuda of Seattle, who did much for Asian American studies in the Pacific Northwest. Bill Hosokawa, *JACL: In Quest of Justice*, is a valuable "company history" with the strengths and weaknesses typical of the genre. I rely on it heavily, along with materials from the James Y. Sakamoto Mss. and the Seattle JACL Mss., both in the University of Washington Archives. For the JACL role in World War II, see chapter 6 below.

somewhat repugnant to many of the Issei, especially to those community leaders who actively supported the ambitions of Japan.

Although the JACL was concerned, almost from its beginnings, with such civil-rights goals as amending the Cable Act so that Nisei women who had forfeited their citizenship by marriage to alien Japanese could get it back, and gaining citizenship for the few Issei who had served in the American military during World War I, its chief thrust was Americanization. The JACL creed, written in 1940, best expresses the Americanized ideology of the more articulate and aggressive Nisei leaders. It stressed accommodation rather than conflict. It swallowed, in one patriotic gulp, the American dream without ever taking notice of its nightmarish qualities for nonwhites:

> I am proud that I am an American citizen of Japanese ancestry, for my very background makes me appreciate more fully the wonderful advantages of this nation. I believe in her institutions, ideals and traditions; I glory in her heritage; I boast of her history; I trust in her future. She has granted me liberties and opportunities such as no individual enjoys in the world today. She has given me an education befitting kings. She has entrusted me with the responsibilities of the franchise. She has permitted me to build a home, to earn a livelihood, to worship, to think, speak and act as I please— as a free man equal to every other man.
>
> Although some individuals may discriminate against me, I shall never become bitter or lose faith, for I know that such persons are not representative of the majority of the American people. True, I shall do all in my power to discourage such practices, but I shall do it in the American way—above board, in the open, through courts of law, by education, by proving myself to be worthy of equal treatment and consideration. I am firm in my belief that American sportsmanship and attitude of fair play will judge citizenship and patriotism on the basis of action and achievement, and not on the basis of physical characteristics. Because I believe in America, and I trust she believes in me, and because I have received innumerable benefits from her, I pledge myself to do honor to her at all times and places; to defend her against all enemies, foreign and domestic; to actively assume my duties and obligations as a citizen, cheerfully and without any reservations whatsoever, in the hope that I may become a better American in a greater America.

This hypernationalism, which was not atypical of second generation American ethnic groups, neither sprang from the Nisei's experience nor accurately reflected their status. It was a declaration of faith, a hopeful vision of what the future might become. Although some Nisei were so Americanized that they actually believed the creed as written, its wording was in part an overreaction to and a conscious rejection of the ethnic heritage seen as retarding the aspirations of the second generation. The creed not only failed to reflect reality but it surely failed to convince many Nisei. Certainly the professional carrot-washer quoted earlier could not have subscribed to it. For these and other reasons, the JACL was a very small part of Japanese America. One source estimates that in Los Angeles County it had only 650 members in 1941 in a population of some 24,000 Nisei.

The JACL was probably weaker in Los Angeles than in the other centers of Japanese America. Because of the relatively large number of potential Nisei voters, and because of the free-wheeling nonorganizational style of southern California politics, some Los Angeles Nisei tried to play ethnic coalition politics, New Deal style. There were, of course, still very few Nisei voters. In 1940 the city had just 5,000 Nisei over 21 years of age, but in 1930 the number had been just over 800.

Ethnic politics did not mean, as it might today, a coalition with other minority groups—most Japanese in America, from the very beginning, have oriented themselves toward the middle and upper classes to which they aspired. Rather, for Nisei, ethnic politics meant shopping around to find majority group candidates who would promise something—almost anything—to them. The English-language pages of the *Rafu Shimpo,* a major outlet for the views of Nisei professionals, rejoiced as early as 1933 that "a young Japanese-American physician—a veteran of World War I—had 'been practically assured' of a position at the Los Angeles County Hospital." The paper noted that both his membership in the American Legion and the sponsorship of a city councilman for whom he had campaigned had played an important part in advancing what the paper called his "vocational prospects." And vocational prospects, particularly for the educated professionals, were central to many Nisei concerns.[34]

But there was one important aspect of the Nisei dilemma that many of the second generation leaders simply tried to ignore and that the JACL never mentioned in its public statements: the growing likelihood of a Japanese-American war. A few Nisei, mostly those who leaned to the left of the political spectrum, joined or endorsed such movements as the boycotting of Japanese goods or protested the shipment of war materials to Japan. A somewhat larger group echoed the patriotic support for Japanese expansion—they were more likely

---

34. Modell, *Japanese of Los Angeles,* pp. 133, 169–70. In Seattle, Clarence Arai ran for the state legislature as a Republican in 1934. He was perhaps the first Nisei candidate for state office. He finished fifth in a field of five. See Hosokawa, *JACL,* pp. 78–79.

to call it defense of Japanese rights—in East Asia. A number of persons in each generation gave at least lip service to the notion that the emerging Nisei generation could somehow bridge the gap between the two Pacific rivals. But the majority, at least in public statements, avoided the issue.

Yet looking closely, one finds an undercurrent of gloom about the future pervading the Nisei generation, at least in some of its more articulate segments. As early as 1937, a second generation student at the University of California, editorializing in a campus magazine, asked his fellow Nisei:

> What are we going to do if war does break out between the United States and Japan? . . . In common parlance we can say "we're sunk." Even if the Nisei wanted to fight for America, what chances? Not a chance! . . . our properties would be confiscated and most likely [we would be] herded into prison camps—perhaps we would be slaughtered on the spot.[35]

As international tensions increased, so did Nisei anxieties. In their insecurity some Nisei tried to accentuate their loyalty and Americanism in a negative rather than a positive way by disparaging their parents' generation, a tactic not unusual among second-generation immigrant groups under pressure. Newspaper editor Togo Tanaka, for example, speaking to a college group in early 1941, insisted that the Nisei must face up to what he called "the question of loyalty." He assumed that, since the Issei were "more or less tumbleweeds with one foot in America and one foot in Japan," real loyalty to America could be found only in his own Nisei generation. Some members of that generation, even before Pearl Harbor, were serving as volunteer informants for the agents of the Federal Bureau of Investigation and for perceptive members of Naval Intelligence, such as Lieutenant Commander Kenneth D. Ringle, helping them to compile lists of the major supporters of Japanese imperialism within Japanese America.[36] A Nisei businessman, a jeweler in Los Angeles, explained to a white newspaperman in the late summer of 1941 that many if not most of the businessmen of the older Issei generation were pro-Japanese rather than pro-American. He expressed the fears of many in his generation: "We talk of almost nothing but this great crisis. We don't know what's going to happen. Sometimes we only look for a concentration

---

35. UC Berkeley *Campanile Review*, Fall 1937.
36. Kenneth D. Ringle Mss., in the possession of the Ringle family, Washington, D.C. See chapter 6 below for details of Ringle's activities in 1941–1942.

camp."[37] But despite these and other tensions, and before the attack on Pearl Harbor would destroy it prematurely, Japanese America was successfully dealing with limitations and was adapting to the American environment.

It is important to point out that credit for the success of that adaptation, as well as for the success of Chinese America and for the greater or lesser successes of the other immigrant groups, must be allotted both to the immigrants themselves and to their environment. Unfortunately, a number of conservative social scientists have chosen to use the relative success of the Chinese and Japanese Americans in the late nineteenth and early twentieth centuries as a kind of intellectual brickbat against contemporary groups within what Gunnar Myrdal has styled "the underclass"—chiefly blacks, Chicanos, and other Hispanic Americans. This so-called immigrant analogy argues, sometimes crudely, sometimes with great statistical and methodological sophistication, that since most members of the earlier immigrant groups have "made it," and since, quite clearly, most members of the underclass have not, the fault must lie somehow within the groups that have not succeeded.

Few of these neo-conservative critics make overtly racist comparisons—some of them are themselves members of the ethnic or racial groups under attack. They use instead such code phrases as "the lack of stable male-headed families," or the "heritage of slavery," or they stress the lack of such cultural mechanisms as "rotating credit associations." Nonetheless, their arguments are, in the final analysis, similar to more obviously racist allegations, such as those attributing the failure of a group to alleged inferior intelligence or to supposedly inferior cultural inheritances. All these critics, however, ultimately share a common point of view: they place the major blame for the failure of some or all underclass groups not on a society that still contains racist, oppressive elements but on some crucial lack in the underclasses themselves. At the same time, these critics exalt the immigrant generations of an earlier age in a way that would have mystified both those immigrant generations and their contemporary opponents. This "blaming the victim" is an age-old way of rationalizing injustice.

Japanese America, like Chinese America before it, was a unique adaptation to unique circumstances. It was largely the creation of one generation, a generation that has now almost passed from the scene. Like all past generations, at least some of its heritage will persist, and that heritage should be studied and even celebrated. But it is also

---

37. Los Angeles *Times,* August 6, 1941.

important that it not be romanticized and that it not be used to attack groups that are now farther down on the American ethnic escalator. And, it should be noted, before the neoconservative social scientists discovered their uses of the Japanese American past, some in the Japanese American community were making the same argument, if more crudely. In July 1963, for example, one Nisei leader's speech was accurately headlined in the Los Angeles *Times:* "Nisei Tells Negroes to Better Themselves."[38]

The Japanese American experience, like the experience of all self-conscious ethnic groups, has some aspects that seem mere variants on the American pattern and some aspects that seem uniquely its own. Earlier, in "Japanese Immigrants," I noted that "the Issei were a small, self-confident group entering a fertile region with a rapidly expanding population. They came with almost all the skills and technological know-how necessary to reach the bottom rungs of the ladder of success. They brought with them the ethnic pride of a successfully emerging nation about to assume the leadership of a continent. They came at a unique time in the history of their two countries: their experience [and the Japanese America they created] cannot be repeated."[39] Only when taking into account a wide range of qualifying factors (see chapter 8 below) can meaningful comparisons be drawn with the experiences of other ethnic groups in the United States.

---

38. Los Angeles *Times,* July 6, 1963.

39. See Roger Daniels, "Japanese Immigrants on a Western Frontier: The Issue in California, 1890–1940," in Hilary Conroy and T. Scott Miyakawa, eds., *East Across the Pacific,* p. 87.

6.

Asian Americans and World War II

That war is a generator of social change is almost a historical cliché, but even clichés need explication and analysis. British historian Arthur Marwick, who has written broadly about the effect of war on western societies in the twentieth century, has attempted to set up a typology:

> War can be broken down into four dimensions. . . . First is the immediate obvious *destructive* and *disruptive* dimension of war: capital is destroyed, peacetime processes are interrupted, people are projected into new situations. Second is the *test* dimension. War brings new stresses, offers new challenges, and imposes new necessities. Institutions adapt; or they may even collapse. . . . In meeting the test of war societies will be forced to change, not necessarily in a desirable direction. Third is the *participation* dimension. . . . As wars more and more involve the participation of hitherto underprivileged groups in the community . . . those groups tend to benefit from such participation. Finally, there is the *psychological* dimension. War . . . is an enormous emotional and psychological experience comparable with the great revolutions in history.[1]

The impact of World War II on American society is just now

---

1. Arthur Marwick, "Problems and Consequences of Organizing Society for Total War," in N. F. Dreisziger, ed., *Mobilization for Total War: The Canadian, American and British Experience, 1914–1918, 1939–1945*, pp. 3–4.

beginning to be assessed by historians and other scholars. There is general agreement that it was a "good war" for the majority of Americans. War and not the New Deal ended the Great Depression and, once the economic equilibrium had been broken, Americans enjoyed a boom that lasted some three decades. Significant wartime gains were made by blacks, women, and the second and third generations of the "new" immigrant groups. These World War II economic gains are generally acknowledged, although scholars continue to disagree about the extent and importance of these changes.

But about the war's impact on Asian Americans there can be no debate: it marked a crucial turning point in the history of each community. Japanese America was simply destroyed, although some of the pieces would be put back together after the war. The impact on Chinese America, although less obvious and less dramatic, was perhaps as decisive. The immediate changes that the war brought to the largest Asian American communities seem contradictory: Japanese America was debased while Chinese America was promoted. The long term changes for each community, however, were similar: in each instance, the center of gravity changed decisively from the Old World to the New.

The changes were of three kinds: changes in the rules by which the Asian American communities were governed by the larger society; changes in the way that these communities regarded themselves; and finally, changes in the racial ideology of the larger society. These last changes were, perhaps, inherent in the long evolution from slavery, segregation, and ostracism toward real freedom, integration, and equality, but their pace was distinctly quickened by the process of fighting a war against forces that were clearly and unambiguously racist.

That the struggle against the Axis produced one of the grossest violations of the constitutional rights of American citizens in our history—the incarceration of more than 70,000 American citizens of Japanese ancestry who were guilty of nothing but having the wrong kind of genes—is an ironic and disgraceful aspect of a war whose stated objective was freedom. But history does not move in straight lines, and its actors often play varied roles. Thomas Jefferson, who proclaimed that "all men are created equal," was a slave holder; Franklin Roosevelt, who proclaimed the "Four Freedoms," ordered Japanese Americans into concentration camps.

Wars often have social effects undreamed of by those who direct them. Just as the American Civil War, despite Abraham Lincoln's initial indifference, eventually became "a war to make men free," the war that began at Pearl Harbor eventually transformed the legal, social, and psychological position of Asians in American society.

For Overseas Chinese accustomed to playing a role in the politics of China, the Sino-Japanese struggles of the 1930s seemed at first just another episode in modern China's long time of troubles. As early as 1931 Chinese Americans were staging peaceful anti-Japanese demonstrations in cities across the United States. But as the intermittent fighting continued, especially after 1937 when there were large-scale battles in Shanghai and elsewhere, support for the Chiang Kai-shek regime grew steadily. Between 1937 and 1945 some $56 million was raised among Chinese in America in support of China's war effort.[2] The heroic Chinese resistance to Japanese aggression, the increasing coverage of Asia in the American press, the growing tensions between Japan and the United States, especially after the bombing of the United States gunboat *Panay* by Japanese planes in Chinese waters in December 1937, all contributed to a new Chinese image in the eyes of many Americans.

Some of that change had been occurring independently. The immensely popular work of novelist Pearl S. Buck, who won a Pulitzer Prize for *The Good Earth* in 1932 and a Nobel Prize in 1938, portrayed the Chinese as long-suffering, sturdy peasants. (Although, it should be noted, when her works were translated into film, the leading roles were taken by Caucasian stars Paul Muni, Katharine Hepburn, and Walter Huston.) It is difficult to overestimate Pearl Buck's importance in the reshaping of the American image of the Chinese in the 1930s and 1940s. As Harold Isaacs put it: "For a whole generation of Americans she 'created' the Chinese, in the same sense that Dickens 'created' for so many of us the people who lived in the slums of Victorian England."[3] The very popular comic strip *Terry and the Pirates* made clear distinctions between Chinese, who were victims and assistant heroes, and Japanese, who were villains. The growing popularity of China and her cause, coupled with the growing unpopularity of Japan, enhanced both the status and the prestige of Chinese Americans in the years prior to World War II.

When Pearl Harbor made allies of China and the United States, the impact on Chinese America was almost instantaneous. By October 1942 sociologist Rose Hum Lee could report that the war had already significantly changed for the better the lives of Chinese Americans.[4] Thirty years later, a Chinese American journalist agreed: "To the men

---

2. Diane Mei Lin Mark and Ginger Chih, *A Place Called Chinese America*, p. 83.
3. Harold Isaacs, *Images of Asia: American Views of China and India*, p. 155. (Originally published as *Scratches on Our Minds*.)
4. Rose Hum Lee, "Chinese in the United States Today," *Survey Graphic* 31 (1942): 419.

of my generation, World War II was the most important historic event of our times. For the first time we felt that we could make it in American society."[5]

Toward the end of the war, in an essay she never published, Lee expressed understandable reservations about the changes in attitude toward the Chinese:

> As violently as Chinese were once attacked, they are now glorified and placed on a pedestal. It is impossible to predict how lasting the change will be. . . . Largely grounded on the sandy loam of sentimentality, one is left conjecturing what the tone of the literature toward the Chinese will be in 1954.[6]

Certainly many of the changes in attitude of the larger society had little or nothing to do with the reality of Chinese America. They reflected, rather, continuing American misperceptions about what was really going on in China. Chiang Kai-shek and, to an even greater extent, his American-educated wife became important political and cultural symbols of the Sino-American partnership. American political leaders publicly extolled "the Generalissimo and Madame." In 1942, for example, on the fifth anniversary of the Marco Polo Bridge incident which had triggered the wider war in China, both Secretary of State Cordell Hull and President Franklin Roosevelt sent public messages to Chiang praising him, the Chinese people, and their struggle. "All the world knows," said FDR, "how well you have carried on that fight which is the fight of all mankind."

In Chungking, China's wartime capital, American Ambassador Clarence Gauss reacted in a realistic private memorandum:

> It is unfortunate that Chiang and the Chinese have been "built up" in the United States to a point where Americans have been made to believe that China has been "fighting" the Japanese for five years, and that the Generalissimo, a great leader, has been directing the energetic resistance of China to Japan and is a world hero. Looking the cold facts in the face, one could only dismiss this as "rot."[7]

---

5. Victor G. Nee and Brett de Bary Nee, *Longtime Californ'*, p. 154.

6. Rose Hum Lee, "Social Attitudes Toward Chinese in the United States, Expressed in Periodical Literature from 1919 to 1944," as cited in Isaacs, *Images of Asia*, p. 120.

7. As cited in Isaacs, *Images of Asia*, p. 187. See also FDR's message to Chiang, February 7, 1942: "The tenacity of the Chinese people . . . is an inspiration to . . . all the peoples of the other United Nations." In his fireside chat of April 28, 1942, FDR put it thus: "We remember that the Chinese people were the first to stand up and fight against the aggressors in this war, and in the future a still unconquerable China will play

Table 6.1
Chinese Americans 1950
Age and Sex Distribution

Age Cohort	Male	% in Cohort	Female	% in Cohort
75+	1145	1.5	181	0.4
70–74	1342	1.7	219	0.5
65–69	2099	2.7	392	1.0
60–64	3152	4.1	595	1.5
55–59	4365	5.7	895	2.1
50–54	5869	7.6	1312	3.2
45–49	6379	8.3	1656	4.1
40–44	6230	8.1	2109	5.2
35–39	6457	8.4	2748	6.9
30–34	5746	7.5	3457	8.6
25–29	7907	10.3	4811	11.9
20–24	6446	8.4	5916	14.6
15–19	4885	6.4	3492	8.6
10–14	4090	5.3	3038	7.5
5–9	3523	4.6	3020	7.5
0–4	7090	9.2	6538	16.2
	76,725		40,415	
Median Age	Males	ca. 34 years	Females	ca. 23 years

SOURCE: United States Department of Commerce. Bureau of the Census. *1950 Census of Population* 3B, table 5, p.19

For the short run, at least, this favorable image was useful to the Chinese American community. Happily not all of its improved position in American life was based on "the sandy loam of sentimentality." Much of the improvement was based on real changes in the nature of the community itself, on real changes in the attitudes of the larger society, and on real accomplishments by Chinese Americans. In addition, wartime sentimentality was constructively exploited to bring

its proper role . . . in the whole world" (Samuel I. Rosenman, comp., *Public Papers and Addresses of Franklin D. Roosevelt* (1942):89–90, 230).

about significant and lasting changes in American immigration and nationality laws.

The demographic changes of the 1940s were quite pronounced. For the first time since the 1870s the total Chinese population rose substantially from 77,000 to 117,000, a jump of just over 50 percent. Close to 20,000 Chinese American babies were born during the decade. For the first time in Chinese American history, the most numerous five-year cohort was composed of persons under five years of age. The Chinese American demographic structure was still badly skewed, but the bottom layer was now the largest (see table 6.1). In addition, the imbalanced sex ratio was further reduced, from 285 males for every 100 females in 1940 to 190 males per 100 females in 1950.

The younger American-born adults—the children of the 1910s and 1920s—assisted in part by the improved economic opportunities of wartime, began to move in significant numbers out of the ethnic economy and into jobs in the professional sphere of the large society. By 1950, as table 6.2 shows, about 7 percent of all Chinese workers were in professional jobs, although the dominance of the ethnic economy was still apparent in the high concentrations of workers in services and petty entrepreneurship.

The educational achievement of Chinese Americans was not significantly higher than that of the general population. Median years of schooling completed was 8.4 for males and 10.3 for the younger and more predominantly native-born females. Just under 8 percent of each sex had been graduated from college.

World War II had a crucial impact on the ways in which Americans defined their cultural identity. As Philip Gleason has written, the war gave unprecedented salience to ideology:

> For a whole generation, the question "What does it mean to be an American?" was answered primarily by reference to "the values America stands for": democracy, freedom, equality, respect for individual dignity, and so on. Since these values were abstract and universal, American identity could not be linked exclusively with any single ethnic derivation. Persons of any race, color, religion or background could be, or become, Americans.[8]

While Gleason may be overstating somewhat the pervasiveness of this cultural pluralism, it was quite pronounced during the war years. Nothing, I think, more clearly indicates this than the successful campaign for the repeal of Chinese exclusion. This campaign resulted

---

8. Philip Gleason, "Americans All: World War II and the Shaping of American Identity," *The Review of Politics* 43 (1981):511–512.

Table 6.2
Occupations, Chinese and Japanese Americans, 1950

Males				
Occupational Group	Chinese	Percentage	Japanese	Percentage
Professional	2,541	6.4	2,722	6.5
Farm	1,186	3.0	13,652	32.5
Managers and Proprietors	8,920	22.5	3,662	8.7
Clerical and Sales	4,512	11.4	3,883	9.2
Craftsmen	1,348	3.4	3,266	7.8
Operatives	6,564	16.6	4,136	9.8
Service	13,746	34.7	4,984	11.9
Laborers (nonfarm)	782	2.0	5,744	13.7
Total persons	39,599	. . .	42,049	. . .
Females				
Occupational Group	Chinese	Percentage	Japanese	Percentage
Professional	914	11.3	1,558	7.5
Farm	66	0.8	3,478	16.6
Managers and Proprietors	658	8.1	791	3.8
Clerical and Sales	3,210	39.6	5,768	27.8
Craftsmen	42	0.5	189	0.9
Operatives	1,711	21.1	4,182	20.2
Service	1,454	17.9	4,572	22.0
Laborers (nonfarm)	47	0.5	214	1.0
Total persons	8,102	. . .	20,752	. . .

SOURCE: United States Bureau of the Census, *1950 Census of Population* 3B, tables 11, 12.

in the first statutory rollback of anti-Asian racism. In retrospect, it can be seen as the hinge on which American immigration policy turned.

Before the war, Chinese exclusion seemed an untouchable cornerstone of American immigration and naturalization policy. A combination of circumstances, however, made the eventual passage of repeal surprisingly easy. The campaign for the repeal of the Chinese Exclusion Acts is a classic example of successful pressure-group politics. As such, it is the subject of a good monograph: Fred W. Riggs, *Pressures on Congress.*[9]

The key organization in the campaign was the Citizens Committee to Repeal Chinese Exclusion and Place Immigration on a Quota Basis. The committee was formed on May 25, 1943; within seven months the repeal had been effected. The crucial figure on the committee was Richard J. Walsh, a New York publisher (the John Day Company and the magazine, *Asia and the Americas*) and husband of novelist Pearl Buck. The committee, which listed more than 150 individuals on its letterhead, was drawn from a wide spectrum of the American upper class and intelligentsia. On the left, it included Roger Baldwin of the American Civil Liberties Union and academic socialist Broadus Mitchell; on the right, it numbered Henry R. Luce of *Time, Life,* and *Fortune* and retired Admiral Harry R. Yarnell among its members.[10]

The committee was able to make a broad appeal that could be varied with its target. In his successful effort to convert Seattle publisher Miller Freeman, the leading Japanophobe of the Pacific Northwest, Walsh used a number of arguments which are worth quoting at length:

> [The Committee] is being formed to support only the broad policy of removing the discrimination against Chinese, and putting them on the basis of equality so far as immigration and naturalization are concerned—that is putting them under the quota law. As you know the Chinese quota would be very small, and very much less than the number of Chinese who now get in illegally. No one so far as I know would advocate any change in the quota system, or letting down the general immigration bars. We believe that if we eliminate the insult to China implied by the present exclusion laws, we can get the active cooperation of the Chinese [not only] in further checking illegal entry into this country, but also in protecting our employment and labor standards. . . .
>
> In writing the other day to the National Commander of the American Legion, I made the point that by getting the cooperation of the Chinese in this way we may even be able to *reduce* the number of Chinese laborers getting into the country. At present, when we discriminate against all Chinese, there is very little inducement to the Chinese authorities to give us any help at all in

9. Fred W. Riggs, *Pressures on Congress: A Study of the Repeal of Chinese Exclusion.* Much of what follows about repeal derives from Riggs.

10. Miller Freeman Mss., UWA, letterhead of committee on letter, Mary Mason to Miller Freeman, July 8, 1943.

stopping illegal entry. But perhaps I shouldn't say such a thing for publication."[11]

Some nativists, of course, were not convinced. Paul Scharrenberg, a long-time labor official whom Earl Warren had made Director of Industrial Relations for the State of California, saw the repeal campaign as a kind of conspiracy. "It is obvious," he wrote, "that a Nation-wide campaign has been organized to wipe out all the exclusion laws and substitute the quota system. The California C.I.O. has already officially endorsed the move and so far as I know, not a single A.F.L. Union has raised its voice in protest."[12] Scharrenberg, who had been a leader in the fight against Asian immigration since before World War I, further bemoaned the fact that

> the present generation has no conception of the long and serious struggle which preceded the enactment of Oriental exclusion laws. Neither do they seem to have any conception of the possible consequences of the repeal of such laws. Unfortunately, I can no longer assume leadership in such a fight, as my present employment as a State officer, prohibits such activity. I have been talking informally to members of the California Joint Immigration Committee and have promises that immediate attention will be given to the subject-matter.

The Joint Immigration Committee was one of several pressure groups that opposed repeal. Its executive secretary, H. J. McClatchy, put the nativist opposition to repeal in its bluntest terms. He rejected the notion that repeal was necessary to aid an ally. "The mere fact that we refuse to modify our immigration laws is not an argument that therefore the Chinese will lay down their arms in surrender." The crucial point, as far as McClatchy and those like him were concerned, was to keep the 1924 Immigration Act intact: "any modification of the Act would be digging a hole in the dike." The issue, for McClatchy, was race:

> We have denied quota to those races which cannot be assimilated here. To say that admission under quota would be 100 or 200 is beside the question. We would be giving up a right to exclude people who would always be a race apart, helping to create another

---

11. Ibid., letter, Richard J. Walsh to Miller Freeman, May 14, 1943.
12. Ibid., letter, Paul Scharrenberg to Miller Freeman, April 19, 1943. For Scharrenberg's role in earlier anti-Japanese movements, see Roger Daniels, *The Politics of Prejudice*, pp. 59, 79, 87.

racial problem, following a route of appeasement bound to lead to friction with other groups not singled out for special favor.[13]

Other nativists saw, correctly, I think, the repeal of Chinese exclusion as a possible turning point in immigration policy. John B. Trevor, one of those who had helped shape the National Origins Act of 1924, felt that

we are up against a powerfully backed movement to repeal the Chinese Exclusion Laws. This movement, of course, is obviously a prelude to undoing the work of twenty years of immigration restrictions. It places in grave peril the provisions of the Act of 1924, which exclude persons ineligible for citizenship.[14]

But the nativists were badly split by the Chinese issue. Nothing better illustrates this than the reactions of Seattle publisher Miller Freeman. Freeman, who had been an anti-Asian crusader since 1917, found the internationalist arguments of the repeal forces compelling. His public support of repeal in October 1943 is worth noting as an important symbol of change:

I am for repeal . . . and for placing China on the quota along with other nations. . . . [T]he Chinese would be allowed only 105 immigrants . . . annually. We should recognize the heroic accomplishments of the Chinese people as a member of the United Nations in the struggle against totalitarianism. The United States has already taken a great step by relinquishing extraterritorial jurisdiction in China. There is no danger that China will follow the example of Japan and attempt to force large numbers of her people on this country. . . .

Unlike Japan, China has never attempted to interject herself in the affairs of this country.[15]

In one sense, the offering of a quota as a kind of reward for good behavior was unprincipled. Indeed, some members of the repeal committee such as sociologist Bruno Lasker briefly held out for a campaign to treat all Asians equally. Others such as Owen Lattimore felt that it might be tactically useful to treat Chinese separately:

---

13. Freeman Mss., UWA, letter, H. J. McClatchy to Miller Freeman, June 25, 1943. McClatchy was the son of V. S. McClatchy (1857–1938) and succeeded his father as Executive Secretary of the California Joint Immigration Committee.

14. Ibid., letter, John B. Trevor to Miller Freeman, April 27, 1943. For Trevor's role in the passage of the National Origins Act in 1924, see John Higham, *Strangers in the Land*, pp. 319–21 and passim.

15. Miller Freeman, "Chinese Exclusion Repeal," Seattle *Post-Intelligencer*, October 16, 1943.

It seems to me that there could hardly be a better time for launching a program for repeal of Chinese exclusion. . . . I personally think it would be good propaganda toward the Japanese at home in Japan if we were to repeal Japanese exclusion as well. It would be a sort of earnest that we are fighting against Japanese militarism and imperialism, not the Japanese people. However, I suppose that at the present time, with California pretty near to a panic over possible Japanese fifth columnists, it would be very difficult to get through such a measure.[16]

Nine bills modifying the Chinese Exclusion Act were introduced into Congress in 1943. The broadest bill, introduced by leftist New York City Representative Vito Marcantonio, would have made the naturalization statutes totally color blind and was never seriously considered. The House finally focused on a measure introduced by Warren Magnuson (D-Wash.) which was debated and passed by the House in October and agreed to by the Senate the next month.

The act was a simple one, in three sections. Section one repealed all or part of fifteen different statutes—enacted between 1882 and 1913—which had effected Chinese exclusion. Section two gave a quota to "persons of the Chinese race" which, under the law, was set at 105 annually. The law was thus specifically racist. A Chinese born in Canada, for example, would be chargeable to the tiny Chinese quota; a white native of Canada could enter as a nonquota immigrant. Section three amended the nationality act to make "Chinese persons or persons of Chinese descent" eligible for naturalization on the same terms as other immigrants.[17]

Passage was aided by a special message to the Congress from President Roosevelt, who used the same kinds of arguments that the committee had pioneered. As commander in chief, he regarded the legislation "as important in the cause of winning the war and of establishing a secure peace." Since China was our ally and her resistance depended, in part, on "the spirit of her people and her faith in her allies," the president argued for a show of support:

We owe it to the Chinese to strengthen that faith. One step in this direction is to wipe from the statute books those anachronisms in our laws which forbid the immigration of Chinese people into this country and which bar Chinese residents from American citizenship.

---

16. Owen Lattimore, as cited in Riggs, *Pressures on Congress*, p. 49. For Bruno Lasker, see ibid., p. 52. Lasker became a member of the committee; Lattimore did not.
17. 57 *Stat.* 600.

Nations, like individuals, make mistakes. We must be big enough to acknowledge our mistakes of the past and correct them.[18]

In addition, Roosevelt pointed out, repeal would silence distorted Japanese propaganda. He argued that the small number of Chinese who could come in would neither cause unemployment nor provide job competition.

But Roosevelt laid primary stress on the foreign-policy aspects of repeal: "While it would give the Chinese a preferred status over certain other Oriental people, their great contribution to the cause of decency and freedom entitles them to such preference. . . . [Passage] will be an earnest of our purpose to apply the policy of the good neighbor to our relations with other peoples." When Roosevelt later signed the bill into law, he reiterated its foreign-policy implications as a war measure affecting mostly persons abroad rather than as a redress of Chinese American grievances:

It is with particular pride and pleasure that I have today signed the bill repealing the Chinese exclusion laws. The Chinese people, I am sure, will take pleasure in knowing that this represents a manifestation on the part of the American people of their affection and regard.

An unfortunate barrier between allies has been removed. The war effort in the Far East can now be carried on with a greater vigor and a larger understanding of our common purpose.[19]

Underscoring the lack of concern for the problems of Chinese America, as opposed to those of China, is the fact that the committee, the Congress, and the president steadily ignored the bills introduced by Representative John Lesinski (D-Mich.) and others which would have allowed the alien wives of Chinese American citizens to enter as citizens. Family unification, later to become a prime factor in immigration legislation, was not considered crucial in 1943, at least not for Asian families.

In keeping with the thrust of the committee's strategy, Chinese Americans were little utilized in the struggle for the bill. Conversely, the Republic of China played an important part in the propaganda campaign. The Chinese consul at Seattle, Kiang Yi-seng, in a July 1943 press statement, assured Americans that the "Chinese people and

---

18. Rosenman, *FDR Public Papers* (1943): 429–430.

19. Ibid., p. 548. Reflecting the spirit in which Chinese exclusion was repealed, the compiler of the index for the 1943 volume, Ken Heckler, entered this and the preceding message under "China." There is no entry for Chinese Americans.

press" were watching "with keenest interest." Repeal, the consul argued, would be a blow to Japan, "a master stroke to give the lie to the Japanese taunt that the United States can talk in terms of racial equality but will not do anything about it." There would not be large-scale immigration, he assured Americans, because the quota would be so small and because "the Chinese people have never been a migratory race." Ignoring the inequities that would continue for Chinese Americans even after passage, Kiang insisted that "the repeal of the Chinese Exclusion Acts places the Chinese people on a footing of actual equality with races of Caucasian or colored descent and it will constitute a milestone in the furtherance of friendship and mutual understanding between our two peoples."[20]

The managers of the bill took great care to keep it untainted by larger issues. Nothing better illustrates this than what occurred when the Japanese American Citizens League offered to testify in favor of the bill. The committee prevailed upon the JACL to withold public support, so that Japanese unpopularity might not adversely affect the bill and so that the inevitable question of quotas and citizenship for all Asians might be forestalled. Legislation on the latter issue was almost a decade away, but within three years two additional measures affecting Asian Americans had been enacted into law.

In July 1946 Congress rewarded other Asian allies by extending quotas and the right of naturalization to "persons of races indigenous to India, and . . . the Philippine Islands" on the model of the 1943 act repealing Chinese exclusion. Underlining the continuing discriminatory nature of American immigration law were provisions for those of "mixed blood." The law defined as Chinese [or Indian or Filipino] "any person as is as much as one-half Chinese blood." Some racist pedant then insisted on putting into the statute books a provision covering a rare and perhaps nonexistent individual, a "quota immigrant who is of one-half Chinese blood and one-half the blood of a race indigenous to India." Such a person would be charged to the quota of the land of her or his birth or, if born in neither country, to the quota of whichever of the two had fewer pending applications.[21]

Of great importance to the Chinese American community was an act making the alien Chinese wives of American citizens—native-born or naturalized—admissible on a nonquota basis. Largely because of this act, legal migration of Chinese boomed—relatively speaking—in

---

20. Freeman Mss., UWA, "Statement" of Dr. Kiang Yi-seng, Chinese consul at Seattle, June 7, 1943.
21. 60 *Stat.* 416.

Table 6.3
Immigration of Chinese by Sex, 1945–1952

Year	Male	Female	Female (percentage)	Total
1945	45	64	59	109
1946	71	162	69	233
1947	142	986	87	1,128
1948	257	3,317	93	3,574
1949	242	2,248	90	2,490
1950	110	1,179	91	1,289
1951	126	957	88	1,083
1952	118	1,034	90	1,152

SOURCE: United States Department of Justice, Immigration and Naturalization Service, *Annual Reports*, 1945–1953.

the immediate postwar years, as table 6.3 indicates.[22] The migration of almost ten thousand Chinese women in eight years had tremendous impact on the structure of Chinese America, which, as late as 1950, contained only twenty-eight thousand women fourteen years of age and older. One must also remember that, while the cultural impact of this relatively large number of adults would serve to reinforce Chinese rather than Chinese American culture, the increased number of families with children would be a major force for acculturation.

Japanese Americans' World War II experience was very different from that of the Chinese. Japan had become the land of the enemy— the enemy who had struck without warning, the enemy whose well-planned military audacity seemed to be the fulfillment of a long racial nightmare—the Yellow Peril. From Vancouver to San Diego, the white population of the Pacific Coast trembled in anticipation of what might happen next. Almost immediately many began to insist that, as a matter of revenge, or safety, or both, persons of "the Japanese race" should be locked up, regardless of age, or sex, or nativity.

The press wasted no time. Contrary to later assessments of a delayed reaction against resident Japanese on the Pacific Coast, the leading newspaper in California, the Los Angeles *Times*, warned on

22. 60 *Stat.* 975.

December 8, 1941, that California was "a zone of danger." The paper called for "alert, keen-eyed civilians" to cooperate with military authorities "against spies, saboteurs and fifth columnists." While invoking the state's vigilante tradition—southern California had experienced a big Ku Klux Klan movement in the 1920s—the *Times* pointed its finger directly at the most likely enemy agents: "We have thousands of Japanese here. . . . Some, perhaps many, are good Americans. What the rest may be we do not know, nor can we take a chance in the light of yesterday's demonstration that treachery and double-dealing are major Japanese weapons."[23]

Such outright incitements to injustice were not confined to West Coast newspapers. Among national columnists, little difference could be noted between the gutter journalism of Westbrook Pegler—who had proposed on December 9 that the United States enter into an atrocity competition with Germany and Japan by killing "100 victims selected out of [our] concentration camps," which Pegler assumed would be set up for "alien Japanese" and others—and the erudite rationalizations of Walter Lippmann—who in a mid-February think piece entitled "The Fifth Column on the Coast," wrote that:

> The Pacific Coast is in imminent danger of a combined attack from within and without. . . . It is a fact that the Japanese navy has been reconnoitering the coast more or less continuously. . . . There is an assumption [in Washington] that a citizen may not be interfered with unless he has committed an overt act. . . . The Pacific Coast is officially a combat zone: Some part of it may at any moment be a battlefield. And nobody ought to be on a battlefield who has no good reason for being there. There is plenty of room elsewhere for him to exercise his rights.[24]

Radio commentators were just as bad or worse. The chief offender on the West Coast air waves seems to have been Mutual Broadcasting System commentator John B. Hughes. Hysteria seems to have infected almost everyone. Columbia Broadcasting System commentator Edward R. Murrow, back for a short time in his native Washington state after having become a media star through his

---

23. Los Angeles *Times*, December 8, 1941. See also Morton Grodzins, *Americans Betrayed*, passim.

24. Pegler in Los Angeles *Times*, December 9, 1941; Lippmann's column appeared in papers of February 12, 1942. For its impact, see Roger Daniels, *Concentration Camps, USA*, pp. 68–70. Lippmann's biographer reports that in the "early 1970s" the pundit still insisted that "it was the right thing to do at the time," but he remembered that the reason was "to protect the Japanese-Americans from the hysterical mobs on the West Coast" (Ronald Steel, *Walter Lippmann and the American Century*, pp. 393–95).

broadcasts from London, told a Seattle audience on January 27, 1942: "I think it's probable that, if Seattle ever does get bombed, you will be able to look up and see some University of Washington sweaters on the boys doing the bombing!"[25]

The psychological impact of the attack on Pearl Harbor was tremendous. In the ensuing crisis, some of the best and worst instincts of the American people came into play. It is one of just two events in the twentieth century—the other is the assassination of John Kennedy—which almost all Americans who were not mere infants at the time can remember vividly. Even today, if asked where they were and what they were doing that Sunday when they first heard the news, they can provide concrete details.

This being true for Americans generally, the impact for Japanese Americans was all the more intense. Not only were they identified with the enemy but almost all facets of their lives were changed, and changed for the worse. In the course of a few months' time, their world was disrupted. The overwhelming majority of them were in some kind of federal custody as hostages of a war they had never made, as victims not of the enemy but of a government most of them had learned to call their own.

I have, elsewhere, described in considerable detail both the decision making process that brought about the incarceration of the Japanese Americans and the nature of that incarceration, so it will only be briefly treated here. First and foremost, it must be understood that whatever significance the relocation, as it is usually called, might have for American history in general, it remains *the* central event of Japanese American history. "Before the war," "after camp"—these and similar phrases punctuate the life history of almost every mainland Japanese American family. It is now quite clear to all but a few diehards and self-serving survivors among its architects and executors that the relocation was wrong. As President Gerald R. Ford stated on February 19, 1976: "We know now what we should have known then—not only was [the] evacuation wrong, but Japanese-Americans were and are loyal Americans."

Although the stated reason for the evacuation was "military necessity," it is now known that politicians and not generals were its prime movers. Had General George C. Marshall and our other top military planners been in charge, Japanese America would have been left largely undisturbed. Our military leaders knew that a full-scale invasion of North America was beyond the capabilities of Japanese

---

25. Freeman Mss., UWA, quoted in letter, Miller Freeman to L. P. Sieg, President, University of Washington, January 29, 1942.

forces, although hit-and-run naval raids were a possibility. Quite properly, however, our society is subject to political and not military decision-making. What is particularly disturbing about the Japanese American situation is that the civilians used a false doctrine of "military necessity" as a rationale for their political decision, and, in a mood of wartime blindness, the Supreme Court of the United States accepted the claim without requiring even a scintilla of evidence.

The destruction of Japanese America began immediately after Pearl Harbor. On the night of December seventh, the Federal Bureau of Investigation, working with lists in part provided by the Office of Naval Intelligence, began taking into custody Japanese Americans who had connections to the Japanese government. These were mostly Issei. The imperial government, as we have seen, had supported and in some cases inspired most of the organizations of the older generation. Similarly Japan had subsidized Buddhism in most places where Overseas Japanese settled. The United States government's security agencies, working on the principle of guilt by association, simply rounded up most of the leaders of the Japanese American community. Officers of the Japanese associations, leaders of local business groups, language-school teachers, and Buddhist priests were arrested, interrogated, and, in most cases, sent to internment camps under the jurisdiction of the Immigration and Naturalization Service. Almost all of these were male enemy aliens, traditional targets in time of war. Unlike naturalized German and Italian resident aliens, the Japanese had been ineligible for naturalization, except for a handful who had served in the American forces during World War I.

In any event, about 1,500 Issei were arrested on the night of December seventh. Eventually more than 2,000 of them were interned in camps in Montana, New Mexico, North Dakota, and elsewhere. These Issei internees have been largely ignored by the historians and chroniclers of Japanese America, mostly because what happened to the rest of the West Coast Japanese was so unprecedented: internment was, after all, fully "legal." But the guidance and stability that these elders might have provided during the ensuing crisis was an important loss to their community. In addition, their story is worth telling for its own sake.

Iwao Matsushita, a gentle and scholarly Seattleite, is the person on whom I will focus; I use him because he left papers that have survived intact and are accessible.[26] But I am convinced that he is not

---

26. Iwao Matsushita Mss., UWA. I hope to publish a collection of Matsushita's letters from Fort Missoula.

unrepresentative. He was born on January 10, 1892, in Fukuoka-ken, and he was graduated from a Kobe high school and from the English Department of the Tokyo University of Foreign Languages in 1914. During his student days in Tokyo, Matsushita had spent a summer teaching Japanese to a British diplomat. After graduation, he had taught English for five years in a high school in Hiroshima-ken.

He came to Seattle in 1919 and worked for Mitsui & Company, chiefly as office manager. He was a *yoin* (hired employee) rather than a *seiin* (formal employee) and so Mitsui laid him off in 1940 when trade between Japan and America was being closed down. He then got a job with the Seattle Japanese Chamber of Commerce compiling trade statistics. His real desire, apparently, had been to get a position teaching Japanese at the University of Washington, and he had pioneered the establishment of a Japanese language course there. Hoping for a permanent appointment, he had taught for a year (1927–1928) without compensation, but despite the positive recommendation of the Department of Oriental Studies, no regular position had materialized.

Matsushita was apparently a prime target because of his employment both by a Japanese firm and by the chamber of commerce. He was picked up just after Pearl Harbor. After being interrogated and held in Seattle for three weeks, he was shipped off at the end of December to the internment facility at Fort Missoula, Montana. His fellow inmates were mostly Italian merchant seamen. Conditions at Fort Missoula were humane and were governed by the Geneva Convention.

The Italian and Japanese prisoners amused one another: "The other night," Matsushita wrote his wife, "we were entertained by a string quartet of the Italian detainees & we were really entranced by their excellent operatic music including Madam Butterfly."[27] That summer, the Japanese came into their own on the diamond:

> We had a baseball match between Japanese & Italian seamen's teams. As it was the first Italo-Japanese game we ever had, almost everybody turned out to see the contest. All players marched into the ground headed by the Italian band, & it was real fun as Italians did not know the rules and made many errors. Our team made an easy 27–7 victory over Italians.[28]

Matsushita taught English, was sometimes allowed out to climb mountains—as a good Seattleite he compared them unfavorably to his

---

27. Matsushita Mss., UWA, postcard, Iwao Matsushita to Hanaye Matsushita, February 28, 1942.

28. Ibid., postcard, Iwao Matsushita to Hanaye Matsushita, July 20, 1942.

"beloved Mt. Rainer"—and was eventually elected "mayor" of the "Japanese Camp." Meanwhile, his wife Hanaye was in deteriorating mental health. She had been evacuated to the assembly center at Puyallup, Washington, and then to the relocation center at Minidoka, Idaho. Matsushita desperately tried to obtain not freedom but incarceration with his wife in Minidoka, where conditions and creature comforts were less pleasant than at Missoula. After almost a year at Missoula, he appealed to Attorney General Francis Biddle:

> I was born a Christian in a Methodist minister's family, educated in an American Mission School, came to this country in 1919 from sheer admiration of the American way of life. I have always been living, almost half and best part of my life, in Seattle, Wash., and never went to Japan for the last twenty-four years, despite the fact there were many such opportunities, simply because I liked this country, and the principles on which it stands.
>
> I have never broken any Federal, State, Municipal, or even traffic laws, and paid taxes regularly. I believe myself one of the most upright persons. I have never been, am not, and will never be potentially dangerous to the safety of the United States. There isn't an iota of dangerous elements in me, nor should there be any such evidence against me. . . .
>
> My wife, with whom I have never been separated even for a short time during last twenty-five years, and who has the same loyalty and admiration for this country, is living helplessly and sorrowfully in Idaho Relocation Center. You are the only person who can make us join in happiness and let us continue to enjoy the American life.[29]

Perhaps as a result of this letter, Matsushita was allowed to file for a rehearing in April 1943. But at the end of December 1943 he was still in Montana, still pleading for "special permission to live with my wife in Hunt, Idaho Relocation Center." He wrote to the United States Attorney in Seattle:

> Many friends of mine who were here with me in 1942 and later transferred south . . . are now enjoying reunion with their families.
>
> My wife, who is ill and under a doctor's care . . . has been patiently waiting for my return for two long years. . . . This was the third Christmas she had to observe so miserably. I don't like her to be tortured like this on account of my being detained here. I like to help her, nurse her, and cheer her up. When I heard a certain wife

---

29. Ibid., letter, Iwao Matshushita to Francis Biddle, January 2, 1943.

died alone without her husband at her side, I simply couldn't but shudder at the thought that the same fate might be falling upon us. As we never lived apart in our married life for 23 years before my apprehension, it is simply unbearable to have to live like this for so long. . . .

I can assure you that there is not one iota of danger to the safety of the American public when I am allowed to live with my wife.[30]

Finally, in mid-January 1944, the Matsushitas were reunited in the concentration camp at Hunt after more than two years of separation.[31] Other internees had been released earlier, and several hundred had chosen repatriation on the exchange ship *Gripsholm*.

The majority of the male Issei and the rest of the Japanese American community were not interned, although there can have been few in the community who were not affected, one way or another, by the wave of internment which took away almost every tenth adult Issei male. Apart from the psychic shocks of the coming of the war and the roundup, all Japanese Americans were affected almost immediately by restrictive government regulations. The community quickly discovered that the legal distinction between citizen and alien was not nearly as important as the distinction between white and yellow, especially if yellow happened to be Japanese. Chinese Americans, especially in the West, became aware of the difference. Many took to wearing buttons that proclaimed positively: "I'm Chinese." Some joined the white persecution with buttons that added: "I Hate Japs Worse than You Do."

Although Attorney General Francis Biddle, in his memoirs, blamed white westerners for what happened to the Japanese Americans—"there was little hysteria for the first few months after Pearl Harbor, almost none until the West Coast suddenly discovered that the Japanese were a menace"—Biddle himself was responsible for the very first act of wartime discrimination against citizens.[32] The Department of Justice issued regulations on December 8 closing our land borders with Canada and Mexico to all enemy aliens and "all persons of Japanese ancestry, whether citizen or alien." Between that time and

---

30. Ibid., letter, Iwao Matsushita to J. Charles Dennis, December 23, 1943. The decision to release him had already been made (see ibid., letter, Edward J. Ennis, Director, Alien Enemy Control Unit, Department of Justice, to Hanaye Matsushita, December 18, 1943). Release policies were, at best, inconsistent.

31. At Minidoka, Matsushita taught American history and English. He eventually returned to Seattle, where he first worked for the War Relocation Authority aiding in resettlement and then secured a position at the University of Washington teaching Japanese. He later was employed in its Far Eastern Library. He died in 1979.

32. Francis Biddle, *In Brief Authority*, p. 209.

March 2, 1942, the official statements of the federal government observed the distinction between alien and citizen Japanese Americans in theory, but in practice its actions affected and almost paralyzed the whole of Japanese America.

In the first place, most of the citizen generation still lived in households headed by enemy aliens: their parents. When the government froze the bank accounts of enemy aliens and closed down American branches of Japanese banks, so much of the community's financial assets were tied up that it became very difficult and in some cases impossible for the ethnic economy to continue to function. Those businesses that depended on continuing lines of credit were simply cut off.

In the second place, continuing raids, with or without search warrants, were made throughout Japanese America from the very outbreak of the war. The following memoranda were exchanged between the army and the Department of Justice on January 6, 1942, but they reflected what had been going on for almost a month. Note particularly the Aesopian language employed to make procedures seem more regular than they were. Biddle, in his memoirs, talks about "spot raids" and "warrants," but the raids became general and warrants often were not used. Under the procedures agreed to within the executive branch, the judiciary was ignored.

> 4. *Searches and Seizures:* A warrant authorizing the search of the premises of an enemy alien for the presence of contraband may be obtained merely on application to the United States Attorney. It is only necessary to support the issuance of such a warrant that it be stated that the premises are those of an enemy alien. In an emergency where the time is insufficient in which to procure a warrant, such premises may be searched without a warrant.[33]

Given the incidence of enemy aliens in the population and the patterns of residential segregation, this meant, for the overwhelming majority of Japanese Americans in the West, that, if not your house or apartment, the house or apartment next door was likely to be the subject of an unannounced search.

> 5. *Mixed Occupancy Dwellings:* The search of mixed occupancy premises or dwellings [that is, places where both Issei and Nisei

---

33. U.S. War Department, *Final Report: Japanese Evacuation from the West Coast,* 1942, pp. 4–6. The quoted paragraphs are from identical memoranda exchanged on January 6, 1942, between General John L. DeWitt and James Rowe, Jr., an Assistant Attorney General.

lived] may be by warrant only. In emergencies involving contraband such as radio transmitters, it may be necessary to keep the premises under surveillance while a search warrant is procured. As previously noted, however, in such an emergency an alien enemy's premises may be searched for contraband without a warrant.

6. *Multiple Searches:* The term "mass raid" will not be employed by the Attorney General. Instructions . . . will permit "spot raids." That is to say, if lists of known alien enemies with the addresses of each are prepared by the F.B.I. and warrants are requested to cover such lists, a search of all the premises involved may be undertaken simultaneously. Thus all of the alien enemy premises in a given area can be searched at the same moment.

Thus, even before the military took over, Japanese America had been deprived by Biddle and the Department of Justice of constitutional protection under the Fourth Amendment, which provides that "the right of the people to be secure in their persons, houses, papers, and effects, against unreasonable searches and seizures, shall not be violated, and no warrants shall issue, but upon probable cause, supported by oath or affirmation, and particularly describing the place to be searched, and the persons and things to be seized." Under wartime conditions, being ethnically Japanese had become, in itself, probable cause.

Although little physical violence was used by the government, what took place in Japanese America can only be described as a reign of terror. Those who wonder today about the relative lack of resistance in the Japanese American community to the demands of the federal authorities should ponder well the cumulative effects of various governmental actions. A teen-aged Nisei girl from San Jose described what happened at her house:

One day I came home to find two F.B.I. men at our front door. They asked permission to search the house. One man looked through the front rooms, while the other searched the back rooms. Trembling with fright, I followed and watched each of the men look around. The investigators examined the mattresses, and the dressers and looked under the beds. The gas range, piano and sofa were thoroughly inspected. Since I was the only one at home, the F.B.I. questioned me, but did not produce sufficient evidence of Fifth Columnists in our family. This made me very happy, even if they did mess up the house.[34]

---

34. War Relocation Authority Mss., Bancroft Library, contained in a collection of letters from Poston, 1942–1945.

What were the tangible results of thousands of these "legal" searches? Attorney General Biddle himself admitted to their fruitlessness in May 1942, *after* the decision to relocate the Japanese Americans had been made:

We have not uncovered through these searches any dangerous persons that we could not have otherwise known about. . . . We have not found among all the sticks of dynamite and gunpowder [most of which came from two Japanese-owned stores, one of which specialized in sporting goods] any evidence that any of it was to be used in a manner helpful to our enemies. We have not found a camera which we have reason to believe was for use in espionage.[35]

But such searches continued, even within the detention camps set up by the army.

Japanese America was in shock as a result of the attacks of both the Japanese and American governments; for the first time in community history there was mass unemployment. Many establishments in the ethnic economy were forced to close their doors, and a sizable percentage of those who worked for Caucasian employers, private and public, lost their jobs one way or another. In Seattle, for example, twenty-seven Nisei young women who worked as clerks in the public schools became the target of a PTA group, which feared that they might sabotage air-raid precautions. "After all," one mother was quoted as saying, "in the event of a raid on the city, they would be the ones to take any calls intended to put the schools on the alert." In a reaction typical of their community response, the Nisei women resigned as a group while stating that their motive was "to prove our loyalty" and contribute to "national unity in spirit." One local paper called the move "a graceful act," while a PTA mother commented, apparently without intended irony, "I think that's very white of those girls."[36]

Within the Japanese American community, leadership naturally devolved on the young citizen Nisei and their chief organization, the Japanese American Citizens League (JACL). Its leaders were stunned, but some of them, at least, realized that a vacuum had to be filled. They tried to assume leadership for the whole community. The JACL had been a tiny minority of a minority. As we have seen in Los Angeles, it had but 650 members in a population of 20,000 eligible Nisei; according to Bill Hosokawa, "in the weeks after the war's

---

35. Biddle, *In Brief Authority*, p. 221.
36. Bill Hosokawa, *JACL: In Quest of Justice*, p. 150.

outbreak, JACL's membership nearly tripled to some twenty thousand as Nisei rushed to join."[37]

Immediately after the war broke out, the JACL had wired President Roosevelt pledging its support and affirming the loyalty of Japanese Americans: the White House turned the telegram over to the State Department, the arm of the government usually designated to communicate with foreigners. The State Department coolly responded by letter that "your desire to cooperate has been carefully noted." In a number of communities, militant JACLers formed patriotic defense communities to mobilize Japanese Americans in the war effort, to publicize their patriotism, and to disassociate themselves from their parents' generation, particularly from its leadership, which they regarded as misguided and even subversive. One such group was the Anti-Axis Committee of the Los Angeles JACL.[38] A leader of that committee, Tokutaro Nishimura "Tokie" Slocum, an Issei (b. 1895) who had gained citizenship through service in the United States Army during World War I, was highly critical of the prewar leadership of both generations:

> We are facing this problem today because of the short-sightedness of the Japanese leaders in America up to this time. They thought only in terms of being Japanese. In order that we not repeat the mistake that our fathers made, we must break our ties with Japan. It is in this time of crisis that we must take advantage of the opportunity to test our mettle. How we meet this problem will determine the destiny of Japanese Americans as Americans. We must not expect comfort or luxury in time of war. Cooperation with the federal government is essential.[39]

His colleague Togo Tanaka, a young journalist and a Phi Beta Kappa graduate of UCLA, spoke on Los Angeles radio station KHTR on the night of December 7. Tanaka told his fellow Nisei: "As Americans we now function as counterespionage. Any act or word prejudicial to the United States committed by any Japanese must be warned and reported to the F.B.I., Naval Intelligence, Sheriff's Office, and local police."[40]

This talk of cooperation between patriotic Nisei and intelligence and law enforcement officers was more than rhetoric. In Los Angeles

---

37. Ibid., p. 160.
38. Cited in John Anson Ford Mss., Box 64, Huntington Library.
39. Hosokawa, *JACL*, p. 168.
40. Ford Mss., Box 64, Huntington Library. Togo Tanaka has denied that he said this.

several Nisei, most if not all of them leaders in the JACL, had been cooperating as informants for some time. This evidence refutes the charge often made by government officials, and never denied by the intelligence specialists concerned, that one of the reasons no Japanese could be trusted was that none of them ever informed on other Japanese.

Evidence of this cooperation is to be found in the files of the Los Angeles Anti-Axis Committee and in the personal papers of the leading naval intelligence specialist on the Japanese Americans, Lt. Commander Kenneth D. Ringle. More, I suspect, could be turned up by use of the Freedom of Information Act to comb FBI files. Ringle's papers, now in the hands of his son, a Washington journalist, give fascinating glimpses into the fuzzy world of prewar counterespionage. Unlike almost everyone else in the government involved with judging Japanese Americans, Ringle had knowledge of the Japanese language and culture, having been a navy language student in Japan from 1928 to 1931. In 1940 he was assigned as a naval intelligence officer in Los Angeles, where, as he put it:

> I made it my business to get acquainted with and know personally the young American of Japanese ancestry, because I believed that the normal Americanization processes of our public schools plus the dying off of the original Japanese stock was reducing the internal menace to our security to negligible proportions. My reasoning was this: The last Japanese to enter the United States legally, did so in 1924. His life and business were here. The Japan he left in 1924 was not the Japan of 1941. If he left there as a young man of 20 in 1924, he had to be thirty-six in 1940, and most of them were over twenty at the time of entry. Hence, the average age of immigrants approached fifty. Of the 150,000 (approximately) persons of Japanese ancestry in the United States in 1940, 60% were American born and American citizens. [The precise numbers were 126,947, and 62.7%.] The service intelligence services, local police, immigration and other Federal agencies had been observing these people for many years and compiling records on many individuals. In the Los Angeles area, where there was the greatest concentration in the United States, some four hundred and fifty dangerous persons, including all the pro-Japanese leaders so far as was known, were arrested as individuals before midnight on 7 December 1941 and were interned. Where then was the potential danger that made it necessary to intern every other person of Japanese ancestry in the Spring of 1942? This I can say with authority. In later careful investigations on both the West Coast and Hawaii, there was never a shred of evidence found of sabotage, subversive acts, spying, or

fifth column activity on the part of the Nisei or long-time local residents. . . . I reported officially in 1941 that it was my considered opinion that better than 90% of the Nisei and 75% of the original immigrants were completely loyal to the United States."[41]

Ringle not only made his views known to his superiors but he published them in *Harper's Magazine* in the autumn of 1942 under the pseudonym of "An Intelligence Officer."[42] He also shared his insights with Curtis B. Munson, a businessman who served as an agent for John Franklin Carter. Carter was running a makeshift intelligence operation for the White House. Carter's operation may charitably be classified "semipro" and was, intellectually at least, a forerunner of the Office of Strategic Services.[43]

In November 1941 Munson sent Carter a report on the Japanese, of which at least a one-page précis was read by Franklin D. Roosevelt. The whole report was sent on to Secretary of War Henry L. Stimson. Munson generally followed Ringle's views, but he transformed the latter's notion that fewer than 10 percent of the Nisei and perhaps 25 percent of the Issei were "not completely loyal." Instead, he uttered a flamboyant prediction that "there are still Japanese in the United States who will tie dynamite around their waist and make a human bomb out of themselves." Munson also claimed to be "horrified" that vital installations such as "dams, bridges, power stations" were completely "unguarded."

It is impossible to demonstrate that Munson's views were of real influence either way in the decision to relocate the Japanese Americans.[44] It is clear, however, that for those who believed Japanese

---

41. Kenneth Ringle Mss., letter, Kenneth D. Ringle to Edward N. Barnhart, February 21, 1952. The Ringle Mss. are in possession of Ringle's son Kenneth, who graciously allowed me to examine them and to copy materials.

42. Kenneth D. Ringle [An Intelligence Officer], "The Japanese in America: The Problem and the Solution," *Harper's Magazine* 185 (1942): 489–97. Ringle's appreciation was written for the War Relocation Authority while he was on TDY to that organization and was given to *Harper's Magazine* by someone at the WRA. Its publication was approved by the Navy Office of Public Relations. After its publication, the office of the Chief of Naval Operations said that it had been approved in error. See Ringle Mss., letter, Rear Admiral H. C. Train to Dillon Myer, October 12, 1942.

43. I reached this conclusion from a perusal of the John Franklin Carter Mss. at the University of Wyoming. Using other materials, Bradley F. Smith, *The Shadow Warriors: O.S.S. and the Origins of the C.I.A.*, has come to the same conclusion. See also Jeffrey M. Dorwart, *Conflict of Duty: The U.S. Navy's Intelligence Dilemma, 1919–1945*, pp. 168–69 and passim.

44. FDR sent Curtis Munson's report to Secretary of War Henry L. Stimson. Stimson Folder, Franklin D. Roosevelt Library (hereafter FDRL), memo, FDR to Henry L. Stimson, November 8, 1941.

to be sinister and treacherous, Munson's irresponsible imaginings and Ringle's cautious notions about loyalty could be used to justify almost anything. It is also clear that there were Nisei who felt that some Japanese Americans were potential spies and saboteurs, which may be taken as one more attribute of their Americanization.

Conversely, the erratic Munson had noted in October 1941 that "the Japs here are in more danger from us than we are from them." Also, in February 1942, observing with horror a process that one of his earlier reports may have helped to promote, Munson warned that "we are drifting into a treatment of the Japanese corresponding to Hitler's treatment of the Jews."[45] Other good advice received by Roosevelt through intelligence sources reporting directly to him included comments by John Steinbeck and the former head of army intelligence Ralph Van Deman. In mid-December 1941 Steinbeck insisted that "there was no reason so far to suspect the loyalty of Japanese-American citizens." In mid-February 1942 General Van Deman described a mass removal of Japanese from the West Coast as unnecessary, impractical, and "about the craziest proposition that I have heard of yet."[46]

Kenneth Ringle had an unrevealed reason to believe that Japanese Americans were not a serious threat. In the spring of 1941 he had organized what E. Howard Hunt would have called a "bag job"; that is, a surreptitious break-in at the Japanese consulate in Los Angeles with the assistance of local police, the FBI, and a criminal he liked to refer to as "our own safecracker." In addition to materials about actual Japanese espionage, none of which involved resident aliens, Ringle found evidence that Japanese officials regarded Japanese Americans of both generations as "cultural traitors" who were not to be relied upon for anything important.[47]

Ringle's sensible views were shared by some senior FBI officials on the Pacific Coast, including both "Nat" Pieper and Richard B. Hood, special agents in charge in San Francisco and Los Angeles.

---

45. President's Secretary's File 122, FDRL, Munson's reports as cited by Smith, *Shadow Warriors*, pp. 100 n9, 433–34. Dorwart, Smith, and I have all seen and used different Munson reports found in different places in Hyde Park.

46. Smith, *Shadow Warriors*, p. 99. Smith also reports two "genuine horrors" in that advice. Atherton Richards, a key subordinate of William J. Donovan in the OSS, wanted the island of Hawaii turned into an "obligatory rendezvous" for "doubtful Japanese," while movie director John Ford, who was making a government film about Pearl Harbor, "believed that the majority of Japanese-Americans were 'tainted' and deserved to have no mercy shown."

47. The story of the "break-in" is told by Ringle's son Kenneth in a feature story in the Washington *Post*, December 6, 1981. For other ONI "surreptitious entries," see Dorwart, *Conflict of Duty*, pp. 38–46.

Although some Nisei had been cooperating with Ringle before Pearl Harbor, it was apparently only on December 19, 1941, that "members of the Anti-Axis Committee came" to Hood at the FBI Los Angeles Field Division and offered him "the facilities of the entire Japanese American Citizens League." What particularly pleased Hood was that while various organizations of both generations had previously offered to cooperate with the bureau, there "had always been a reluctance on their part to furnish any specific derogatory information concerning any organization or individual." At that meeting and after, as Hood reported to his superiors in January 1942, the JACLers were giving the FBI two things it wanted very much: new names of possible subversives and "the present addresses of several individuals who were the subjects of custodial dentention memorandums and whose present whereabouts were unknown to this office."

Hood included the names of eleven persons, largely Kibei, who had been denounced as disloyal by informants supplied by the Anti-Axis Committee. In addition, the committee had furnished the FBI with lists of all Kibei JACLers in Los Angeles and had promised to deliver a similar list for San Pedro.[48] Despite this cooperation, when Hood testified before a congressional committee at the beginning of March, he complained that "there has not been the response that we feel we should be getting at a time like this," and he agreed when a congressman interpolated that "they are not quite as anxious to inform against their fellow Japanese as some other groups are."[49]

The overwhelming majority of Japanese Americans played a passive role, waiting to see what their government would do with them. Most assumed, long before the event, that they would have to move. As it turned out, not quite all of the West Coast Japanese had to move. Those who lived in the eastern half of Washington and Oregon were not subject to evacuation. Although fewer than one thousand Japanese lived in that area before the war, it did mean that, unlike California, Washington and Oregon continued to have some Japanese residents at liberty throughout World War II.

Had "the rules of the game" been made clear to the Japanese American community, it would have been better able to cope. Instead,

---

48. Ringle Mss., R. B. Hood, Special Agent in Charge, Federal Bureau of Investigation, "Memorandum: Re Japanese Activities, Los Angeles," January 20, 1942. No fewer than sixteen copies of this report were circulated within the bureau, the army, and the navy. For "Nat" Pieper, see Daniels, *Concentration Camps, USA*, p. 39. See also Josephine W. Duveneck, *Life on Two Levels: An Autobiography*, p. 226.

49. U.S. Congress, House, Select Committee Investigating National Defense Migration, *Hearings*, 77th Cong., 2d sess., 1942, p. 11701 (hereafter cited as Tolan Committee, *Hearings*). For parallel activity in Seattle, see below.

there was not only confusion but some actual misinformation was disseminated by the federal government. Although rumors had been circulating in the Japanese American community since the outbreak of war, by mid-February 1942, when Roosevelt signed Executive Order 9066, it was clear that some Japanese were going to be evacuated and that the army was going to be in charge.

In a move that was unrelated to the rest of the evacuation and that was conducted under different authority, the United States Navy at the end of February 1942 had evicted the 500 families that lived on Terminal Island, a strategic location within the Port of Los Angeles. The navy was not concerned about where these families went. Almost all of the Terminal Islanders simply found someplace else to live in Los Angeles County and therefore they were later evacuated by the army as well.

First official notice of evacuation was given to the general population in Lt. General John L. DeWitt's Public Proclamation No. 1, issued on March 2, 1942. The proclamation announced that "such persons, or classes of persons as the situation may require will by subsequent proclamation be excluded from all of Military Area No. 1. . . . [Later the proclamation singled out] Any Japanese, German or Italian alien, or any person of Japanese Ancestry [as its subjects]."[50] The rest of the West Coast was designated Military Area No. 2 (see map 6.1). Military Area No. 1 coincided with the eventual evacuation zone with one significant difference: the eastern half of California, designated as part of Military Area No. 2, was eventually cleared of Japanese by the army. This was done even though DeWitt's first proclamation had plainly stated that "the designation of Military Area No. 2 as such does not contemplate any prohibition or regulation or restriction." During most of March 1942, Japanese in Military Area No. 1 were allowed to move although they were required to file a "Change of Residence Notice" before moving. According to the army's figures, almost half of the 10,000 Japanese who had moved from Military Area No. 1 to avoid being rounded up had then moved to the California portion of Military Area No. 2, where the army got them anyway.

What we now call the evacuation and relocation of the Japanese Americans began on March 24 when Lt. General DeWitt, the West Coast commander, issued a "Civilian Exclusion Order" ominously

---

50. Public Proclamation No. 1 and a number of other documents may be found most conveniently in U.S. Congress, *House Report 2124*, 77th Cong., 2d sess., 1942, pp. 293–351. See also ibid., *House Report 1911*. These are interim reports of the Tolan Committee, issued in May and March 1942.

Map 6.1
Original evacuation zones, March 1942

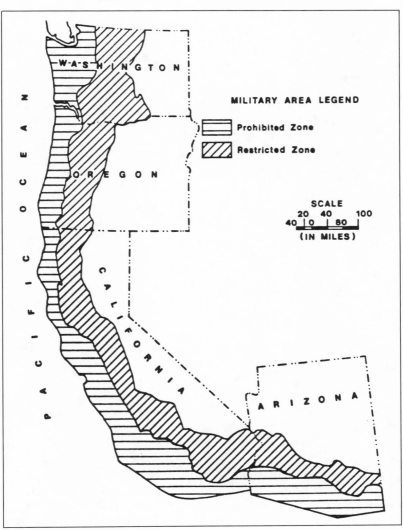

This map shows the area from which Japanese Americans were relocated. The shaded areas represent the original "Military Area No. 1," initially divided into "prohibited" and "restricted" zones, by General De Witt's Proclamation No. 1, March 2, 1942. Eventually, all Japanese in California were relocated; in the other three states those living in unshaded portions were allowed to remain. (Adapted from U.S. Department of War, *Final Report: Japanese Evacuation from the West Coast 1942* [Washington, 1943], fig. 9, p. 88)

Map 6.2
The WRA camps, 1942–1946

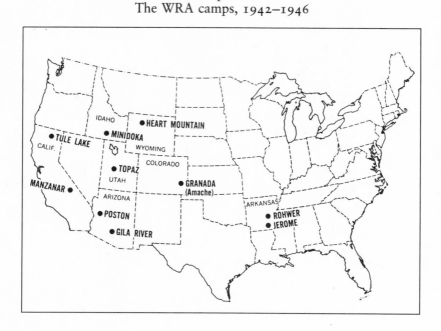

designated "No. 1."[51] Although it affected only some fifty Japanese families living on Bainbridge Island near Seattle, we can now see that it was a dress rehearsal. What happened there set the patterns for the incarceration of more than 100,000 persons, some 70,000 of them native-born American citizens. The Bainbridge Islanders were given six days to be ready to go where the army sent them. As no local facility was yet ready, they were sent all the way to southeastern California, to the camp at Manzanar (see map 6.2). The army, aided by technocrats on loan from the Census Bureau, then divided the rest of the area to be evacuated into 107 districts, with about 1,000 Japanese in each.[52] These districts were evacuated between the end of March and early June. No Japanese family knew long beforehand just

51. Civilian agencies and the local military were given notice on March 20, four days earlier. See U.S. War Department, *Final Report*, pp. 519–21.

52. Roger Daniels, "The Bureau of the Census and the Relocation of the Japanese Americans: A Note and a Document," *Amerasia Journal* 9, no. 1 (1982): 101–05. Census Bureau official Calvert L. Dedrick was an Orwellian figure who suggested the ultimate euphemism, calling the whole removal-incarceration process a "residential control program." See National Archives, Record Group 210, Report of the Special Meeting of Federal Advisory Council, San Francisco, March 16, 1942.

when its time would come, as the army deliberately withheld news of evacuations so that advance information "would not reach any affected person within the evacuation district" before the appointed time.

The army's *Final Report* explained that a seven-day timetable was planned for each "normal Evacuation district":

A. Posting of the Exclusion Order throughout the area: From 12:00 noon of the first day to 5:00 A.M. the second day.

B. Registration of all persons of Japanese ancestry within the area: From 8:00 A.M. to 5:00 P.M. on the second and third days.

C. Processing, or preparing evacuees for evacuation: From 8:00 A.M. to 5:00 P.M. on the fourth and fifth days.

D. Movement of evacuees in increments of approximately 500: On the sixth and seventh days.[53]

Once the notice was posted, evacuees were instructed to bring only those possessions they could carry and were told that the government would store, "at the sole risk of the owner," more substantial household items. They were ordered to bring "bedding and linens (no mattress)," "toilet articles," "extra clothing," "knives, forks, spoons, plates, bowls and cups," and "essential personal effects." No pets were allowed. All over Japanese America, family animals were given away, set free, or, in many cases, simply destroyed. Personal items and household goods could not be shipped to the assembly centers.

Families, whenever possible, were moved as units. Individuals were allowed to move before evacuation if that move would unify a family. Families were not told where they were being sent. Most went to hastily improvised facilities fairly close to home. The fifteen assembly centers were mostly fairgrounds and race tracks with minimum added facilities. Many of the Seattleites were taken to the state fairgrounds at Puyallup and put into the stalls that had once held livestock; many of the Angelenos were taken to luxurious Santa Anita racetrack, but the horse stalls in which they were placed were hardly luxurious. Most centers had no running water or heat; the toilets and scant bathing facilities were communal and without partitions. All was surrounded by mud or dust and, of course, barbed wire, searchlights, and armed soldiers. Male and female, young and old, alien and citizen, every Japanese person remaining in the affected area was in some kind of custody by early summer of 1942.

---

53. U.S. War Department, *Final Report*, pp. 92–100, includes a specimen "Civilian Exclusion Order" and "Instructions."

While many today question the behavior of the Japanese Americans in 1942—"Why did they go so meekly?"—few who have considered the climate of opinion and the possible alternatives believe that Japanese America could have done otherwise than it did. No political group in the larger community—neither the American Civil Liberties Union, which reluctantly urged compliance, nor even the American Communist party, which viewed incarceration of Japanese Americans as a way of defending the Soviet Union—would have supported them. (The few Japanese American Communists supported their own relocation as necessary fuel for the locomotive of history. Party activists such as Karl Yoneda limited their dissident activities within the camps to circulating petitions for a second front in Europe.)

Most Japanese Americans went quietly when they were called, with fear and bitterness in their hearts. The young leaders of the Japanese American Citizens League had been called upon to make an agonizing decision. In the weeks after Pearl Harbor, as we have seen, they had pledged their loyalty as American citizens and had tried to behave as patriotic citizens in a national emergency. Rarely were they allowed to do so.

In Seattle a group of Japanese American women volunteers, including Mrs. Clarence Arai, wife of the Nisei lawyer and JACL leader, had been doing volunteer work under the auspices of the local chapter of the American Red Cross. Shortly after Pearl Harbor, the FBI padlocked the club rooms where they had been meeting and confiscated their working materials. As the chairman of the volunteer special services for the Seattle Red Cross told the story the next year, Mrs. Arai came to her in mid-December and suggested that the local chapter try to get the materials, including about 750 "comfort" kits for service men. The Seattle chapter had a quota of 1,000 such kits and were finding it very difficult to finance the contents, "about one dollar's worth of comfort articles." The FBI did eventually turn over the contents "plus many hundred pounds of candy wrapped in pound boxes, but kept the [kit] bags, which were found stamped 'Japanese Club'. . . . we took the contents to fill our own bags. Fearing possible sabotage, we returned all the candy."[54]

In early 1942 before any official announcements had been made, the JACL leadership had apparently decided to cooperate with the government, no matter what. It is difficult to see, even some forty years later, any viable alternatives to some form of cooperation. But

---

54. Freeman Mss., UWA, letter, Mrs. Otis Floyd Lamson, Member National Committee, Camp and Hospital Services, American Red Cross, to Miller Freeman, July 21, 1942.

the enthusiastic mode of cooperation which the JACL eventually developed makes its rational position in 1942 vulnerable to the attacks of community dissenters four decades later.

Initially, most JACL leaders assumed that the government would differentiate between civilian and alien, between loyal and disloyal. Nonetheless, by late February 1942, when a previously established Select Committee of the House of Representatives investigating "National Defense Migration" held hearings on the West Coast, the JACL position of total accommodation to the government's wishes had already been decided. The testimony given by its spokesmen at the public sessions of the Tolan Committee (named for its chairman, Democrat John H. Tolan from Oakland), was markedly conciliatory in tone. In San Francisco, for example, National Secretary Mike Masaoka of the JACL testified in a prepared statement on February 23:

> When the President's recent Executive order was issued, we welcomed it as definitely centralizing and coordinating defense efforts relative to the evacuatio[n] problem. Later interpretations of the order, however, seem to indicate that it is aimed primarily at the Japanese, American citizens as well as alien nationals. As your committee continues its investigations in this and subsequent hearings, we hope and trust that you will recommend to the proper authorities that no undue discrimination be shown to American citizens of Japanese descent.[55]

If, however, evacuation were deemed a matter of "military necessity," then Masaoka and the JACL would submit:

> With any policy of evacuation definitely arising from reasons of military necessity and national safety, we are in complete agreement. . . . If, in the judgment of military and federal authorities, evacuation of Japanese residents from the West Coast is a primary step toward assuring the safety of this Nation, we will have no hesitation in complying with the necessities implicit in that judgment.

Similar statements came from JACL leaders all along the coast. In Portland, Hito Okada, national treasurer of the JACL, testified on February 26:

> . . . so far as evacuation is concerned, I believe that the aliens should be evacuated. . . . as far as our alien parents are concerned, they are

---

55. Tolan Committee, *Hearings*, pp. 11137–48.

willing to go wherever the United States government wants them. They are not arguing on that point at all. As far as ourselves are concerned, as citizens, we have our homes here, and like other American citizens, we like to have the opportunity of defending them. However, for the best interests of the Nation, we are willing to sacrifice our homes, our money, and our lives if necessary in order that the United States might win this war.[56]

When asked directly by Chairman Tolan whether he thought "wholesale evacuation" was the answer, Okada hedged: "Well, I have heard pro and con. I haven't made up my mind as to that. I have talked to several of our officials, and one said, mass evacuation; another one said partial evacuation. I haven't made up my mind myself. However, I believe if it is necessary, from the danger standpoint, then all should be evacuated."

In Seattle, on February 28, James Y. Sakamoto, a past JACL national president, insisted that Japanese Americans were loyal and that his organization, "both locally and nationally, has, let us say, 'turned in' people [to the FBI] whom we thought should be checked into." Sakamoto argued that mass evacuation was unnecessary, but, like the others, he insisted: "We will be only too happy to be evacuated if the Government orders us, because we feel that the basic loyalty at a time such as this is to obey the order of the Government to which we owe true allegiance."[57]

Sakamoto made it clear that he would have preferred a system in which the citizen generation assumed a kind of loose protective custody for the generation of their parents: "We can have a registration system where every alien must report, let us say, twice a week, to our Japanese American Citizens League headquarters, and if they do not come in to register twice a week, we will report these persons to the Federal Bureau of Investigation, and a check-up will be made."

Of fifteen Japanese Americans who testified, only two directly opposed evacuation. They were James and Caryl Omura, who published a small (circulation ca. 500) Nisei magazine as an avocation. James Omura insisted that the JACL was "leading the American-born Japanese along the wrong channels."[58]

Owing in large part to the leadership supplied by JACLers there

---

56. Ibid., pp. 11353–56.
57. Ibid., pp. 11470–78.
58. Ibid., pp. 11229–33. In an interview in Salt Lake City in March 1983, and in correspondence, James Omura, who "voluntarily" relocated in Denver, could give no "reason" for his behavior. Omura did suggest that his acculturation largely outside of the Japanese American community might be a factor.

was nothing approaching mass resistance or even noncooperation with the army's evacuation orders. Several thousand persons were able to move themselves far enough east so that they were not affected by the evacuation orders, but perhaps as many others moved away from the coast to the interior of California only to find that the entire state was eventually declared a prohibited area.

Only a handful of individuals resisted by deliberately and overtly challenging the legality of the orders which discriminated between citizens of Japanese ancestry and other Americans. There was no communication between these individuals. As one of the most significant protestors, Gordon K. Hirabayashi, explained it later, he had thought that many other individuals would challenge the regulations in one way or another. He was quite surprised that more did not.[59] In part the lack of protest was owing to the accommodationist stance of the JACL; it also was owing to the successful attacks by the JACL on those who did protest.

Apologists for the JACL such as Bill Hosokawa have argued, I think correctly, that the national organization had little choice. Noncooperation as a mass phenomenon could have had disastrous results for the community as a whole. The fairly rapid postwar improvement of the Japanese American image is certainly, at least in part, a fruit of the wartime accommodation of the JACL and most Japanese Americans.

Hosokawa quotes with approval Mike Masaoka's statement in a postwar memoir:

> Both [JACL President Saburo] Kido and I were quite surprised and pleased that there was practically no public outcry or challenge against the decision to cooperate with the Army. We believed that such total compliance indicated the general agreement of the evacuees that cooperation was indeed proper under those tumultuous and threatening conditions.[60]

But the dark side of that compliance, which Hosokawa and others refuse to discuss, is the fact that the JACL tried to stifle all dissent within the community. The JACL leadership not only attempted to impose its views on all Japanese Americans but deliberately denigrated and tried to deprive of all community support those who opposed the wartime tyranny of the American government. The JACL attacked Japanese Americans who, in 1942, attempted to test the

---

59. UWA, interview with Gordon Hirabayashi by Roger Daniels, February 1981.
60. Hosokawa, *JACL*, p. 160.

evacuation in the courts and who, in 1944 and 1945, resisted the draft on grounds of conscience.

On April 7, 1942, for example, as the forced mass evacuation was starting, JACL National Secretary and Field Executive Mike Masaoka issued a "Bulletin" to all JACL chapters urging that no one support Minoru Yasui of Portland, Oregon. Yasui was an attorney and reserve officer who had deliberately violated the curfew and was asking JACL support for the test case he intended to appeal to the Supreme Court of the United States.

> National Headquarters is unalterably opposed to test cases to determine the constitutionality of military regulations at this time. We have reached this decision unanimously after examining all the facts in light of our national policy of: "the greatest good for the greatest number."
>
> We recognize that self-styled martyrs who are willing to be jailed in order that they might fight for the rights of citizenship, as many of them allege, capture the headlines and the imaginations of many more persons than our seemingly indifferent stand. We realize that many Japanese and others who are interested in our welfare have condemned the JACL for its apparent lackadaisical attitude on the matter of defending the rights and privileges of American citizens with Japanese features.[61]

It is impossible to reconcile Masaoka's 1942 concern about the condemnation of "many Japanese and others" with his postwar memoir stating that there "was practically no public outcry or challenge" to JACL policies. There were many such challenges, and subsequent community strife sometimes resulted in violence. This violence, which the incarcerated people wreaked not on their government oppressors but upon each other, stemmed partly from resentment over the usurpation of community power and authority by the JACL minority.

In his 1942 "Bulletin" Masaoka gave eleven reasons to justify the JACL position in denying support to Yasui. These are worth summarizing here:

1. As "good Americans" we should do what our government tells us.
2. To oppose evacuation would be a violation of the JACL's pledge of "whole-hearted cooperation" to FDR.

---

61. JACL, Office of the National Secretary, San Francisco, Bulletin 142, "Re: Test Cases," April 7, 1942. A copy of this document was furnished from the files collected by Aiko Herzig-Yoshinawa for the Commission on Wartime Relocation and Internment of Civilians. Aiko Herzig-Yoshinaga did much to make the commission's work a success.

3. JACL has "continually cooperated" in the hope that our cooperation would inspire a reciprocal cooperation.
4. The "gracious acceptance of all army regulations and orders" is
   "our contribution to the nation."
5. Public opinion is opposed to any resistance. Any challenge could be
   construed as sabotage.
6. Even winning a case [which Masaoka doubted would occur] would
   be a loss, as the general public would resent it. Anyway, we will all
   be evacuated before the Supreme Court acts. "It would appear more
   sensible" to defer all suits until after the war, if ever. "We do not
   intend to attempt to win a case and lose good will."
7. If we challenge the military we may irritate them into treating us
   worse. "Whatever may be said against the procedure followed by
   the Army in conducting this evacuation is one thing, but no one can
   gainsay the statement that they have been tolerant, fair, and as
   reasonable as possible in their treatment of this problem. We do not
   intend to force them to change their attitude on this matter."
8. Attorney General Biddle has argued that no legal challenge to the
   government would prevail.
9. The American Civil Liberties Union has decided not to challenge the
   evacuation. "We are not disposed to question the wisdom of the
   American Civil Liberties Union on questions of this kind."
10. Test cases bring "unfavorable publicity." Masaoka then quotes a
    letter from Hearst's San Francisco *Examiner* attacking Minoru
    Yasui and suggesting that all Japanese Americans be discharged
    from the Army because of his actions: "Yasui [the letter continued]
    took advantage of an American education, going to the University of
    Oregon, and paid that back with the usual Japanese treachery."
    Masaoka reasons that "since our motives are too often misunder-
    stood . . . we believe that test cases should not be made. We do not
    intend to create any unnecessary excuses for denouncing the Japa-
    nese as disloyal and dangerous."
11. Failure to mount a challenge, Masaoka insists, is not "giving up" the
    rights of citizenship but merely "temporarily suspending" some of
    them "in the greater aim of protecting them for all time to come."
    After victory "our rights and privileges will be returned because we
    cooperated."

In a closing peroration reminiscent of Christian eschatology,
Masaoka insists that if Japanese Americans remain meek, they may
inherit the earth. "Because our sacrifice is greater, let us trust that our
rewards in that greater America which is to come will be that much the
greater."

In December 1942 when Minoru Yasui had lost his case in the

Portland Federal District Court, JACL National Treasurer Hito Okada wrote from Salt Lake City to a Caucasian sympathizer. Okada claimed that the organization's policy of cooperation had been justified because "concessions," such as work furloughs, indefinite furloughs, student relocation, and resettlement, would not have been acceded to by the army if the JACL had acted otherwise. Dillon Myer, head of the War Relocation Authority (WRA), had apparently counseled nonparticipation in the case. According to Okada, Myer had told JACL leaders in a closed session: "Do not irritate the Army." Okada and other JACL leaders were concerned because Yasui was receiving much community support. "Our young people have flocked to his cause . . . they do not see the broader aspects of how it may affect the Resettlement Program being pushed by the WRA."[62]

The JACL position of acquiescence to almost anything the government proposed is not unique in the history of American minority group leadership. One is reminded of Booker T. Washington, who also preached the gospel of accommodation, cooperated with the more enlightened members of the white power structure, North and South, and did everything within his power to silence such militant critics as W. E. B. DuBois.

The problems of effective minority group leadership in an overtly racist democracy are more numerous and more difficult than many critics wish to recognize, but one striking feature of minority group leadership in twentieth century America has been the unwillingness of leaders to tolerate a diversity of opinion and tactics within their own group. Minority group leaders have each desired, for obvious reasons, to be the sole voice of their group. And the majority society, for equally understandable reasons, has wanted only one leader to speak for the whole minority group. Japanese American leadership has characteristically been seen as group rather than individual leadership. Mike Masaoka never spoke for himself but always for the collective leadership of the community or the organization. When he retired in the 1970s, the highest accolade that could be paid him was to call him "Mr. JACL."[63]

---

62. Letter, Hito Okada to Mildred Bartholomew, December 4, 1942. This letter was shown to me by Aiko Herzig-Yoshinaga. It is impossible for me to estimate how many young people "flocked" to the cause of Minoru Yasui. Some mimeographed documents in my possession from a Relocation Center (Minidoka?) speak of a Civil Liberties League being formed to support Yasui claiming membership of "300 nisei." The three undated pages are headed "Civil Liberties League." I judge them to date from Fall 1942.

63. I have treated this subject at greater length in my essay, "The Japanese," in John Higham, ed., Ethnic Leadership in America, pp. 36–63. I have benefited from

But, it must be remembered, for almost all of the more than 100,000 West Coast Japanese Americans neither tactics nor strategy were involved. They simply obeyed the orders that came down from the government. Between late March and the end of October 1942, the assembly centers were filled and then emptied, and Japanese Americans were shipped off to the more permanent relocation centers. That second move also meant a change of custody, as assembly centers were run by the army while relocation centers were run by a newly created civilian agency, the War Relocation Authority (WRA). (The exception to this generalization was the camp at Manzanar, which served both as an assembly center and a relocation center: it passed to WRA control on June 1, 1942.)

All but one of the assembly centers—again Manzanar, located in the California desert near Death Valley, was the exception—were close to the centers of Japanese America in a familiar climate where friends could bring packages and exchange brief greetings. The relocation centers, conversely, were deliberately placed in Godforsaken spots in alien climes where no one had lived before and no one has lived since. Two of the relocation centers, Poston and Gila River in Arizona, were located on unused portions of American Indian reservations. Tule Lake in northern California, Minidoka in Idaho, Heart Mountain in Wyoming, Topaz in Utah, and Amache in Colorado were all in desolate western locations with extreme heat in summer and bitter cold in winter; most were part of uncompleted federal reclamation projects. The two camps in the eastern part of the country—Rohwer and Jerome in Arkansas—were on land that the New Deal's Resettlement Administration had intended to distribute to dispossessed tenant farmers. The smallest camps, Amache and Jerome, each held about 7,500 persons; the largest, the complex on the Colorado River at Poston, held just over 18,000.

When the decision to evacuate was made in February, no one in the government had any clear idea of what was going to happen to the Japanese American people. The army was determined that none be left at liberty on the West Coast. Major General Allen W. Gullion, the Provost Marshal General, and his aide Colonel Karl R. Bendetsen, and a few other army bureaucrats originally envisaged the creation of a system in which all enemy aliens, not just Japanese Americans, would be under their jurisdiction for the duration. But General George C. Marshall and his staff quickly scotched that idea, as they did not want to tie up large numbers of troops.

discussions on this topic with John Higham, August Meier, and Elliott Rudwick, and with my student Mark Cowett.

The civilian War Relocation Authority was created on March 18, and Milton S. Eisenhower, the scholarly brother of Dwight Eisenhower and a bureaucrat in the Department of Agriculture, was named its first director. Eisenhower had been told of his pending appointment one week before it became official. After hectic trips to the West Coast—Eisenhower makes it clear in his memoirs that he "knew very little about the problems of the Japanese Americans"—he called a meeting with governors of ten western states, or their designated representatives, at Salt Lake City on April 7. Eisenhower's notion was that he would establish "small inland camps on the model of Civilian Conservation Corps camps which would serve as staging areas for the evacuees as they were moved into private jobs as soon as possible and could resume something like a normal life." As Eisenhower tells the story, which is largely supported by a transcript of the meeting, the governors, with the exception of Ralph Carr of Colorado, were vehemently opposed.

> One governor shouted: "If these people are dangerous on the Pacific coast they will be dangerous here! We have important defense establishments, too, you know." Another governor [Nels Smith of Wyoming] walked close to me, shook his fist in my face, and growled through clenched teeth: "If you bring the Japanese into my state, I promise you they will be hanging from every tree."[64]

After this meeting Milton Eisenhower returned to Washington and reported that he saw "no alternative to the unhappy one of creating evacuation camps where the people could live in modest comfort, do useful work, have schools for their small children, and thus retain as much self-respect as the horrible circumstances permitted." Thus, by early April the decision was made to place a whole people in what were, in fact, concentration camps; the decision was made not by the military but by civilian bureaucrats under pressure from elected representatives

---

64. Milton S. Eisenhower, *The President Is Calling*, pp. 95–127, treats his WRA experience. His recent biographers Stephen E. Ambrose and Richard H. Immerman cogently suggest that "despite all his efforts on behalf of the Japanese-Americans, Eisenhower must live with the knowledge that he presided over a policy according to which the Nisei were, in his own words, 'needlessly uprooted and subjected to indignities of historic proportions'" (*Eisenhower, Educational Statesman*, pp. 59–65). Other errors surface in his memoirs. Eisenhower thought that his successor was named "Meyer" and that "when the war was over a special court was established to cover a major portion of the economic losses of the Japanese-Americans" (*The President Is Calling*, p. 127). When Eisenhower died, the New York *Times* could find space in an obituary of twenty-eight column inches for only one euphemistic sentence about his WRA career: "In 1942 he was named director of the War Relocation Authority, resettling residents of Japanese ancestry" (New York *Times*, May 3, 1985).

of the people. Six days before the meeting with the governors, Eisenhower had expressed his disapproval of the whole process: "I feel most deeply [he wrote his old boss, Agriculture Secretary Claude Wickard] that when the war is over and we consider calmly this unprecedented migration of 120,000 people, we as Americans are going to regret the unavoidable injustices that may have been done."[65]

Milton Eisenhower continued to execute "avoidable injustices" until the middle of June; then he resigned. He never spoke or wrote to the president about righting these injustices. In his letter of resignation, Eisenhower went so far as to tell the president that "public attitudes have exerted a strong influence in shaping the program and charting its direction. In a democracy this is unquestionably sound and proper."

Eisenhower also gave the president his "considered judgment" that the "great majority" of the evacuees had "an essential Americanism." He guessed that 80 to 85 percent of the Nisei were "loyal," which for many security-minded officials would be ample justification for the whole evacuation and relocation program. He also estimated that only 50 percent of the Issei were even "passively loyal," and he suggested that those of either generation "who prefer the Japanese way of life" be sent to Japan. He also asked that the president issue a strong public statement in behalf of the loyal Nisei, institute a more liberal wage policy, and ask Congress to enact a special program of rehabilitation for the evacuees after the war.[66]

More than thirty years later, when he published his memoirs, Milton Eisenhower still could not blame himself for anything that had happened and he still deluded himself about the system he had helped to establish.

We called the relocation camps "evacuation centers." Never did we think of them as concentration camps. Technically, the Japanese-Americans were not restricted to the camps, although in fact they could not return to the Pacific coast and movement without safeguards would probably have endangered their lives, at least in the beginning.

There are three misstatements of fact in that short paragraph. First, the notion that Japanese Americans could not be safe and free

---

65. National Archives, Record Group 16, "Correspondence of the Secretary of Agriculture, Foreign Relations, 2-1, Aliens-Refugees," Letter, Milton Eisenhower to Claude Wickard, April 1, 1942.

66. President's Personal File 4849, FDRL, letter, Milton Eisenhower to FDR, June 18, 1942.

anywhere in the United States was obviously false: some twenty thousand Japanese Americans were at liberty all through the war. While most if not all of them suffered discrimination, that has been the plight of nonwhite Americans for more than three centuries. Second, the notion that "technically" Japanese Americans were free to leave the camps was also untrue. The guards and barbed wire were not there to keep people out. Third, there was the whole vexed question of whether the places in which Japanese were confined should be called "concentration camps."

Franklin Roosevelt himself had no problem with this term. He used it in press conferences to describe the camps. But after realizing what had happened in the Nazi extermination camps, American officials went to great lengths to avoid use of the word. Others have also resisted using the term. Some victims of the Nazis, for example, insist that the term "concentration camp" can only be used to describe their own experience. In fact, the term goes back to the late nineteenth century and stems from Spanish General Valeriano Weyler's policy of "reconcentration" in Cuba—really more like our own strategic hamlet program in Vietnam—and from the British use of the term for their camps for Boer civilians during their conquest of much of South Africa.

Our concentration camps were places where men, women, and children, citizen and alien, were detained. On the basis of one executive order a whole community, the West Coast Japanese, was ordered from its homes and confined without a trace of due process or even an allegation of personal guilt. Japanese Americans were all judged guilty, deprived of much of their real property, and incarcerated, some of them for more than three years, merely by reason of ancestry.

There was no organized physical torture and there was little brutality in the camps run by the WRA. They were not death camps: they cannot be compared to Buchenwald or the Gulag Archipelago. More persons were born in them than died in them. But they were places in which persons were confined; the camps were ringed with barbed wire and with guard towers manned by armed soldiers. And although they were not extermination camps, the American system of humane concentration camps did inflict death on some of its inmates.

The most outrageous instance occurred at the central Utah camp called Topaz just before sunset on the evening of April 11, 1943. James Hatsuki Wakasa, age 63, was shot to death by a sentry from a guard tower.[67] Apparently no person in the camp, either resident or

---

67. The Wakasa material comes from the War Relocation Authority report, "The

WRA official, witnessed the shooting, and the army quickly entered the center and removed the corpse. The first reports released to the press stated that the old man "was attempting to crawl through the fence," but later investigation by the government indicated that this was a lie and part of a coverup initiated almost immediately by the army officer in charge, First Lieutenant Henry H. Miller, commanding officer of the small local military police detachment.

James Wakasa, an Issei bachelor, had been in the United States for forty years. He was a chef by profession and, during World War I, had served the United States Army as a civilian instructor in cooking at Fort Dodge, Iowa. Unfortunately for him, he was not considered important enough to have been interned. The Military Police detachment commander claimed that four warnings had been given to Wakasa before the firing of the single shot that had killed him.

After the shooting, the Military Police detachment had been put on alert; its men were issued Thompson submachine guns and gas masks, and they remained in that aggressive posture for almost forty-eight hours. During that period, the troops harassed and menaced the inmates. At about 10 A.M. Monday, the day after the homicide, part of a committee of inmates investigating the incident approached the area where the body was found. According to an affidavit, they were forced to disperse:

> An Army "jeep" came speeding up from the north on the road beyond the fence and, upon seeing us, came to an abrupt halt. [The inmates said that they, themselves, were about thirty-five feet inside the fence.] The driver stood up from his seat, turned to his companion, and grabbed the sub-machine gun from the latter's hand. He jumped off the jeep and came dashing to the fence pointing his gun at us [and said]: "Scatter or you'll get the same thing that the other guy got."
>
> We immediately obeyed his orders. . . . His companion was heard to emit a loud laugh, one of derision.

Since James Wakasa had been a Japanese national, the Spanish government, the power that represented Japanese interests in the United States, had to be notified. A Spanish vice-consul from San Francisco and a representative from the American State Department soon arrived. Before that, a group of army officers from nearby Fort Douglas had come to investigate. The military rejected, typically, any

---

Wakasa Incident," written by Topaz Reports Officer Russell Bankson. It may be found in a collection of papers Bankson gave to the University of Washington Archives, titled "U.S., War Relocation Authority."

civilian jurisdiction, either by the county sheriff or by the WRA, but promised its own investigation. The officer in charge, a Lt. Colonel Meek, refused to answer eleven questions about the incident put to him by the WRA acting project director.

One of the issues in dispute was how the Memorandum of Understanding between the War Department and the WRA should be interpreted. The memorandum provided that the functions of military police included apprehension and arrest of evacuees and the use of such force "as may be necessary." After the shooting of Wakasa, Lt. Colonel Meek interpreted this to mean, under what he said was "usual procedure," that a command given three times to halt and a shot thereafter constituted an "arrest" as military men understood it. This, of course, was nonsense, as the appropriate military regulations spoke of force commensurate with the situation.

Both the army and the WRA conducted independent investigations. The WRA investigation, which included a post mortem, indicated the following:

> 1. The perforating wound was front to back and "entered the thoracic cage 3rd rib 2 1/2 cm left of mid-sternal line. No powder burn. There is an exit wound measuring 1 cm by 5 cm jagged posteriorly at 6th thoracic vertebra 3 cm right of mid thoracic line.

This evidence was incompatible with the sentry's story that he had shot Wakasa while the inmate was crawling through the fence. It indicates that Wakasa had been facing the guard tower from which the shot came.

> 2. The body was found from 40 to 65 inches inside the fence, that is, its nearest point was more than three feet away and its farthest point was five feet away from the fence. The center of a considerable bloodstain was approximately five feet from the fence.

The army held an inquiry on April 13 which resulted in a court-martial and acquittal for the sentry at Fort Douglas on April 28. Lieutenant Miller did sign, apparently on the instruction of his superiors, a letter promising three things: that the armament carried by his men would be reduced; that the Military Police would not again enter the project center without clearance from the WRA; and that his men would not "molest, injure or exercise any unusual surveillance upon the evacuees of Topaz Center."

While these concessions were, in effect, a confession of error, they were far from meeting the demands of an angry committee of evacuees. The committee wanted clarification about whether "any evacuee going through the fence in an irregular manner can be shot to death by the military police"; wanted the sentry tried in open federal court; and argued that Military Police should shoot at "residents" only in self-defense.

It is clear that the "Wakasa incident," as WRA chronicler Russell Bankson has termed it, was an aberration. Nonetheless—for James Wakasa at least—Topaz, "jewel of the desert," was a death camp.

For most of the "incarcerated people," as the WRA liked to call them, the relocation experience involved dislocation, discomfort, anxiety, and boredom. There were disturbances and "incidents" at most if not all of the camps, but they were exceptional events punctuating a routine of tedium. What we must remember is that a population of nearly 120,000 persons was uprooted, deprived of most of its personal possessions, moved in most instances at least twice, and confined for the better part of three years. Life in the assembly and relocation centers has been described in nonfiction and fiction and has even been depicted with reasonable accuracy on network television. It will not be chronicled in detail here. Eventually the camps became American communities with many of the same kinds of communal institutions that existed in the larger society—schools, libraries, hospitals, newspapers, churches, and even a very circumscribed self-government.

But the camps had one institution not normally present in American society: communal feeding in mess halls. The incarcerated people lined up with trays three times a day to eat wholesome, starchy, and cheap food not usually prepared in the most appetizing manner. We know from the meticulous records kept by Colonel Karl R. Bendetsen's paper soldiers that the average cost of feeding a person in an assembly center was 38.19 cents per day: at the same time the army spent only 50 cents per day on food for active soldiers. Naturally, the food was complained about. But many, especially parents, lodged a more important complaint: the destruction of the traditional family meal was increasing the distance between parent and child. There is no evidence that anyone in the government ever considered spending the money to provide kitchen facilities for individual families or small groups of families.

Housing, unlike feeding, was largely on a family basis. Families were housed in what the WRA called "apartments." These were actually rooms, originally without partitions, of certain standardized sizes. Larger families occupied more than one room. At Topaz, which was typical, there were five basic room sizes: one dimension was 20 feet, the other was 8, 12, 16, 20, or 24 feet. Thus, the largest apartment was a room of 480 square feet. Such an apartment would often be assigned to a family of six. By April 1943 when the camp population had begun to decline, the average family member had 114 square feet of living space; that is, an area 6 by 19 feet. None of the apartments had running water; all eventually had electricity. Heating systems varied: most inmates remember having difficulty keeping warm in winter. There was no air conditioning or cooling system of any kind.[68]

The schools were largely staffed by Caucasian teachers, many of whom were quite dedicated. As federal employees they were paid significantly more than was usual for teachers in the surrounding communities. Despite woeful shortages of such things as scientific equipment, the schools managed to inculcate or maintain, on the surface at least, a great deal of idealism under the circumstances. One of the high-school commencement orators at the Topaz graduation in January 1944 felt that his generation of Japanese Americans, because of the camp experience, had a special mission in the struggle for a peaceful postwar world: "We nisei must set an example for the peoples of the earth by overcoming the bitterness caused by evacuation among the peoples of this nation. We must think, talk and act equally and friendly toward caucasians, negroes and other orientals as hate has never yet overcome the problem of hate."[69]

Significant also, as Harry Kitano has pointed out, was the shedding of minority status. All of the typical "high school activities— a yearbook, football, and basketball teams, cheerleaders, student body organizations, scholarship society—were available, and, for the first time, young Nisei were able to feel themselves in the majority, and to run things. They became student body leaders, athletic, political, and social heroes—roles usually reserved for Caucasians in the everyday world."[70]

Adult education classes were also available. At the Minidoka Relocation Center in Idaho, for example, by February 1943 thirty-two different subjects were taught in forty-six sections with an enrollment of nearly one thousand. The subject matter ranged from accounting to vegetable gardening. The most popular classes were: Americanization, with 260 students; secretarial courses, with 185 students; American History, with 101 students; and American Government, with 56 students. All but eleven of the sections were taught by Japanese Americans.[71]

Librarians, often with the help of Caucasian colleagues on the outside, quickly established libraries inside the places of incarceration.

---

68. War Relocation Authority Mss., UWA, "The Housing Crisis at Topaz."
69. Ibid., "Second Commencement at Topaz."
70. Harry H. L. Kitano, *Japanese Americans.*
71. Kaoru Ichihara Mss., UWA, *Minidoka Adult Education Bulletin* (20 pp. mimeo), March 1943.

One of the first of these, at the assembly center in Portland, Oregon, was established on May 16, 1942, just two weeks after the center opened. The Portland Library Association provided approximately a thousand books for the center and the Portland Public Library donated specialized supplies: ink pads, date stamps, and charge cards. Individuals contributed current magazines such as *Reader's Digest, Life,* and *Time.* Later, the public school system chipped in with about a thousand texts and readers.

The library, housed in two small buildings, was constructed with evacuee labor; as the Nisei librarians reported happily, the shelves were made to order: "we can see and reach even the top shelf without squinting and stretching or climbing stools." Circulation quickly reached 150 books a day—not counting school books and magazines—a high figure for a population of some four thousand, many of whom could not read English. (Anything in Japanese was barred from the assembly centers; later this restriction was relaxed.) Before the Portland assembly center was closed in mid-September 1942, the library had circulated almost two books per inhabitant.[72]

From the very earliest days of the evacuation, camp newspapers and newsletters existed. These semiofficial organs, ostensibly put out by the inmates but always "supervised" by the camp administrations, varied in quality and subtlety. At the worst, they were fawning examples of collaboration.[73] At Manzanar, for example, on April 11, 1942, the following appeared:

> The citizens of Manzanar wish to express in public their sincere appreciation to General John L. DeWitt and his Chiefs of Staff, Tom C. Clark and Colonel Karl R. Bendetsen, for the expedient way in which they have handled the Manzanar situation. The evacuees now located at Manzanar are greatly satisfied with the excellent comforts the general and his staff have provided for them. . . . Thank you, general!

Although one would like to think that the article was written in the tradition of Jonathan Swift, the evidence clearly indicates that it was just bootlicking. The attitude expressed was one of resigned cooperation.

The "Farewell Edition" of the *Evacuzette,* the mimeographed

---

72. Fukano Family Mss., UWA, reports by Kiyoko, Yasuko, and Haruko Tsuboi (9 pp., typescript), n.d.

73. All of the camp and assembly center newspapers are available on microfilm from the Library of Congress. My understanding of them has been heightened by the research of my student Mark Henning.

semiweekly of the Portland assembly center, is probably representative. Summarizing "Health," a staff member wrote: "Medically speaking, there [is] no group of people in any concentration camp or any community of 3,500 people, who are better taken care of, at no expense to themselves, than the people at present confined to the Portland Assembly Center." Regarding health and sanitation measures, all were routinely immunized against typhoid and smallpox, with children getting shots for whooping cough and diptheria as well. A 64-bed emergency hospital and outpatient clinic was set up, with back-up services available at two local hospitals and the University of Oregon Medical School Clinic. Nisei doctors, dentists, and nurses were available.

As for general living conditions, the medical staff wrote that food was "moderately well balanced . . . in adequate amounts" and "although quarters were not very good, and very windy in places, plenty of fresh air was accessible at night. Plenty of good water was furnished, and hot water was provided in sufficient quantities to allow a person to take a bath every other day."

The summary ended on a relatively positive note: "Yes, there are many things lacking at this Center so far as the promoting of health is concerned but the full resources of the Government are being placed at the people's disposal to safeguard health."

Even Minoru Yasui, who was challenging the whole process in the courts, counseled good cheer and resignation. Admitting that their stay had been "a chaos of soul-stagnating boredom, of restrictive regulations, and of physical discomforts," Yasui was pleased that the Portland center evacuees had "thus far endured without violence." Although he looked forward to eventual release, he warned his fellow evacuees to "be prepared to undergo greater sacrifices." Nevertheless, he urged them to "go forth, not with sadness or with heavy hearts, but firm with the conviction that we shall unceasingly dedicate ourselves to the perpetuation of the democratic ideals and the principles of freedom."

The most negative comment came from Managing Editor Sho Nojima. Upon discovering that the Washington and Oregon evacuees were going to be in "segregation" in Wyoming and Idaho, Nojima reported himself "shocked . . . to an inexpressible degree." Probably, like most of the Nisei optimists, he had thought that after a relatively brief incarceration, the demonstrably loyal would be paroled into the interior.

Self-government in the relocation process was a matter of convenience each side. The United States at first acted through the army and through the Wartime Civil Control Administration (WCCA) of Lt. General DeWitt. Later the government acted through the WRA and found it useful to have some evacuees govern, regulate, and manipulate their fellow Japanese Americans: this was simpler and certainly cheaper than having large staffs. From the government's point of view the Japanese who implemented its orders were, in essence, trustees in a prison system, monitors in a crowded school. From the point of view of the impounded people themselves, or most of them, there were clear advantages in having some of their own empowered to help shape not basic policy—that came down from Washington—but, rather, the day-to-day execution of that policy.

The words "collaborator" and "collaborationist" have been given a bad name by the World War II experience in Norway and elsewhere. But no terms more aptly describe most of those who exercised authority within the Japanese American community. It has been suggested that the self-government groups inside America's concentration camps be compared to the *Judenrats* or Jewish councils, which the Nazis set up to aid in their governance of the Jews of Germany and occupied Europe. Similarities exist, but there is one overriding, fundamental difference: the men of the *Judenrats,* however unwittingly, were collaborating in the extermination of their people; the Japanese men who helped supervise the evacuation and relocation were collaborating in a process that eventually led to freedom for most of their people. Nevertheless, in each case, some of the oppression was effected by the collaborators. They themselves would argue, probably correctly, that Caucasians would have been even more oppressive. But then and later, collaboration itself was one of the factors that led to disunity and discord among the oppressed.

The history of the relocation is punctuated by disagreements and sometimes violence within the evacuated community. I know of no documented instance in which that violence was directed, initially, against Caucasian oppressors. The chief targets—and the easiest ones—were the Japanese American collaborators. Usually stigmatized as *inu*—literally "dog" but in the camp context "informer"—some of the collaborators eventually had to be rescued by the government from their own people, taken out of camps, and protected temporarily in isolation units. Larry Tajiri, Managing Editor of the *Pacific Citizen,* the JACL organ, wrote in 1943 to a sympathetic Caucasian that "of thirty men beaten by gangs at the relocation centers, twenty-nine were prominent members of the J.A.C.L."[74]

The most thoroughgoing example of evacuee self-government of

---

74. *Common Ground* Mss., Immigration History Research Center, Folder "L. Tajiri," letter, Larry Tajiri to Margaret Anderson, March 8, 1943. I learned of this document through my student Deborah A. Overmyer.

which I know occurred in the assembly center constructed on the state fairgrounds at Puyallup, Washington, a center some of the inmates named "Camp Harmony." Nowhere else did inmates have as much direct control over other inmates; in addition, nowhere else was the characteristic collective or group leadership of the Japanese American community replaced by the leadership of a dynamic individual. The leader was James Y. Sakamoto, a maverick whose flamboyant life and career would have stood out in any prewar ethnic community but nowhere more so than in contrast with the "grey flannel" conservative style adopted by almost all of the other successful Japanese American leaders.

Sakamoto was born in Seattle in 1903 to parents whose 1894 arrival in the Northwest made them pioneer Issei.[75] He first appears in the public record as a seventeen-year-old schoolboy chosen to testify before a committee of the United States House of Representatives investigating Japanese immigration. He seems cocky and bright, assuring his interrogators that he is loyal to America and not to Japan. The brief interchange below, between the high school boy and a Colorado Republican representative, gives us some notion of his personality and self-assurance:

> Mr. [Howard H.] Vaile: Well, you know you are claimed as a citizen by Japan and also by the United States?
> Mr. Sakamoto: I don't care. I was born here.
> Mr. Vaile: Is it your intention to remain an American citizen [or] be a Japanese citizen?
> Mr. Sakamoto: Why should I not remain an American? I was born here, and why should I go back there? This is my home.
> Mr. Vaile: You intend to remain an American citizen?
> Mr. Sakamoto: Well, nobody is going to stop me.[76]

Despite his obvious intelligence, Sakamoto did not excel in high school except in athletics. He had a reputation as a drinker and a "hell raiser." He left Seattle after graduating from Franklin High School, played semipro baseball, and became a professional welterweight prize fighter. He also worked as English editor of the New York *Japanese American Daily News* and, he often said, "studied at

---

75. Much of what follows comes from biographical materials in the James Y. Sakamoto Mss., UWA. See also Hosokawa, *Nisei*, pp. 182–83, 195–97; and idem, *JACL*, pp. 26–29, 158–59, 271–72 and passim.

76. U.S. Congress, House, Committee on Immigration and Naturalization, *Japanese Immigration Hearings*, 66th Cong., 2d sess., 1921, pp. 1198–1201. A garbled version of this testimony was printed in T. Iyenaga and K. Sato, *Japan and the California Problem*, pp. 223–29.

Princeton—too short a period to mention." In 1927, apparently as a result of injuries suffered in the ring, including detached retinas, he went blind. Returning to Seattle he established an English language weekly, the *Japanese American Courier,* which he managed to keep going until the relocation stopped its publication. He also became involved in Japanese American organizational politics, helped to establish the JACL, and became its second national president, serving from 1936–1938.

Sakamoto's *Japanese American Courier* was very much a vehicle of accommodation. It was also quite conservative, politically and ideologically. In February 1931, for example, Sakamoto supported Herbert Hoover's notions of voluntarism. He suggested that there was no real Depression, maintaining that if everyone would just cooperate with the president, the country could "do away with unemployment."[77] Like almost all of the Japanese American press, his paper was essentially an apologist for imperial Japanese ambitions in China, deriving most of its news of Asia from *Domei* and other Japanese sources. As the crisis between Japan and America worsened, Sakamoto expressed his alarm to his sister in a letter of April 1941:

> There are strong possibilities of this nation becoming more involved in the present world crisis than it is now. The relations with Japan in particular are not improving. . . .
>
> After all, we are like a Yo-shi [adopted child] to America. If we are not to disgrace the people of Yamato we are honor bound to remain loyal Americans. Search your own heart, Katie, you've never been to Japan. America has always been your country. Despite the trials and tribulations our parents had to go through fighting discrimination and prejudice, I know that you still love America just as I do. . . .
>
> I might have given you a little scare by saying that we have to accept the worst if we become involved but I, personally, feel that it won't be that bad. During the last world war German Americans suffered a great deal of discrimination. People in this country have become much more enlightened since that time. Of course, we must expect the worst but depending on our ownselves as loyal American citizens we can do much to retain and advance our just position in American life.[78]

When war did come, Sakamoto and others quickly formed a JACL Emergency Defense Council with Sakamoto as chairman. The

---

77. Sakamoto Mss., UWA, letter, James Y. Sakamoto to Kasagi, February 6, 1931.
78. Ibid., UWA, letter, James Y. Sakamoto to Mrs. K. Iyenaga, April 4, 1941.

committee was created to cooperate with various federal bodies, including the Federal Bureau of Investigation. Another early JACL president, Clarence Arai, a local lawyer who had run unsuccessfully as a Republican for the Washington State legislature in 1934, was named chairman of a committee to "report subversive activities in the Community to the FBI."[79] As with other JACL groups, the Seattle members assumed that their community included spies and subversives. Sakamoto wrote of this in a letter to Franklin Roosevelt, after it was clear that there would be an evacuation:

> We know there have been dissident elements among us, often unknown to ourselves. We know that some of the customs brought from abroad do lay some members of our parent [generation] open to suspicion even yet. We, like our fellow citizens, have complete confidence in the all-seeing eye of the Federal Bureau of Investigation. We have seconded their efforts when told what it was they were searching for and we shall continue to do so.[80]

By the time the evacuation from Seattle to the Puyallup assembly center began in late April 1942, a remarkable and perhaps unique arrangement had been made between the army and the local JACL leaders. According to one contemporary account, the acting provost marshal for Washington and Oregon Lt. Colonel Paul B. Malone suggested to the local leaders that they run the assembly center. In addition, the civilian hired by the army to run the camp, Robert (Bob) Turner, was a personal friend of Sakamoto.[81]

As it worked out, James Y. Sakamoto became "Chief Supervisor" of the "Japanese Staff." Under him were persons in charge of "Personnel," "Intelligence," "Operations," and "Supply," which were each given military-style nomenclature such as G-1, G-2. The camp was divided into four geographical areas, designated A, B, C, and D. One JACLer was placed in charge of each area with an evacuee staff under him. The Japanese staff was the means by which orders were transmitted to the incarcerated people. Sakamoto made this clear in his "Memo No. 1":

> The Chief Supervisor . . . is the only channel through which the actual administrators of the Camp (Japanese Staff) may do business with the WCCA staff. In turn the Chief Supervisor will communi-

---

79. Ibid., UWA, minutes, JACL Emergency Defense Council, December 12, 1941.
80. Ibid., UWA, letter, James Y. Sakamoto to Franklin D. Roosevelt, March 23, 1942.
81. Seattle JACL Mss., UWA, letter, Bill Hosokawa to Office of the National Secretary, JACL, May 7, 1942.

cate with the WCCA staff only through Bob Turner or someone duly delegated to represent him.[82]

All of this, the JACLers insisted, was for the benefit of their fellow inmates. The same memo claimed that "THE ADMINISTRATIVE WORK OF THE HEADQUARTERS STAFF IS BEING CONDUCTED BY REPRESENTA- TIVES OF THE INHABITANTS OF THE CAMP SERVING AS A LIAISON BODY BETWEEN THE WCCA AUTHORITIES AND THE CAMP POPULATION." But, it must be emphasized, this was a role that the JACLers arrogated to themselves. The incarcerated people of the Puyallup assembly center were not asked if they wished to be so represented. When, after some time in camp, the volume of complaints and general "grousing" began to build, Sakamoto arranged for a vote of confidence. This was taken by a show of hands at a head-count formation. Dissidents claimed, then and later, that the overwhelming endorsement Sakamoto thus received would have been greatly reduced, if not overturned, had there been a secret ballot and time to organize opposition. Surviving documents as well as interviews suggest that life at Puyallup was even more regimented and controlled than at other assembly centers.

It has been argued that JACLers were interested in exercising power for its own sake.[83] Sakamoto and his helpers, like JACLers generally, sincerely believed that enthusiastic cooperation with their own oppressing government was the best way to ensure decent treatment during the relocation. Even more important, they believed it was the way to get better treatment after the war. To this end they not only obeyed orders and helped to execute those orders, but also, as we have seen, they tried to stop any Japanese Americans from protesting. National officers went so far as to send gifts of fruit and vegetables throughout the war to high government officials such as Secretary of War Henry L. Stimson and Assistant Secretary of War John J. McCloy. Many JACL leaders were among the first to volunteer for military service when that privilege was restored to Japanese Ameri-

---

82. Hiroyuki Ichihara Mss., UWA, includes a small collection of administrative documents generated by the Japanese American staff at Puyallup.

83. Paul R. Spickard addresses this problem in "The Nisei Assume Power: The Japanese Citizens League [sic], 1941–1942," *Pacific Historical Review* 52 (1983): 147–74. Spickard overstates Issei-Nisei tensions and has inflated notions about what the JACL leaders might have done (e.g., "even prior to evacuation, they had done little to protect Japanese Americans against such abuses as searches and seizures," p. 172). He interprets most of their actions in very unfavorable light, concluding that "when, in the winter of 1941–1942, the federal government offered [the JACL leaders] a chance to move the Issei aside in a swift manner, they seized the opportunity with enthusiasm" (p. 174). It is one thing to criticize the young Nisei leadership; it is another to make them out to be monsters.

cans. But at the same time, it must be noted that some of the JACL clearly enjoyed their power, which flowed not from their own people but from the federal officials with whom they collaborated.

Right from the start they gained advantages. The Seattle JACL office, which helped to coordinate the physical evacuation, was allowed to move to the Maryknoll School in the last area to be cleared of Japanese. From there, with the WCCA and the army in an adjoining office, the JACL helped to make the process a smooth one. Partially as a reward, the JACL was allowed to take files and office equipment to Puyallup, although that was clearly against DeWitt's regulations.[84]

Sakamoto's correspondence would suggest that the evacuation period, particularly during his weeks as chief supervisor at "Camp Harmony," was perhaps the most satisfying of his life. This should not be surprising. Sakamoto had been a marginal ethnic leader and proprietor of a significant but struggling newspaper. The months at Puyallup were the only time that he exercised real power. He hoped to continue his leadership in the relocation center at Minidoka, but it and the other camps were run by the WRA staff. There was no place for Sakamoto to exercise the kinds of leadership and power that he had enjoyed in post-Pearl Harbor Seattle and at "Camp Harmony."

For the rest of the war Sakamoto was limited to concocting chimerical schemes for group and individual relocation and to writing letters of exhortation to others. His postwar fate was even sadder. He had lost his newspaper, the *Japanese American Courier,* in the evacuation and did not have the capital to reestablish it. Eventually a job was found for him as a telephone solicitor for the St. Vincent de Paul Society in Seattle. In 1955 he was run over and killed by an automobile on his way to work. Never, after leaving Puyallup in the fall of 1942, had he exercised significant leadership.

While Sakamoto's leadership during the evacuation was both more effective and more spectacular than that exercised by other local JACL leaders, other such leaders exercised authority in every West Coast locality with a sizable Japanese community and in every assembly center. The move to relocation centers, for a wide variety of reasons, weakened greatly the authority and influence of the JACL and its leaders. This did not come about overnight, but within the camps the JACL influence waned steadily after the middle of 1942.

In the first place, as we shall see, the progressive relaxations of government policy made it easier and easier for young adult Nisei to leave camp. Not only did many JACL leaders leave the relocation

---

84. Seattle JACL Mss., UWA, letter, Bill Hosokawa to Office of the National Secretary, JACL, May 7, 1942.

centers for college, employment, and the military but also the number of those in the incarcerated community who had been its natural constituency—the young, the acculturated, the upwardly mobile—was constantly shrinking. In the second place, the policy of the JACL called for more and more sacrifice: at first it merely required submission to authority; later it asked the community to encourage its sons to volunteer to fight for the government that had incarcerated them. In the third place, continued incarceration in the bleak and alien relocation centers caused increasing bitterness. And finally, as the "loyal" Nisei departed, the weight of opinion of the "neutral" or "disloyal" Issei and Kibei increased. Power and influence in that part of the community which remained incarcerated began to shift back to the older generation and its less acculturated offspring.

According to the War Relocation Authority, 120,313 Japanese Americans had been in its custody at one time or another, as table 6.4 indicates.[85] By the end of 1944, as the mass exclusion orders were being revoked under pressure from the Supreme Court, the population of the camps was down to 79,763. Some 40,000 persons had left camp during 1942–1944. The earliest departures were made by those furloughed to harvest crops or to attend college in 1942. Others had left as a result of enlisting in the military. Later, still more were drafted right out of the concentration camps. A few hundred were repatriated to Japan on one of the voyages of the exchange ship, the Swedish liner *Gripsholm*. 1,990 had died in camp, while 6,485 new American citizens were born behind barbed wire.[86] By far the largest number to leave were those whom the WRA described as "applicants for leave clearance." The government claimed that it had the authority to recall any of those on leave, but apparently that authority was exercised in only one instance, bringing back a family of three which had allegedly aided in the flight of an escaped German prisoner of war. Each successive relaxation of WRA rules involved not only a fight within the government but, in most instances, a further division within the Japanese American community.

Even as the evacuation began—while the Japanese American community sweltered in the made-over stables and livestock pavilions of the assembly centers without clear knowledge of where they were to

---

85. I am using WRA figures, as printed in U.S. Department of the Interior, War Relocation Authority, *WRA: A Story of Human Conservation*, pp. 196–211. The Army earlier gave somewhat different figures. See U.S. War Department, *Final Report*, pp. 381–83.

86. This includes 128 deaths and 504 births, but not six stillbirths, in assembly centers between March 21 and October 30, 1942. U.S. War Department, *Final Report*, p. 202.

Table 6.4
Movement into and Out of WRA Centers, 1942–1946

Numbers of Persons	In	Numbers of Persons	Out
90,491	Assembly centers	54,127	To West Coast
17,915	Direct evacuation	52,798	Relocated to interior
5,981	Born in camp	4,724	To Japan
1,735	From INS internment camps	3,121	To INS internment camps
5,179	Seasonal workers (allowed to work harvests, then to camp)	2,355	To armed services
1,275	Penal and medical institutions	1,862	Died
1,118	Hawaiian Islands	1,322	To institutions
219	Voluntary residents (mostly non-Japanese)	4	Unauthorized departures
120,313	Total persons	120,313	Total persons

SOURCE: War Relocation Authority, *The Evacuated People: A Quantitative Description*, Washington, D.C., 1946, pp. 8, 128.

be sent or what was to become of them—some West Coast college presidents and other academics began a salvage operation to get college-age students out of custody and into schools. With a few exceptions, notably President Rufus B. von Kleinsmid of the University of Southern California, West Coast academics were sympathetic to the aspirations of their Japanese American students.[87] President Lee P. Sieg of the University of Washington, for example, arranged to have special commencement ceremonies held at the Puyallup assembly center, as did several Seattle public high schools.

The key academic, because of his influence and prestige, was President Robert Gordon Sproul of the University of California. Sproul, who had headed the university since 1930, was much more conservative than many of his colleagues and refused to criticize the evacuation itself. Claiming that he was neither "in a position to pass judgment" on the military aspects of the evacuation nor prepared to say that "public opinion would have tolerated any other course," he

---

87. For details, see Daniels, *Concentration Camps, USA*, pp. 98–101; and Robert W. O'Brien, *The College Nisei*.

treated the evacuation as a "necessary evil." In late April 1942 Governor Culbert Olson of California, in a letter perhaps drafted by Sproul, wrote to Franklin Roosevelt that "unless some special action is taken, the education of those who might become influential leaders of the loyal American born Japanese will abruptly be closed. Such a result would be injurious not only to them, but to the nation, since well-trained leadership for such persons will be needed after the present war." Olson proposed that qualified students be allowed to continue their education in whichever non-West Coast institutions would accept them.

Roosevelt sent this letter to United States Commissioner of Education John W. Studebaker for preparation of a reply. For about two weeks the issue was discussed within the administration. According to Berkeley Provost Monroe Deutsch, who was the academic administrator most involved in the struggle to get the students back into colleges, presidential advisor Harry L. Hopkins was a key advocate for the Japanese Americans. Some War Department officials became convinced that continuing the education of the Nisei was a good idea. Milton Eisenhower of the WRA may have been working toward such a goal even before Olson's letter arrived; he reports that he encouraged Roosevelt to act positively upon it. By the middle of May, Roosevelt was convinced. He signed a positive reply to Olson which Studebaker had drafted. Before the 1942–1943 school year started, Roosevelt promised Olson that "qualified American-born Japanese students will be enabled to continue their education in inland institutions." The president assured the governor that Milton Eisenhower and his "Japanese Relocation Authority" [sic] would work out a plan "which will meet with your entire approval." Roosevelt insisted that "I am deeply concerned that the American-born Japanese college students shall be impressed with the ability of the American people to distinguish between enemy aliens and staunch supporters of the American system."

In his somewhat roseate memoirs, Milton Eisenhower, after quoting Roosevelt's statement above, observed in 1974 that he "felt that the President had gained an insight into the human problem that, had it come in February rather than May, might have prompted him to decide against mass evacuation."[88] This was, I think, a misreading of the president. When Roosevelt had approved Stimson's request for authority to put mass evacuation into effect, he had urged him to "be as reasonable as you can." That decision had been an expedient proposed by responsible subordinates. It might have been politically

---

88. Eisenhower, *The President Is Calling*, p. 121.

dangerous not to have made it. From then on Roosevelt, who was not vicious, allowed and even at times encouraged a gradual amelioration; there could have been no politically safer place to start than with American-born college students, especially since he had support from the West Coast educational establishment. Only *after* mass evacuation was the government—or some parts of it—prepared to try to distinguish between loyal and disloyal.

Eisenhower and the educators put together a most successful program that got some 4,300 young persons out of assembly centers and WRA camps and into interior colleges and universities. Although federal financial aid for the students was suggested, it was never granted, but students and other relocatees were provided with train or bus fare to their destinations. The majority of the students were aided by private philanthropy, most of it organized by various Christian groups. A coordinating body based in Philadelphia, the National Japanese American Student Relocation Council, headed by Clarence E. Pickett, executive secretary of the Quaker social-service agency the American Friends Service Committee, performed yeoman service. The students were exhorted to "do well" in school, and it was stressed that their behavior might have important consequences for those still in confinement. This was a heavy burden to place on young people, and many of their letters showed the strain.

From the University of Colorado one student wrote to Berkeley Provost Monroe Deutsch that "it was a thrill to become accustomed to feeling 'free' . . . most of us realize our most important mission [is] being 'good-will ambassadors', and to show that we are also loyal Americans." The college Nisei also tried to keep a low profile, as a University of Nebraska student reported: "all of us have tried to avoid being seen in conspicuous groups and have tried to spread out as much as possible." Not all schools were willing to accept Nisei students, and some that had accepted them quickly forced them to leave when local patriots protested. Milton Eisenhower was "still distressed" thirty-two years later when he remembered the kinds of excuses that some educators offered for their behavior toward Nisei students.

But before any significant number of students was released for return to school, some evacuees were "temporarily" released from assembly centers to help harvest crops. The first such group consisted of fifteen persons who went from the Portland assembly center to southeastern Oregon—east of the prohibited zone—to thin sugar beets. A report from this group sometime in June 1942, when it had grown to "about a hundred Japanese," gives a good picture of the first significant relaxation of the evacuation. Its unknown author, who may have been sent there from the assembly center at Puyallup, was letting people still in WCCA custody know what conditions were like:

At the present time we are required to stay at [the] Farm Security Administration [camp at Nyssa, in the southeastern corner of Oregon consisting] of canvas tents, size 14 by 12, equipped with small wood and coal cook stoves. There are board floors but no boarded side-walls. Neither are there any windows nor means of locking the doors. You may cook by yourself with your own utensils or eat in the mess hall which will cost approximately 75¢ per day.

Good hot showers are available at all times. Good laundry rooms and ironing rooms are provided. At the present time the camp consists of 72 tents, now occupied by about a hundred Japanese, mostly from Gresham, Oregon [a rural area outside Portland]. There is one water faucet to every ten tents, 3 persons in a tent. A First-aid clinic with a nurse is provided and a doctor is available twice a week.

At the present time there is an acute shortage of sugar beet thinners. Sugar beet thinning will be over in about two weeks. Thereafter there will be plenty of work hoeing onions, corns, lettuce, peas, beans, and potatoes. Also hoeing and harvesting of beets and hay pitching.

There are some apple orchards where pickers will be needed. If a group should move into a private farm, there will be other types of work available, such as tractor driving, team work and [irrigation] work. Most of the common labor is done on contract basis and after a week or ten days experience, an ordinary person should earn from four to five dollars a day. Any of this work or living quarters cannot be recommended for city people. At the present there are not stores in the camp. The nearest town is 4 miles from the camp. You may go shopping if accompanied by proper officials. You are not permitted to stop in town on the way to and from work. The employers furnish the workers transportation to and from work. Some workers travel as far as 40 miles from camp to work.

The camp is on a self-governing basis except for one camp manager. We are required to be in the camp area between the hours of 8:00 P.M. AND 6:00 A.M. There are no restrictions on lights-out, no guards, no fence but you cannot go out of the camp unless accompanied by some F.S.A. official or your employer. Other Japanese residing in the same vicinity have no restrictions whatsoever. The attitude of people in that community is very favorable towards the Japanese. It is expected that, within a short time, laborers will be permitted to move into the bunk houses of individual farmers who will have responsibility for their safety.[89]

---

89. Seattle JACL Mss., UWA, "Report By Token Crew from Nyssa, Oregon," n.d.

This paradoxical situation highlights the inconsistency of government relocation policy from its outset. Japanese Americans living outside of Lt. General DeWitt's prohibited areas were at liberty. The first Japanese Americans sent by the government to such an area, after having been rounded up and placed in confinement, were left in a condition that can only be described as semifree. As more and more Japanese were "furloughed" to help in harvests—some 10,000 during 1942—the paradox became more and more apparent. Though they were incarcerated and deprived of their own farms, the West Coast Japanese Americans nonetheless made important contributions to the agricultural war effort, even in 1942. But instead of the tidy profits enjoyed by most other American farmers during the war, they received the low wages reserved for migrant agricultural workers.

The ironic aspects of the Army-mandated evacuation were heightened when a branch of the army itself began to recruit Japanese Americans right out of the assembly and relocation centers.[90] Like every part of the American government, the army lacked personnel skilled in foreign languages. It had trained a few officers in Chinese and Japanese in the 1920s and 1930s, but apart from these "language officers," who had learned their language as individuals while living abroad, the army had no organized way to provide language skills until late 1941.

At that time a small army language school, the forerunner of today's Defense Language Institute, was established at the Presidio in San Francisco to teach Japanese. It employed a number of Asian nationals and Americans of Asian ancestry as instructors. As a part of the Western Defense Command's insistence that the Pacific Coast be cleared of Japanese, the school had to be relocated, in winter, from California to Minnesota, a move that did not endear General DeWitt and his subordinates to the army linguists.

Staffing the language school created serious problems. Most personnel available to it as instructors were specialists in studies such as medieval Japanese literature: the school needed translators of military messages and technical manuals. The school, which was a part of military intelligence, might be strengthened by the recruitment of some Japanese Americans in military custody. The language school

---

90. Material on the military intelligence based on Masaharu Ano, "Loyal Linguists: Nisei of World War II Learned Japanese in Minnesota," *Minnesota History* 45 (1977): 273–87; Tamotsu Shibutani, *The Derelicts of Company K*; Joseph D. Harrington, *Yankee Samurai*; documentary materials, including a typescript history of military intelligence during World War II, which were housed in 1974 at the Office of Military History in Washington, D.C.; and an interview with Brig. Gen. John Weckerling (Ret.) dated October 1973.

officials hoped to find Kibei who had been noncommissioned officers in the Japanese military. Such persons would know Japanese military terminology. They never found even one such person, but starting in July 1942 they recruited instructors and then students from among the Japanese American population in and out of camp. The commandant of what became the Military Intelligence Service (MIS) language school, Lt. Colonel Kai E. Rasmussen, had obtained War Department authority to recruit directly from the camps. The results of that recruiting sent the Western Defense Command, Colonel Karl R. Bendetsen, and California law enforcement officers into a virtual tizzy. As Bendetsen later described it:

> Col. Rasmussen, from his school in Minnesota, sent a detail in to Manzanar to gather up a few enlistees. . . . [The recruits] came down [from] Manzanar on the train, in company of a noncommissioned officer and an officer. By jove, when they got to Los Angeles, the whole town was in a tail spin for the entire night upon reports of seeing Japanese there. . . . Here is what happened. For example, one Japanese was seen and then a hundred reports would come in on him, and the police think that there were probably a hundred Japanese and their prowler cars were out, and we couldn't get it straightened out until the next morning.[91]

This recruiting, and later the draft, brought some 6,000 Japanese Americans to the MIS school, first at Camp Savage, Minnesota, and then at nearby Fort Snelling. Perhaps 5,000 of the graduates were sent overseas to various parts of the Pacific theater. Some served in headquarters units, others with frontline organizations such as Merrill's Marauders in Burma. They translated captured documents, monitored radio traffic, interrogated prisoners, and otherwise used their linguistic skills to help defeat the nation from which their ancestors had come. Unlike the well-publicized exploits of the Japanese American fighters in Italy and France—the 100th Battalion and the 442nd Regimental Combat Team—the feats of the Japanese American intelligence specialists received almost no public notice. Their accomplishments were a minor but significant aspect of our war effort.

The whole question of training linguists points up the schizoid way in which the American government attacked some problems. Although almost all of the experts on the Japanese Americans were against mass evacuation, that policy was adopted by the government.

---

91. National Archives, Record Group 394, transcript of telephone conversation, Col. Karl Bendetsen and Col. William P. Scobey, February 17, 1943.

After the evacuation decision had been made, the officers of the Western Defense Command, who had been its chief military instigators along with the officers of the Provost Marshal General's staff, fought hard to keep tight restrictions and they opposed, in vain, the use of Japanese Americans by the military. Both the army and the navy, of course, needed linguists. The army, thanks to men such as Lt. Colonel Kai Rasmussen and General John Weckerling, eventually decided to use the Japanese Americans. But they had greatly overestimated the linguistic abilities of the American-born Japanese. One account states that of the first 3,700 Nisei interviewed, only 3 percent could speak Japanese fluently, another 4 percent could be considered fairly proficient, and another 3 percent knew just enough to make their training seem worthwhile. In the early days of the war, standards were high. Journalist Bill Hosokawa, one of those whom Lt. Colonel Rasmussen interviewed early, reported later: "I thought I could boast a fair speaking knowledge of the language, but he quickly proved me completely inadequate. . . . First he asked me to read a high school text. I could make out perhaps two or three characters in a hundred." With what the journalist later remembered as "ill-concealed disgust," Lt. Colonel Rasmussen eventually dismissed him, remarking in Danish-accented English (Rasmussen was foreign-born): "Hosokawa, you'd make a helluva Jap."[92]

But as the war dragged on, standards for linguists, as for everything else, dropped. The army, having initially decided to use only qualified ethnic linguists, eventually simply used ethnics. By late 1944 the army was sending to the MIS school whole units of Japanese Americans who had been trained for infantry combat. Most of them had no proficiency in Japanese; many lacked skills in any language. Some of these later became what Tamotsu Shibutani called "the derelicts of Company K." The United States Navy, which was more ethnically exclusive than the army, organized its Japanese language training on a different principle. It selected the brightest young reserve officers it could find: all of them were Caucasian and hardly any had even the slightest background in either Japanese language or culture.

An entirely separate attitude toward military service for Japanese Americans was to be taken by the Selective Service System.[93] Up to the time of Pearl Harbor, Japanese American citizens were treated like

---

92. Bill Hosokawa, "Our Own Japanese in the Pacific War," *American Legion Magazine* (July 1964): 15–17, 44–47.

93. Much of the material on the draft comes from Selective Service System, Special Monograph No. 10, *Special Groups*, 2 vols., one of a series published between 1949 and 1953. Especially useful is the section, "Japanese Americans," 1:113–42.

other citizens. According to selective service records, 3,188 American citizens of Japanese ancestry had been inducted into the armed forces by November 1941. Others had enlisted or had entered military service with National Guard units. The relative racial egalitarianism of the Selective Service System had been mandated by law: the Selective Training and Service Act of 1940 had been one of the first to contain a nondiscrimination clause:

> In classifying a registrant there shall be no discrimination for or against him because of his race, creed or color, because of his membership or activity in any labor, political, religious or other organization. Each registrant shall receive equal and fair justice.

Shortly after Pearl Harbor, however, some army commanders began to transfer recently inducted Nisei to the enlisted reserve; in other words, they discharged them from active duty. The same thing happened to some Nisei who had enlisted; others remained on active duty with their units. Some were removed from their units and were made permanent KPs (kitchen police) or were given other menial assignments; still others were placed in special labor battalions. The discharges of recent inductees evoked protest from General Lewis B. Hershey, the director of the Selective Service System, who complained of the futility of inducting men only to see them separated from active duty and sent back to civilian life. Accordingly, on March 30, 1942, a confidential telegram was sent to all state directors of selective service informing them that no more registrants of Japanese extraction would be accepted by the army for induction. That this and other special regulations affecting Japanese American citizens were illegal under the Selective Training and Service Act seems not to have seriously bothered anyone. The "confidential" policy was formalized on September 14, 1942, when a directive sent to all local draft boards provided that "registrants who are Japanese or of Japanese extraction or parentage" be treated as if they were aliens and placed in draft classification "IV-C." Prior to that date, many local boards had simply placed Japanese Americans in classification "IV-F."[94]

Even as the draft status of Japanese Americans was being changed, the army was having second thoughts about using general Japanese American manpower as opposed to the special linguists being utilized "secretly" by military intelligence. (It was not discussed generally in the press, but it was certainly no secret in Minneapolis, where large numbers of khaki-clad Nisei GIs went on pass every weekend.) Just six days after Roosevelt's Executive Order 9066, a

---

94. Selective Service System, *Special Groups* 2: 9.

middle-level intragovernmental group, the Joint Evacuation Board composed of both military and civilian representatives, formally proposed that special efforts "be made to draft or enlist American citizens of Japanese extraction into the armed forces and [employ them] where they can be of service to their country and where they are least likely to fall under suspicion, justified or unjustified."[95]

Almost three months later, Assistant Secretary of War John J. McCloy, after being prodded by Milton Eisenhower, agreed that "it might be well to use our American citizen Japanese soldiers in an area where they could be used against the Germans." He may have been thinking of the Nisei 100th Battalion of the Hawaiian National Guard, which had been federalized shortly after Pearl Harbor and sent to Camp McCoy, Wisconsin, *without its weapons*.[96] In mid-July a general staff board of the army was set up to investigate the possibility of utilizing Japanese American manpowers.

Lt. General DeWitt and his subordinates vehemently objected to this change of policy. They argued, quite logically, that if the government could make judgments about the loyalty of civilians in order to draft them, the whole costly evacuation program was largely unnecessary. Nevertheless, the army announced officially in January 1943 that a special Japanese American combat unit would be formed. This became the famous 442nd Regimental Combat Team.

President Franklin Roosevelt soon publicly endorsed this policy change. In a letter to War Secretary Henry L. Stimson he wrote: "No loyal citizen of the United States should be denied the democratic right to exercise the responsibilities of his citizenship, regardless of his ancestry. . . . Americanism is not, and never was, a matter of race and ancestry." At the time of this letter, about one-hundred thousand persons were still behind barbed wire in relocation centers. But, in the words of an anonymous Selective Service System historian, everyone recognized that the new policy "marked [a] step in the gradual relaxation of restrictions against the use of Japanese Americans in the armed forces." Roosevelt himself put it thus in his February letter to Stimson: "This is a natural and logical step toward the reinstitution of Selective Service procedures which were temporarily disrupted by the evacuation from the West Coast."

---

95. Daniels, *Concentration Camps, USA*, pp. 112–13, 145–48, covers the decision-making process in greater detail. Roger Daniels, *The Decision to Relocate the Japanese Americans*, expands on this and prints a number of documents not readily available elsewhere.

96. The best account of Japanese American troops in Europe is Thomas D. Murphy, *Ambassadors in Arms*, which treats of the 100th Battalion. See also Orville C. Shirey, *Americans: The Story of the 442nd Combat Team*.

Despite the President's notions about Americanism and natural steps, even the voluntary enlistment of Nisei was hedged about with special requirements. The volunteers, as the selective service policy statement indicated, "will be limited to persons who were born in the United States or its Territories, and who speak English." If the volunteer were in a relocation center, as over 90 percent of the young men of military age still were, he had to fill out, in addition to the usual "Application for Voluntary Induction" (DSS Form 165), a brand new form in quadruplicate: "Statement of United States Citizen of Japanese Ancestry" (DSS Form 304A). This latter form, created after conferences between selective service officials and representatives of the army and the navy, was a variant of an existing selective service form: "Alien's Personal History and Statement" (DSS Form 304).[97] Both forms clearly violated the nondiscrimination clause of the Selective Training and Service Act. Prospective Japanese American volunteers had to list, among other things, religion and membership in religious groups, membership in organizations, five references other than employers, contributions made to "any society, organization or club," and magazines and newspapers subscribed to or customarily read." In addition, they had to answer two final questions determining willingness (1) to serve on combat duty, wherever ordered, in the armed forces, and (2) to swear unqualified allegiance to the United States and to foreswear any allegiance to Japan. (For details see pp. 261 ff.)

In a little over a month, 1,138 eligible persons had volunteered for induction from within relocation centers, as table 6.5 indicates. The erratic pattern from camp to camp probably reflects the quality of leadership in the inmate populations and in the WRA administration, as well as the skill of the recruitment teams. It is certainly no accident that Minidoka, where most of the Seattleites from "Camp Harmony" had gone, had a voluntary induction rate much higher than that of any other camp. The JACL, of course, viewed the formation of the combat team as a partial vindication of its position. But, even as the call for volunteers was going out, an emergency meeting of the JACL in Salt Lake City called for the reinstitution of the draft and for a halt to the

---

97. Form 304 and its variants are printed in Selective Service System, *Special Groups*, 2: 142–54. The original versions read:

27. Have you had in the past or do you now have any obedience to the Japanese Emperor or any other foreign government? If yes, do you hereby foreswear that allegiance or obedience? If you have had or now have such allegiance or obedience and do not foreswear it, why do you not do so?
28. Do you hereby declare your loyalty and allegiance to the United States? If not, why?

Table 6.5
Japanese American Volunteers and Inductees, by Relocation Center, 1943–1945

Relocation Center	A Citizen Males Ages 18–37 March 1943	B Volunteers to 29 March 1943 (1)	C Ratio A:B	D Volunteers to 20 January 1944 (1)	E Inducted after 20 January 1944 (2)
Topaz, UT	1,475	111	13.29:1	80	392
Poston, AZ	3,405	228	14.93:1	116	495
Gila River, AZ	2,210	114	19.39:1	84	403
Granada, CO	1,580	121	13.06:1	117	377
Heart Mountain, WY	1,970	45	43.78:1	38	347
Jerome, AK	1,578	33	47.82:1	37	15
Manzanar, CA	1,809	97	18.65:1	42	132
Minidoka, ID	1,601	298	5.37:1	219	375
Rohwer, AK	1,608	34	47.29:1	15	259
Tule Lake, CA	2,270	57	39.82:1	57	
Total persons	19,506	1,138	17.14:1	805	2,795

SOURCES: A and B, from Selective Service System, *Special Groups* 2:202; C, my computation; D and E, from War Relocation Authority, *WRA: A Story of Human Conservation,* p. 202. See also chap. 6, n99, below for comments on statistics of military service.

(1) Includes both those who were accepted and those who were not.
(2) Includes only those who were accepted.

policy of classifying citizen Japanese Americans in IV-C, a category reserved for unacceptable aliens.

As the selective service historian pointed out, not only did a segregated unit accentuate the discrimination against Japanese Americans, but since the only way that a Japanese American could enter the armed forces was through voluntary induction, he was a further victim of discrimination. Many in the community thought that establishing a special unit was "merely a device to set up a 'suicide group'." Certainly the fact that Japanese Americans were concentrated in a regimental combat team and not scattered throughout the army in the services of supply and other noncombat units meant that Japanese American soldiers suffered a higher percentage of casualties than did the army at large.

By January 1944 the government was finally ready to reinstitute the draft for Japanese Americans, in and out of camp. All registrants were sent four copies of DSS form 304A. If they were found "acceptable" after a perfunctory loyalty check, they were processed for induction somewhat like other registrants. Those found "unacceptable" were kept in draft classification IV-C. By November 18, 1944, even Japanese aliens were allowed to volunteer for induction. Once accepted, they were still faced with discriminatory procedures. The restrictions on assignment were changed so that Japanese American inductees could be sent as individual replacements to the European and North African theaters, but most were still sent to the 442nd Regimental Combat Team. Top priority, however, went to the Military Intelligence Service Language School in Minnesota, which had first call on any person of Japanese ancestry who was linguistically qualified. The selective service historian reports that "so great was the need for registrants who could speak Japanese the War Department issued waivers of certain physical defects as well as of age to procure the services of these men."[98]

Each of these changes created what selective service liked to call "local board problems." Japanese Americans who had registered for the draft before relocation were still assigned to West Coast boards, so many Japanese Americans were hard for their boards to find. Some local boards "were somewhat averse" to forwarding for induction any registrant of Japanese ancestry. Japanese American inductees were sometimes ordered to report to their original local boards in the very places from which they were still excluded. The transportation of Japanese American inductees to induction stations was a "problem"; food service was hard to get because many restaurants simply would not serve "Japs." Eventually the Selective Service System violated its own regulations by allowing Japanese American draft registrants to apply directly to Washington to have their boards changed rather than having to apply through state directors of selective service.

For men who were still in relocation centers, the draft procedure was somewhat different. They were eventually transferred to a board in the vicinity of the relocation center; the Selective Service System was unwilling either to set up boards inside relocation centers or to have preinduction physicals held there. Potential draftees were simply taken by bus to the nearest outside facility where their preinduction and induction physicals were combined, thus providing one more example of discriminatory treatment by selective service.

Altogether, according to selective service records, some 23,000 Nisei, about half from the continental United States, served during World War II. They were almost equally divided between Europe and the Pacific theaters. Of the 25,500 registrants of "Japanese extrac-

---

98. Selective Service System, *Special Groups* 1:125.

tion" who were processed for induction, more than 22,000 were actually inducted. The historian of selective service simply remarks that, "considering the size of the Japanese American population group, these figures are impressive," without making any comparative analysis. Many of the young Japanese American soldiers who fought in France and Italy were farmers and sons of farmers. Had they been white, they would have received deferments as essential agricultural workers. There were no occupational deferments for Japanese Americans.

As is well known, Japanese American soldiers in both the European and Pacific theaters compiled a magnificent record. The 442nd Regimental Combat Team, in particular, was showered with well-deserved honors, including seven Presidential Unit Citations and a reputation as the most decorated unit of its size in the army. While participating in seven major campaigns in Italy and France it suffered 9,486 casualties. Its members, and members of the 100th Infantry Battalion which it eventually absorbed, were awarded 18,143 individual decorations, including a Congressional Medal of Honor, 47 Distinguished Service Crosses, 350 Silver Stars, and more than 3,600 Purple Hearts. The Congressional Medal of Honor, one of only 29 awarded during the war, was given posthumously to Private First Class Sadao S. Munemori.[99]

The whole "Go For Broke" tradition of the Japanese American troops was a useful tool in the public rehabilitation of Japanese Americans which began during the war. Nonetheless, too many writers, in celebrating the exploits of Japanese American fighting men, have ignored the ambiguity and bitterness felt by many if not most of them.

The two letters that follow, each written in early 1944 from Camp Shelby, Mississippi, by a Nisei volunteer, can be read as a hypothetical dialogue betwen Nisei soldiers.[100] The first comes close

---

99. Quotation and statistics from Selective Service System, *Special Groups* 1:141. In October 1947, army cargo ship *Wilson Victory* was renamed the *Private Sadao S. Munemori*. The WRA gave somewhat different data, stating that between November 1940 and December 1945, 25,778 Japanese Americans entered the armed forces—438 officers and 25,340 enlisted men—with an estimated 13,528 from the mainland and 12,250 from Hawaii. See U.S. Department of Interior, War Relocation Authority, *WRA: A Story of Human Conservation*, p. 202. The Selective Service System reported that between November 1940 and November 1946, 22,237 Japanese were inducted, 13,448 of them from Hawaii. See Selective Service System, Table 55, *Special Groups* 2: 113–14. I presume, therefore, that the 33,000 figure in the text of *Special Groups* 1:142, is a typographical error for 23,000. It is not clear if either set of figures includes the 1,400 men of the 100th Battalion, who were federalized Territorial National Guard.

100. Both letters are in the collection of materials assembled by Russell Bankson,

to being stereotypical in its presentation of the "Go For Broke!" canon. The second gives voice to perhaps equally common views that most of the celebrants of the Japanese American war experience have chosen to ignore. The first Nisei asked that his letter be read to the draftees. "They're just like me," he wrote, "so I thought I'd give them reasons why I volunteered:"

So you want to know how it feels to be a volunteer? I'll tell you short and snappy! It's hell! No lie! Why did I ever join? Maybe for patriotic reasons or maybe my pals joined up! I'd rather believe the latter!

What am I fighting for? For the chance of returning to California? I may never reach there! Regardless of uniform I'm called a Jap! Yep lets face it! Wot am I fighting for? I'll tell you! I'm fighting so that my parents can live here—I'm fighting so that my kid brothers and sister can get an education here! That's what I'm fighting for? Sure, I'll be called a Jap, what of it? We'll be called that for generations to come! But thats a small detail. My parents were given a home and a living far superior to Japan. They (US) gave me an education and [a] chance to prove I got what it takes! That's what I'm fighting for! To reclaim myself! I don't blame this country, I never blame this country, I never will! The evacuation was a *Military* necessity, not because the caucasians hated us—get that out of your heads. Disregard the petty discriminations—look at it with a broad view point, good gravy! We're too narrow-minded. Sure we're called Japs—the more to fight to show them we're Americans. The 100th and 442nd have proved it so you're being drafted. So wot? Now's the chance to show them we're not just sitting complacently on our seats! Prove [it] to them and they'll change their minds! That's why I volunteered! Yes-sir! To fight for the rights of my parents, myself, and kid-brothers and sister. To fight for opportunities that are plentiful. But don't expect them to come to you. What do you want, service with a smile?

I sound nuts and illogical yet that's how I feel.

The second volunteer was much less willing to overlook his own growing awareness of discrimination within the military:

I've been hoping and praying that my friends would never have to go through the stuff we've been experiencing lately. When I think of the young kids of high school age, some of them fellows

---

University of Washington Archives. They are typed copies. Each is addressed to "Mr. Ernst." The first is undated; the second is dated February 19, 1944. I have made minor emendations in spelling and punctuation.

whom I had charge of as recreation leader in Tanforan, having hardest and *dirtiest* branch of the Army, without any choice of their own, it just makes me sick. Compare them with any whites, yes, even Negros. They have all kinds of opportunities to get into whatever branch of service they may choose, places where their talents and education may be fully utilized and also places which may offer you a decent career after the war. Compare their chances with ours. We have only the infantry (one regiment), the artillery (one battalion), and engineers (one company) open to us. They say our outfit is one of the most intelligent in the service. However I've found out, and so have many others with a reasonable amount of education, that education means next to nothing here. We need no initiative or foresight—they even tell us the exact spot in which to dig. All we need here are strong legs and backs and nothing else.

When I was in recruit school training we were surprised to see fellows with Air Corps insignias placed in our midst. We asked why they were sent here. They told us that the only reason was because they were part Japanese. Can you imagine a flight instructor, aviation cadet in advanced training, aerial gunner, and a number of headquarters men "shanghaied" into the lowest branch of the Army just because they had a trace of Japanese blood in their veins? Many others have been sent here from other camps because somewhere down the family line was a Japanese. Fellows are being sent here from other camps and the general trend seems to segregate them all into this one concentration camp. Pretty pictures have been painted by such papers as "Pacific Citizen," but I wish you could actually be here and get a first hand picture of everything. You asked me about the morale of the fellows. After asking around we've all come to the conclusion that despite the propaganda that goes out, morale is about as low as our flat arches. Can you blame us when so many fellows have been "mis-placed" here? For example, an engineer graduate put in a cannon company, a chem. engineer and others of equal position put into rifle companies and told that they cannot get transfers. Any white or negro after finishing his basic training has a fair chance of transferring out to a unit where his previous education and training can be fully utilized. Compare them with us and you can readily see why we think the idea of drafting niseis under the illusion that they are on equal terms with whites just *stinks*. I never fully realized how little democracy meant until I got into the Army. When they ask me what I'm fighting for and against whom, I tell them that my first enemy is right here in the U.S.—the American Legion, the short-sighted American public, etc. The Germans are only secondary.

Just the other day the call came out for more volunteer replacements for Italy. As not enough volunteered, names were picked out of a hat. Mine was one of several chosen. I spoke to the colonel and told him my lack of training for anything like overseas combat but evidently training means nothing. I went through the program of overseas processing but was rejected for the present because of poor eyes. I was told that I'd probably catch a later boat over.

When I think of those swell, young, fine "American" boys who will be drafted into a segregated outfit, after being promised that nisei draftees will be taken in without discrimination, I'm almost certain that the purpose of the volunteers has been completely defeated.

If the reinstitution of selective service caused differences of opinion among volunteers already in the army, it is not surprising that it created tremendous divisions within the relocation centers. Eventually draft resisters within the camps provided the major element of the "left opposition," a term I have coined to describe the stance of some professedly "pro-American" Japanese Americans in resisting what they felt were unconstitutional orders of their own government. (The term does not denote a Marxist viewpoint. Japanese American Marxists, inside the American Communist party or out, took an uncompromising position of all-out support for the war: after all, the Soviet motherland was in danger.) These resisters can be differentiated from what might be called the "right opposition," those Japanese Americans who, for one reason or another, rejected American ideals and professed their allegiance to Japan.

The existence of this bipolar resistance has been all but ignored in the literature, which has stressed the compliance of the Japanese Americans—what William Petersen has dubbed the "model minority" phenomenon. In 1969, for example, in the first book adequately to survey the Japanese American experience, Harry H. L. Kitano argued, in a section labeled "Japanese Nonresistance," that political, economic, social-psychological, and cultural factors all contributed to the passivity with which Japanese Americans submitted to their fate.[101] More recently, many politically aware *Sansei* and *Yonsei* (third and fourth generation persons) have "attacked" the generations of their parents and grandparents for not resisting.[102]

---

101. Kitano, *Japanese Americans*, pp. 44–46.
102. This presumed lack of Japanese American resistance would seem to mimic the "Sambo thesis" put forth by Stanley Elkins to explain the nonresistance of blacks to

The myth of the almost totally docile Japanese Americans, like most successful myths, contains elements of truth. There was little violent resistance, and there were no desperate attempts at mass escape. Even sustained mass civil disobedience rarely occurred. A major factor in the relative compliance of the Japanese American community, of course, was the deliberately accommodationist position taken by the JACL. As we know, its leaders hoped that cooperation with oppression might not only ameliorate wartime persecution but might ensure better treatment after the defeat of Japan. The postwar treatment of the Japanese American is still viewed by most JACLers and by many if not most Japanese Americans as demonstrating the essential correctness of that strategy.

Although their community leadership was rarely challenged after 1942, committed members of the JACL were a minority of the Japanese American population; those opposed to the JACL were also a minority. The majority of the incarcerated people were passive or at least politically dormant most of the time. The "right opposition" was openly pro-Japanese and anti-American. Its members were largely Issei and its leaders were often Kibei; that is, American-born Japanese who had received a significant part of their education in Japan. It must be emphasized, however, that only a minority among the Issei and Kibei took an active part in the right opposition. It was they who fostered pro-Japanese cultural movements such as martial arts training, and, presumably, it was they who assaulted JACL leaders within the camps. The JACL leaders bitterly opposed these "disloyals" and finally encouraged the War Relocation Authority to place them in special segregation camps. If Japanese Americans were scapegoats for many white Americans, Kibei were scapegoats for many Nisei. When, for example, a distinguished artist and University of California professor was brutally beaten in camp by an unknown assailant, the incident was characterized as a "typical Kibei attack from the rear with a lead pipe."[103]

Although the right opposition was clearly a small minority of the camp population, its demonstrations sometimes received great support from the larger population. This was true of the most serious outbreak of violence in the entire evacuation: the Manzanar riot of December 6, 1942. Reports of the riot appeared in newspapers commenting on the first anniversary of Pearl Harbor. On the evening

---

slavery which, in turn, drew upon the presumed nonresistance of the concentration camp victims of the Third Reich. See Stanley Elkins, *Slavery*.

103. President's Files, Berkeley, University of California Archives (hereafter UCA), letter, Monroe W. Deutsch to John W. Nason, April 27, 1943.

of December 5 Fred Tayama, a Los Angeles restaurateur and a leading JACL official, was attacked by an unknown group of inmates and beaten seriously enough to require hospitalization.[104] Although he could not identify his attackers, the WRA arrested "the usual suspects"—Kibei malcontents. Chief among these was Harry Y. Ueno, whose major demonstrable offense had been an attempt to organize a union of kitchen workers inside Manzanar. He not only had agitated for better working conditions but had also accused WRA officials and employees of appropriating rationed sugar and meat intended for evacuees, thus intensifying the food anxieties often present among imprisoned people.

Ueno's arrest sparked a mass demonstration led by the most effective agitator in the camp, Joe Kurihara, a Hawaiian Nisei. A wounded World War I veteran of the United States Army, Kurihara was understandably embittered by his imprisonment (although another ex-doughboy inmate of Manzanar, Tokataro Slocum, was a staunch defender of the necessity for and correctness of the evacuation). According to Bill Hosokawa, Kurihara swore, after he was arrested and placed behind barbed wire, "to become a Jap a hundred percent and never do a day's work to help this country fight this war."[105] After listening to Kurihara and others, the assembled demonstrators demanded: first, the release of those arrested; and second, an investigation of Manzanar by the Spanish consul. Some speakers also urged further violence against Fred Tayama and other *inu* who were suspected, correctly in some cases, of having urged the WRA to segregate the Kibei malcontents and other members of the right opposition. Meetings throughout the day repeatedly incited to violence: death lists and blacklists of alleged informers and other enemies of the people were read over loudspeakers. Almost all of those targeted for vengeance were JACL leaders, many of whom held positions of authority under the WRA.

After some fruitless negotiations with the Manzanar administration, another and more heated mass meeting was held about 6:00 P.M. More death lists were read, and the crowd was exhorted to kill Tayama immediately. One group from the mass meeting invaded the hospital to "get him" (he was successfully hidden under a bed), while

---

104. The Manzanar Riot is a set piece in most of the histories of the relocation. The most detailed treatment is Arthur A. Hansen and David A. Hacker, "The Manzanar 'Riot': An Ethnic Perspective," in Arthur A. Hansen and Betty E. Mitson, eds., *Voices Long Silent: An Oral Inquiry into the Japanese American Evacuation*, pp. 41–79. S. K. Embrey, Arthur Hansen, and Betty Mitson, eds., *Manzanar Martyr*, appeared too late to utilize here.

105. Hosokawa, *Nisei*, p. 362.

another group went to the jail, presumably to free the prisoners. Some accounts say that these demonstrators hurled rocks at WRA security personnel, others that the abuse was all verbal; in any event, no casualties were reported among the security personnel.

The WRA authorities then called in the soldiers who guarded the camp but who did not normally effect discipline within it. The soldiers, who seem not to have had riot training, pushed the crowd back from the jail but failed to disperse it. The troops then teargassed the crowd of several hundred, mostly teen-agers and young men, some of whom were there out of curiosity rather than conviction. The crowd fled from the gas and dispersed but later regrouped. Then, apparently without orders (as would happen at Kent State three decades later), the troops fired into the crowd of unarmed young Americans approximately their own age. They used submachine guns, shotguns, and rifles, killing two young men and wounding at least ten others. One soldier was hit by a ricochet.

In retrospect, it is clear that an inept camp administration was at least partly responsible for the Manzanar riot, but the WRA did not draw that conclusion. Rather, in an official report, it insisted that the crisis "cleared an air that had become heavy with distrust."[106] Sixteen persons whom it regarded as troublemakers were removed to an isolation facility at Moab, Utah; even more indicative of the administration's problems was the evacuation of sixty-five of its chief supporters among the inmates, leaders of the JACL faction at Manzanar, to an abandoned Civilian Conservation Corps camp in the Mojave Desert for their own protection.

Within Manzanar, a general strike took place and black armbands of mourning were worn. According to Togo Tanaka, one of the suspected *inu,* two-thirds to three-quarters of Manzanar residents wore the armbands. Some, he felt, wore them under coercion. For about a month no real work activities other than routine housekeeping details took place at Manzanar, which then returned to "normal."

One of the differences between the killings at Manzanar and the previously noted killing of James Wakasa at Topaz (which was to occur four months later in April 1943) was that in the Wakasa case, the WRA was seen as the defender of the inmates against the army. At Manzanar, the WRA was seen as unleashing the army against the inmates.

The killings at Manzanar and Topaz were idiosyncratic—the

---

106. War Relocation Authority, *WRA: A Story of Human Conservation,* pp. 49–51.

result of local blunders rather than of national policy. Beginning in February 1943, however, a new WRA policy caused trouble everywhere and created unnecessary dissension among the evacuated people. The army was about to distribute a questionnaire to male volunteers for military service (DSS Form 304A) in order to determine their loyalty. The WRA also decided to determine loyalty by means of a companion questionnaire addressed to all inmates, not just male volunteers. The WRA's purpose was twofold: first, to expedite the relocation of individuals out of the camps; and second, to separate those regarded as disloyal, especially the troublemakers, from the bulk of the incarcerated people.

The chosen instrument was incredibly inept. The WRA used a minor variant of the selective service questionnaire, retitling it "Application for Leave Clearance." Everyone over age seventeen was obliged to fill one out. "Leave clearance" was bureaucratic language for an application to obtain release from camp. Many of the inmates, particularly the Issei, had no desire to leave. But the most serious problems were with questions 27 and 28, variants of the questions that ended the form issued to army volunteers (cf. fn. 97, *supra*):

27. Are you willing to serve in the armed forces of the United States on combat duty, wherever ordered?

28. Will you swear unqualified allegiance to the United States of America and faithfully defend the United States from any or all attack by foreign or domestic forces, and foreswear any form of allegiance or obedience to the Japanese emperor, to any other foreign government, power or organization?

It is hard to overstate the inappropriateness of putting these questions to the entire adult incarcerated population. Granted that the WRA had had less than a month's notice of the army's plans, and granted that it was easier to use an already prepared form with a new heading. It was, nevertheless, stupid. Question 27 made no sense for elderly Issei or for females of any age. Question 28, which despite its clumsiness had a certain relevance for American citizens, was totally inappropriate for Issei, who were by law ineligible for naturalization. Any Issei who signed such a questionnaire would be voluntarily assuming stateless status at a time when forced repatriation of alien Japanese was being discussed in Congress and the press. Eventually the WRA realized part of its error and reworded question 28, for Issei only, to read: "Will you swear to abide by the laws of the United States and to take no action which would in any way interfere with the war effort of the United States."

But the greatest unreasonableness of all, which the WRA clung to and which Director Dillon Myer defended a quarter of a century later in his memoirs, was the notion that the government could accurately determine the loyalty of a whole people by having each of them fill out a questionnaire.[107] The result would not have been so disastrous had the questionnaire been what it was labeled: an application for leave clearance required only of those individuals seeking release. The one thing that can be said in partial expiation was that Dillon Myer and the WRA, unlike General John L. DeWitt and the Western Defense Command, were convinced that most of the Japanese Americans were loyal. They believed that their loyalty could be determined, and they saw the changed military policy as a way to "clear" the name of the majority of their captives. They also saw it as a way of identifying dissidents—persons whom they regarded as disloyal and whom they hoped to segregate.

The issuance of the questionnaire in early 1943 triggered what is usually called "the registration crisis." The questionnaire served to divide further the incarcerated community and to widen fissures that exist today. Objections to the questionnaire were numerous; everyone in camp already had good reasons not to trust the United States government. Some felt question 28 to be a trap for Nisei—that if they foreswore allegiance to Japan they were admitting that such allegiance had once existed. Many answered question 27 conditionally, with such answers as "Yes, if my rights as a citizen are restored," or "No, not unless the government recognizes my right to live anywhere in the United States." Some answered "No" to both questions because they felt primary loyalty to Japan; others answered "No–No" because they resented their treatment. Large numbers for a time refused to fill out the questionnaire at all. Many others, however, viewed the question-naire, like the opportunity to volunteer for military service, as an excellent opportunity to salvage their lives. One "Yes–Yes" respon-dent, who had also volunteered for military service, explained his position to Provost Monroe Deutsch of the University of California: "[It was] a hard decision. . . . I know that this will be the only way that my family can resettle in Berkeley without prejudice and persecution."[108]

Of the nearly 78,000 inmates who were liable for registration, almost 75,000 eventually filled out the questionnaires. Approximately 6,700 answered "No" to question 28 and thus were labeled "disloyal" by the WRA. Nearly 2,000 more qualified their answers to that crucial question: the bureaucrats treated almost all qualifications as if they were "No" answers. A few hundred—more ambivalent or perhaps

---

107. Dillon S. Myer, *Uprooted Americans*.
108. President's Files, UCA, letter, K. O. to Monroe Deutsch, March 15, 1943.

shrewder—simply left the question blank. The overwhelming majority—more than 65,000 persons—answered "Yes" to question 28.[109]

An analysis of the answers by camp shows that internal conditions could modify the results significantly. Originally persons were sent to a certain camp for geographic or administrative convenience of the government: there was no a priori reason for any single camp to be more or less loyal than another. At nine of the ten camps, registration patterns were similar. At five camps, everyone registered. At four others, a total of 36 individuals—10 aliens and 26 citizens—refused to register. At the tenth camp, Tule Lake, California, more than one-third of the camp's eligibles, a total of 3,218 individuals—1,856 aliens and 1,360 citizens—refused to register.

Dorothy S. Thomas and Richard S. Nishimoto, who have studied Tule Lake, suggest that egregious administrative blunders were largely responsible for the high degree of nonregistration and "disloyalty" at Tule Lake. Another probability exists. I am convinced that, just as the exceptionally "patriotic" showing of volunteers at Minidoka was owing, at least in part, to the leadership of James Y. Sakamoto and others, the "antipatriotic" showing at Tule Lake was owing in part to effective leadership in that cause. Bill Hosokawa, in suggesting that coercion by militant "disloyals" was also a factor, is making the same point in a negative way.[110]

These antipatriots were the heart of what I have termed the "right opposition." After the registration crisis showed that so many of them were at Tule Lake to begin with, the WRA chose to make that camp its segregation center, shipping there those who had either declared themselves disloyal or who had refused to put their loyalty in terms that the WRA could accept. The WRA planned to ship all "loyal" Japanese Americans out of Tule Lake.

The transfer plan never quite worked out the way the bureaucrats had wished. Eventually, more than 18,000 Japanese Americans were in the segregation center at Tule Lake. About one-third were persons the WRA had decided should be segregants; another third were members of their families. The final third were "Old Tuleans," as Thomas and Nishimoto have called them, many of whom simply did not want to move again. As one such Issei put it at the time: "Tuleans who are staying are often doing so because they didn't want to move. Those who are coming in here are among the worst because

---

109. Data from table in War Relocation Authority, *WRA: A Story of Human Conservation*, pp. 199–200.

110. Dorothy S. Thomas and Richard S. Nishimoto, *The Spoilage*, pp. 82–83; Hosokawa, *Nisei*, p. 365.

they wouldn't bother to pack and come here unless they were fairly bad."

Another Issei told the University of California investigators that he had refused to register because he thought that those who registered would have to leave Tule Lake. Others feared that "Leave Clearance" would become mandatory. Two Nisei brothers from Venice, California, ages 20 and 23, explained that: "We'd like to sit in Tule Lake for a while. We don't want to relocate. The discrimination is too bad. I see letters from people on the outside. There are fellows in Chicago who want to come back [to camp] but who are not allowed in."

Some not only stated their "disloyalty" positively but also took the further step of applying for repatriation or expatriation. (The government always called it repatriation, even for those born here.) A young Nisei mother who had applied for repatriation explained her actions:

> I have American citizenship. It's no good, so what's the use? . . . I feel that we're not wanted in this country any longer. Before the evacuation I had thought that we were Americans, but our features are against us. . . . I found out about being an American. It's too late for me, but at least [in Japan] I can bring up my children so that they won't have to face the same kind of trouble I've experienced.

I find it impossible to categorize the above statement as "disloyal." Of course, the government did.[111] Reasoned disillusionment is surely a more accurate description.

Tule Lake also housed a large number of persons who not only expressed active loyalty to Japan and Japanese ideals but who expressed violent antipathy to anything American. As Dorothy Thomas and Richard Nishimoto (*The Spoilage,* 1946) and Rosalie Wax (*Doing Fieldwork,* 1971) have made clear, Tule Lake eventually resembled a prison camp in which inmates and keepers became so polarized that for weeks "shooting, beatings and murder" became the order of the day.[112] Both of the above-mentioned books were written

---

111. The preceding three quotations cited in Thomas and Nishimoto, *The Spoilage,* pp. 93, 95–96, 111.

112. Rosalie H. Wax, *Doing Fieldwork: Warnings and Advice.* Wax, now a distinguished anthropologist, was a graduate student working as a participant observer at Tule Lake for the Thomas and Nishimoto study. See also idem, "The Development of Authoritarianism: A Comparison of the Japanese-American Relocation Centers and Germany" (Ph.D. diss., University of Chicago, 1951); idem, "Reciprocity as a Field Technique," *Human Organization* 11 (1952): 34–37; idem, "The Destruction of a Democratic Impulse," *Human Organization* 12 (1953): 11–21; idem, "Twelve Years

from participant observer notes. Valuable as they are—particularly Wax's 1971 reflections on her 1944–1945 experience—a modern historical evaluation of the Tule Lake experience is probably the most pressing need on the research agenda of Japanese American studies. But even without such a study, it is clear that Tule Lake represents the most reprehensible aspect of the relocation center experience. Perhaps what is to be wondered at is that there was only one Tule Lake, although one was more than enough.

Yet, many "loyal" Japanese Americans applauded the decision to segregate the "disloyals." As one put it, writing from Topaz in late 1943, "the disloyal ones have been segregated and sent to Tule Lake. As a result the place is very peaceful now with the radical element gone. [It] certainly was a good idea . . . something they should have done a long time ago."[113]

For a time, Tule Lake was more than the civilian WRA could handle. The camp was turned over to the army and placed under martial law. Some inmates accused others of being *inu*. Several serious beatings and at least one murder occurred. During the period of army control, an evacuee was shot and killed by a sentry who, although exonerated by both civilian and military courts, seems to have overreacted.

Within the Tule Lake community, a vigorous minority movement arose for what was called "resegregation." Its proponents, militant pro-Japanese desirous of being sent to Japan, objected to the presence of the majority at Tule Lake who, despite their presumed "disloyal" status, had no desire to go to Japan. Eventually more than one-third of the population at Tule Lake, 7,222 persons, made formal application to go to Japan. Almost 65 percent of these were American-born who had renounced their citizenship.

Congress made renunciation easier by passing the so-called Denationalization Act of 1944. Attorney General Francis Biddle and the Justice Department drafted and promoted the passage of this act on the erroneous estimate that 300 to 1,000 citizens might avail themselves of its provision. The department's "expert" on Japanese Americans, Edward J. Ennis, who later became head of the American Civil Liberties Union, explained that three pressing concerns supported passage of the act: first, a fear that the courts might eventually declare continued detention of American citizens unconstitutional, and Justice wanted some way to hold on to "disloyals"; second, the

Later: An Analysis of Field Experience," *American Journal of Sociology* 63 (1957): 133–42.

113. President's Files, UCA, letter, T. K. to Monroe Deutsch, October 17, 1943.

fear that militant "disloyals," once released, might be dangerous; and third, the hope that the bill would induce militant "disloyals" to renounce their citizenship, so that they could then be detained.[114]

It is unwise to draw hard conclusions about "disloyals," especially "militant disloyals," even from requests for expatriation/repatriation to Japan or renunciations of citizenship. Motivation was varied, and we must always remember that the internal and external pressures on inmates were tremendous. For many in Tule Lake and the nine other camps as well, the thought of being thrust back, virtually penniless, into a hostile, wartime Caucasian world was frightening. A Nisei girl expressed this fear:

> Are they going to kick us out? What good will that do, when we don't want to get out? My mother said that segregation was a dirty trick, bringing us here with so much trouble and now it doesn't mean a thing. We hope that by renouncing citizenship, we will be allowed to stay here, but we are not sure.[115]

Her doubts were well advised. Even renunciation was not enough. Before the war was over many renunciants were, as they would put it, "being evicted" from Tule Lake as the WRA liquidated the camps in 1945–1946.

Surely no sadder comment on wartime democracy in America can be made than that thousands of her own people had been conditioned by mistreatment to prefer a Tule Lake to freedom. Even the hard core of the Tulean right opposition, the ones who taught and took the martial-arts classes, who created and believed the rumors about mythical Japanese naval victories, who knew and preferred Japan to America, might have behaved differently had their treatment been different.

This was certainly true of the group I have termed the "left opposition." Its activities were clearly within the American tradition of reasoned protest. But these protesters also brought the wrath of the WRA and the enmity of the JACL down upon themselves.[116] The left opposition came to the fore during the registration and segregation crisis of 1943 and the ensuing controversy over the reapplication of the draft to persons still in confinement. Its activities were centered in one camp—Heart Mountain, Wyoming—perhaps because the neces-

---

114. Thomas and Nishimoto, *The Spoilage*, pp. 355–56.

115. Ibid., p. 23.

116. I have described the Heart Mountain resistance at greater length in *Concentration Camps, USA*, pp. 118–29. See the sources therein cited. See also Douglas W. Nelson, *Heart Mountain: The Story of an American Concentration Camp*.

sary leadership developed there, or perhaps because the local WRA administration was particularly unsympathetic. The chief local official, Project Director Guy Robertson, later wrote that it had been necessary "to avoid too much leisure" on the assumption that evacuees would have had too much time to organize and agitate. In his final report, Robertson had complained about a plague of "factions":

> There were factions who refused to believe in anything inaugurated by the administration. . . . The administration were *inu* . . . and the evacuees who cooperated were called worse. . . . They considered the WRA as the government, making no distinction between the different sections of the government . . . they caused a great deal of difficulty.

In this and other documents generated by Robertson, we get a picture of a man unable to cope, always ready to blame everything but his own ineptitude for whatever went wrong. At Heart Mountain a lot went wrong. From the time inmates began to move in during the latter part of 1942, the story of the camp was filled with dissension and organized protest. As its historian Douglas W. Nelson has observed, work details, pay scales, food, living conditions, shortages of coal all sparked conflict between inmates and the administration and eventually between groups of inmates.

But only with the registration crisis in February 1943 did the struggles at Heart Mountain take on an ideological cast. According to community analyst Forrest LaViolette, when the "Leave Clearance" questionnaires were first handed out, many in the camp felt betrayed: "It's a trick. Sign that application for leave and they'll throw you out to starve." Almost all of the Issei in the center quickly complied with the administration's request and filled out the questionnaire. But elements of the Nisei population resisted, organizing the Heart Mountain Congress of American Citizens which, like the JACL, excluded the alien generation.

The Heart Mountain Congress not only attacked the WRA but insisted that "the JACL is not truly representative of the citizens . . . [and] should be willing to step aside if Niseidom cannot get together under its banner." The leader of the congress, Frank T. Inouye, made it clear from the start that his protests were not at all pro-Japan but were, rather, in the American tradition: "We *must demand* that our name be cleared; and have it read to the world that there has never been a justification for our evacuation, and that we are fighting, not to redeem ourselves or to clear our names, but for what we have always believed in."

For several weeks the majority of the Heart Mountain Nisei boycotted the questionnaires despite a good deal of cajoling and exhortation from government representatives. Finally, after the army had agreed to accept conditional answers to questions 27 and 28, every Nisei in camp filled out a questionnaire: but of some 3,800 Nisei registrants, 126 refused to answer question 28, 104 gave qualified answers, and 278 answered "No." In other words, 1 Nisei in 7 at Heart Mountain would not cooperate fully. The 278 who answered "No" were mostly not members of the left opposition. Many of them apparently answered "Yes–Yes."

Not surprisingly Heart Mountain ranked as one of the least productive camps in terms of volunteers for the army: only 45 of 1,970 military-age males had volunteered by the end of March 1943. This so frustrated Project Director Robertson—like any bureaucrat he wanted his unit to have a good record—that he addressed an open letter to the camp's Issei insisting that it was their responsibility, not his, "to see that Heart Mountain maintains at least a comparable position with other centers" in meeting its quota of volunteers. Robertson claimed that a "life-long stigma will be borne by their children who fail to assume their responsibility in a democratic government." This was too much for even the long suffering Issei leadership to stomach. Its council, the block leaders, replied that there was no way that alien inmates could be blamed for the failure of a program initiated by the very government that had placed them behind barbed wire.

Robertson's staff apparently took its cues from its leader. An official government report described staff sentiments at Heart Mountain after the registration crisis:

> An intensification of caste feeling, based on belief in moral superiority and lack of understanding of evacuee position. Manifest in such statements as "It's about time we got hard boiled." "A Jap's a Jap. This proves it." "They don't appreciate what we do for them." "Might as well drop this sentimental attitude and be realistic." Etc.

The same report described the mood of the inmates: their "sense of injustice deepened. . . . Bitterness over loss of citizenship increased [and] cynicism and spiritual discouragement" grew. One can trace this growing malaise in the steadily increasing number of persons who formally applied to go to Japan. Up to February 1943, there had been 42 such applications. In the next two months, 364 more persons had signed up, and by August 1943 the total number of Heart Mountain requests had grown to 800, about 8 percent of the camp population. A majority were persons who had answered "Yes" to both the crucial questions.

When the segregation process began in September 1943, it was hailed by the camp newspaper, the Heart Mountain *Sentinel*, as "a necessary and overdue measure" that would be welcomed by "loyal residents." By the end of that month, 903 persons had been shipped from the Wyoming camp to Tule Lake, including 352 adult aliens, 309 adult citizens, and 242 children, almost all of whom were citizens. But unlike either Manzanar or Tule Lake, no overt anti-Americanism surfaced at Heart Mountain. The camp's historian has reported his inability to find even "*one* expression of or reference to pro-Japanese or anti-American sentiment."

One of the justifications for the segregation program had been that, with the "disloyals" gone, relocation centers could become peaceful, unified communities. This never happened at Heart Mountain. After segregation, organized protest not only increased in frequency but it bore greater consequences. Many leaders and adherents of the left opposition were still in camp after segregation, either because they had answered "Yes" to questions 27 and 28, or because they had so qualified their answers that they were not segregated.

One such leader was Kiyoshi Okamoto. Born in Hawaii, Okamoto was educated in Los Angeles and became a construction engineer, breaking out of the employment pattern that had stifled most prewar Nisei. He had never been to Japan and could not speak Japanese. A supporter of the antiregistration and antivolunteer movements among Heart Mountain Nisei, Okamoto became more outspoken after segregation. As he explained it later, he became increasingly disturbed by what he considered "un-American practices" at Heart Mountain. These included specific incidents of brutality and discrimination by Caucasian staff members, the substandard living and working conditions of the evacuees, and the denial of free speech. His own growing awareness of the general injustice of the whole evacuation led him in November 1943 to form a "Fair Play Committee of One." He began to agitate among his fellow prisoners about doing something to clarify the legal status of the incarcerated. Soon Okamoto was running open forums in camp. He attracted enough followers to form a Fair Play Committee, but the committee had little impact until after the announcement of the reinstatement of the draft for Japanese Americans by Secretary of War Henry L. Stimson on January 20, 1944.

The Heart Mountain *Sentinel*, which spoke in this instance for both the camp administration and the JACL, quickly hailed the war secretary's announcement as "the most significant development in returning Japanese Americans to full civic status." The next issue admitted that it would be "misleading and inaccurate" to say the news "brought joy to the hearts of all draft-age men," but the editors tried to forestall trouble by urging Heart Mountaineers to avoid another "senseless" round of "endless questions" and "picayune issues."

Kiyoshi Okamoto and the Fair Play Committee obviously felt otherwise; by mid-February 1944, for the first time, they had allies outside the camp. Samuel Menin, a Denver attorney, advised them about their legal rights. James Omura, who had been one of the two Nisei publicly to attack the JACL and its accommodationist position during the Tolan Committee hearings, and who was English language editor of the Denver *Rocky Shimpo,* opened the newspaper's columns to the Fair Play Committee. The committee raised enough money to purchase a mimeograph machine and began to distribute its own bulletin inside Heart Mountain, where the *Rocky Shimpo* circulated as well. Project Director Robertson and local selective service officials warned committee members against counseling draft resistance. The evacuee dissidents replied that they were merely advising Nisei to get a clarification of their rights. An FBI investigation in February 1944 could find no indictable behavior. At the end of February the first seventeen Heart Mountain draftees boarded the bus to take their draft physicals. Anthropologist Asael T. Hansen, one of many social scientists who worked for the WRA, advised the camp administration in early March that the draft crisis was over and that, at the most, two or three individuals might refuse to take their physicals.

At about this time, the evacuee community council, usually an arm of the camp administration, circulated a petition to President Roosevelt accepting the draft but mildly protesting other aspects of government policy. Opposed by the Fair Play Committee, the petition became a test of strength. Only slightly over one-third of the camp's adults were willing to sign, much to the disappointment of both the administration and its JACL supporters. Shortly thereafter, the strength of the Fair Play Committee began to appear. In the first half of March, twelve Nisei refused to board the bus to take their draft physicals. Draft resistance had begun.

The *Sentinel* launched an attack on the committee and its members: "During the last week, in the hidden recesses of boiler rooms and latrines, behind closed doors and under the cover of darkness, leaders of the Fair Play Committee have fired with fanatical zeal the weaker members and departed from their mimeographed statements which are purposely toned down for public consumption."

The *Rocky Shimpo* issued a counterblast insisting that the *Sentinel* staff had "purchased a seat in the great gallery of bigots, racist demagogues, autocrats and fascist-minded. . . . [The paper had] deserted justice, fair play, equal rights and all that are revered in our constitution and in the government of our United States."

The real debate was about the nature of loyalty and Americanism. The *Sentinel* suggested that the leaders of the Fair Play Committee had answered questions 27 and 28 untruthfully, which implied that they should be sent to Tule Lake. The committee insisted that the "patriotism equals submission" formula of the *Sentinel* and the JACL constituted genuine disloyalty to American democracy and its traditions.

At one level, the *Sentinel* couched its argument against the Fair Play Committee in pragmatic rather than ideological terms. It suggested that "fighting against issues that are beyond our control . . . is a waste of time and space." On another level, the *Sentinel* insisted that the fallacy of the resisters' case was "the contention that a restriction of our rights means a loss of those rights. We don't lose any rights unless the [C]onstitution itself is changed. . . . If the Supreme Court rules evacuation was constitutional, then we will not have been deprived of any rights."

Many Heart Mountain draft eligibles were won over to the militant position. By the end of March 1944, 54 of the 315 evacuees ordered to report for physicals had failed to do so. Later that month, emboldened both by its success and by the lack of any retribution, the Fair Play Committee broadened its attack and began to agitate for a general strike at Heart Mountain. Predictably, the WRA reacted. Washington informed Project Director Robertson that a reexamination of the papers of Kiyoshi Okamoto, the committee leader, had uncovered evidence of "disloyalty": he was quickly taken into custody and sent off to Tule Lake. Reacting to Okamoto's transfer, another committee leader, Isamu Horino, wishing to dramatize the lack of freedom, publicly announced that he would leave Heart Mountain. Horino tried to walk through the main gate in broad daylight. Naturally the military police stopped him. The WRA took this act as *prima facie* evidence of disloyalty. Horino, too, was shipped off to Tule Lake.

A third leader of the Fair Play Committee, twenty-seven-year-old Paul T. Nakadate, had committed no overt act. Nonetheless, he was subjected to a long interrogation by the project director about his loyalty under the guise of a "leave clearance hearing." Nakadate, who had answered "Yes" to both questions, believed that "democracy is sharing of equal responsibilities and sharing of equal rights." Since he felt that his treatment had been unequal, he could no longer say whether he would serve in the United States Army (he had not yet been called). These and similar answers and statements—Nakadate was obviously being very careful about what he said—failed to satisfy the project director. With the approval of WRA headquarters, Nakadate was also shipped off to Tule Lake.

But the administration was not just after leaders. At Robertson's urging, a reluctant United States Attorney caused the arrest, in late March and early April, of all fifty-four evacuees who had refused induction. This, coupled with its leaders' exile, was intended to break the back of the Fair Play Committee. The WRA also wanted the committee's outside voice stilled and its exiled leaders imprisoned.

On April 1, 1944, Project Director Robertson had written to his chief, Dillon Myer, arguing that James Omura's editorials in the Denver *Rocky Shimpo* bordered on "sedition." Robertson asked for an investigation of the newspaper, whose assets were being administered by the Alien Property Custodian because its proprietors were enemy aliens. The following week, in what can hardly have been a coincidence, the *Sentinel* attacked Omura as "the number one menace to the post-war assimilation of the Nisei." The *Sentinel* insisted that Omura was "responsible for wrecking the lives" of the jailed draft resisters and that he was "prostituting the privileges of freedom of the press to advocate an un-American stand." By the end of the month, federal officials had seized Omura's records and correspondence, and the Alien Property Custodian had fired him and his staff. With its leaders gone, many of its stalwarts imprisoned, its outside voice silenced, the Heart Mountain resistance seemed broken. But a victory in court would have made it stronger than ever.

Even before his "deportation" to Tule Lake, Okamoto had written to the American Civil Liberties Union (ACLU) asking for help in testing the constitutionality of drafting citizens who were behind barbed wire. In mid-April ACLU Director Roger Baldwin, in a public letter (Okamoto's letter had been private) disassociated himself and his organization from the Fair Play Committee and its cause. The dissidents had, Baldwin admitted, "a strong moral case" but, he insisted, "no legal case at all." He admonished Okamoto that "men who counsel others to resist military service are not within their rights and must expect severe treatment."

What caused Roger Baldwin to release his letter publicly is not clear, but a letter from Project Director Guy Robertson to Dillon Myer implies that someone at the JACL's Salt Lake City headquarters had requested him to do so. In any event, the major spokesman for civil liberties in the United States had supported the JACL position: its adherents were jubilant. "ACLU TAKES ISSUE WITH OKAMOTO" was headlined in the *Sentinel*. Letters from Nisei in the army were printed to buttress the accommodationist position, and the United States Army Air Force arranged for Sergeant Ben Kuroki, the first Japanese American war hero, to visit Heart Mountain. The visit, reported Project Director Robertson, had "a very good effect on the general morale of the people."

On May 10, 1944, a federal grand jury in Cheyenne, Wyoming, indicted the Heart Mountain draft resisters, whose numbers had grown to sixty-three. They were tried there the following month in what remains the largest single mass trial for draft resistance in our history. The defense, by Denver lawyer Samuel Menin, argued that the defendants had violated their orders to take physicals only to clarify their ambiguous draft status and that no felonious intent was involved. The court was not impressed. Federal District Judge T. Blake Kennedy found all sixty-three guilty, sentenced them to three years imprisonment each, and questioned their loyalty in a memorandum: "If they are truly loyal American citizens they should embrace . . . the opportunity to discharge the duties [of citizenship] by offering themselves in the cause of our National Defense."

Defense attorney Samuel Menin filed an appeal restating his original contention. Menin also argued that the defendants had been deprived of their liberty without due process of law by being held in a relocation center. The appeal was denied in March 1945 by the Tenth Circuit Court of Appeals in Denver and the Supreme Court declined to hear the case.

In the meantime the WRA caused charges to be brought against other Heart Mountain resisters and one of their allies. The same federal grand jury that had indicted the draft resisters had also returned indictments against seven members of the Fair Play Committee's executive council (including Kiyoshi Okamoto and Paul Nakadate, who had been sent to Tule Lake) and Denver editor James Omura for unlawful conspiracy to counsel, aid, and abet violations of the selective service act. The indictments were kept secret by federal authorities until after the June convictions of the draft resisters. A few days after the convictions, the Heart Mountain *Sentinel*, perhaps in on the secret, argued that those who encouraged the draft resisters not to report "deserve[d] penitentiary sentences even more than those convicted." On July 21, 1944, the indictments were made public and the eight defendants were arrested.

The seven evacuee defendants were represented by A. L. Wirin, a southern California ACLU attorney whose views about the relocation and other matters were often more libertarian than those of the national body. James Omura was defended by Denver attorney Sidney Jacobs, who tried unsuccessfully to get a separate trial for the editor on the grounds that he had never seen any of the other defendants before they appeared in court together. (He had corresponded with some of them.) The government contended that the Fair Play Committee was a conspiracy against the selective service system in particular and the war effort in general. Editor Omura was found innocent, but all seven evacuees were found guilty and sentenced to terms of two and four years' imprisonment.

After the verdict, Nisei war hero Ben Kuroki, who had been a government witness, told the press: "These men are fascists in my estimation and no good to any country. They have torn down [what] all the rest of us have tried to do. I hope that these members of the Fair Play Committee won't form the opinion of America concerning all Japanese Americans."

Attorney A. L. Wirin filed an appeal contending that there was insufficient evidence and that the judge's instructions to the jury were improper. More than a year later, the Tenth Circuit Court of Appeals in a 2–1 decision upheld Wirin's second contention while rejecting the first. The defendants were free.

But even while this persecution was going on, resistance at Heart Mountain continued. Between the start of the first trials in the summer of 1944 and the closing of the camp in November 1945, 22 more men were indicted and convicted for draft resistance, bringing the total of such convictions at Heart Mountain to 85. To put that resistance into numerical perspective, more than 700 Heart Mountain men did board the bus for their draft physicals and 385 were inducted; of these, at least 11 were killed and 52 wounded.

The Heart Mountain draft resistance had little national impact and was all but ignored by scholars for a quarter of a century, partly because the Supreme Court refused to review the convictions. The so-called Japanese American cases of 1943 and 1944 received national attention. In these cases the Supreme Court of the United States put its imprimatur on most of the process by which the Japanese American people were uprooted and deprived of both their property and their liberty. The case that had most disturbed the JACL, that of Minoru Yasui, fell by the wayside. Instead, three obscure and very different individuals became the focus of the legal struggles over the evacuation.

The first case to be decided by the Supreme Court was that of Gordon K. Hirabayashi, who in 1942 had been a senior at the University of Washington. A Quaker whose parents had been converted to Christianity in Japan, Hirabayashi had already applied for and received conscientious-objector status before the attack on Pearl Harbor. Sometime in early 1942 he had decided to bear witness against the whole evacuation process: he had chosen to start with the curfew regulations. Although he had also refused to report for evacuation, his Seattle attorney, inexperienced in appellate procedure, had failed to make the right kind of record in the federal district court, so Hirabayashi's case challenged only General John L. DeWitt's curfew proclamation and its enforcement.[117] The Court decided the

---

117. UWA, interview with Gordon Hirabayashi by Roger Daniels, February 1981.

Hirabayashi case in favor of the government 9–0. The case was heard in May 1943 and was reported the next month.

The *Hirabayashi* decision, written by Chief Justice Harlan Fiske Stone, remains a grotesque example of how "patriotism" can distort a judicial mind. His biographer tells us that Justice Stone in this decision shrank "judicial review of the war powers almost to the vanishing point." For Justice Stone, the chief point was neither the civil rights of Gordon K. Hirabayashi nor even the Constitution, but whether the United States had "the power to wage war successfully." In an opinion that wandered erratically over the history of Japanese in the United States, the Chief Justice argued that the discrimination suffered by the Japanese had intensified their solidarity and inhibited their assimilation, thereby making them what we would now call security risks. Stone explicitly condoned the racially discriminatory aspects of the treatment of Japanese Americans. "Because racial discriminations are in most circumstances irrelevant and therefore prohibited, it by no means follows that, in dealing with the perils of war, Congress and the Executive are wholly prohibited from taking into account those facts . . . which may in fact place citizens of one ancestry in a different category."[118]

Justice Stone had wanted his opinion "written in such a way as to suggest that all avenues of legal relief were foreclosed to the Japanese evacuees," but others, including Justices Hugo Black and William O. Douglas, wanted the decision decided on narrower grounds. The conservative point of view prevailed, but Black and Douglas, usually paladins of civil liberty, were not supporters of the Japanese. Black, who silently assented in *Hirabayashi,* put his views on the record in the *Korematsu* case and in an interview, years later. Douglas, who filed one of three concurring opinions, unsuccessfully tried to get Stone to remove his statement about race discrimination, quoted above, because it "implies or is susceptible to the inference that the

---

Some material on the Hirabayashi defense may be found in the papers of Arthur Barnett and Mary Farquharson in the same repository.

118. 320 *US* 81 (1943). The literature on the so-called Japanese American cases is quite large. The pioneer interpretation is Eugene V. Rostow, "Our Worst Wartime Mistake," *Harper's Magazine* 191 (1945): 193–201; and idem, "The Japanese American Cases—A Disaster," *Yale Law Journal* 54 (1945): 489–533. The latter is reprinted in idem, *The Sovereign Prerogative*. Other important early analyses include Milton R. Konvitz, *The Alien and the Asiatic in American Law;* Nanette Dembitz, "Racial Discrimination and the Military Judgment: The Supreme Court's Korematsu and Endo Decisions," *Columbia Law Review* 45 (1945): 175–239; Sidney Fine, "Mr. Justice Murphy and the Hirabayashi Case," *Pacific Historical Review* 33 (1964): 195–209. Peter Irons, *Justice at War*, reveals the inner history of the cases from the prosecutorial side.

Japs who are citizens cannot be trusted because we have treated them so badly."

Justice Douglas's opinion simply abdicated, temporarily, almost any judicial restraint on the military in a time of crisis: "We cannot sit in judgment of the military requirements of that hour." Douglas then went on to deny the appropriateness of racial discrimination in Stone's decision: "Detention for reasonable cause is one thing. Detention for ancestry another." Despite Douglas's unwillingness publicly to embrace racial discrimination, his opinion had the same effect. Perhaps his final statement about Hirabayashi—"It is sufficient to say that he cannot test in that way the validity of orders as applied to him"—was intended as a clue to future appellants. But one suspects that even if Hirabayashi's attorneys had found the "way"—habeas corpus—the Court would not have opened the gates of the concentration camps in mid-1943.

A second concurrence was by the Court's newest justice, Wiley B. Rutledge. Obviously troubled by the more sweeping aspects of Stone's opinion, Justice Rutledge agreed with the result but insisted that "it does not follow that there may not be bounds beyond which [military authority over civilians] cannot go."

The third concurring opinion, by Justice Frank Murphy, was originally written as a dissent. But the patriot overruled the judge as he toned his dissent down slightly under pressure to conform with Felix Frankfurter and other colleagues. But even toned down, Murphy's was a strong statement:

> The broad provisions of the Bill of Rights . . . are not suspended by the mere existence of a state of war. . . . Distinctions based on color and ancestry are utterly inconsistent with our traditions and ideals.
>
> Today is the first time, so far as I am aware, that we have sustained a substantial restriction of the personal liberty of citizens of the United States based on the accident of race or ancestry. . . . It bears a melancholy resemblance to the treatment accorded to members of the Jewish race in Germany. . . . This goes to the very brink of constitutional power. [In his original dissent, Murphy had said "over the brink."]

In his conclusion Murphy served public notice that the issue of the relocation was not settled: "When the danger is past, the restrictions imposed on [Japanese Americans] should be promptly removed and their freedom of action fully restored."

In retrospect it is hard to see what external dangers still existed in mid-1943 when Murphy and the others wrote. This was more than a year after the rout of the Japanese carrier forces at Midway. But, of course, once a government takes a false step it usually continues to justify it. The second and third Japanese American cases did not come before the Court until December 1944, when victory was in sight, when Japanese American troops had already won significant victories in combat, and when tens of thousands of Japanese Americans had been released from camps to civilian life in the interior and on the East Coast.

The first of two cases handed down on December 18, 1944—a real "black Monday" for the Constitution—involved Fred Korematsu, California-born and a graduate of an Oakland high school. By that time the ACLU, which had refused to support Gordon Hirabayashi as it had refused to support the Heart Mountain resistance, was willing to file a brief amicus curiae which focused on the main issue: "whether or not a citizen of the United States may, because he is of Japanese ancestry, be confined in barbed-wire stockades euphemistically termed Assembly Centers or Relocation Centers—actually concentration camps."[119]

Justice Hugo Black wrote the majority opinion. The unanimity of 1943 had disappeared. Although there had been no changes in the Court's personnel, three justices dissented. Black stressed four justifications for what the military had done.

> 1. The presence of an indefinite number of disloyal persons of Japanese ancestry.
> 2. Because of the impossibility of determining loyalty of individuals quickly, temporary exclusion of the whole group was deemed by appropriate authorities a military necessity.
> 3. Subsequent to exclusion many refused to swear unqualified allegiance and others requested repatriation or expatriation. [This, of course, refers to the registration and segregation crisis of 1943. Events of that year could not provide legal justification for a 1942 decision.]
> 4. In wartime, citizenship carries heavier burdens than in time of peace.

Justice Black took note of the ACLU brief and the points raised by the dissenters. As had Justice Douglas in the *Hirabayashi* case, he insisted that prejudice and racism had nothing to do with the case.

> Regardless of the true nature of the assembly and relocation centers—and we deem it unjustifiable to call them concentration camps with all the ugly connotations that term implies—we are

---

119. To be more precise, the ACLU withdrew from the Hirabayashi case after having been involved initially. See the correspondence between Mary Farquharson and Roger Baldwin in the Farquharson Mss., UWA. Korematsu is 323 *US* 214 (1944).

dealing specifically with nothing but an exclusion order. To cast this case into outlines of racial prejudice, without reference to the real military dangers which were presented, merely confuses the issue. Korematsu was not excluded from the Military Area because of hostility to him or his race.

Black carefully circumscribed the scope of his opinion, writing that "we uphold the exclusion order as of the time it was made and when the petitioner violated it."

Twenty-three years later, in an interview with the New York Times, Justice Black defended his record in franker language:

> I would do precisely the same thing today. . . . We had a situation where we were at war. People were rightly fearful of the Japanese in Los Angeles [Korematsu lived in the San Francisco Bay Area], many loyal to the United States, many undoubtedly not, having dual citizenship—lots of them. They all look alike to a person not a Jap. Had they [imperial Japanese forces] attacked our shores you'd have a large number of them fighting with the Japanese troops. And a lot of innocent Japanese-Americans would have been shot in the panic. Under the circumstances I saw nothing wrong in moving them away from the danger area.[120]

Justice Felix Frankfurter, concurring in Black's opinion, wanted to put a little more distance between the army and the Court, a distance he had not found necessary to establish in 1943. "To find that the Constitution does not forbid the military measures now complained of does not carry with it approval of that which Congress and the Executive did. That is their business, not ours."

Three justices dissented in the *Korematsu* case: Justices Owen Roberts, Robert Jackson, and Frank Murphy. Justice Roberts, whose false reports about Japanese American sabotage at Pearl Harbor had fueled the hysteria that resulted in the evacuation, discerned a significant difference between *Hirabayashi,* in which he had silently concurred, and *Korematsu:* "This is not a case of keeping people off the streets at night. . . . It is a case of convicting a citizen . . . for not submitting to imprisonment in a concentration camp solely because of his ancestry." Roberts could uphold curfew restrictions based on race, but he could not condone evacuation. He denied vehemently any possible distinction between reporting for evacuation and being detained in an assembly or relocation center. The whole process, according to Roberts, was "a cleverly designed trap to accomplish the

---

120. New York *Times,* September 25, 1971. The interview was published four years later as part of Black's obituary.

real purpose of military authority, which was to lock him in a concentration camp." Justice Roberts also took issue with the notion, in Douglas's concurrence in *Hirabayashi* and in Black's decision in *Korematsu*, that the proper procedure would have been for Fred Korematsu to submit to governmental authority, be taken off to camp, and then file for a writ to get out. Roberts questioned "a new doctrine of constitutional law that one indicted for disobedience to an unconstitutional statute . . . must obey it . . . and then, and not before, seek, from within prison walls, to test the validity of the law."

Justice Robert Jackson, who as prosecutor at Nuremberg would be able to make judgments about the military decisions of German generals, was unable at the end of 1944 to make judgments about American generals. He said there was no way for him to determine whether Lt. General DeWitt's orders were based on sound military judgment: "But even if they were permissible military procedures, I deny that it follows that they are constitutional. If, as the Court holds [Korematsu's evacuation was constitutional], then we may as well say that any military order will be constitutional and have done with it."

Justice Jackson, paradoxically, would have found for Fred Korematsu and ordered his immediate release, but he did "not suggest that the courts should have attempted to interfere with the Army in carrying out its task. But I do not think that [the Court] may be asked to execute a military expedient that has no place in law under the Constitution."

The third dissent, by Justice Frank Murphy, went farther than the other two. Finding nothing mysterious about military decision-making, Murphy used DeWitt's mendacious *Final Report,* testimony taken by congressional committees, and material from the ACLU brief to weigh the evidence. His conclusion was straightforward: the exclusion order, made while the federal and state courts were open, went "over the brink of constitutional power" and into "the ugly abyss of racism." DeWitt's orders and proclamations met no reasonable test, according to Murphy. In summary, they deprived American citizens of equal protection under the laws, as provided by the Fifth Amendment. Murphy, a Catholic, found the orders akin to "excommunicating them without benefit of a hearing . . . [depriving] them of all their constitutional rights to procedural due process. . . . This dangerous practice of protective custody, as proved by recent European history, should have absolutely no standing as an excuse for the deprivation of the rights of minority groups."

After examining in detail the various charges made against the Japanese American community and quoting some of General DeWitt's choicer rhetoric, Justice Murphy concluded with a defense of what we now call "cultural pluralism":

A military judgment based upon such racial and sociological considerations is not entitled to the great weight ordinarily given to judgments based upon strictly military considerations. . . . I dissent, therefore, from this legalization of racism. . . . All residents of this nation are kin in some way by blood and culture to a foreign land. Yet they are primarily and necessarily a part of this new and distinct civilization of the United States. They must accordingly be treated at all times as the heirs of the American experiment and as entitled to all the rights and freedoms granted by the Constitution.

It is worth noting that not even Justice Murphy looked behind General DeWitt to see Secretaries Stimson and McCloy and, of course, President Roosevelt himself as the real violators of the constitutional rights of the Japanese Americans. Similarly, in the *Hirabayashi* case, Justice Frankfurter had supported what he called the decision of "Congress and the Executive," subtly reversing the order of responsibility. The Roosevelt Court simply did not point fingers at its creator.

It did, however, have more to say on the situation of Japanese Americans. In a companion decision to the *Korematsu* case, handed down the same day (December 18, 1944), the Court unanimously agreed that it was impermissible to hold loyal citizens in detention against their will. The case involved Mitsuye Endo, a Japanese American woman, a native Californian and a permanent civil servant of that state who had a brother serving in the armed forces of the United States.[121] She had been relocated to the camp at Topaz. Shortly after arriving there, she had applied for a writ of habeas corpus. She could have applied successfully for leave clearance and have been released, since she was clearly employable in the civilian economy, but she had refused to apply. Since she would not comply with its procedures, the WRA opposed her writ. The ACLU, in its brief for her, stressed three points: first, the government was without power to detain a citizen against whom no individual charges had been instituted; second, segregation and detention of citizens on the basis of ancestry was patently unconstitutional; and third, since she was being kept behind barbed wire involuntarily and without due process, she was entitled to release without complying with WRA regulations.

Justice William O. Douglas wrote for the Court. Rather than finding that Congress and the executive had erred in setting up an agency to keep American citizens in protective custody without due process of law, Douglas instead ruled, against all of the evidence, that only the WRA had exceeded its authority in detaining citizens against

---

121. 323 *US* 283 (1944).

their will. According to Justice Douglas, Congress intended "to place no greater restraint on the citizen than was clearly and unmistakably indicated by the language they used." The unconstitutional villain of the piece, according to Douglas, was not the president, the Congress, or the army, but the WRA! "Whatever power the War Relocation Authority may have to detain other classes of citizens, it has no authority to subject citizens who are concededly loyal to its leave procedures."

Justice Douglas's opinion is historical nonsense. Congress surely knew what the WRA intended. Its chief criticism of the WRA had not been that it was violating the rights of citizens but that it was "coddling Japs." Although there were no dissents from Douglas's decision—not even Justice Frankfurter wanted to keep Mitsuye Endo in confinement—Justices Roberts and Murphy, in separate concurrences, complained of the flaws in Douglas's opinion and the failure of the Court to come to grips with the real constitutional issues. The *Endo* decision left a whole range of issues unsettled, issues that further test cases might have raised: What of citizens who had refused to sign loyalty questionnaires? or who had said "No" to both questions? or who had otherwise provided answers that had not satisfied the bureaucrats of the WRA? These questions were never raised because the cases were never brought to trial. The cases were never brought because the organizations responsible for bringing such cases (the ACLU and the JACL) were essentially satisfied with the *Endo* decision.

The *Endo* decision, as Morton Grodzins put it, has clearly weakened the constitutional protections of "all Americans" during wartime.[122] All three of the above decisions, which still stand as precedents, mean that a citizen who has been deprived of liberty and property by military fiat must obey such orders without resistance and, as Justice Douglas suggested in *Hirabayashi*, must find an appropriate means to challenge the order through the courts. For Mitsuye Endo, who found the appropriate means, the challenge took more than thirty months during which time she was detained behind barbed wire even though, in Justice Roberts's words, she should have been "free to come and go" as she pleased.

For the JACL, however, the events of 1943–1944—starting with the acceptance of volunteers for the 442nd Regimental Combat Team and ending with the *Korematsu* and *Endo* decisions—did more than vindicate its past behavior. They also helped pave the way for the postwar rehabilitation of the image of the Japanese American community and for the very real social, economic, and political gains to be

---

122. Morton Grodzins, *Americans Betrayed.*

made by that community in the decades that followed. The transition from "treacherous Jap" to "model minority" within less than a generation must surely be one of the more rapid changes in our history. From the late 1940s on, it has been possible to describe Japanese Americans much as William Petersen did in his widely read 1966 article, "Success Story: American Style."[123] But success has its costs, and the success of the Japanese American community has been no more cost free than any other.

In the first place, all members of the community did not participate in the success. Many Issei were simply destroyed by the confiscation of their property and their hopes. They never recovered. Thousands of both generations, soured by bitter experience, chose repatriation/expatriation to Japan where, apparently, they had great difficulty in finding acceptance. In the second place, even for those who remained in the United States and enjoyed the material and psychic benefits of success, there were costs often above and beyond those that other upwardly mobile Americans paid for their success, costs that in some cases became apparent only when their offspring of the third and fourth generations, the Sansei and Yonsei, began to ask the Japanese American equivalent of the old question: "What did you do in the war, Daddy?"

Some of the bitterness of the war years resurfaced in 1981, when the Carter-appointed Commission on the Wartime Relocation and Internment of Civilians held hearings across the country. Long pent-up tears were shed in public and formerly whispered accusations were spoken aloud. As with any other significant historical event, the relocation of the Japanese Americans continues to affect lives that did not exist when it occurred.

None of this should be forgotten: at the same time, none of this should be allowed to obscure the fact that, despite its degradations, World War II marks a positive turning point in the Asian American experience. Before the war, as we have seen, the Chinese American and Japanese American communities, although they contained more American citizens than aliens, still faced largely toward Asia and were still largely shut out of the mainstream of American life. After World War II—and for Chinese Americans it can be argued that the war lasted until 1949—the identification with America became predominant. This is not to say that discrimination ended then—it has not fully ended yet and is not likely to do so soon—but rather to argue that the depths had been plumbed and the ascent had begun.

---

123. William Petersen, "Success Story, Japanese American Style," *New York Times Magazine*, January 6, 1966. See also idem, *Japanese Americans: Oppression and Success*.

7.

Asian Americans and the Cold War, 1945–1960

I f World War II marked the decisive turning point in the history of Asian America, the fifteen years after the war signaled a period of dramatic and largely positive change. Although many Chinese Americans suffered from the growing unpopularity of what almost all Americans simply called "Red China," Japanese Americans basked in the growing warmth of American postwar relationships with Japan. In the immediate postwar years, the still tenuous nature of Asian America was manifest in the degree to which foreign rather than domestic events played the preponderant role. In the 1950s domestic events became paramount, with changes in immigration and naturalization statutes and the belated admission of Hawaii to statehood. It was a clear sign that the center of gravity of both Chinese and Japanese America was shifting to this side of the Pacific.

The first major domestic events were the closing of the relocation centers and the slow return of most mainland Japanese Americans to the West Coast. Of significance also was a White House ceremony celebrating the achievements of the Japanese American combat forces. Changes in law included, in 1948, the passage of the Japanese American Claims Act and, in 1952, the McCarran-Walter Immigration Act. Although the latter maintained most of the unattractive features of the old National Origins Act and added a few new, ugly details of its own, this cold war measure nevertheless marked the full turning of the tide of immigration law. The statutory anti-Asian discrimination that had begun with the Chinese Exclusion Act of 1882 was now largely a thing of the past: all nations now had at least a token quota, and racial bars to naturalization which had been on the books since the founding of the republic were totally down.

Even more important than the changes in law were the changes in American ideology. The United States was still patently a white man's country, but the notion was beginning to prevail that equal opportunity—or something approaching it—ought to be given at least lip service. Few things are more difficult to chronicle and calibrate than changes in what Carl Becker has called "climates of opinion." Nonetheless, sometime between June 1941, when Franklin Roosevelt issued Executive Order 8802 establishing a Fair Employment Practices Commission, and June 1952, when Congress dropped the racial and ethnic bars to naturalization, some kind of Rubicon in American policy had been crossed.[1]

To be sure, racist attitudes and blatant discrimination continued—and even prevailed at times. One could simply say, as John Morton Blum has done, that "blacks . . . lost the battle for victory at home" during World War II, but this seems an overly negative evaluation of what happened in those years.[2] It is certainly true that FDR's ringing statement—"There shall be no discrimination in the employment of workers in defense industries because of race, creed, color, or national origin"—did not end employment discrimination and, in many instances, did not even modify it. But it is also true that the tide did turn.

In 1944, when Gunnar Myrdal characterized the growing tensions between America's egalitarian pretensions and its racist practices as an "American dilemma," the discrepancy was becoming more and more difficult for intellectuals and national leaders to justify.[3] What had been, for all practical purposes, a regional "dilemma" was becoming a national "dilemma," involving by 1950 some fifteen million black persons, or one American in ten. Under these circumstances, it became much easier to relax the bars for fewer than one million Asian Americans, more than one-third of whom lived in the faroff territory of Hawaii.

---

1. Oscar Handlin places this change a little earlier. "Somewhere, in the mid-1930's there was a turn. Americans ceased to believe in race, the hate movements began to disintegrate, and discrimination increasingly took on the aspect of an anachronistic survival from the past rather than a pattern valid for the future" (Oscar Handlin, *Race and Nationality in American Life*, p. 141).

2. John Morton Blum, *V Was for Victory: Politics and American Culture During World War II*, p. 220.

3. Executive Order 8802, June 25, 1941, cited in Samuel N. Rosenman, comp., *The Public Papers and Addresses of Franklin D. Roosevelt* (1941): *The Call to Battle Stations*, pp. 233–37. See also Gunnar Myrdal, *An American Dilemma*.

The presence of large numbers of blacks and other members of what Myrdal would later call the "underclasses" made it easier for Asian Americans to move up the ethnic escalator. That upward movement was assisted by international complications, since American racism was no longer just a domestic affair. In contradistinction to the post World War I era, when Americans had said that they wanted to be left alone—"We seek no part in directing the destinies of the World" was the way Warren Harding had put it in his 1921 inaugural address—after World War II, most American leaders continued to press Roosevelt's claims to leadership of what increasingly came to be called the "Free World."

Since most of the inhabitants of the world were not white, this self-imposed leadership role placed further strains on the already weakened racial and ethnic barriers in the United States. This curious combination of causes—a relaxation of discrimination at home and an aspiration to universal leadership abroad—produced, and was a product of, that changed climate of opinion in which Asian Americans for the first time made steady and uninterrupted social and economic progress. None of this, however, would have been easy to predict at the end of World War II.

When the war ended in August 1945, about 44,000 Japanese Americans were still incarcerated in relocation centers. The Supreme Court's decision in the *Endo* case had not freed them. In the first place, the decision had done nothing either for the noncitizen Issei or for Nisei whose loyalty was deemed doubtful by the government. In the second place, although the WRA was determined to depopulate and close down the centers as soon as possible, for many Japanese Americans of each generation the camps had become a haven in a world that seemed to them wholly hostile. There can be no sadder commentary on the destructive effects of the government's abuse of Japanese Americans than the fact that, even after the war was over, a third of the Japanese American people were not only still in camps but many of them literally had to be forced to leave. As the WRA itself described it: "The Government placed the remaining evacuees under direct compulsion to leave. The evacuees unable to make up their minds, or who refused to leave, were given train fare to the point of evacuation."[4]

Two-thirds of the Japanese American people were no longer in camp. As we have seen, about 23,000 persons were serving in the army, the only branch of the service which would accept them. This included perhaps 100 Nisei women who had been accepted into the

---

4. U.S. Department of the Interior, *Impounded People*, p. 218.

Women's Army Corps. The rest of the Japanese American people on the mainland had left the camps and had reentered, however tentatively, the mainstream of American life. It would be more precise to say that most of them had entered the mainstream of American life for the first time, because Nisei economic life in the Rocky Mountain West, the Midwest, and the East was quite different from the life they had lived in prewar Japanese America.

There were major differences. For one, the generational struggle was over: the day of the Issei had passed. It was "life without father" or mother, as the new communities were largely Nisei and Sansei, especially at first. When parents joined children and grandchildren, they did so almost as guests (see table 7.1). In addition, there were major cultural and economic changes. Economically there was no longer an ethnic economy to shelter Japanese Americans; culturally there were no longer established ethnic institutions to shape their lives. There were now neighborhood clusters of Japanese, but no real *Nihonmachi* (Japantowns).

Although it would be an overstatement to say that the new Japanese American communities in such cities as Chicago, Minneapolis, Denver, or Cleveland were fully integrated—they were not so at the end of the war and, in fact, are not so now—the degree of interaction with majority whites was, of necessity, greatly increased. Even in Chicago, the greatest new population center of Japanese Americans, as late as 1950 there were some 11,000, down from a postwar peak of at least twice as many.[5] In consequence of this decentralization, most Japanese Americans were employed in the larger economy. When we compare the postwar life patterns of Japanese in the Midwest with prewar life patterns in West Coast urban centers, we will see how drastically Japanese American life had been transformed.

Both Franklin D. Roosevelt and his War Relocation Authority had high hopes that, after the war, the new Japanese American

---

5. Census data for Chicago show 390 ethnic Japanese in 1940, and 11,051 in 1950. Illinois figures were 462 and 11,646, respectively. There was an intercensal peak, which Michael D. Albert estimates at 23,000, for the start of 1946. Masako K. Osako says, "nearly 30,000 Japanese-Americans moved to Chicago" (p. 326), but I think that this is too high a figure. Part of the problem is that Chicago was a way station through which many persons passed while moving to more permanent destinations. Albert's as yet unpublished dissertation is the best single work treating postwar Japanese American Chicago. Cf. table 2:4 and table 5:1 in Michael D. Albert, "Japanese American Communities in Chicago and the Twin Cities" (Ph.D. diss., University of Minnesota, 1980). See also Masako K. Osako, "Japanese-Americans: Melting into the All-American Pot," in Peter d'A. Jones and Melvin G. Holli, eds., *Ethnic Chicago*, pp. 313–44, 377–80.

Table 7.1
Japanese Americans 1950
Age and Sex Distribution

Age Cohort	Male	% in Cohort	Female	% in Cohort
75+	1422	1.8	401	0.6
70–74	2771	3.6	690	1.1
65–69	4219	5.5	1173	1.8
60–64	4705	6.2	2097	3.2
55–59	2138	2.8	3281	5.1
50–54	3072	4.0	3937	6.1
45–49	3323	4.3	2889	4.5
40–44	2545	3.3	2067	3.2
35–39	4282	5.6	3520	5.4
30–34	7894	10.3	6494	10.0
25–29	9998	12.6	9576	14.8
20–24	8003	10.5	7780	12.0
15–19	4940	6.4	4662	7.2
10–14	4355	5.7	3874	6.0
5–9	5472	7.2	5281	8.1
0–4	7308	9.6	7196	11.1
	76,447		64,918	
Median Age	Male ca. 28 years		Females ca. 26 years	

SOURCE: United States Department of Commerce. Bureau of the Census. *1950 Census of Population* 3B, table 4, p. 18.

communities would contain the majority of the Japanese American population. But this was not to be. The intervention of the Supreme Court in the *Endo* case, the unexpectedly rapid ending of the war, the closing down of the camps, and even the action of the WRA itself in sending those who made no positive decision about leaving camp back to their former home areas, all contributed to frustrating the planned decentralization of Japanese Americans (see table 7.2). A significant reduction did occur in the prewar West Coast concentration. By 1950, instead of almost nine out of ten mainland Japanese living in the three Pacific states, the ratio had dropped to almost seven out of ten. Put another way, before wartime relocation about one Japanese American in twenty had lived in states east of the Rockies; afterward, almost one in three did. Had a census been taken in late 1946, surely a much higher percentage would have been found in the Midwest and East. But the roots many had put down there were relatively weak. If the restrictions against returning to the West Coast had not been relaxed so soon, if the war had lasted longer, and if the reaction to their return had been more severe, a different pattern might have ensued.

A glance north of the 49th parallel provides an instructive comparison, as the experience of the Japanese Canadians was in many respects similar to that of their American cousins. In Canada, a similar prewar clustering occurred along the coastal strip of British Columbia: its density was somewhat higher; the census of 1941 showed more than 95 percent of Japanese Canadians living there. The expulsion and relocation of Japanese Canadians began within days of that in the United States, and Canadian Prime Minister William Lyon Mackenzie King was as convinced of the desirability of breaking up the West Coast concentration as was Franklin Roosevelt. But in Canada, where there was no judicial review of governmental acts, the prohibition against Japanese Canadians returning to their former British Columbia homes was kept in effect more than five years longer than the similar prohibition in the United States. Coastal British Columbia was not reopened to Japanese Canadians until April 1, 1949. The result was a spectacular shift in population (see table 7.3).[6]

In Canada, two-thirds of the Japanese Canadians remained east of the Rockies: in the United States, more than two-thirds of the Japanese Americans returned to the region where they had once lived. In Canada, Toronto replaced Vancouver as the most populous center of Japanese residence: in the United States, Los Angeles continued to be the urban area in which the largest number of Japanese Americans lived.

Although more than two-thirds of Japanese Americans did return to the Pacific region, in many instances that return was not really a homecoming. Not only were there flurries of hostile demonstrations, particularly in rural areas, but many thousands had lost their homes, especially their farms, in one way or another. While agriculture

---

6. For more detailed U.S.-Canadian comparisons, see Roger Daniels, "The Japanese Experience in North America: An Essay in Comparative Racism," *Canadian Ethnic Studies* 9, no. 2 (1977): 91–100; idem, "Japanese Relocation and Redress in North America: A Comparative View," *The Pacific Historian* 26, no. 1 (1982): 2–13; idem, "Chinese and Japanese in North America: The Canadian and American Experiences Compared," *The Canadian Review of American Studies* 17 (1986): 173–86, and the works therein cited.

Table 7.2
Japanese American Population, by Census Regions and Selected
States, 1940 and 1950

Region or State	1940	Percentage	1950	Percentage	Change 1940–1950
United States	126,947	100.0	141,768	100.0	+11.7
Pacific	112,353	88.5	98,310	69.3	−12.5
Mountain	8,574	6.8	14,231	10.0	+66.0
W.N. Central	755	0.6	2,738	1.9	+262.6
E.N. Central	816	0.6	15,996	11.3	+1,860.3
Mid-Atlantic	3,060	2.4	6,706	4.7	+119.2
W.S. Central	564	0.4	1,334	.9	+136.5
E.S. Central	43	...	328	.2	+662.7
South Atlantic	442	0.3	1,393	1.0	+215.2
New England	340	0.3	732	.5	+115.3
California	93,717	73.8	84,956	59.9	−9.4
Illinois	624	.5	11,646	8.2	+1,766.3
Washington	14,565	11.5	9,694	6.8	−34.4
Colorado	2,734	2.2	5,412	3.8	+98.0
Utah	2,210	1.7	4,452	3.1	+101.4
New York	2,538	2.0	3,893	2.7	+1,433.9
Oregon	4,071	3.2	3,660	2.6	−10.1
Ohio	163	.1	1,986	1.4	+1,118.4
Idaho	1,191	.9	1,980	1.4	+66.2
New Jersey	298	.2	1,784	1.3	+498.7
Michigan	139	.1	1,517	1.1	+991.3
Minnesota	51	...	1,049	.7	+1,956.9

SOURCE: U.S. Census.

continued to be a major occupation of Japanese in the West, that concentration was greatly reduced in the postwar years. The 1940 census showed that more than two out of five Japanese employed in the three West Coast states (41.4 percent) were in agriculture; the 1950 census showed that just under one in three working Japanese in the West was so employed (32.5 percent). The 1960 census for

Table 7.3
Japanese Canadian Population, by Province, 1941 and 1951

Region or Province	1941	Percentage	1951	Percentage	Change Percentage 1941–1951
Canada	23,149	100.0	21,663	100.0	−6.4
British Columbia	22,096	95.5	7,169	33.1	−67.6
Ontario	234	1.0	8,581	39.6	+3,567.1
Alberta	578	2.5	3,336	15.4	+477.2
Manitoba	42	0.2	1,161	5.4	+2,664.3
Quebec	48	0.2	1,137	5.2	+2,268.8
All other	151	0.7	279	1.3	+84.8

SOURCE: Census of Canada

California showed that only one in five employed Japanese (20.9 percent) was still in agriculture. In twenty years the percentage of Japanese employed in western agriculture had been cut about in half. Agriculture, however, still employed a disproportionate number of Japanese. By 1960 agriculture employed fewer than one white Californian in fifty (1.7 percent), so that Japanese were more than ten times as concentrated in farming as were whites.[7] (See also table 6.2.)

That Japanese Americans were, as the economists put it, "economically disadvantaged" by the relocation is axiomatic. For many years historians, including me, have cited the figure $400,000,000 as a conservative estimate of Japanese American property losses. We have attributed that figure to the Federal Reserve Bank (FRB) of San Francisco, which had been assigned quasi-fiduciary authority over Japanese American property in March 1942. We now know that this figure was a postwar invention. The bank had made not the slightest attempt, then or later, to estimate the total value of Japanese American property. Until further research is done, we simply will not know its valuation. Clearly, it was worth hundreds of millions of dollars.[8]

---

7. Employment data from various censuses. 1940 data are conveniently compiled in U.S. War Department, *Final Report, Japanese Evacuation from the West Coast, 1942*, pp. 416–18. 1950 data from U.S. Dept. of Commerce, Bureau of the Census, *Census of Population, 1950*, "Special Reports," 3B:41. 1960 data are conveniently compiled in California, Dept. of Industrial Relations, Division of Fair Employment Practices, *Californians of Japanese, Chinese, Filipino Ancestry*, pp. 33–34.

8. Perhaps the earliest appearance of the $400,000,000 figure in an official

In its self-congratulatory report at the end of 1942, the FRB concluded that its program had

> historical significance in that it accomplished the evacuation of an entire racial group from a wide area in a limited period of time, an operation unique in the nation's history. That it was conducted without serious incident during a period of war and strong animosity against the Japanese was the result of a high degree of restraint displayed by both the evacuees and the persons with whom they had dealings.[9]

By contrast, Sandra C. Taylor, the leading authority on the bank's handling of evacuee property, has concluded that the program was

> hastily-devised, ill-conceived, and procedurally sloppy. . . . The white community, for the most part anxious to be rid of its unwelcome neighbors, was quick to victimize them. The bank agents could only prevent the grossest abuses, and then only for a few of the thousands uprooted. . . . Hampered by inadequate time and inability or unwillingness to apprehend or punish the exploiters, the [bank personnel] failed, and in their failure they too became victims of a misguided policy.[10]

---

document came in August 1954, when JACL official Mike Masaoka testified, without contradiction, that "the Federal Reserve Bank of San Francisco . . . estimated that there was a loss of $400 million in actual money losses out of the evacuation" (U.S. Congress, House, *Japanese American Evacuation Claims*. Hearings before Subcommittee No. 5 of the Committee on the Judiciary, 83rd Cong., 2d sess., 1954, p. 15). That figure has become part of the folklore of the evacuation. In 1983 consultants to the Commission on the Wartime Internment and Relocation of Civilians "estimated" such losses, in 1945 dollars, as between $108 million and $164 million in income and between $41 million and $206 million in property, for a total of $149 to $370 million. Despite a great deal of statistical hocus pocus, there is no reason to have confidence in the "data," as the requisite research was simply not done. As the consultants themselves admitted, "we have had to make assumptions and use data that are less than ideal" (Arnold et al., *Economic Losses*, p. 7). By applying inflationary formulae and investment assumptions, they arrived at a range of losses running from $1.2 to $6.4 billion. All the above estimates were adjusted to reflect the payments that some Japanese Americans received under the Japanese American Claims Act of 1948, which the consultants estimated at $25 million in 1948 dollars. See Frank S. Arnold et al., *Economic Losses of Ethnic Japanese as a Result of Exclusion and Detection, 1942–1946.*

9. [Federal Reserve Bank, San Francisco], "Report of the Federal Reserve Bank of San Francisco as Fiscal Agent of the United States on Its Operations in Connection with Evacuation Operations in Military Areas No. 1 and No. 2 during 1942" (San Francisco, 1942), 22 pp. + 75 exhibits, at p. 22.

10. Sandra C. Taylor, "The Federal Reserve Bank and the Relocation of the Japanese in 1942," *The Public Historian* 5 (1983): 9–30, at p. 30.

An examination of the FRB's publications yields further evidence of its essential unconcern for the Japanese American people. A 1943 article piously entitled "Work in the Evacuees' Interests in the Federal Reserve Bank of San Francisco," is actually concerned only with the economic impact on California agriculture of the removal of Japanese Americans.[11] When Japanese Americans began to return to the West Coast, the FRB made no effort to make amends for its wartime misfeasance, which it has never acknowledged. There is no reason, almost four decades later, to question the judgment of Thomas and Nishimoto in 1946 "that every evacuee incurred some loss, that many of them suffered severe and irreparable losses, both tangible and intangible, and that the burden fell more heavily upon the small owner than the large."[12]

In addition to what was lost, any Japanese American balance sheet must also consider what was not gained. The war years from 1942 to 1945 were, for most Americans, years of relative prosperity, years in which old debts were paid and savings and investments were increased. But, generally, even those Japanese whose assets were not depleted stood still. They and their families would always suffer from being a step or two behind where they would have been if the government had only let them continue to live industrious and productive lives.

It is instructive to note that much of the political leadership of California behaved in a responsible way as the Japanese started to return, and it is fascinating if fruitless to ponder whether, if political leaders had acted similarly in 1941–1942, the evacuation would have been found "necessary." Many of these leaders were relatively recent converts to racial and ethnic tolerance. Los Angeles Mayor Fletcher Bowron, who as late as mid-1943 had insisted that his city wanted none of its "Japs" back, held a public ceremony at city hall as the first evacuees trickled back in January 1945 to reassure them that "We want you and all other citizens of Japanese ancestry who have relocated here to feel secure in your home."

A similar if slower turnabout was made by California Governor Earl Warren. Warren was opposed to the return of any Japanese Americans to California before the end of the war. Interestingly enough, as attorney general in 1942, Warren had feared Japanese American espionage and sabotage. As governor in November 1944, he feared only the reactions of anti-Japanese Californians. Japanese who had been released from camp, the governor said, should not be

---

11. *Federal Reserve Bulletin*, Washington, D.C., April, 1943.
12. Dorothy S. Thomas and Richard S. Nishimoto, *The Spoilage*, p. 16.

allowed to return because of possible "civil disturbances" that might impede the "war effort." When, however, the bar was lifted by the federal government under the spur of the Supreme Court's decision, Warren immediately urged the people of California to support the federal government's action.[13]

While not all state and local government officials behaved as responsibly—and some of the least responsible were rural law enforcement officials—no one who had taken the pulse of wartime California would have predicted that the return of the Japanese Americans would be as free of violence as it was. John Modell has cited a series of polls taken in Los Angeles during 1943 showing that, far from being prepared to welcome Japanese back, 64 to 74 percent favored "a constitutional amendment after the war for the deportation of all Japanese from this country."[14] Not only did Angelenos largely refrain from violence when Japanese Americans began to return (thirteen months after the last of the polls just cited) but by 1948 they joined the rest of the state's voters in rejecting, by a ratio of better than three to two, a ballot proposition that would have made the alien land laws even harsher. The California alien land laws themselves fell before the state supreme court in 1952; those of other states became moot in the same year as federal law eliminated the category of "aliens ineligible to citizenship."

Some elected federal officials, such as Senator Warren G. Magnuson (D-Wash.), continued to agitate for harsh measures against Japanese Americans even after they had begun their return to the West Coast. At the end of April 1945, for example, Magnuson demanded a "clear cut" policy on Japanese residing in the United States, asserting that "One class of Japanese should be shipped off to Japanese territory on the first boat we can spare. . . . They are the alien Japanese and the American-born Japanese who have indicated by act or implication their loyalty to Hirohito."[15]

Nor was anti-Japanese activity limited to the public sector. In one of the most publicized anti-Japanese actions, the American Legion post in Hood River, Oregon, removed the names of all sixteen local Japanese American servicemen from the city's honor roll. This and other racist acts by American Legion posts from Seattle to Hollywood created largely unfavorable comment in *Life* magazine and other national media. Trade unions, in many instances, not only kept up prewar discriminations but also tried to erect new ones. Most notorious were

13. Roger Daniels, *Concentration Camps, North America*, pp. 158–70.
14. John Modell, *The Economics and Politics of Racial Accommodation*, p. 188.
15. Seattle *Post-Intelligencer*, April 29, 1945.

the efforts of Dave Beck's Teamsters in the Pacific Northwest. In the summer of 1945 some of the first returning Japanese American farmers around Seattle could get their produce handled only by having sympathetic white clergymen deliver their crops to the downtown wholesale produce markets to disguise its origin.

One of the few unions actively to support Japanese American reentry into the labor force was Harry Bridges' International Longshoremen's and Warehousemen's Union, which, in a celebrated incident, actually suspended and then expelled anti-Japanese union leaders and threatened to suspend a whole local in Stockton, California, for discriminatory activities. It should be noted, however, as Harvey Schwartz, the historian of this incident has pointed out, that the strenuous action taken by the international union against its local was governed largely by the union's desire to organize successfully in Hawaii.[16]

The residential patterns of the returning Japanese were changed significantly. In the larger cities of prewar Japanese settlement, the Japantown clusters had tended to be in the old central cities. With the evacuation, however, the former Japanese areas became the homes of new migrants to the western cities, often blacks and Mexican Americans. While some returning Japanese Americans managed to reestablish themselves in their old neighborhoods, others were unable to do so and still others did not want to do so, particularly when many of their new neighbors would be black. Many—particularly the younger, upwardly mobile Nisei families—wanted to join the migration to suburbia which was one of the most pronounced population shifts of the postwar era. Central city ethnic neighborhoods—the old *Nihonmachis*—in the postwar era would contain a smaller fraction of the Japanese American population of cities such as Seattle, San Francisco, and Los Angeles. In some places, such as the city of Gardena in greater Los Angeles, suburban centers of Japanese population would develop;[17] in other places, such as the area in and around Seattle, Japanese population would become more widely dispersed. In each of those instances, however, a central city ethnic center endured and became a commercial and cultural center for the ethnic community. One of the many tensions within the postwar ethnic community would come from the unwillingness of many prosperous suburban Nisei to spend much of their time and energy in reestablishing such centers,

---

16. Harvey Schwartz, "A Union Combats Racism: The ILWU's Japanese American 'Stockton Incident' of 1945," *Southern California Quarterly* 62 (1980): 161–76.

17. Cathy Lynn Tanimoto, "Changing Japanese Ethnicity: A Case Study of Gardena, California" (M.A. thesis, Louisiana State University, 1975).

often many miles from where they lived, and the resentment of Issei and more traditional Nisei who felt that the suburban Nisei were not showing proper solidarity with the community.

The larger changes in West Coast urban population almost certainly help to explain the relative weakness of the postwar anti-Japanese campaign, if, in fact, the sporadic hostility can be called that. In contrast with the fewer than 100,000 ethnic Japanese who returned after the war, more than three million newcomers came to the West Coast between 1940 and 1950; in 1944 alone, according to one estimate, more than 1,100,000 persons moved to California. Significant numbers of these newcomers were blacks and Mexican Americans. By the 1950 census, blacks outnumbered Asians in the region. There were some 500,000 blacks and 200,000 Asians in a region with a population of nearly 14.5 million.[18]

Even before Japanese Americans began to return to the West Coast, the strongly accommodationist views of the JACL and its leaders began to prevail, at least among the Nisei. Most members of that generation apparently came to believe, as the JACL leaders always had, that the only way they could ever win a place for themselves in America was by being better Americans than most. In the immediate postwar years, an enlarged and expanded JACL became the voice of the Japanese American community. For some twenty years after the relocation, the JACL had few overt challenges from either within or without the community, although there were those, such as San Francisco attorney Wayne Collins, who viewed its posture with contempt and referred to the leaders of the organization as "JACkals." But no significant group within the community publicly questioned the correctness of the position the JACL had taken in 1942 and had continued to maintain. That it had paid dividends in the postwar era cannot be doubted. Given the small numbers of the Japanese American community, the JACL lobbying operation, run for decades by

18. Population data are as follows:

1940					1950				
State	Black	%	Asian	%	State	Black	%	Asian	%
CA	124,306	1.8	167,643	2.4	CA	462,172	4.4	188,931	1.8
OR	2,565	0.2	6,797	0.6	OR	11,529	0.8	6,864	0.5
WA	7,424	0.4	19,226	1.1	WA	30,691	1.3	17,960	0.8

SOURCE: U.S. Census

Mike Masaoka, must be ranked as one of the most effective in the nation.

The two great postwar triumphs of the JACL were the Japanese American Claims Act of 1948 and the naturalization provisions of the McCarran-Walter Immigration Act of 1952. Although each was a flawed triumph, the passage of these statutes represented fulfillment of two major goals that the organization had set at its 1946 national convention in Denver. The JACL actively participated in the National Leadership Conference on Civil Rights, supported fair housing bills, antilynching and antipoll tax bills, and filed amicus curiae briefs in a chain of civil rights cases leading up to *Brown* v. *Board of Education* (1954). In turn, the organization gained support for the measures that it cared about most from the whole civil rights coalition.[19] In addition, it was able to get the cooperation of the federal government and the support of some of those who had been responsible for the incarceration.

The first major fruit of this curious coalition of oppressed and oppressors was the Japanese American Claims Act of 1948. The act did not question the propriety of the evacuation. As the Report of the Senate Committee on the Judiciary put it: "The question of whether the evacuation of the Japanese people from the West Coast was justified is now moot. The Government did move these people, bodily, resulting losses were great, and the principles of justice and responsible government require that there should be compensation for such losses."[20] The bill had the "unanimous support of the Government departments concerned as well as the entire delegation of west coast Congressmen."[21] Among those who testified for it were John J. McCloy, former Assistant Secretary of War, Francis Biddle, former Attorney General, and Dillon S. Myer, former head of the WRA. Secretary of the Interior J. A. Krug, writing for the Truman administration, outlined some of the burdens that the Japanese American had borne:

> The evacuation orders gave the persons affected desperately little time to settle their affairs. The government safeguards that were designed to prevent undue loss . . . were somewhat tardily instituted, were not at once effectively publicized among the evacuees, and were never entirely successful. . . . Continued exclusion increased the losses. Private buildings in which evacuees stored

---

19. For an "in-house" description of the JACL accomplishments, see William K. Hosokawa, *"Better Americans in a Greater America,"* n.p., n.d., but ca. 1968.

20. U.S. Congress, Senate, *Report 1740*, 80th Cong., 2d sess., 1948, p. 2.

21. Ibid., *Report 1531*, 80th Cong., 2d sess., 1948, p. 2.

their property were broken into and vandalized. Mysterious fires destroyed vacant buildings. Property left with "friends" unaccountably disappeared; goods stored with the Government were sometimes damaged or lost. Persons entrusted with the management of evacuee real property mulcted the owners in diverse ways. Tenants failed to pay rent, converted property to their own use, and committed waste. Prohibited from returning to the evacuated areas even temporarily to handle property matters, the evacuees were unable to protect themselves adequately. Property management assistance given by the War Relocation Authority on the West Coast, although it often mitigated and often prevented loss, could not completely solve the problem there, complicated as it was by difficulties in communication with absent owners and local prejudice.[22]

The Report of the House Committee on the Judiciary observed, in recommending that the bill "do pass," that the argument had been made

> that the victims of the relocation were no more casualties of the war than were many millions of other Americans who lost their lives or their homes or occupations during the war. However, the argument was not considered tenable, since in the instant case the loss was inflicted by a voluntary act of the Government without precedent in the history of this country. Not to redress these loyal Americans in some measure for the wrongs inflicted upon them would provide ample material for attacks by the followers of foreign ideologies on the American way of life, and to redress them would be simple justice.[23]

Despite such rhetoric, the redress was only partial. The Japanese American Claims Act, which was signed into law in July 1948 and later extended and modified, set off seventeen years of litigation; the last claim filed was not settled until 1965. Congress appropriated just $38 million to settle all claims. Claims were allowed only for "damage to or loss of real or personal property" and could not include such normal economic considerations as good will, anticipated profits, earnings, or interest. In all, some 23,000 claims were filed aggregating $131 million in damages. The Department of Justice, which administered the processing of claims, moved with agonizing bureaucratic

---

22. Letter, J. A. Krug to Joseph W. Martin, Jr. (Speaker of the House), March 17, 1947, printed in U.S. Congress, House, *Report 732*, 80th Cong., 1st sess., 1947, pp. 2–4.

23. House *Report 732*, p. 5.

slowness and inefficiency. In addition, many of its lawyers went to great lengths to see that the government was not "cheated" by its former victims. In what was perhaps the most outrageous legal interpretation, a young Nisei farmer near Seattle had his adjudicated award cut in half because he had a Caucasian wife. The Justice Department reasoned that since Washington was a community property state, he was entitled to only half the award. His wife, who had not been forced to accompany her husband and small children to the concentration camp, was entitled to nothing.[24]

During all of 1950, just 210 claims were cleared and only 73 people were actually compensated: at that rate, it would have taken more than a century to process all the claims. Under such circumstances, it is little wonder that many claimants, particularly the older Issei, were willing to settle their claims for a few cents on the dollar. One ninety-two-year-old accepted $2,500 for a $75,000 claim because he was convinced that he would not live long enough to settle the matter in the courts. In some cases, the government spent more money adjudicating a claim than the claim was worth. Bill Hosokawa has reported that the government spent over $1,000 in settling a $450 claim.

In addition to the actual losses, there were the lost opportunities, opportunities that continue to affect the economic status of the Japanese American community. As economist Kenneth Hansen put it some two decades ago: "The Nisei are paying the price today in the loss of opportunity and gains which they would have made had [the relocation and incarceration not occurred]. Losses are still being compounded because of constantly increasing evaluations of often valuable lands they were forced to let go."[25]

Despite its economic, legal, and moral shortcomings, the Japanese American Claims Act was an important symbol of the improved image of the Japanese American people as well as a partial vindication of the accommodationist strategy and tactics of the JACL. But at the same time that the federal government was ameliorating the economic conditions of the Japanese Americans, the State of California was endeavoring to make them worse. Between 1944 and 1948 some eighty escheat cases were filed against Issei by the State of California, continuing an assault begun during the war by liberal Democratic Attorney General Robert W. Kenny. A score of these prosecutions were "successful," and the state took land and other assets worth

---

24. This and similar cases are documented in several partially restricted collections on Japanese American agriculture in the Archives of the University of Washington, Seattle.

25. As cited by Audrie Girdner and Anne Loftis, *The Great Betrayal*, pp. 436–37.

about a quarter of a million dollars from Issei-headed families. This process came to an end in 1952 when the California Supreme Court declared the Alien Land Acts, which dated back to 1913, unconstitutional.[26] A case challenging the acts had gone to the United States Supreme Court, which, although it had found for the Japanese appellant on technical grounds, had let the laws stand. Since four justices—Black, Douglas, Murphy, and Rutledge—had written angry concurrences denouncing the acts, it is clear that had California not negated the land laws, the Warren Court would have.[27]

Within California, and elsewhere on the West Coast, it was apparent that popular attitudes were changing. In 1948, four years before the alien land laws were struck down, the remnants of the old anti-Japanese political coalition—including "patriotic" groups such as the Native Sons of the Golden West, some business and farming groups, some labor unions, and a variety of politicians of both parties—had succeeded in placing an anti-Japanese measure on the California ballot which would have made the land laws even harsher. As we have seen, this measure went down to a resounding defeat in the general election, with almost 59 percent of those voting rejecting it. Never before had an anti-Asian measure been defeated by a popular vote in California. Although it should be remarked that just over two voters in five favored further discrimination, the change from the well-nigh unanimous anti-Japanese attitudes of the war years was striking. Only four years earlier, as we have seen, in September 1944 a public opinion poll in California's largest city had shown that 74 percent of the respondents had favored a constitutional amendment to deport "all Japanese from this country" and to forbid all further Japanese immigration.[28]

While changes in postwar attitudes toward Japanese Americans accompanied a steady improvement of the *Nikkei* (persons of Japanese ethnicity) image, the reputation of Chinese Americans fluctuated as events in China altered Sino-American relationships. During World War II, the changes had been almost all positive. Chinese American men and women had contributed significantly to the war effort; according to selective service data, almost 16,000 Chinese Americans

---

26. *Fujii* v. *State* 38 *California Reports, 2nd Series* 7/8 (1952). The decision by Justice Stanley Mosk, a quondam World Federalist, found the statute, among other things, in violation of the United Nations Charter!

27. *Oyama* v. *California* 332 US 633. For a good discussion, see C. Herman Pritchett, *Civil Liberties and the Vinson Court*, pp. 118–22.

28. For polls, see John Modell, *Economics and Politics of Racial Accommodation*, p. 188.

served in the military between 1940 and 1946. Because there were no Chinese American units, Chinese were generally integrated. About 1,600 even served in the navy, some in commissioned ranks.[29] William Der Bing, head of protocol and community affairs for NASA in the 1970s, has described some of the obstacles he overcame in his successful attempt to get a wartime commission as a naval aviator.

> They were reluctant to give me the application forms. I said, "Either I get them here or I can get them from my Congressman." The minute I mentioned "Congressman," the next thing I knew I had a pile of papers. Even in the Navy, there were some real good men, but the majority didn't want a "Chinaman" in their outfit. They made every remark possible to harass you.
>
> Personally, I was told that "No Chinaman will ever fly in my outfit." I was told that by a doctor—a Navy doctor. He gave me a physical. He said, "I want you to know that I would do anything I can to fail you in your physical." I looked at him and said, "If you do, it would be the most dishonest thing that an officer in this United States Navy would ever do to another member of the United States Navy." I put it just this way.[30]

The mixed and uneven nature of Chinese American "success" in the immediate post-World War II era can be illustrated by two incidents. A well-to-do former Kuomintang officer, Sing Sheng, moved into the middle-class San Francisco suburb of Southwood. After some turmoil about his presence, an informal neighborhood referendum found 174 persons voting against him, 28 for him, and 14 without opinion. But when the event was publicized, Sheng and his family received invitations to move to scores of communities across the nation. Eventually they settled peacefully in the northern California town of Sonoma. In the Midwest a fraternity at Northwestern University revoked an invitation it had made to Sherman Wu, the son of a former Nationalist officer, because at least seven Caucasian pledges had said that they would not enter the fraternity if it took Wu. Again there was a counterreaction: two other fraternities at Northwestern offered to pledge the young Chinese American, who was understandably hesitant: "If they are sincere enough," the New York *Times* reported him as saying, "I may join one. I don't know yet."[31]

---

29. The precise number is 15,998, which covers enlistments and inductions, September 1940 through October 1946. Of those, 14,377 were in the army and 1,621 in the navy. U.S., Selective Service System, Special Monograph 10, *Special Groups* 2:13.
30. Diane Mei Lin Mark and Ginger Chih, *A Place Called Chinese America*, p. 96.
31. Harold R. Isaacs, *Images of Asia*, pp. 123–24.

During this period American relations with China, which had enjoyed a kind of honeymoon just before and during World War II, became terribly complicated. The news was filled with the ignominious defeats of Nationalist armies, the development of "two Chinas," and the "Who lost China?" debate in American domestic politics. In addition, the Chinese intervention in the Korean War in late 1950 and ugly stories about Chinese "brainwashing" of American prisoners of war all combined to transform American attitudes from what Harold R. Isaacs has called the "Age of Admiration (1937–1944)" into a brief "Age of Disenchantment (1944–1949)." This was followed by a lengthy "Age of Hostility," which endured, with some modifications, until 1971–1972. "Ping-pong diplomacy" then burst on the international sports scene, and President Richard M. Nixon's trip to China, spectacularly covered on television, ushered in a new wave of good feeling toward China. The political cartoonists' symbol for China changed from a menacing armed giant to a giant panda.[32]

Even more complex were our postwar views of the Chinese people. Both Harold Isaacs and his critic, Stuart Creighton Miller, agree that the prewar American image of the Chinese had been unitary, regulated almost exclusively by American relations with and attitudes toward China.[33] The postwar image had become plural. There were now, in American eyes at least, two Chinas: Mao Tse-tung's Communist China, pagan and threatening; and Chiang Kai-shek's capitalist China, Christian and supportive. After the Chinese intervention in the Korean War, many of the same forces in American politics which had stressed the "Who lost China?" theme now introduced the "unleash Chiang Kai-shek" variation. This fantasized, as Lyndon Johnson would in another war, that Asian "boys" could do the dirty, nasty fighting on the ground, leaving the clean war of bombing, strafing, and shelling to the American technologists.

But the major dynamic of the cold-war era was ideological rather than racial. Depending on their politics, there were good or bad Chinese. Our insistence, during the negotiations at Panmunjon, that Chinese prisoners of war had a right to opt for one China or the other—an option that we had failed to give to Soviet prisoners of war after World War II—is merely one example of how the cold war influenced almost every aspect of American policy. Even more significant for Asian Americans would be the way in which the cold war would lead to modifications in our immigration and refugee policies.

---

32. Ibid., p. 71.
33. Stuart Creighton Miller, *The Unwelcome Immigrant: American Images of the Chinese, 1785–1882.*

Another important factor was that the Chinese American population itself had changed considerably. As Rose Hum Lee pointed out in the mid-1950s, about half of the Chinese American population was then native born and was American in its attitudes. This population, reinforced by emigré Chinese Nationalist officials and their children, was becoming increasingly middle class. It was not only disassociating itself from the problems and concerns of American Chinatowns but was striving, rather consistently, for acculturation if not assimilation into the larger American society.[34] One is tempted to say that, just as international developments had produced two Chinas, domestic developments had produced two Chinese Americas, but that would be a gross oversimplification.

The cold-war atmosphere of the 1950s affected Chinese Americans both positively and negatively as their ancestral homeland became, in the eyes of many, the chief American antagonist. There were some significant positive aspects of the Asian cold war for Chinese America. The American postwar refugee and displaced person program had originally included only Europeans. The 1950 Refugee Act, for example, had reserved 4,000 spaces for "European refugees from China," largely white Russians and members of the Shanghai Jewish community. In 1953, for the first time, Asians were designated admissible refugees as 2,000 visas were reserved for "refugees of Chinese origin" who were vouched for by the government on Taiwan.[35] This tiny trickle was the start of an Asian refugee stream, which in the late 1970s and early 1980s became, with the so-called boat people and other Southeast Asian refugees, a major component of American immigration.

But other cold-war effects were negative. The fact that China had become an enemy made many in the Chinese American community wonder whether they would have to endure the kind of treatment that had been meted out to Japanese Americans during World War II. This natural anxiety was heightened in 1950 when Congress passed the Emergency Detention Act, which, after thirteen paragraphs of purple rhetoric about a monolithic worldwide Communist conspiracy, provided for a presidential declaration of an "Internal Security Emergency." Under this statute, which remained on the books for

---

34. Rose Hum Lee, "The Integration of the Chinese in the United States," unpublished paper cited in Isaacs, *Images of Asia*, p. 124.

35. 67 *Stat.* 401. For a summary of U.S. refugee policy, see Roger Daniels, "American Refugee Policy in Historical Perspective," in J. C. Jackman and Carla Borden, eds., *The Muses Flee Hitler: Cultural Transfer and Adaptation, 1930–1945*, pp. 61–77. For the Shanghai Jewish community, see David Kranzler, *Japanese, Nazis and Jews*.

twenty-one years, the attorney general was empowered to "apprehend and ... detain ... each person as to whom there is reasonable ground to believe that such person probably will engage in, or probably will conspire with others to engage in, acts of espionage or sabotage." The parallels between this statute and the process by which Japanese Americans were incarcerated during World War II are so striking that it is little wonder that many Chinese Americans feared that they, too, might be found guilty simply by reason of ancestry. The statute, however, was really aimed at ideological rather than ethnic "enemies" of the republic.[36]

More tangible fears were created by the renewed prosecutorial activities of two separate arms of the Department of Justice: the FBI and the Immigration and Naturalization Service. The FBI's activity was aimed at subversive individuals, real and imagined. At the end of the war almost the entire Chinese American establishment supported the Kuomintang, although a few radicals supported the Communists in China and an even smaller number were members of the American Communist party.

At the time of Mao Tse-tung's victory, about 5,000 Chinese nationals were resident in the United States on nonimmigrant visas. Some of them were highly trained professionals. Perhaps a majority were graduate students, many of them attending the most prestigious American institutions. These stranded professionals and students represented very different strata of the Chinese population than had the previous immigrants, legal or illegal, who had been largely southern peasants. One such student, Donald Tsai, who had come to study at Pomona College in 1941 and had gone on to do graduate work at M.I.T., recently told interviewers:

36. 64 *Stat.* 1019. In justifying the pending repeal, then Deputy Attorney General Richard Kleindienst wrote: "Unfortunately, the legislation has aroused among many citizens of the United States the belief that it may one day be used to accomplish the apprehension and detention of citizens who hold unpopular beliefs and views. In addition, various groups, of which our Japanese-American citizens are the most prominent, look upon the legislation as permitting a reoccurrence of the roundups which resulted in the detention of Americans of Japanese ancestry during World War II. It is therefore quite clear that the continuation of the Emergency Detention Act is extremely offensive to many Americans. In the judgment of this Department, the repeal of this legislation will allay the fears and suspicions—unfounded as they may be—of many of our citizens. This benefit outweighs any potential advantage which the act may provide in a time of internal security emergency" (letter to Sen. James O. Eastland, December 2, 1969, printed in Roger Daniels, *The Decision to Relocate the Japanese Americans*, pp. 131–32).

Many students came from China on scholarships from the Chinese government, although I myself did not come as a scholarship student. Those were very difficult scholarships to obtain, through competitive examinations, and so on. And the reason why you see so many Chinese people in the United States who are eminent professionals, teachers, and so forth is that many of these were, indeed, the scholarship students. . . . When they arrived, the war occurred and they were either cut off or decided not to return, and they have indeed made out very well. . . .

Some of us had to work, as did numerous other people. I did various kinds of jobs, library, binding room, tutor. . . . I went to M.I.T. for graduate school. M.I.T. was my father's school also. He studied mining engineering there in 1910 or thereabouts. . . . All of the students were planning to go back to China. There was no thought of staying.

Yet, in the event, a majority of these students did stay, making them the first important segment of the postwar "brain drain" that saw more and more technical and professional personnel from lesser developed countries migrate to the United States and other nations. Some eventually went to Taiwan. A very few, including some highly trained scientists, chose to go back to the People's Republic. The most prominent such person was physicist Hsue-shen Ts'ien, who is considered to be the "father" of the first Chinese satellite.[37]

Although very few made the physicist's choice, every year that passed after the Nationalist debacle in 1949 and the retreat to Taiwan saw more and more Chinese Americans, new and old, reach a *modus vivendi* with the mainland regime. (It must be noted that, unlike European refugees and immigrants, most of whom are vehemently anti-Communist, many Chinese refugees here since the 1950s hold friendly views toward the People's Republic. They visit China even though they do not wish to return permanently. It is beyond the scope of this work to examine this phenomenon in detail, but surely two of its causal components are: first, the fact that Chinese everywhere, regardless of ideology, are pleased by the stature and respect that Mao Tse-tung and his successors have given China and the Chinese; and second, the traditional Chinese acceptance of those who seem to have received the "mandate of Heaven.") Some of the most conservative institutions in Chinese America, the family associations, ran afoul of the FBI because of their continuing communication with related clan

---

37. Donald Tsai, interview in Mark and Chih, *Chinese America*, pp. 104–5. For Hsue-shen Ts'ien, see Borys Lewytzkyj and Juliusz Stroynowski, *Who's Who in the Socialist Countries*, p. 638.

groups in China. As late as 1969, J. Edgar Hoover would testify about security risks before a congressional committee:

> The blatant, belligerent and illogical statements made by Red China's spokesmen during the past years leave no doubt that the United States is Communist China's No. 1 enemy. . . . Red China has been flooding the country with propaganda and there are over 300,000 Chinese in the United States, some of whom could be susceptible to recruitment either through ethnic ties or hostage situations because of relatives in Communist China. . . . In addition up to 20,000 Chinese immigrants can come into the United States each year and this provides a means to send illegal agents into our Nation. . . . There are active Chinese Communist sympathizers in the Western Hemisphere in a position to aid in operations against the United States. [This last was a jab at Canada, which had recognized the People's Republic and was providing a haven for draft resisters.][38]

Nothing more clearly demonstrates the mixed effect of the cold war on American domestic legislation than the passage of the McCarran-Walter Immigration Act of 1952. Sponsored by two of the country's premier "Red hunters," Senator Pat McCarran of Nevada and Representative Francis E. Walter of Pennsylvania, it became law only over the veto of President Harry S. Truman. Truman's chief complaints were that the law was not liberal enough and that it continued the National Origins Quota System, which was "false and unworthy in 1924 [and] even worse now."[39] In addition, the bill also expanded the ideological and moral bases for denying admission to the United States and made deportation for a wide variety of "offenses" much easier, although it should be noted that cold-war liberals did not object much to these latter provisions.

Cold-war liberals, such as President Truman, wanted abolition of the quota system, allocation of visas without regard to national origin, race, creed or color, and flexible annual admissions set at one-sixth of one percent of the most recent census.[40] Cold-war conservatives, such as Senator McCarran, insisted that the law did "not contain one iota of racial and religious discrimination" because it totally eliminated any racial, religious, or ethnic bars to either immigration or natural-

---

38. As cited in Stanford L. Lyman, "Red Guard on Grant Avenue: The Rise of Youthful Rebellion in Chinatown," in idem, *The Asian in North America*, p. 198.

39. The 1952 Immigration and Nationality Act is 66 *Stat* 163; Truman's veto may be found in Harry S. Truman, *Public Papers, 1952–53*, p. 182.

40. President's Commission on Immigration and Naturalization, *Whom We Shall Welcome.*

ization. The new eligibility for all Asians to become naturalized citizens had eliminated the category of aliens ethnically or racially ineligible to citizenship. This was the category on which so much discriminatory legislation, such as the Alien Land Acts, had been based. What neither conservatives nor liberals realized was that, despite tiny ethnic quotas (205 Chinese and 185 Japanese per annum), the combination of unrestricted naturalization after 1952 and the family reunification provisions of the McCarran act meant that relatively large numbers of Asians were able to immigrate into the United States legally during the 1950s.

Family reunification provisions—which had begun for the Chinese wives of American citizens under the terms of a 1946 act—made the close relatives of United States citizens nonquota immigrants. In consequence, wives, children, parents, brothers, and sisters of citizens were able to come in as nonquota entrants. In addition, some Asians came in under the provisions of the War Brides Act of 1945, the Alien Fiancées or Fiancés Act of 1946, and the Refugee Relief Act of 1953. These immigrants, too, were not chargeable to the tiny Asian quotas.[41] As a result, in the 1950s some 45,000 Japanese and some 32,000 Chinese were able to enter legally as immigrants despite a quota system that ostensibly limited immigration to a total of about two thousand for each group for the entire decade. As has been the case with immigration legislation so many times before and since, the legislators and the bureaucrats who advised them had no accurate conception of even the short-term impact of their lawmaking.

For Asian Americans, therefore, the 1952 act marked the full turning of the tide of immigration restriction, a tide that had begun, at the federal level, with the naturalization statute of 1870 and the Chinese Exclusion Act of 1882. The post-1952 system had its clearly racist aspects—a quota immigrant of British birth but Chinese ethnicity would still be charged to the tiny, oversubscribed Chinese quota rather than to the large (65,361), undersubscribed British one. Nonetheless, it provided ways for Asian American groups with an established population base here to expand their number significantly (see table 7.4).

---

41. The War Brides Act of 1945, properly, "Admission of Alien Spouses and Alien Minor Children of the United States Armed Forces," is 59 *Stat* 659; for intendeds, see the act of June 29, 1946, "Admission of the Alien Fiancées or Fiancés of Members of the Armed Forces of the United States," 60 *Stat.* 339; for Chinese wives of American citizens, see the act of August 9, 1946, "To Place Chinese Wives of American Citizens on a Nonquota Basis," 60 *Stat* 975. The Refugee Relief Act of 1953 is 67 *Stat* 401. By 1952 there was a double Chinese quota: 100 for China—really Taiwan—and 105 for "Chinese," who could be of any national origin.

Table 7.4
Migration of Ethnic Chinese and Japanese to the United States by Sex, 1950–1960

Year	Chinese				Japanese			
	Male	Female	Total	Percentage Female	Male	Female	Total	Percentage Female
1950	110	1,179	1,289	91.5	16	29	45	64.4
1951	126	957	1,083	88.4	45	161	206	78.2
1952	118	1,034	1,152	89.8	153	4,581	4,734	96.8
1953	203	890	1,093	81.4	198	2,291	2,489	92.0
1954	1,511	1,236	2,747	45.0	685	3,377	4,062	83.1
1955	1,261	1,367	2,628	52.0	708	3,435	4,143	82.9
1956	2,007	2,443	4,450	54.9	1,342	4,280	5,622	76.1
1957	2,487	2,636	5,123	51.5	765	5,357	6,122	87.5
1958	1,396	1,799	3,195	56.3	868	5,559	6,427	86.5
1959	2,846	3,185	6,031	52.8	810	5,283	6,093	86.7
1960	1,873	1,799	3,672	49.0	824	4,812	5,636	85.4
Total	13,938	18,525	32,463	57.1	6,414	39,165	45,579	85.9

SOURCE: U.S. Department of Justice, Immigration and Naturalization Service, *Annual Reports,* 1950–1960, table 10, "Immigrants Admitted by Race, Sex, and Age." NOTE: This table yields different totals than does the INS compilation by country. For example, the latter table (table 14, 1960), gives for 1951 a total of 1,821 for "China," 198 for "Japan"; for 1960, 4156 for "China" and "Hong Kong," and 5,471 for Japan. "China" (INS) included "Formosa." In other words, in 1951 at least 738 of the entries from China and Formosa were not ethnic Chinese, and at least 153 of the entries from Japan were not ethnic Japanese. For 1960, at least 484 of the entries from China, Formosa, and Hong Kong were not ethnic Chinese, but at least 165 of the entries listed as Japanese entered from places other than Japan.

The government also provided a way, the so-called confession system, for such long-established illegal immigrants as the "paper sons" and "ghosts" of Chinese America to regularize their status. Starting as an administrative innovation, the confession system was written into the statute books in 1957.[42] Under its terms, paper sons and others who had achieved entry by fraudulent means might be able to regularize their status if a close relative—spouse, parent, or child— were a citizen of the United States or a permanent resident alien. The

42. Act of September 11, 1957.

act, passed at a time when cold-war rhetoric still prevailed and many of the institutions of Chinese America still felt themselves besieged by the Department of Justice, gave a great deal of discretion to officials of the Immigration and Naturalization Service (INS), an agency Chinese Americans had learned to distrust. Thus, while many Chinese Americans were able to regularize their status under this humanely conceived statute, many others, probably a majority of its potential beneficiaries, were too distrustful of the government to risk taking advantage of its benefits.

Sometimes the INS used information gained under the confession program selectively, to exclude or deport those favorable to the People's Republic. Many Chinese Americans believe that the INS was often abetted by informers in the service of the Chinese Nationalist regime. Maurice Chuck, publisher of a leftwing newspaper, the San Francisco *Journal,* felt himself to have been singled out by the INS:

> My grandfather used the name of Chuck to come to this country, so naturally my father was under the same name and became a citizen of this country. . . . What happened was [that] they arrested me and tried me and used my father's confession as evidence against me. They didn't use it against my father. . . . So it's very obvious that the reason that they put on this so-called "confession" program was to aim at some particular individuals. They tried to deport me to Taiwan but my activities here in this country were so totally against the Chiang Kai-shek government, it's like sending me to a firing squad. So I got all these professors from U. C. Berkeley and other places to prove that because of my political activities, it's absolutely impossible to deport me to Taiwan.[43]

The renewed immigration of the 1950s, which brought new life to the Chinese American community, also brought new attacks. Perhaps the most traumatic attack came as a result of the activities of Everett F. Drumwright, United States consul general in Hong Kong. In December 1955, Drumwright made a report to the State Department about what he called "a fantastic system of passport and visa fraud." He later argued that the Chinese Communists were using the system to infiltrate agents into the United States. In March 1956, agents of the INS conducted a series of raids to seize illegal immigrants in the Chinatowns of both the East and West Coasts. The protest of the Chinese American establishment, interestingly enough, stressed economic losses rather than human-rights violations. In a complaint

---

43. Mark and Chih, *Chinese America,* p. 104.

couched to appeal to the Eisenhower administration, New York City Chinese leaders claimed that the immigration raids were resulting in losses of $100,000 weekly to merchants there.[44]

Obviously, illegal immigration has happened and continues to happen. No one who has read Maxine Hong Kingston's marvelous book, *The Woman Warrior*, with its evocations of "ghost" names and dual lives, can underestimate the impact that illegal status has had on the Chinese American community.[45] But from the 1950s on, illegality was surely less and less important, both statistically and psychologically, as more and more of the Chinese American population were native-born or naturalized citizens, and as more humane immigration legislation and procedures allowed greater numbers of Chinese to enter the United States legally.

The long-delayed grant of statehood to Hawaii in 1959 was an important victory for Asian Americans: in the subsequent election a Chinese American and a Japanese American became members of the United States Congress, the first Asian Americans to be elected by a largely Asian American constituency. (The first Asian American congressman was Dalip Singh Saund [1899–1973], born in India and elected to the House of Representatives in 1956, where, for six years, he represented a district embracing California's Imperial Valley and containing a largely white electorate.)

There were three major reasons for the long delay in the admission of Hawaii to statehood. First, none of the other overseas territories had ever been seriously considered for admission. Second, doubts had constantly been raised about the loyalty of Hawaii's population before World War II. Those doubts were decisively settled during the war itself, but new ones were raised during the 1950s when Hawaii had its own "Red scare." This centered on charges that the most powerful union in the islands, the International Longshoremen's and Warehousemen's Union, was controlled by Moscow. Third, and clearly most important, was the matter of race. Although some 90 percent of Hawaii's half-million people in 1950 were American citizens, most of them native born, a considerable majority was what the census still called "nonwhite," so that, if admitted, Hawaii would be the only state in twentieth-century America to have a "nonwhite" majority. Ernest Gruening remembered that, after several Japanese Americans had testified during hearings held in Honolulu in 1937, Representative John E. Rankin (D-Miss.) turned to him and said,

---

44. For details, see the New York *Times*, March 4, 17, 18, and 24, 1956.
45. Maxine Hong Kingston, *The Woman Warrior*.

"Mah Gawd, if we give them folks statehood we're lahkley to have a senator called Moto."[46]

By the usual standard, Hawaii had long had all of the necessary attributes for statehood, and the development of mass air transportation after the end of World War II had made its continued territorial status an anachronism. As Charles and Mary Beard put it, Hawaii had

> unequivocally met every test applied to 29 other territorial applications into the union. It is a paradox that the United States should still permit so vital a part of itself to remain in the inferior status of a territory when that part fulfills each and every one of the historic qualifications for statehood and is eager to assume the burdens and responsibilities of full equality as well as to enjoy its privileges.[47]

Popular opinion, too, seemed to support Hawaiian statehood. A series of eleven public opinion polls taken on the mainland between 1946 and 1954 showed majorities in favor of statehood swelling from 60 percent to 70 percent. Reflecting that majority view, statehood bills passed the House in 1947, 1950, and 1953, but the Senate refused to agree. While opponents of Hawaiian statehood came from every section of the nation, the core of the opposition was from southern senators, including Eastland of Mississippi, Smathers of Florida, Ellender of Louisiana, Connally of Texas, and Johnston and Thurmond of South Carolina. Although there was much talk of Hawaii being "tinctured with communism" (Eastland), Strom Thurmond made it quite clear that his objections were more racial than ideological. Quoting with approval Rudyard Kipling's bromide, "East is East, and West is West, and never the twain shall meet," the Dixiecrat-turned-Republican stressed the "impassable difference" between Hawaiians whose ancestors came from Asia and Americans whose ancestors came from Europe. Important objections also came from some leaders of Hawaii's missionary-descended elite, such as Walter F. Dillingham and newspaper-owner Lorrin P. Thurston, who feared that popular sovereignty would erode their control. Hawaiian lawyer-scholar J. Garner Anthony put it nicely when he told a congressional committee in 1950 that "any argument against statehood must be bottomed either upon disbelief in democracy, self-interests, or ignorance of American history."[48]

---

46. This section draws heavily on the account in Gavin Daws, *Shoal of Time*, pp. 381–91. See also, Ernest Gruening, *Many Battles: The Autobiography of Ernest Gruening*, p. 230.

47. As cited in Ruth Tabrah, *Hawaii: A Bicentennial History*, p. 191.

48. As cited in Daws, *Shoal of Time*, p. 383. J. Garner Anthony, Hawaii's attorney general during World War II, has written a useful account of *Hawaii Under Army Rule*.

When statehood came, it quickly brought about something that racists had long dreaded—a Chinese senator. But Hiram Leong Fong, born in Honolulu in 1907, was no mandarin. He was, in fact, like so many of his fellow Republican senators in the post–World War II era, a "self-made" millionaire. More typical of the kinds of representatives that Hawaii would send to Washington was Democrat Daniel Ken Inouye, a Japanese American (as have been five of the nine persons to represent the Aloha State in the United States Capitol since 1959).[49] Except for his Japanese ethnicity, Inouye, born in Hawaii in 1924, is a representative American political type. A wounded war hero—he had lost an arm fighting with the 442nd in Italy—he used his veteran base to become one of the unbeatable politicians.

It would be hard to overstate the importance of Senators Fong and Inouye, and those Asian American congresspersons who have followed them, in terms of their impact on Asian American self-image and confidence. The Hawaiians, along with three Japanese American congressmen from California, represent Asian American political power.[50] There would come a time, in the late 1970s through early 1980, when the United States Senate would be three percent Japanese American (Daniel Inouye, D-Hawaii; Spark Matsunaga, D-Hawaii; and S. I. Hayakawa, R-Calif.) and zero percent black. This real representation, as opposed to symbolic, was an important component of the self-confidence that much of the leadership of Asian American communities began to feel in the decades after the 1950s. Hawaiian statehood, which triggered this process, was thus important to Asian Americans everywhere, not just to those in the islands.

---

49. The following have served as members of Congress from Hawaii: Oren E. Long, (1899–1965), served in Senate, 1959–1963; Hiram L. Fong, (1907–), served in Senate, 1959–1977; Daniel K. Inouye, (1924–), served in House, 1959–1963; served in Senate, 1963– ; Spark M. Matsunaga (1916–), served in House, 1963–1977; served in Senate, 1977– ; Thomas P. Gill, 1922–), served in House, 1963–1965; Patsy T. Mink, (1927–), served in House, 1965–1977; Daniel K. Akaka, (1924–), served in House, 1977– ; Cecil Heftel, (1924–), served in House, 1977–1987; Patricia Saiki (1930–), served in House, 1987– . Long was born in Nebraska; the rest were born in Hawaii. Fong and Saiki were elected as Republicans; the rest were elected as Democrats.

50. The following Japanese Americans have been elected to Congress from California: Samuel I. Hayakawa (1906–), served in Senate, 1975–1981. Norman Y. Mineta (1931–), served in House, 1975– . Robert T. Matsui (1941–), served in House, 1979– . Hayakawa was born in Canada; the others, who spent time in Relocation Centers, were born in California. Hayakawa was elected as a Republican; the others were elected as Democrats.

Data from the census of 1960 can be construed into a group portrait of each community at a nodal point in its development, providing a kind of socioeconomic comparison. The census found just over 700,000 in the two communities: 473,170 Japanese and 236,084 Chinese. These figures are not comparable with those of previous censuses because, for the first time, the population of Hawaii was included. Hawaii in 1960 contained more than two-fifths of the total Japanese American population (207,230 or 43.8 percent) and one-sixth of the total Chinese American population (39,152 or 16.6 percent). In the continental United States, very significant population increases were recorded for the decade, 87.6 percent for the Japanese population and 67.4 percent for the Chinese. Despite this much more rapid rate of growth than that of the general population, the two Asian American communities amounted to only .3 of 1 percent of the population of the nation.

Even after a decade of significant immigration, each community was still overwhelmingly native born: 78.5 percent of the Japanese Americans and 60.5 percent of the Chinese Americans fell into this category. The heavily female immigration of the 1950s, particularly among the Japanese, had changed the sex ratios dramatically. In the Chinese community, male dominance had dropped from 65.5 percent in 1950 to 57.4 percent in 1960, while in the Japanese community females actually outnumbered males.

In 1950 Japanese males had accounted for 54.1 percent of the population; in 1960 they were only 48.5 percent. The new Japanese American female preponderance was largely the result of the migration of young women. In the age cohorts 20 through 39 years, foreign-born women outnumbered foreign-born men by just over four to one, or 29,608 to 7,337. The difference here, some 22,000 more females, was larger than the number by which all Japanese females exceeded Japanese males. In areas where military brides made up a particularly large percentage of the ethnic population, the sex ratios were even more striking: in Texas, for example, females made up almost two-thirds (64.2 percent) of the Japanese American population.

Among the Chinese Americans, males outnumbered females in every five-year census cohort of both foreign and native born. The least unbalanced Chinese sex ratios were in the settled communities of Hawaii: for the entire state, Chinese males were 51 percent of the ethnic population; for the Honolulu metropolitan area, they were only slightly less predominant (50.8 percent). Chinese communities in California were a little less male-dominated than were the outlying centers. Of the nine mainland metropolitan areas with the largest Chinese American populations, the three California centers (San Francisco/Oakland, Los Angeles/Long Beach, and Sacramento) were between 54.8 and 56.2 percent male, while the six outlying centers (New York, Chicago, Boston, Seattle, Washington, D.C., and Philadelphia) had ratios between 58.3 and 62.2 percent.

Both ethnic communities remained heavily concentrated in the West. Four-fifths (82.2 percent) of Japanese Americans lived in just four Pacific states (California, Hawaii, Washington, and Oregon), while three-fifths (60.6%) of the less concentrated Chinese Americans resided there. Concentration also prevailed elsewhere. More than nine of ten Japanese Americans (92.6 percent) were found in just twelve states, while the same fraction of Chinese Americans (91.6 percent) were found in thirteen states and the District of Columbia. The percentage of mainland Japanese on the West Coast was 68.3, down only 1 percent from the 1950 figure, while the percentage in California was marginally higher, 60.0 as opposed to 59.9.

Although there was no significant difference between the median ages of the two communities (28.4 years for the Japanese population, 28.3 years for the Chinese), the age and sex distributions were dissimilar. Still reflecting the bachelor-immigrant pattern, Chinese males were significantly older than Chinese females, with a median age of 30.9 years for the former and 25.2 years for the latter. In the Japanese community, where the pattern had been affected by the bride immigration, women were only slightly older than men, with a median age of 28.6 to 28.2 years, respectively. The most numerous single five-year Japanese cohort by age and sex consisted of females between 30 and 34 years of age. In the Chinese community, more "normal" cohort patterns were beginning to emerge at the younger end of the age spectrum. The two most numerous single cohorts consisted of Chinese of both sexes under five years of age and those between 5 and 9 years of age. In both communities, reflecting the prewar immigration patterns, males predominated among the elderly. Among those of age 65 and over, 56.4 percent of the Japanese and 75.1 percent of the Chinese were males.

Quite different patterns of educational achievement in the two communities were apparent. While gross figures indicated that Japanese were somewhat better educated—they had a median of 12.1 years of schooling (12.2 for males, 12.1 for females) as opposed to a median of 11.1 years (10.7 for males, 11.7 for females) for Chinese—analysis of the data shows that larger percentages of Chinese had either no education or a great deal of it. The seeming parity or advantage for females disappears when we examine the very well educated. At the lower end of the educational spectrum, only 2.8 percent of Japanese males and 3.7 percent of Japanese females over age 14 were recorded as having had no formal schooling, while more than one-seventh of the similar Chinese population was so recorded (14.7 percent for males, 15.2 percent for females). Japanese educational superiority continued when those having at least a high-school diploma were counted: just over half of the Japanese (56.1 percent of the males and 55.3 percent of the females) and just under half of the Chinese (44.1 percent of the males and 48.3 percent of the females) were listed as high-school graduates or better. But when only college graduates were enumerated, significantly more Chinese than Japanese, and significantly more males than females were listed. Among Chinese, more than one-sixth of the males (16.5 percent) and more than one-eighth of the females (12.5 percent) had college degrees, while among the Japanese almost one-eighth of the males (11.9 percent) and about one-sixteenth of the females (6 percent) were graduates.

Given this high level of education, the 1960 census data show that income for both Asian American groups is surprisingly low. Japanese American men had a median income of $4,304, while Chinese American men earned only about four-fifths of that amount, or $3,471. Asian American women, of course, made much less: Japanese American women earned only 46 percent as much as their male counterparts, a median of $1,967, while Chinese American women did slightly better, relatively and absolutely, bringing in 60 percent as much as Chinese American men, a median of $2,067.

It is relatively easy to explain the depressed earnings of Asian Americans. Long established patterns of discrimination, exclusion from some of the best-paid sectors of the economy, particularly from those sectors in which effective unionization had occurred, and the economic losses of the war period for the Japanese Americans, all contributed. Asian Americans continued to be concentrated in certain sectors of the economy. Among Japanese, more than one-fourth (25.2 percent) provided services; more than one-fifth (21.1 percent) were in wholesale and retail trade, and about one-seventh (14.2 percent) were in agriculture, forestry, and fishing. In the blue-collar jobs: only 16.5 percent were in manufacturing and 5.7 percent were in construction. Among Chinese, over one-third (36.7 percent) were in wholesale and retail trade, more than one-fourth (26.2 percent) provided services, and almost none (1.2 percent) were in agriculture, fishing, and forestry. As compared with Japanese, even fewer Chinese Americans were in the well-paid blue-collar jobs: 14 percent in manufacturing and 1.9 percent in construction.

To make these education, income, and employment data more meaningful, they should not be compared with national averages. National averages are depressed by the inclusion of the South, where standards were low and where very few Asians lived. The data should be compared instead with the averages for the region in which most of them lived. Perhaps the most meaningful single comparison would be within California. Such comparison has been made easier by superb statistics for 1959 and 1960 which the California Fair Employment Practices Commission published in 1965. These statistics clearly show, as do the national data, that both Chinese Americans and Japanese Americans had become somewhat better educated than the white majority, although we must understand that the "white" data are somewhat depressed by the inclusion of what the census bureau calls "Spanish surname" figures.

In general, in American society there is a direct relationship between education and income: the more education, the more income. But in both California and the nation, this was not true for Asian Americans. In California, although college graduates were 11 percent more likely to be found among Japanese males than among white males, and 24 percent more likely among Chinese males, white men made considerably more money. For every $51 earned by a white male Californian, Japanese males received $43 and Chinese males received $38. If one looked only at the relatively affluent, the disparity was even greater. A white man's chances of receiving an annual income of $10,000 or more were 78 percent better than those of a Chinese male in California, and 57 percent better than those of a Japanese. Chinese and Japanese Californians, however, made significantly more than other "nonwhite" minority groups: for example, about 7 percent of Chinese and Japanese men 25 years of age and older had incomes of $10,000 or more, while for Filipinos and other "nonwhites," only about 1 percent had such incomes.[51]

What the data demonstrate is that more and more Japanese and Chinese Americans were achieving middle-class status and were doing so at a much faster rate than were other minority groups. At the same time, their heritage within American society, and the continuing prejudice of that society retarded their material progress to a greater degree than their educational achievements alone would have predicted. While it was no longer necessary for college graduates to become "professional carrot washers," and while more and more of the younger Asian Americans were finding niches in the larger economy rather than in the ethnic economy, there were still significant barriers, both real and psychological, to their advancement within that economy.

One of the patterns that was readily discernible was that although well-trained Asian American college graduates could find suitable employment with relative ease, it was still very difficult for them to gain promotion to supervisory and higher administrative positions. A

---

51. Dept. of Industrial Relations, FEPC, *Californians*, pp. 11, 44–47.

large number of interviews conducted with such persons in California in the 1960s would indicate that perhaps the greatest barrier was a reluctance of employers to place Asian Americans into positions in which they could hire and fire whites. In addition, these same interviews indicated that some Asian Americans were reluctant to be placed into such positions. Both phenomena were clearly carryovers from the recent, more racist past.

Certainly, no rational observer in 1942 would have dared to predict the amount of progress toward equality that Asian Americans would have made by 1960. But, just as certainly, there should be no attempt to deny that discrimination and deprivation continued. In the years after 1960, however, the denial was to be made time and again. In addition, the relative success of the largest Asian American groups was to be used as a kind of rhetorical club to belabor those minority groups whose measurable progress had been less outstanding.

8.

Epilogue:
Since 1960—the Era of
the Model Minority

Since 1960 there have been significant changes for Asian Americans, changes that, however important, can only be briefly noted here. In the last twenty-five years, the whole philosophical basis of American immigration law has been revamped as the quota system of the old National Origins Act has been scrapped. Also, for the first time, Asia has surpassed Europe as a source of immigrants. Foreign affairs have continued to have a major effect on the Asian American condition: the misbegotten war in Vietnam produced a massive exodus of Asian refugees which helped to swell the incidence of persons of Asian ancestry and birth to the highest proportion in our history. By the 1980s the United States Congress was ready, after four decades, at least to consider some kind of redress for the victims of the wartime incarceration of the Japanese Americans. But prior to all of these changes, a basic change took place in the minds of most Americans toward Asians, a change best described by a misleading catchword: "model minority." Initially applied only to Japanese Americans, by the 1970s the term was increasingly used to describe successful, upwardly mobile Asian Americans of any ethnicity.

The appellation "model minority" was perhaps used for the first time in the most influential single article ever written about an Asian American group. "Success Story, Japanese American Style," by demographer-sociologist William Petersen, appeared in the *New York Times Magazine* on January 6, 1966.[1] The author, then a faculty

---

1. William Petersen, "Success Story, Japanese American Style," *New York Times*

member at the University of California at Berkeley, was reacting against student radicalism and its accompanying countercultural lifestyle. He not only praised the achievements of Japanese Americans but he used their experience as a way of denigrating "problem" minority groups. Through their good example, Petersen chose to attack, from a conservative point of view, what he felt was an erosion of standards of American life. In the process he developed the phrase "model minority," using the term "model" in two senses: first, as a way of praising the superior performance of Japanese Americans; and second, as a way of suggesting that other ethnic groups should *emulate* the Japanese American example. The unstated major premise of Petersen's argument was that Horatio-Alger-bootstrap-raising was needed for success by such "non-achieving" minorities as blacks and Chicanos, rather than the social programs of Lyndon Johnson's Great Society. Once posited by Petersen, this insidious theme would be picked up, gradually, by a host of conservative publicists and theorists, most notably by Thomas Sowell.[2]

The notion that Japanese Americans had performed in a superior fashion was not new. Four years earlier, for instance, in *The Politics of Prejudice,* I myself had observed that despite decades of sustained mistreatment "the vast bulk of California's Issei and their descendants were . . . superlatively good citizens."[3] What was new in William Petersen's approach was the blanket denigration of other groups and of the efforts of social scientists and government to manage and organize social change. Petersen laid out the bones of his argument in three early paragraphs. After quickly encapsulating the discrimination and injustice suffered by Japanese Americans, he argued:

Magazine, January 6, 1966, pp. 20 ff. For the spread of the concept, see Harry H. L. Kitano and Stanley Sue, "The Model Minorities," *Journal of Social Issues* 29, no. 2 (1973): 1–9.

2. See especially Thomas Sowell, *Race and Economics;* and Thomas Sowell, ed., *Essays and Data on American Ethnic Groups.* One difference between Petersen and Sowell is that Petersen, in 1966, included Chinese Americans with "Negroes, Indians, Mexicans, . . . and Filipinos" as nonachieving nonwhites. Sowell differentiates them. Data available a year before Petersen wrote indicated clearly that education and income patterns for Chinese and Japanese in California were far different from the others. See California, Department of Industrial Relations, FEPC, *Californians of Japanese, Chinese and Filipino Ancestry.* Nathan Glazer has argued with great insight that the 1965 immigration act, along with the Civil Rights Act of 1964 and the Voting Rights Act of 1965, marked a brief "national consensus as to how we should respond to the reality of racial and ethnic group prejudice and . . . difference" idem, *Affirmative Discrimination,* p. 3.

3. Roger Daniels, *The Politics of Prejudice,* p. v.

Generally this kind of treatment, as we all know these days, creates what might be termed "problem minorities." Each of a number of interrelated factors—poor health, poor education, low income, high crime rate, unstable family pattern, and so on and on— reinforces all of the others, and together they make up the reality of slum life. And by the "principle of cumulation," as Gunnar Myrdal termed it in *An American Dilemma,* this social reality reinforces our prejudices and is reinforced by them. When whites defined Negroes as inherently less intelligent, for example, and therefore furnished them with inferior schools, the products of these schools often validated the original stereotype.

Once the cumulative degradation has gone far enough, it is notoriously difficult to reverse the trend. When new opportunities, even equal opportunities, are opened up, the minority's reaction to them is likely to be negative—either self-defeating apathy or a hatred so all-consuming as to be self-destructive. For all the well-meaning programs and countless scholarly studies now focused on the Negro, we hardly know how to repair the damage that the slave traders started.

The history of Japanese Americans, however, challenges every such generalization about ethnic minorities. . . . Barely more than 20 years after the end of the wartime camps, this is a minority that has risen above even prejudiced criticism. By any criterion of good citizenship that we choose, the Japanese Americans are better than any other group in our society, including native-born whites. They have established this remarkable record, moreover, by their own almost totally unaided effort. Every attempt to hamper their progress resulted only in enhancing their determination to succeed. Even in a country whose patron saint is Horatio Alger, there is no parallel to this success story.[4]

Later in the article, after pointing out that blacks were the "minority most thoroughly imbedded in American culture, with the least meaningful ties to an overseas fatherland," Petersen attributed the Japanese American ability to "climb over the highest barriers" at least "in part [to] their meaningful links with an alien culture." Some of Petersen's remarks were a sophisticated restatement of the dictum of the father of American sociology William Graham Sumner: "Stateways cannot change folkways." In other words, government programs are useless.

The "success" or "nonsuccess" of minority groups, individuals,

---

4. Petersen, "Success Story," pp. 20–21.

or even nations, is much more complex than writers such as Petersen and Sowell would indicate. Simplistic comparisons between immigrant groups are not particularly meaningful. The generalized form, known as "the immigrant analogy," has usually run something like this: "The Germans, the Irish, the Jews, the Poles, and so forth, have 'made it.' Why can't the blacks? Immigrants came to this country poor, they were discriminated against, and look at them now. Blacks want everything given to them. Blacks aren't willing to work for success the way others have." The specialized form of the immigrant analogy was not new either. It had been used by some Japanese American leaders years before Petersen's article appeared. In January 1960, for example, Haruo Ishimaru, housing committee chairman of the San Francisco JACL, prefaced his testimony before the United States Commission on Civil Rights with the statement: "I am representing the most angelic of minorities in this community."[5]

Several problems exist with the immigrant analogy. Petersen and others who use it tend to ignore those members of the paragon group who didn't "make it" (the Issei bachelors, for example, or the old men of Chinatown), just as they tend to ignore successful blacks. In the final analysis, of course, immigrant groups, however defined, are abstractions: what we really have are collections of individuals who, to a greater or lesser degree, identify with one another. When, for example, one speaks of the success of the so-called WASP, one must ignore the most WASPish group in the country, the whites of Appalachia. In addition, success always has a price, whether for the individual or for the group.

None of this is to argue that group comparison is wrong—this book has been, in part, a group comparison—but to argue that such comparisons should be, as much as possible, value free. For example, to note that Japanese Americans are overrepresented in agriculture and that Chinese Americans are underrepresented in that occupational grouping says nothing about the quality of either group. Only the differing histories of each group can explain how and why this particular occupational specialization has come about. Nor can past mistreatments be meaningfully compared. There is no way, as Harry Kitano has put it, "to compare the scars." One can narrate, analyze, and try to explain.

Nonetheless, it is clear to me, as much of the foregoing has indicated, that despite a different history, Chinese Americans, *en bloc*, present to some observers a profile similar to that of the Japanese Americans. But any meaningful comparative understanding of the

5. U.S. Commission on Civil Rights, *Hearings*, 1960, p. 777.

position of immigrants and their descendants in host countries must take into account several major factors, including (1) the relative social position and time of entry of the particular immigrant or ethnic group in the social hierarchy of the host country—or what Harry Kitano and I have called "the step on the ethnic escalator"; (2) the demographic structure of the immigrant community; (3) the relative level of technological skills and attitudes prevailing both in the immigrant/ethnic group and in the host society; (4) the legal situation and status of the group involved; (5) the traditions and attitudes of both the immigrant/ethnic group and the larger society; and (6) the social, economic, and political climates of the countries involved.[6]

While Petersen's article was being written, the Immigration Act of 1965 was beginning to take effect. That act, which was not fully operative until July 1, 1968, totally scrapped the old quota system. Instead of giving quota spaces to nations, 120,000 spaces were reserved for natives of the Western Hemisphere on a first-come, first-served basis, with no limitations on the number from any one country; another 170,000 spaces were reserved for natives of the Eastern Hemisphere, with a 20,000 maximum on nationals of any one country. A series of other preferences and priorities were established, and the act assumed a probable annual immigration of between 350,000 and 400,000. In 1971 about 370,000 immigrants were admitted. Only 96,000, or just over one-fourth, were from Europe, the traditional major source of immigrants. Asia contributed slightly more, with 103,000 or almost 28 percent. More than two-fifths came from the New World, with 50,000 legal Mexican immigrants presenting the largest single national bloc. Immigration figures from Asia have since been supplemented by very large numbers of refugees from South-East Asia, many of whom have been ethnically Chinese. These immigrants have come during and after our intervention in the Vietnamese War, swelling the Asian American population significantly (see table 8.1).

By 1980 Japanese Americans, who had been the largest Asian American ethnic group for half a century, were outnumbered by Chinese and Filipinos. Despite the much more rapid growth rates for the Asian American groups (total population for the nation increased only 11.5 percent in the decade 1970–1980), they still represented only a tiny fraction: 3.26 million in a population of 226.5 million, or 1.4 percent.

---

6. Roger Daniels, "On the Comparative Study of Immigrant and Ethnic Groups in the New World: A Note," *Comparative Studies in Society and History* 25 (1983): 401–04.

Table 8.1
Asian American Population, 1970 and 1980

Ethnic Group	1970	Percentage Increase from 1960	1980	Percentage Increase from 1970
Chinese	435,062	84.3	806,027	85.3
Filipino	343,060	88.9	774,640	125.8
Japanese	591,020	25	700,747	18.5
Asian Indian	ca. 76,000		361,544	475.7
Korean	69,130		354,529	412.8
Vietnamese			261,714	

Source: U.S. Census

By the 1980s journalists like Bruce Nelson of the Los Angeles *Times* were hailing "people of Asian ancestry" as "the nation's best-educated and highest-income racial group." *Newsweek,* in a feature article, simply extended Petersen's slogan: "Asian-Americans: A 'Model Minority'." Using preliminary 1980 census data, *Newsweek* pointed out that "Asian-Americans now enjoy the nation's highest median family income: $22,075 a year compared with $20,840 for whites." At Harvard, where Asian Americans comprised more than 8 percent of entering freshmen in 1982, Professor Stephan Thernstrom described "Oriental students" as "the most hard-working, disciplined people imaginable. . . . I don't know when they sleep." At the University of California at Berkeley, more than 21 percent of the undergraduates are recorded as Asian Americans, or about four times their incidence in the state.

These kinds of statistics have misled some journalists and scholars into believing that discrimination against Asians in the United States is a thing of the past. Robert Higgs, for example, argued in 1977 that in the United States "apparent prejudice against [Japanese] . . . has virtually disappeared."[7] Others, however, have understood the ambiguous nature of the status of Asian Americans in contemporary America. Bryan Man, writing in 1978, examined carefully the achievement patterns of Chinese and "white" men in California and Hawaii

---

7. Bruce Nelson, "Asians Come on Strong," Los Angeles *Times,* October 10, 1982; Martin Kasindorf et al., "Asian-Americans: A 'Model Minority'," *Newsweek,* December 6, 1982; Robert Higgs, *Competition and Coercion,* p. 127.

in 1960 and 1970. He concluded that race, country of birth, migration experience, and the social structure of American society all had continuing effects. "While some Chinese equal or surpass whites in occupational achievements," he wrote, "it is quite clear that many Chinese achieve less than their white counterparts, all things being equal. This fact, then, calls upon us to seriously question the notion that the Chinese are a 'model minority'."[8]

Certainly the economic success of some Asian Americans has been spectacular. Two of the first one-hundred persons on *Forbes'* *Magazine*'s 1983 list of the "richest" Americans were Chinese: An Wang, the 63-year-old proprietor of Wang Laboratories was fifth on the list with an alleged $1.6 billion; and Kyupin Philip Hwang, the 46-year-old head of TeleVideo Systems, was thirty-first on the list with $575 million.[9] One should not minimize either the economic or the psychic importance of such individual accomplishments, or the accomplishments of such highly visible achievers as the Japanese American members of Congress mentioned earlier. Nevertheless, it seems to me that the transformation of collective communal self-images, while impossible to quantify, is much more significant.

For a variety of reasons, both Chinese and Japanese Americans in the 1960s and particularly in the 1970s, developed a positive and dynamic sense of where they were and where they wanted to go. Certainly the following factors must be included as causal components of that change:

1. An increase in numbers, both relative and absolute
2. An improvement in status in both law and custom
3. Increased perception and awareness by the majority society of other ethnic groups—blacks, Chicanos, Puerto Ricans, and very recent migrants from Central America and the Caribbean—deemed more threatening to middle-class values
4. The growing international status of both China and Japan
5. The ethnic revival—real and imagined—of the 1960s and 1970s
6. An increase in American cosmopolitanism, which embraced

---

8. Bryan Dai Yung Man, "Chinese Occupational Achievement Patterns: The Case of a 'Model Minority'" (Ph.D. diss., University of California at Los Angeles, 1978). The quotation is from the abstract, in *Dissertation Abstracts International* 39:3172A (1978). The socioeconomic "bipolarization" is commented on perceptively in Wen H. Kuo, "Colonized Status of Asian-Americans," *Ethnic Groups* 5 (1981): 227–51.

9. *Forbes'* list, as cited in Cincinnati *Enquirer*, September 30, 1983.

foreign foods, cultures, and even brides (but rarely husbands) from Asian countries and ethnic groups

This increased self-confidence enabled some community leaders to demand better treatment. Early in the 1970s Chinese American civic leaders from both coasts made it clear that many of their constituents were in dire need of federal assistance. Irving S. K. Chin, chairman of the Chinatown Advisory Council to the Borough President of Manhattan, told a United States Senate committee that Chinese, as a "silent minority," had not previously protested because of "their English language deficiency and a lack of familiarity with the American governmental system," "fear of government," lack of political "clout," and philosophical and cultural reluctance to engage in political activities. Ling-chi Wang, a San Francisco community activist and later chairman of the Asian American Studies Department at the University of California at Berkeley, spoke to the same committee about the "silent" Chinese of San Francisco. Wang advocated manpower training programs for his community which were, he said, "long overdue," "much needed," and "relevant." Describing conditions in San Francisco's inner-city Chinatown, Wang cited data showing that unemployment was almost double the citywide average, that two-thirds of the living quarters were substandard, and that tuberculosis rates were six times the national average. He found the greatest Chinese American social problems involved discrimination, educational handicaps, lack of marketable skills, language barriers, citizenship requirements, and culturally biased and irrelevant tests.[10]

How can these complaints of deprivation and poverty be squared with reports about "model minorities" and of superior educational achievement? The fact is that Chinese Americans are of very different kinds. Chinese Americans themselves draw sharp distinctions: the American-born Chinese (the ABCs) tend to be college-educated, to have middle-class occupations, and to live outside of the inner-city Chinatowns; and the recent immigrants (the FOBs, "fresh off the boat") tend to be poorly educated, deficient in English, to live in Chinatowns, and to ply the low-wage service trades or sweatshop manufacturing enterprises typical of the inner city. Of course, many

---

10. Chin appeared before the Subcommittee on Education of the Senate Committee on Labor and Public Welfare; Wang appeared before the same committee's Employment, Manpower and Poverty Subcommittee. Their testimony can be found in Integrated Education Associates, *Chinese-Americans*, pp. 12–17, 18–28. For an analysis of some recent Chinese immigrants of high achievement, see Edwin Clausen, "Chinese Intellectuals in the U.S.: Success in the Post World War II Era," in Douglas W. Lee, ed., *The Annals of the Chinese Historical Society of the Pacific Northwest*, pp. 121–59.

Table 8.2
Years of School Completed, Japanese and Chinese Americans
25 Years and Older, 1970

Level of Schooling	Years Completed	Japanese Americans		Chinese Americans	
		Number	Percentage	Number	Percentage
None		6,465	1.8	25,205	11.1
Elementary	1–4	8,361	2.4	11,522	5.1
	5–7	22,340	6.3	24,296	10.7
	8	29,970	8.5	12,780	5.6
Secondary	1–3	43,301	12.2	22,121	9.7
	4	138,946	39.3	48,071	21.2
College	1–3	48,001	13.6	24,929	11.0
	4	56,323	15.9	58,241	25.6
Total number of persons		353,707	...	227,165	...

SOURCE: United States Bureau of the Census, *1970 Census of Population: Japanese, Chinese, and Filipinos in the United States* (PC[2]–1G), tables 3 and 18, Washington, D.C., 1973.

recent Chinese immigrants are both middle-class and well-educated; some have brought a good deal of capital with them. But large numbers of recent Chinese immigrants have been poor.

Census data on the years of school completed by adults show both the bifurcated nature of the contemporary Chinese American community and its differences from the Japanese American community, which has received very little immigration (see table 8.2). The gross data for the two communities were similar: 68.8 percent of Japanese Americans were high-school graduates as compared with 68.1 percent of Chinese Americans; Japanese Americans had completed 12.5 median school years as compared with 12.4 for Chinese. But more than one-fourth of Chinese American adults had not completed elementary school, about the same percentage as were college graduates, whereas for Japanese Americans, the comparable figures were about one-tenth not completing elementary school and almost one-sixth college graduates. This reflects not a different cultural attitude toward education but, rather, generational differences. Only about one-fifth (20.9 percent) of all Japanese Americans in 1970 were foreign born, as opposed to nearly half (47.1 percent) of Chinese Americans.

Some of the ambiguities of Chinese American life in the post-World War II years are suggested in the two autobiographies of California ceramicist, Jade Snow Wong, who was born in San Francisco in 1922.[11] The first, *Fifth Chinese Daughter* (1945), has been reprinted often and is widely used in public schools, while the second, *No Chinese Stranger* (1975), went quickly out of print. The differences between these two books show, among other things, the increasing self-confidence that many Chinese and Japanese Americans began to feel in the 1960s and 1970s. There are, of course, constants between the two volumes. Wong underplays her own accomplishments—no reader of her early work learns that she is an outstanding ceramicist—and she stresses her inner feelings. She provides special insights into being both Chinese American and female. Writing in the third person, she tells us that

> until she was five years old, Jade Snow's world was almost wholly Chinese, for her world was her family.... Respect and order—these were the key words of life. It did not matter what were the thoughts of a little girl; she did not voice them.... She must always be careful to do the proper thing. Failure to do so brought immediate and drastic punishment. Teaching and whipping were thus almost synonymous.... Thus, life was a constant puzzle. No one ever troubled to explain.

The puzzle becomes worse when a male Wong is born and she "realizes that she herself was a girl, like her younger sister, unalterably less significant than the new son in the family." By the time she is fourteen, her life is

> darkened by the stubborn, unhappy struggle which began between her and her family. The difficulty centered around Jade Snow's desire for recognition [but] the conflict remained under the surface for nearly two years because of the Wong's peculiarity in refusing to recognize or discuss emotional issues.

When her father refuses to support her college attendance—he will pay for his son's—Wong complains that

---

11. I must note here two greatly talented contemporary Chinese American authors: playwright Frank Chin and novelist Maxine Hong Kingston. Kingston's work is indispensable, whether one speaks of *The Woman Warrior*, with its twentieth-century focus, or of *China Men*, with its evocation of the whole spectrum of the overseas Chinese experience. Her sources include family traditions, memory, and folklore. She is essential to any understanding of the nature of Chinese America.

she was trapped in a mesh of tradition woven thousands of miles away. . . . Acknowledging that she owed her very being and much of her thinking to those ancestors, she could not believe that this background was meant to hinder her further development, either in American or China. Beyond this point she could not think.

Supporting herself, she attends first San Francisco City College and then Mills College, an expensive private women's school across the bay, and begins to live a life of her own. *Fifth Chinese Daughter,* which has been the subject of bitter attacks by some male Asian American critics, is clearly a work of its time—1945.[12] Toward the end of the book, Wong describes her postcollege relationship with her family, which was still uneasy, but easier:

> When she entered the Wong household she slipped into her old pattern of withdrawal, and she performed her usual daughterly duties . . . in the role of an obedient Chinese girl. But now . . . she could return to another life in which she fitted as an individual.

This duality, this "torn-ness" between Chinese and American, is no longer expressed in *No Chinese Stranger,* published in her fifty-third year. Wong now lives in a different America: she has visited the new China. She retells some of the incidents of the first book, and, since the angle of vision is different and she is different, the stories, while not really different, are, nevertheless, not quite the same. Most important of all, Wong is at peace with herself. Says she, leaving the third person:

> My future is in this land where Daddy and his progeny have sunk their roots around the rocks of prejudice. . . . With strong belief in our purpose, it may not be folly for the determined, with the hearts of children, to attack the high mountain of prejudice in our own way. When we die our children and grandchildren will keep on working until, some day, the mountain will diminish. Then there will be no Chinese stranger.

Wong's books can be read as a nonfiction *bildungsroman;* as a story of education, but an education peculiarly and particularly ethnic; as Chinese American, yet with overtones that resonate to many other immigrant memoirs and women's autobiographies.

Despite her specialness, Wong can, to a degree, stand as surrogate

---

12. See, for example, the intemperate remarks in Jeffrey Paul Chan et al., eds., *Aiiieeeee! An Anthology of Asian-American Writers.* Preceding quotations are from Jade Snow Wong, *Fifth Chinese Daughter,* pp. 2–3, 27, 90–91, 110, and 168; and idem, *No Chinese Stranger,* p. 366.

for hundreds of thousands of mute, unknowable Chinese American lives. By no stretch of the imagination can her experience be called typical. Even Jade Snow Wong's father, who seems almost stereotypically patriarchal, like some of the characters in *Flower Drum Song*, was an atypical Chinese American of his generation. As an immigrant convert to Methodism he, unlike most of his fellows, was able to bring over his family. I would suggest, nonetheless, that the growing self-confidence of the 1975 book (as opposed to the 1945 volume) reflects a communal change in attitude, a change brought about, at least in part, by an increasing sense of security about the place of Chinese Americans in our national life. Such feelings were doubtless heightened by President Nixon's China trip and by the acknowledged success of more and more Chinese in American life.

Increased psychological security was also an important factor in Japanese American life. Because there was a central event in Japanese American history—the wartime evacuation and incarceration—to which almost the entire community eventually responded, one can look at its collective behavior as it began, in the 1970s and 1980s, to come to grips with its own past. Perhaps the turning point in community attitudes was the campaign to gain a pardon for Iva Ikuko Toguri, the so-called Tokyo Rose.

Toguri, born in Los Angeles on July 4, 1916, was graduated from UCLA in June 1941. A few weeks later she sailed to Japan to visit a critically ill aunt. As were hundreds of other Nisei (mostly Kibei), Toguri was trapped in Japan by the outbreak of the war. During the war she was one of several persons, some of them allied prisoners of war, who made English-language broadcasts beamed at American troops. The propaganda value of these broadcasts was dubious, at best; troops listened to them largely for the popular American music that comprised the bulk of the programs.

Toguri was under great pressure from Japanese authorities to renounce her American citizenship, but she steadfastly refused to do so. When, after being cleared by American occupation authorities, she was able to return to the United States, the Department of Justice had her indicted on eight counts of treason. A trial in the summer of 1949 resulted in her conviction on one count—"that on a day during October, 1944, the exact date being to the Grand Jurors unknown, the defendant in the offices of the Broadcasting Corporation of Japan did speak into a microphone concerning the loss of ships." She was sentenced to ten years in jail and served six years and two months.[13]

---

13. For the best account of her life, see Masayo Duus, *Tokyo Rose: Orphan of the Pacific*.

As legal historian Stanley Kutler has demonstrated, her prosecution was based on testimony that the Justice Department knew was false. This need not concern us here, although anyone interested in the quality of justice in cold-war America should learn about it.[14]

During her trial, and for years afterwards, the ethnic community put as much distance as possible between itself and Toguri. After all, she seemed to represent exactly what Japanese Americans had been accused of and incarcerated for: treachery. One Japanese American columnist wrote that Toguri, whether guilty or not, had

> played fast and loose with the well-being of Americans of Japanese ancestry. The Japanese Americans, like other American minorities which have become subjected to discrimination, have a group responsibility which arises from the fact that an individual's acts, particularly when they are of a criminal nature, are used to reflect on the integrity of the group as a whole.

And, to point up what he obviously considered Toguri's irresponsibility, he hailed "the feeling of group responsibility which impelled the Nisei G.I.'s to acts above and beyond the call of duty."[15]

After her release from prison in January 1956 she moved to Chicago, where her father had established a successful business. Except for an occasional newspaper story, Toguri was ignored by the larger Japanese American community until the early 1970s. In 1973 Clifford I. Uyeda, a San Francisco pediatrician and community activist, learned from John Hada, a retired lieutenant colonel in the United States Army, about Toguri's trial, which had been the subject of Hada's master's thesis.[16] Convinced that she had been wronged,

---

14. Stanley I. Kutler, "Forging a Legend: The Treason of 'Tokyo Rose'," *Wisconsin Law Review* 6 (1980), pp. 1341–82; reprinted in idem, *The American Inquisition: Justice and Injustice in the Cold War*. One other Nisei, Tomoya Kawakita, a Kibei, was tried and convicted for treason. A member of the Japanese Army, Kawakita was a hated guard, called "Meatball" by his victims, at a camp for U.S. prisoners of war. He was sentenced to death, but this was commuted to life imprisonment by President Eisenhower. President Kennedy pardoned him—more than a decade before Toguri would be pardoned—and he was expatriated to Japan. *U.S. v. Kawakita* 96 Fed Supp 824 (1950).

15. The columnist quoted is Larry Tajari, *Pacific Citizen*, June 19, 1948, as cited by Isami Arifuku Waugh, "The Trial of Tokyo Rose," *Bridge*, February 1974, pp. 5–12, 40–46. See also John Juji Hada, "The Indictment and Trial of Iva Ikuko Toguri d'Aquino" (M.A. thesis, University of San Francisco, 1973); and David A. Ward, "The Unending War of Iva Ikuko Toguri D'Aquino," *Amerasia Journal* 1, no. 2 (1975): 26–35.

16. Clifford I. Uyeda, *A Final Report and Review: The Japanese American Citizens League National Committee for Iva Toguri*, is an invaluable account. For the major publication of the committee, see Japanese American Citizens League, National

Uyeda became the guiding spirit of the campaign for a pardon for Toguri after he learned that pardon requests filed by her attorneys had been turned down by both the Eisenhower and Johnson administrations. Despite a distinct reluctance to become involved on the part of some "old timer JACLers," the national organization did, eventually, support the campaign. Additional support was garnered from the larger community and from politicans. Media coverage was mostly sympathetic and included a segment on *Sixty Minutes*. The campaign was ultimately successful, and President Gerald R. Ford granted the pardon on his last day in office. The willingness, however reluctant, of the Japanese American community to support the campaign for Toguri's pardon would suggest its growing psychological security. The Toguri campaign was almost noncontroversial within the community by the time of its successful resolution.

The reverse has been true of the ongoing struggle for "redress." This campaign has not only been traumatic but has resulted in the opening of old communal divisions and the creation of new ones. It is impossible to say just when the organized movement for redress began: by the late 1960s, Japanese American groups in San Francisco, southern California, and Seattle had begun to agitate for compensation for wrongs suffered during World War II. Sometimes the word "reparations" was used, but eventually the softer term "redress" was generally accepted.

During the late 1960s, attitudes began to change within the Japanese American community toward the relocation and the advisability of publicly discussing it. In 1967, for example, when the University of California Extension Division sponsored an all-day symposium to commemorate the twenty-fifth anniversary of Executive Order 9066, no representative of the JACL was willing to participate.[17] But in the early 1970s a series of "pilgrimages" was begun to Manzanar and other relocation centers. Successful campaigns were waged to declare as historical landmarks the two relocation centers within California, Manzanar, and Tule Lake. In the course of the struggle to commemorate Manzanar, conservative forces within California objected strenuously, but futilely, to the wording on

---

Committee for Iva Toguri, *Iva Toguri (d'Aquino): Victim of a Legend*. A second edition is dated 1976. Independent of Uyeda's efforts, a 1974 resolution of the National Council of the JACL recognized the injustice done to Toguri and asked her if she wished assistance. Nothing came of it.

17. The conference, "It Did Happen Here," was organized by Roger Daniels and Harry H. L. Kitano. Former California Attorney General Robert W. Kenny came to say *mea culpa*. The organizers could not find anyone willing to defend the correctness of the relocation.

the plaque to be erected, especially to the use of the term "concentration camp." Lillian Baker, an activist in the right wing of the Republican party in California, emerged at this time as a vocal and peripatetic opponent of any form of redress for Japanese Americans and of any suggestion that the evacuation had been either improper or unnecessary.[18]

In the meantime, on February 19, 1976, the thirty-fourth anniversary of the signing of Executive Order 9066, Gerald R. Ford issued Presidential Proclamation 4417, which formally revoked the wartime document and apologized for the relocation. Calling attention to the bicentennial celebrations, Ford insisted that "an honest reckoning" must take account "of our national mistakes as well as our national achievements."

> We know now [the president continued] what we should have known then—not only was that evacuation wrong, but Japanese Americans were and are loyal Americans. On the battlefield and at home, Japanese Americans—names like Hamada, Mitsumori, Marimoto, Noguchi, Yamasaki, Kido, Munemori and Miyamura— have been and continue to be written into our history for the sacrifices and contributions they have made to the well-being and security of this, our common Nation.[19]

Although the full story of the Ford proclamation has not yet been told, its issuance has been a milestone in the transformation of the image of the Japanese American people—a transformation that began in the

---

18. Lillian Baker, *The Concentration Camp Conspiracy*. The text of the Manzanar plaque reads:

Manzanar

In the early part of World War II, 110,000 persons of Japanese Ancestry were interned in relocation centers by Executive Order No. 9066, issued on February 19, 1942. Manzanar, the first of ten such concentration camps, was bounded by barbed wire and guard towers, confining 10,000 persons, the majority being American citizens. May the injustices and humiliation suffered here as a result of hysteria, racism and economic exploitation never emerge again.

The Tule Lake text was similar but shorter. It did not refer to Tule Lake's history as a segregation center. For this movement, see Sue K. Embrey, ed., *The Lost Years, 1942–1946*, and Tule Lake Plaque Committee, Northern California–Western Nevada District Council, Japanese American Citizens League, *Tule Lake*. Manzanar and Tule Lake are California Registered Landmarks, Nos. 850 and 850-2, dated 1973 and 1979, respectively.

19. *Federal Register*, vol. 41, no. 35, February 20, 1976. For a brief account of the JACL's campaign to get Executive Order 9066 repealed, see Bill Hosokawa, *JACL: In Quest of Justice*, pp. 339–41.

summer of 1942 when some Nisei were let out of camps to attend college and others were recruited for military intelligence. It has also provided important impetus to the campaign for redress.

Preliminaries of the redress campaign were started as early as 1970, when the JACL passed the first of three successive resolutions calling for legislation to make amends for "the worst mistakes of World War II." They were initiated by dissident activists from within and without the national organization. Little came of these resolutions. The JACL leadership neither opposed nor acted on them. Edison Uno, perhaps the most influential of the proponents of redress, suggested in late 1976 that it would take "at least ten years" to get any meaningful action from the national group.[20] After Uno's untimely death, Clifford Uyeda, who had led the successful campaign for the Toguri pardon, took up the struggle and became chairman of the JACL National Committee for Redress. The 1978 JACL convention in Salt Lake City marked a turning point in the redress campaign and provided a dramatic confrontation between its backers and their opponents.

Before the convention, the redress committee had published an important statement of the case for redress. It referred directly to the parallel experience of German Jews, a comparison that would have been unthinkable for the organization a few years earlier:

> German Jews experienced the horrors of the Nazi death camps Japanese Americans experienced the agonies of being incarcerated for an indeterminate period. Both were imprisoned in barbed wire compounds with armed guards. Both were prisoners of their own country. Both were there without criminal charges, and were completely innocent of any wrongdoing. Both were there for only one reason—ancestry. German Jews were systematically murdered en masse—that did not happen to Japanese Americans, but the point is that both Germany and the United States persecuted their own citizens based on ancestry.[21]

The pamphlet went on to point out that the West German government had paid $25 billion in restitution to Jews and that another $10 to $15 billion was still to be paid. While no dollar figure was suggested, the committee statement closed by arguing that

> redress for injustices of 1942–1946 is not just an isolated Japanese American issue; it is an issue of concern for all Americans.

---

20. Conversation with Edison Uno, Lethbridge, Alberta, Canada, November 1976.

21. National Committee for Redress, Japanese American Citizens League, *The Japanese American Incarceration: A Case for Redress.*

Restitution does not put a price tag on freedom or justice. The issue is not to recover what cannot be recovered. The issue is to acknowledge the mistake by providing proper redress for the victims of injustice, and thereby make such injustices less likely to recur.[22]

Having prepared the groundwork, Uyeda and his committee unveiled their full proposal at the biennial JACL convention at Salt Lake City later that summer. It asked for $25,000 in per capita payments to individuals or heirs forced out by General John DeWitt's orders. It also called for a trust fund of $100 million to be set up for the benefit of Japanese Americans, to be administered by Japanese Americans. The proposal was unanimously adopted by the national council. In addition, Uyeda was elected national president, the first person so elected who had not previously either headed a chapter or been in the JACL administrative hierarchy.

But conservative forces within the organization, the community, and the nation were shocked that a "model minority" should make such strident demands. At the convention's closing banquet, S. I. Hayakawa, who had been elected to the United States Senate from California as a Republican in 1976, admonished Japanese Americans to stop looking back and to concern themselves instead with future problems. Too polite to attack the JACL at its own convention, Hayakawa pulled no punches in a postbanquet interview. A story the next morning in the Salt Lake City *Tribune,* which was distributed nationally by the wire services, clarified his position:

> The Japanese American Citizens League has no right to ask the U.S. government for reparations for Japanese American citizens placed in relocation camps during World War II, according to Sen. S. I. Hayakawa . . . "Everybody lost out during the war, not just Japanese Americans," and the JACL asking for $25,000 in redress for each Japanese American placed in relocation camps was "ridiculous."

The next year, in an essay that ranged widely over the Japanese American experience, Hayakawa aligned himself with Thomas Sowell's views about race in America. He went so far as to suggest that the wartime incarceration was good for the Japanese Americans.

> As one talks with Nisei today—they are now in their fifties and sixties—one gets the impression that the wartime relocation, despite the injustices and economic losses suffered, was perhaps the

---

22. As cited in Hosakawa, *JACL,* p. 347.

best thing that could have happened to the Japanese-Americans of the West Coast. As many say, the relocation forced them out of their segregated existence to discover the rest of America. It opened up possibilities for them that they never would have known had they remained on farms in Livingston or fishing boats in San Pedro.[23]

This infuriated many in the Japanese American community. They delighted in pointing out that Hayakawa, who was Canadian-born, had spent the war in Chicago and had not experienced relocation. His California constituency was conservative, not ethnic. Nonetheless, significant numbers of Japanese Americans, for a variety of reasons, rejected redress. Some insisted that no amount of money could compensate them for their suffering; others saw redress as a kind of welfare; still others thought it best not to reopen the wounds of the past. In the early stages of the redress campaign, Japanese Americans were probably divided on the issue much as John Adams had imagined that colonial Americans were divided on the American Revolution—about a third favored it, another third opposed it, and the final third was uncommitted or indifferent. For Japanese Americans in the late 1970s, much of the "unconcern" and even opposition to redress may have stemmed, at least in part, from a healthy skepticism that anything would come of it.

The initial negative reactions from the community, plus the practical concerns voiced by members of the small Japanese American congressional delegation, caused the JACL's redress committee, then headed by Sansei activist John Tateishi (b. 1939), who had spent some of his childhood in the camp at Manzanar, to switch tactics. Instead of asking for direct redress, the JACL agreed to support a bill introduced on August 2, 1979, which called for appointing a commission "to determine whether a wrong was committed against those American citizens and permanent residents relocated and/or interned as a result of Executive Order Numbered 9066 and other associated acts of the Federal Government, and to recommend appropriate remedies." The

---

23. "*Giri* to One's Name: Notes on the Wartime Relocation and the Japanese Character," in S. I. Hayakawa, *Through the Communication Barrier*, pp. 131–37; quotation from pp. 135–136. *Giri*, according to Hayakawa, is "the duty to keep one's reputation unblemished." Edith Blicksilver writes: "Most families were not weakened but strengthened by the indignities they endured" ("The Japanese American Woman, the Second World War, and the Relocation Camp Experience," *Women's Studies International Forum* 5, nos. 3/4 [1982]: 353). For careful anthropological study of aging Nisei that has produced more cautious and, I believe, sounder conclusions, see Donna L. Leonetti, *Nisei Aging Project Report*.

commission was to be called the Commission on Wartime Relocation and Internment of Civilians (CWRIC).

This tactical switch was viewed by some community activists, both inside and outside of the JACL, as a "sellout." The neutrality of the language—"to determine whether a wrong was committed"—enraged them. Two groups, one informal, the other formal, emerged in opposition to the JACL. The informal group, centered in Seattle, supported a bill introduced by Representative Mike Lowry (D-Wash.) which called for a payment of $25,000 to each survivor and his or her heirs plus other provisions. The formal group supporting the Lowry bill was an organization called the National Council for Japanese American Redress based in Chicago and headed by William Hohri, a Nisei. It also initiated lawsuits seeking billions in damages from the federal government.

The JACL switch was caused partly by Senator Hayakawa's refusal to support any measure directly calling for cash payment, and partly by the feeling of many supporters of the legislation, including the very influential Senator Henry M. Jackson (D-Wash.), that it was necessary to establish a "record" on which the Congress could act. In March 1980 hearings were held before the Committee on Governmental Affairs of the United States Senate. A number of witnesses and statements demonstrated a broad spectrum of support—only William Hohri opposed the bill—and later that year Congress passed the bill creating the commission.[24]

The commission, appointed in the last days of the Carter administration by the president, the president pro-tem of the Senate (Warren G. Magnuson, D-Wash.), and the Speaker of the House (Thomas P.

---

24. U.S. Congress, Senate, *Commission on Wartime Relocation and Internment of Civilians Act, Hearing before the Committee on Governmental Affairs*, 96th Cong., 2d sess., 1980. The eight witnesses were: Roger Daniels, Jerry Enemoto, William Hohri, Mike Masaoka, Robert T. Matsui, Norman Y. Mineta, Clarence M. Mitchell, Diane Yen-Mei Wong, and Jim Wright. Quotation ("record") from Senator Henry Jackson, interview, March 18, 1980.

Since I have been directly involved in the campaign for redress, it is proper that I make what lawyers call my "interest" explicit. On March 18, 1980, I testified, at the request of the government, before the Senate hearings in support of the establishment of a commission. When the commission was established, I served, from time to time, as a consultant to it, participated in a briefing for the commissioners, wrote several memoranda, answered staff questions, helped to brief counsel, etc. In a document submitted to the commission by the JACL, I contributed an introduction which found monetary redress "entirely appropriate," although it did not recommend a specific amount. Finally, I read and commented on a draft version of the historical portion of the text, but not the footnotes, of what became *Personal Justice Denied*. Over a period of almost three years I received from the government, in compensation and for expenses, the approximate equivalent of one-month's salary.

O'Neill, D-Mass.) originally consisted of seven members: Joan Z. Bernstein, chair, the former general counsel of the Department of Housing and Urban Development; Daniel E. Lundgren, vice-chair, a Republican representative from Long Beach, California; Edward W. Brooke, former Republican senator from Massachusetts; Arthur S. Fleming, chair of the Civil Rights Commission and former Secretary of Health, Education and Welfare; Arthur J. Goldberg, former justice, Supreme Court of the United States; William M. Marutani, federal judge in Philadelphia and the only Japanese American on the commission; and Hugh B. Mitchell, former Democratic senator from Washington.

In the early weeks of the Reagan administration, Republican Senator Ted Stevens of Alaska realized that some of his constituents, Aleuts, were also evacuated under provisions of Executive Order 9066, and the act creating the commission was amended so that the scope of its investigation included "Aleut civilians, and permanent residents of the Aleutian and Pribilof Islands." Stevens, who was majority whip in the Republican controlled Senate, also wanted to have a representative of the Aleut people named to the commission; Speaker O'Neill insisted that, if the Senate got to name another member, the House should have the same right. This was agreed to: the Senate selected the Reverend Ishmael V. Gromoff, a priest of the Russian Orthodox church who was an official spokesman for the Aleut people and of Aleut ancestry. Then, as Washington legend has it, Speaker O'Neill decided that, if "they name a priest, I'll name a priest," and he named Father Robert F. Drinan, the Jesuit head of Americans for Democratic Action and former Democratic Representative from Massachusetts for the ninth spot on the commission.[25] Given the distinctly liberal composition of the commission, it was all but a certainty that the relocation would be condemned and that some kind of redress would be recommended to Congress. Political expediency suggested that the figure be somewhat below the $25,000 originally asked for by the JACL.

The commission met, held hearings in Washington and around the country, published a report, and made recommendations. It's impact on the Japanese American community was significant. The very existence of the CWRIC forced large numbers of the survivors to

---

25. For an account of the evacuation of the Aleuts, see Dorothy Knee Jones, *A Century of Servitude: Pribilof Aleuts under U.S. Rule*, pp. 107–18. I have the O'Neill quote from three sources that are reasonably reliable. Washington insiders speculated with great glee about President Reagan's reactions when he learned that he was committed to sign a commission for Father Drinan.

come to grips—often publicly at hearings or in community meetings—with their own long-suppressed feelings about their wartime experiences. Some of the televised hearings on the West Coast became quite disorderly. The hearings and communitywide discussion clearly provided a catharsis. The overwhelming body of the testimony, both from Japanese Americans and from officials who supervised one or another aspect of the program, was sympathetic to redress and was critical of what had been done during the war. Abe Fortas, for example, who, as Undersecretary of the Interior, supervised the War Relocation Authority after February 1944, testified that

> I believe that the mass evacuation . . . was a tragic error . . . I cannot escape the conclusion that racial prejudice was its basic ingredient. . . . I think that it is clear—perhaps it was always clear—that the mass evacuation order issued by General DeWitt was never justified.[26]

But the two key surviving officials able to testify, Karl R. Bendetsen and John J. McCloy, continued to support the positions that they had taken during the war. On the one hand, Bendetsen, who had once boasted that he had "conceived method, formulated details and directed evacuation of 120,000 persons of Japanese ancestry from military areas," now claimed that he was just obeying orders, referred the CWRIC to his own *Final Report* of 1943, and was generally defensive.[27] McCloy, on the other hand, totally ignored his own key role and concentrated on the defense of his chief, Henry L. Stimson, and of Franklin D. Roosevelt. The crux of his testimony was to urge the CWRIC to conclude

> after an objective investigation, that under the circumstances prevailing at the time and with the exigencies of wartime security, the action of the President of the United States and the United States

---

26. "Statement of Abe Fortas Before the Commission on Wartime Relocation and Internment of Civilians, June 14, 1981," 7 pp., typed, in my possession.

27. "Written Statement of Karl R. Bendetsen for the Commission on Wartime Relocation and Internment of Civilians, July 8, 1981," 17 pp., typed, in my possession. It is clear that Bendetsen used material from his oral history interview available at the Truman Library. Both Bendetsen documents must be used with extreme caution. Bendetsen minimizes his own anti-Japanese bias and explains away his influence on the decision to relocate. Conversely, in each document, Bendetsen claims to have made decisions that were in fact made by others (e.g., the choosing of sites for WRA centers). "Oral History Interview with Karl R. Bendetsen by Jerry N. Hess, New York City, New York, October 24, November 9 and November 21, 1972," Harry S. Truman Library, Independence, Mo. For his earlier boast, see *Who's Who in America*, (1946–1947 edition), p. 173.

Government in regard to our then Japanese population was reasonably undertaken and thoughtfully and humanely conducted. There has been, in my judgment, at times a spate of irresponsible comment to the effect that this wartime move was callous, shameful and induced by racial or punitive motives. It was nothing of the sort.

I know of the decisions that were made, and I think that I know who made them, and I think I know generally what the motivation was of those individuals who made them. . . .

I therefore believe in the interests of all concerned, the Commission would be well advised to conclude that President Roosevelt's wartime action in connection with the relocation of our Japanese-descended population at the outbreak of our war with Japan, was taken and carried out in accordance with the best interests of the country, considering the conditions, exigencies and considerations which then faced the nation.[28]

Early in 1983 the CWRIC released its report, *Personal Justice Denied*. Its argument and conclusions were fully in line with prevailing scholarship. The crucial paragraph in the report's summary read as follows:

The promulgation of Executive Order 9066 was not justified by military necessity, and the decisions which followed from it—detention, ending detention and ending exclusion—were not driven by analysis of military conditions. The broad historical causes which shaped these decisions were race prejudice, war hysteria and a failure of political leadership. Widespread ignorance of Japanese Americans contributed to a policy conceived in haste and executed in an atmosphere of fear and anger at Japan. A grave injustice was done to Americans and resident aliens of Japanese ancestry who, without individual review or any probative evidence against them, were excluded, removed and detained by the United States during World War II.[29]

Quite deliberately, the CWRIC did not couple its report and its recommendations. The report itself drew largely favorable press and television coverage. To be sure, many conservative papers delighted in placing the blame on FDR, and a number of letters to the editor

---

28. McCloy testimony, November 3, 1981, as cited in CWRIC, *Personal Justice Denied: Report of the Commission on Wartime Relocation and Internment of Civilians*, pp. 383–84. Although dated December 1982, the report was not released until February 24, 1983.

29. CWRIC, *Personal Justice Denied*, p. 18.

wondered why, if the Japanese had started the war, we should apologize for locking them up.

But John J. McCloy attacked the CWRIC Report head-on in an "Op Ed" essay in the New York *Times*. Insisting that the whole issue had been artificially created by what he called the "Japanese-American lobby," McCloy claimed that bowing to that lobby would "perpetrate injustice." Appealing to popular prejudices, McCloy, who never mentioned his own role in the relocation, deliberately conflated Tokyo and Little Tokyo.

> The historic reality is that the wartime Japanese Government made the evacuation necessary. If any compensation is owing, the responsibility lies with the Government, whose sneak attack set in train the dislocation, death and misery of millions, including the privations suffered by the innocent ethnic Japanese on the West Coast. After all, the dead American sailors, marines and soldiers of Pearl Harbor, Iwo Jima and Okinawa and the dead Japanese and their kin will never be "compensated" for their "dislocation." . . . An insufferable element of the commission's effort to condemn our officials is the imputation of "racial prejudice" and "war hysteria" to deceased statesmen. . . . [T]o associate ignorant prejudice with Mr. Stimson and other senior officials is an affront to their memory and a total misconception of the facts and of their characters. . . . What have we come to when Americans are asked to shoulder the blame, to finance and conduct inquiries into their "guilt" and pay for the consequences of an indisputable act of aggression by Japan?[30]

In June 1983, just before its legislative mandate expired, the CWRIC issued five recommendations for redress to Congress. First, it called for a joint resolution of Congress, to be signed by the President, recognizing a grave injustice and offering apologies. Second, it recommended presidential pardons for those who had been convicted of violation of the various statutes establishing and enforcing the evacuation. Third, it urged that Congress direct appropriate parts of the executive branch to treat with liberality Japanese American applicants for restitution, status, and entitlements lost because of World War II. It gave as an example any applications for review of the less-than-honorable discharges, which many were given on grounds of ethnicity in the months after Pearl Harbor. Fourth, it recommended that

---

30. John J. McCloy, "Repay U.S. Japanese?," New York *Times*, April 10, 1983. The *Times*, which did not object to the relocation during World War II, deplored it in the 1980s but opposed any tangible redress.

Congress appropriate money to establish a special foundation to "sponsor research and public educational activities . . . so that the causes and circumstances of this and similar events may be illuminated." And fifth, in its most important and expensive recommendation, it urged Congress to appropriate $1.5 billion "to provide personal redress to those who were excluded," as well as to fund recommendation four. It called for a one-time per capita compensatory payment of $20,000 to each of the estimated 60,000 survivors of the relocation. This would cost $1.2 billion.

Recommendations one through four were adopted unanimously; Representative Daniel E. Lundgren dissented from recommendation five. The commissioners also recommended, with Representative Lundgren again dissenting, that a $5 million fund be set up for the "beneficial use" of the Aleuts and that each of the few hundred surviving Aleuts who were evacuated during World War II be given a direct per capita payment of $5,000. Finally, addressing itself to history, the commission quoted poet W. H. Auden:

> We are left alone with our day, and the time is short and
> History to the defeated
> May say Alas but cannot help or pardon. . . .

and expressed its belief that "though history cannot be unmade, it is well within our power to offer help, and to acknowledge error."[31]

Press reaction, which was generally favorable to the notion of an apology, argued that $1.5 billion was too much money. A bill to effectuate the CWRIC's recommendations was quickly introduced and an initial hearing took place in late July 1983. The testimony of Representative Lundgren, the sole dissenter from the CWRIC recommendations, was politely negative. Lundgren continued to support the historical analysis of *Personal Justice Denied* and the idea of a Congressional apology. He opposed monetary redress for a variety of reasons, but especially because

> it is inappropriate that present day taxpayers should be held accountable for actions that occurred 40 years ago. Should we pay monetary redress for the abhorrent practice of slavery or the inhumane treatment of Indians 100 years ago? . . .
> Carried to its logical extension, such a principle of restitution could have untold consequences. Should the Chinese be paid back for their underpaid role in helping the railroads open the American West? Should people of German ancestry be compensated for being denied rights in World War I? Should we return to Black Americans

---

31. CWRIC, "Press Release," 17 pp. [n.d., but June 15, 1983].

the plantations on which their families worked for over 200 years?[32]

Although Lundgren's argument was a chain of non sequiturs—the bill provided for redress for survivors only—his last point, that the possible claims of black Americans could reach astronomical amounts, raised a truly frightening specter for many.

It took more than five years after the submission of the CWRIC recommendations for a bill to pass both houses and become law. Although redress seemed to have majority support, and bills enacting the recommendations were introduced into both houses in the Ninety-eighth and Ninety-ninth Congresses, none passed. Finally, in August 1988, redress was enacted. The $20,000 payments to individuals will begin in January 1990, and spread over ten years; older persons are to be paid first. Perhaps 60,000 persons who were incarcerated are still alive. Many more will surely die before they are paid, but any persons who die after the bill was signed into law may have their compensation inherited by survivors. Survivors of persons who died before that time will not be compensated. About half of those incarcerated by their government are already beyond any earthly redress.

Reflecting on the events of recent years, it has been all too easy for superficial observers, or for those with particular axes to grind, to argue that prejudice against Asians is no longer a significant problem. This misperception has not been shared by most leaders in the Chinese American and Japanese American communities. These leaders, of course, have witnessed tremendous progress of recent years. They have also been aware that discrimination, both covert and overt, still exists. Covert discrimination exists largely in that Asian Americans of high achievement do not gain the kind of status and rewards received by whites of similar accomplishments. As noted previously, Asian American income levels have not been proportional to their educational attainments. And overt discrimination has clearly been exacerbated both by the economic downturns of the 1970s and 1980s and by the displacement of American technology by Japanese technology in the auto industry and elsewhere. One bizarre and tragic incident in a Detroit suburb must stand as surrogate for innumerable others.

On the night of June 19, 1982, Vincent Chin, a 27-year-old

---

32. "Testimony of Congressman Daniel E. Lundgren, 42d District, California, before the Senate Judiciary Committee Subcommittee on Administrative Practice and Procedure, July 27, 1983," 6 pp., mimeographed. The hostile opposition was led by John J. McCloy, who appeared on public and commercial television to oppose any form of redress.

American-born draftsman of Chinese ancestry, went with three friends to a topless bar, the Fancy Pants Tavern in Highland Park, to celebrate his impending marriage. Some racial slurs were made by Ronald Ebens, a 43-year-old unemployed auto industry foreman, who thought that Chin was Japanese. A scuffle ensued, and the participants were asked to leave the bar. Later that night, Ebens and his 23-year-old stepson Michael Nitz, who had been in the bar scuffle, spotted Chin in a fast-food restaurant. They waited for him to leave and, while Nitz held him, Ebens beat him with a baseball bat so severely that he died four days later. Originally charged with second-degree murder, the white pair, in a plea bargain, were allowed to plead guilty to manslaughter. Then Wayne County Circuit Judge Charles Kaufman fined each auto worker $3,780 and placed him on three-years' probation. Naturally there was an outraged community reaction. In a tactic reminiscent of the Scottsboro case of the 1930s, a "Justice for Vincent Chin" committee was formed, petitions were circulated, and the victim's mother made a cross-country tour to raise funds for legal expenses. The protests eventually forced a federal investigation, which produced a federal indictment of Ebens for depriving Chin of his civil rights. (A re-indictment for the homicide would have been double jeopardy.) Tried and found guilty, Ebens was sentenced to twenty-five years in prison. That conviction was reversed on appeal because of judicial errors. When the case was re-tried, in 1987, Ebens's attorney persuaded the jury that the deadly assault was not racially motivated, so the auto worker went free. Later that year a civil suit against Ebens was settled by a court-approved agreement whereby Ebens agreed to pay, over time, $1.5 million to Chin's estate.

Most anti-Asian American incidents have not involved death or even physical harassment. But by the mid-1980s, as stories in the national media have made clear, there is growing concern not just about violence but about anti-Asian attitudes at all levels of American society. Japanese American and Chinese American communities have been affected in different ways. For Japanese Americans, the chief factor has been the growing resentment of the industrial success of Japan, a resentment linking auto workers, their bosses, and some of their political representatives. Some UAW locals have printed and distributed bumper stickers reading "Toyota-Datsun-Honda = Pearl Harbor" and "Unemployment—Made in Japan." Although national UAW officials disassociate themselves from such sentiments, the bumper stickers have been found at their union's Detroit headquarters. Visitors to Detroit-area auto plants have found racist anti-Japanese posters and graffiti all but ubiquitous; and likening auto plant unemployment to an "economic Pearl Harbor" has become almost automatic in the industry.

Similar prejudice has spewed from the executive suites: perhaps the worst offender is Bennett E. Bidwell, Chrysler's executive vice-president for sales and marketing, who has suggested that the best way to stem car imports would be to charter the *Enola Gay* (the B-29 that dropped the first atomic bomb). Michigan political leaders such as Democratic Senator Donald W. Reigel, Jr., have echoed the auto industry's rhetoric about "an economic Pearl Harbor," and Representative John D. Dingell, a Michigan Democrat whose father had called for concentration camps for alien Japanese almost four months *before* Pearl Harbor, has complained about American jobs being taken by "little yellow men."

Gallup polls, not quite comparable, have indicated that between 1980 and 1982 the percentage of Americans with "favorable attitudes" toward Japan fell from 84 to 63 percent. But millions of Americans have continued to buy Japanese products, which suggests that feelings are mixed. The New York *Times* has quoted one Maine man as saying "I'm not going to give the American auto industry a couple of thousand dollars more just to be patriotic." Commenting on both the Chin murder and the trade/unemployment issue, Floyd Shinomura, JACL president and a law professor at the University of California at Davis, has noted that "the Vincent Chin case reminds us that non-Asian Americans tend to see all Asians as foreigners. The Japanese trade issue tends to affect us negatively because we become much more visible."

For Chinese Americans, the problems of the 1980s have been much more complex. As we have seen, refugees and immigrants swelled their population, which nearly doubled between 1970 and 1980. Many of these immigrants have been poor, exploited, and, to a degree, crime-ridden. A series of gang shootings in Chinatowns on both coasts, highlighted by a mass execution of thirteen Chinese in an after-hours gaming establishment in Seattle by recent immigrants from Hong Kong, has produced a minor wave of stories and books about the dangers of the Triad Societies, sometimes called the Chinese Mafia.

Chinese have thus become more economically and socially diverse by the 1980s, while the Japanese Americans, whose population has had only very slight infusions from abroad after the early 1960s, have become more uniformly middle-class. Under the pressures of what leaders of both groups see as a backlash, efforts have been made to form a united front of Asian Americans, or at least of Chinese Americans and Japanese Americans. One such leader, Oakland attorney Alan S. Yee, has observed that both Chinese Americans and Japanese Americans can relate to the Chin murder because most of them have experienced racial prejudice at one time or another.

That's what really unites all Asian groups on this issue even though the Asian-American community has traditional divisions. But we find that, from the outside, we're all perceived as the same, and, despite an image as "model minorities," we see the search for the scapegoat still there.

Model minorities or scapegoats? Obviously neither stereotype is or can be accurate. The one and a half million Chinese and Japanese Americans enumerated by the 1980 census cannot be placed in a single pigeonhole. Those whose families have been here more than a generation or so have achieved, on the average, more than members of most ethnic groups who arrived at the same time. An extraordinary number of individual Chinese and Japanese Americans have achieved distinguished or at least prominent places for themselves in American life. (For obvious physical reasons, Asian Americans have not made a significant impact in most American professional sports, but there are few if any other spheres where they have not made their mark.) But even the most successful still encounter slights, ranging from the polite but obtuse comment, such as "How well you speak English!" to the affrontive gesture, such as the word "Jap" spray-painted on a Sacramento congressman's garage.[33]

Diana Fong, writing about "America's 'Invisible Chinese'" on the "Op-Ed" page of the New York Times, summarizes the current situation succinctly:

We're still not fully integrated into the mainstream because of our yellow skin and almond eyes. Much has changed in 100 years [since the exclusion act], but we still cannot escape the distinction of race.[34]

---

33. Material about the 1980s comes from a variety of sources, including personal observation. Especially useful were the following newspaper articles: David Smollar, "Violence, Slurs—U.S. Asians Feel Trade Backlash," Los Angeles Times, September 14, 1983; and Robert Lindsay, "The New Asian Immigrants," New York Times Magazine, September 10, 1983, pp. 22 ff.

34. Diana Fong, "America's 'Invisible' Chinese," New York Times, May 1, 1982. See also Gene Oishi, "The Anxiety of Being a Japanese-American," New York Times Magazine, April 28, 1985, pp. 54, 58–60, 65.

Selected Bibliography

Manuscripts

American Loyalty League. Seattle. University of Washington. Archives.

Barnett, Arthur. Seattle. University of Washington. Archives.

Bendetsen, Karl R. Independence, Missouri. Harry S. Truman Library. Oral History Interview.

California Federation for Civic Unity. Berkeley. University of California. Bancroft Library.

California Joint Immigration Committee. Berkeley. University of California. University Library. Documents Division.

Carter, John Franklin. University of Wyoming. Coe Library.

Commission on Wartime Relocation and Internment of Civilians. Washington, D.C.

Common Ground. St. Paul, Minnesota. Immigration History Research Center.

Conn, Stetson. Washington, D.C. Office, Chief of Military History. United States Army.

Conrad-Duveneck Collection. Stanford. Hoover Institution. Archives.

Farquharson, Mary. Seattle. University of Washington. Archives.

Ford, John Anson. San Marino, California. Box 64. Huntington Library.

Freeman, Miller. Seattle. University of Washington. Archives.

Fukano Family. Seattle. University of Washington. Archives.

Hirabayashi, Gordon K. Interview. Seattle. University of Washington. Archives.

Hirakawa, Kihachi. Seattle. University of Washington. Archives.

Ichihara, Hiroyuki. Seattle. University of Washington. Archives.

Ichihara, Kaoru. Seattle. University of Washington. Archives.

Japanese American Research Project Archives. UCLA.

Johnson, Hiram W., III. Berkeley. University of California. Bancroft Library.

Kenny, Robert W. Berkeley. University of California. Bancroft Library.

Knox, Frank, Collection. Washington, D.C. Washington Navy Yard. Office of Naval History.

Matsushita, Iwao. Seattle. University of Washington. Archives.

Metcalf, Victor H. Berkeley. University of California. Bancroft Library. Scrapbook pertaining to discrimination against Japanese in San Francisco. 1906.

Morgenthau, Henry, Jr. Hyde Park, New York. Franklin D. Roosevelt Library. Diary.

Olson, Culbert L. Berkeley. University of California. Bancroft Library.

Pacific Coast Committee for American Principles and Fair Play. Berkeley. University of California. Bancroft Library.

Phelan, James D. Berkeley. University of California. Bancroft Library.

Port Blakely Mill Company. Seattle. University of Washington. Archives.

President's Files. Berkeley. University of California. Bancroft Library. Archives.

Records of the Adjutant General. Washington, D.C. National Archives. Record Group 407.

Records of the Office of Government Reports. Suitland, Maryland. Washington National Records Center. Record Group 44.

Records of the Office of Provost Marshal General. Washington, D.C. National Archives. Record Group 389.

Records of the Secretary of Agriculture. Washington, D.C. National Archives. Record Group 16.

Records of the Secretary of War and the Assistant Secretary of War. Washington, D.C. National Archives. Record Group 107.

Records of the 10th U.S. Circuit Court of Appeals. Denver, Colorado. Federal Records Center.

Records of the War Relocation Authority. Washington, D.C. National Archives. Record Group 210.

Records of the Western Defense Command. Washington, D.C. National Archives. Record Group 394.

Ringle, Kenneth D. Washington, D.C. Ringle family.

Roosevelt, Franklin D. Hyde Park, New York. Franklin D. Roosevelt Library.

Rowell, Chester H. Berkeley. University of California. Bancroft Library.

Sakamoto, James Y. Seattle. University of Washington. Archives.

Seattle JACL. Seattle. University of Washington. Archives.

Stilwell, Joseph W. Stanford. Hoover Institution. Archives. Diary.

Stimson, Henry L. New Haven. Yale University. Diary.

War Relocation Authority Collection. Bancroft Library.

War Relocation Authority Collection. Los Angeles. University of California. Special Collections.

War Relocation Authority Collection. Seattle. University of Washington. Archives.

Articles, Books, Dissertations, and Theses

Abbott, Edith. *Immigration: Select Documents.* Chicago: University of Chicago Press, 1924.

Albert, Michael D. "Japanese American Communities in Chicago and the Twin Cities." Ph.D. dissertation, University of Minnesota, 1980.

Almaguer, Tomas. "Racial Domination and Class Conflict in Capitalist Agriculture: The Oxnard Sugar Beet Workers Strike of 1903." *Labor History* 25 (1984): 325–50.

Ambrose, Stephen E., and Immerman, Richard H. *Milton S. Eisenhower, Educational Statesman.* Baltimore: Johns Hopkins University Press, 1983.

Anders, Steven E. "The Coolie Panacea in the Reconstruction South." M.A. thesis, Miami University, 1973.

Anderson, David L. "The Diplomacy of Exclusion, 1876–1882." *California History* 57 (1978): 32–45.

Ano, Masaharu. "Loyal Linguists: Nisei of World War II Learned Japanese in Minnesota." *Minnesota History* 45 (1977): 273–87.

Anthony, J. Garner. *Hawaii Under Army Rule.* Palo Alto: Stanford University Press, 1955.

Archdeacon, Thomas. *Becoming American: An Ethnic History.* New York: Free Press, 1983.

Arensmeyer, Elliott Campbell. "British Merchant Enterprise and the Chinese Coolie Labor Trade: 1850–1874." Ph.D. dissertation, University of Hawaii, 1979.

Armentrout-Ma, [L.] Eve. "Big and Medium Businesses of Chinese Immigrants in the Untied States, 1850–1880: An Outline." *Bulletin of the Chinese Historical Society* 13, no. 7 (1978): 1–5.

_____. "A Chinese Association in North America: Pao-huang Hui from 1899 to 1904." *Ching-shih wen-t'i* 3 (1978): 91–111.

_____. "Chinese in California's Fishing Industry, 1850–1941." *California History* 60 (1981): 142–57.

_____. "Chinese Politics in the Western Hemisphere, 1893–1911: Rivalry between Reformers and Revolutionaries in the Americas." Ph.D. dissertation, University of California at Davis, 1977.

_____. "Urban Chinese at the Sinitic Frontier: Social Organizations in United States' Chinatowns, 1849–1898." *Modern Asian Studies* 17 (1983): 107–35.

Arnold, Frank S.; Barth, Michael C.; and Langner, Gilah. *Economic Losses of Ethnic Japanese as a Result of Exclusion and Detention, 1942–1946.* [n.p.]: ICF Incorporated, June 1983.

Arreola, Daniel. "Locke, California: Persistence and Change in the Cultural Landscape of a Delta Chinatown." M.A. thesis, California State University, Hayward, 1975.

Baker, Lillian. *The Concentration Camp Conspiracy: A Second Pearl Harbor.* Glendale, CA: AFHA Publications, 1982.

Bamford, Mary. *Angel Island: The Ellis Island of the West.* Chicago, 1917.

Barth, Gunther. *Bitter Strength: A History of the Chinese in the United States, 1850–1870.* Cambridge: Harvard University Press, 1964.

Bell, Daniel. *The End of Ideology.* Glencoe, IL: Free Press, 1960.

Bell, Reginald. *Public School Education of Second-Generation Japanese in California.* Stanford: Stanford University Press, 1935.

Biddle, Francis. *In Brief Authority.* New York: Doubleday & Co., 1962.

Bigler, John. *Governor's Special Message.* Sacramento, 1852.

Billington, Ray. A. *The Protestant Crusade, 1800–1860.* New York: Macmillan Co., 1938.

Blicksilver, Edith. "The Japanese American Woman, the Second World War, and the Relocation Camp Experience." *Women's Studies International Forum* 5, nos. 3/4 (1982): 351–53.

Blum, John Morton. *V Was for Victory: Politics and American Culture During World War II.* New York: Harcourt Brace Jovanovich, 1976.

Bodnar, John. *The Transplanted: A History of Immigrants in Urban America.* Bloomington: Indiana University Press, 1985.

Bonacich, Edna, and Modell, John. *The Economic Basis of Ethnic Solidarity: Small Business in the Japanese American Community.* Berkeley and Los Angeles: University of California Press, 1980.

Bowen, James L. "Yung Wing and His Work." *Scribner's Monthly Magazine* 10 (1875): 106–08.

Brown, Richard Maxwell. "Historiography of Violence in the American West." In *Historians in the American West,* edited by Michael P. Malone, pp. 234–69. Lincoln: University of Nebraska Press, 1983.

Brunhouse, Robert L. "Lascars in Pennsylvania." *Pennsylvania History* 7 (1940): 20–30.

California. Department of Industrial Relations. Division of Fair Employment Practices. *Californians of Japanese, Chinese, Filipino Ancestry.* San Francisco, 1965.

California. Senate. *Journal of the Senate of the State of California, 1905.* Sacramento, 1905.

Campbell, Persia Crawford. *Chinese Coolie Emigration to Countries within the British Empire.* London: P. S. King & Son, 1923.

Caroli, Betty Boyd. *Italian Repatriation From the United States.* Staten Island, NY: Center for Migration Studies, 1974.

Carranco, Lynwood. "Chinese Expulsion from Humboldt County." *Pacific Historical Review* 30 (1961): 329–37.

_____. "Chinese in Humboldt County, California: A Study in Prejudice." *Journal of the West* 12 (1973): 139–62.

Caughey, John W. *Their Majesties the Mob.* Chicago: University of Chicago Press, 1960.

Chamberlain, John. *Farewell to Reform.* New York: Liveright, 1932.

Chan, Jeffrey Paul; Chin, Frank; Inada, Lawson; and Wong, Shawn Hsu, eds., *Aiiieeeee! An Anthology of Asian-American Writers.* Washington, D.C.: Howard University Press, 1974.

Chan, Kim M. "Mandarins in America: The Early Chinese Ministers to the United States." Ph.D. dissertation, University of Hawaii, 1981.

Chan, Loren B. "The Chinese in Nevada: An Historical Survey." *Nevada Historical Society Quarterly* 25 (1982): 266–314.

_____. "Example for the Nation: Nevada's Execution of Gee Jon." *Nevada Historical Society Quarterly* 18 (1975): 90–106.

Chan, Sucheng. "Chinese Livelihood in Rural California: The Impact of Economic Change, 1860–1880." *Pacific Historical Review* 53 (1984): 273–307.

_____. *This Bittersweet Soil: The Chinese in California Agriculture, 1860–1910*. Berkeley and Los Angeles: University of California Press, 1986.

Char, Tin-yuke, and Char, Wai Jane. "The First Chinese Contract Laborers in Hawaii, 1852." *Hawaiian Journal of History* 9 (1975): 128–34.

Chen, Chia-lin. "A Gold Dream in the Blue Mountains: A Study of Chinese Immigrants in the John Day Area, Oregon, 1870–1910." M.A. thesis, Portland State University, 1972.

Chen, Ta. *Chinese Migrations*. U.S. Department of Labor. Bulletin of the Bureau of Labor Statistics, No. 340. Washington, D.C., 1923.

_____. *Emigrant Communities in South China: A Study of Overseas Migration and Its Influence on Standards of Living and Social Change*. New York: Institute of Pacific Relations, 1940.

Cheng, Lucie, and Bonacich, Edna, eds. *Labor Immigration under Capitalism*. Berkeley and Los Angeles: University of California Press, 1983.

Chin, Art. *Golden Tassels: A History of the Chinese in Washington, 1857–1977*. Seattle: Art Chin, 1977.

Chin, Doug, and Chin, Art. *Uphill: The Settlement and Diffusion of the Chinese in Seattle, Washington*. Seattle: Shorey Bookstore, 1973.

Chinese Historical Society of America. *The Life, Influence and the Role of the Chinese in the United States, 1776–1976*. San Francisco, 1976.

Chinn, Thomas W., ed. *A History of the Chinese in California: A Syllabus*. San Francisco: Chinese Historical Society, 1969.

Chiu, Ping. *Chinese Labor in California, 1850–1880*. Madison: State Historical Society of Wisconsin, 1963.

Chow, Willard T. *The Reemergence of an Inner City: The Pivot of Chinese Settlement in the East Bay Region of the San Francisco Bay Area*. San Francisco: R & E Publishers, 1977.

Choy, Philip P. "Golden Mountain of Lead: The Chinese Experience in California." *California Historical Quarterly* 50 (1970): 267–76.

Christgau, John. "Collins versus the World: The Fight to Restore Citizenship to Japanese American Renunciants of World War II." *Pacific Historical Review* 54 (1985): 1–31.

Chu, Yung-deh Richard. "Chinese Secret Societies in America: A Historical Survey." *Asian Profile* 1 (1973): 21–38.

Chung, Sue Fawn. "The Chinese American Citizens' Alliance: An Effect in Assimilation." Honors thesis, University of California, Los Angeles, 1965.

Clark, Lovell C. "Nativism—or Just Plain Prejudice?" *Acadiensis* 10 (1980): 163–71.

Clausen, Edwin. "Chinese Intellectuals in the U.S.: Success in the Post–World War II Era." In *The Annals of the Chinese Historical Society of the Pacific Northwest*, edited by Douglas W. Lee, pp. 121–59. Seattle: The Society, 1983.

Cohen, Lucy M. *Chinese in the Post–Civil War South: A People without a History*. Baton Rouge: Louisiana State University Press, 1984.

Collins, Donald E. *Native American Aliens: Disloyalty and Renunciation of Citizenship by Japanese Americans during World War II*. Westport, CT: Greenwood Press, 1985.

Commission on Wartime Relocation and Internment of Civilians. *Personal Justice Denied: Report of the Commission on Wartime Relocation and Internment of Civilians.* Washington, D.C., 1982.

Commons, John R. et al., eds. *A Documentary History of American Industrial Society.* 9 vols. Cleveland: A. H. Clark, 1910.

Condit, Ira M. *The Chinaman as We See Him.* Chicago: F. H. Revell, 1900.

Conroy, F. Hilary. *The Japanese Frontier in Hawaii, 1868–1898.* Berkeley and Los Angeles: University of California Press, 1953.

Conroy, Hilary, and Miyakawa, T. Scott, eds. *East Across the Pacific: Historical & Sociological Studies of Japanese Immigration & Assimilation.* Santa Barbara: Clio Press, 1972.

Conte, James T. "Overseas Study in the Mejii Period: Japanese Students in America, 1867–1902." Ph.D. dissertation, Princeton University, 1977.

Coolidge, Mary Roberts. *Chinese Immigration.* New York: Holt, 1909.

Corbett, P. Scott, and Corbett, Nancy P. "The Chinese in Oregon, c. 1870–1880." *Oregon Historical Quarterly* 78 (1977): 73–85.

Cowan, Robert E., and Dunlop, Boutwell. *Bibliography of the Chinese Question.* San Francisco: Bancroft, 1909.

Crane, Paul, and Larson, Alfred. "The Chinese Massacre." *Annals of Wyoming* 12 (1940): 47–55, 153–60.

Cronin, Kathryn. *Colonial Casualties: Chinese in Early Victoria.* Melbourne: Melbourne University Press, 1982.

Cross, Ira B. *History of the Labor Movement in California.* Berkeley and Los Angeles: University of California Press, 1935.

Culley, John J. "World War II and a Western Town: The Internment of the Japanese Railroad Workers of Clovis, New Mexico." *Western Historical Quarterly* 13 (1982): 43–61.

Dahlie, Jorgen. "The Japanese Challenge to Public Schools and Society in British Columbia." *Journal of Ethnic Studies* 3 (1974): 10–24.

Daniel, Cletus E. *Bitter Harvest: A History of California Farmworkers, 1870–1941.* Ithaca: Cornell University Press, 1981.

Daniels, Roger. "American Historians and East Asian Immigrants." *Pacific Historical Review* 43 (1974): 448–72.

_____. "American Refugee Policy in Historical Perspective." In *The Muses Flee Hitler: Cultural Transfer and Adaptation, 1930–1945,* edited by J. C. Jackman and Carla Borden, pp. 61–77. Washington, D.C.: Smithsonian Institution Press, 1983.

_____. "The Bureau of the Census and the Relocation of the Japanese Americans: A Note and a Document." *Amerasia Journal* 9, no. 1 (1982): 101–5.

_____. "Changes in Immigration Law and Nativism since 1924." *American Jewish History* 76 (1986): 159–180.

_____. "Chinese and Japanese in North America: The Canadian and American Experiences Compared." *The Canadian Review of American Studies* 17 (1986): 173–186.

_____. *Concentration Camps, North America: Japanese in the United States and Canada during World War II.* Melbourne, FL: Krieger, 1981.

_____. *Concentration Camps, U.S.A.: Japanese Americans and World War II*. New York: Holt, Rinehart & Winston, 1972.

_____. *The Decision to Relocate the Japanese Americans*. Philadelphia: Lippincott, 1975.

_____. "The Decisions to Relocate the North American Japanese: Another Look." *Pacific Historical Review* 51 (1982): 71–77.

_____. "The Japanese." In *Ethnic Leadership in America,* edited by John Higham, pp. 36–63. Baltimore: Johns Hopkins University Press, 1978.

_____. "Japanese America, 1930–1941: An Ethnic Community in the Great Depression." *Journal of the West* 24, no. 4 (1985): 35–50.

_____. "The Japanese Experience in North America: An Essay in Comparative Racism." *Canadian Ethnic Studies* 9, no. 2 (1977): 91–100.

_____. "Japanese Immigrants on a Western Frontier: The Issei in California, 1890–1940." In *East Across the Pacific: Historical and Sociological Studies of Japanese Immigration and Assimilation,* edited by H. Conroy and T. S. Miyakawa, pp. 76–91. Santa Barbara: Clio Press, 1972.

_____. "Japanese Relocation and Redress in North America." *The Pacific Historian* 26, no. 1 (1982): 2–13.

_____. "Majority Images—Minority Realities: A Perspective on Anti-Orientalism in the United States." *Perspectives* 2 (1976): 209–62.

_____. "The Melting Pot: A Content Analysis." *Reviews in American History* 9 (1981): 428–33.

_____. "On the Comparative Study of Immigrant and Ethnic Groups in the New World: A Note." *Comparative Studies in Society and History* 25 (1983): 401–04.

_____. *The Politics of Prejudice: The Anti-Japanese Movement in California and the Struggle for Japanese Exclusion.* 1962. 2d. ed. Berkeley and Los Angeles: University of California Press, 1978.

_____. *Racism and Immigration Restriction*. St. Charles, MO: Forum Press, 1974.

_____. "Westerners from the East: Oriental Immigrants Reappraised." *Pacific Historical Review* 35 (1966): 373–83.

_____, ed. *Anti-Chinese Violence in North America*. New York: Arno Press, 1978.

Daniels, Roger, and Kitano, Harry H. L. *American Racism: Exploration of the Nature of Prejudice*. Englewood Cliffs, NJ: Prentice-Hall, 1970.

Daniels, Roger, Taylor, Sandra C., and Kitano, Harry H. L., eds., *Japanese Americans: From Relocation to Redress*. Salt Lake City: University of Utah Press, 1986.

Davids, Jules, ed. *The Coolie Trade and Chinese Emigration*. Vol. 17. *American Diplomatic and Public Papers: The United States and China*. Wilmington, DL: Scholarly Resources, Inc., 1973.

Davis, Winfield J. *History of Political Conventions in California, 1849–1892*. Sacramento: California State Library, 1893.

Daws, Gavin. *Shoal of Time*. New York: Macmillan Co., 1968.

Deal, David M. "Chinese Labor in Walla Walla." *Chinese Historical Society of America, Bulletin* 12, no. 10 (1977): 2–6.

DeGraaf, Lawrence B. "Recognition, Racism, and Reflections on the Writing of Western Black History." *Pacific Historical Review* 44 (1975): 22–51.

De Lorme, Ronald L. "The United States Bureau of Customs and Smuggling on Puget Sound, 1851 to 1913." *Prologue* 5 (1973): 77–88.

Dembitz, Nanette. "Racial Discrimination and the Military Judgment: The Supreme Court's Korematsu and Endo Decisions." *Columbia Law Review* 45 (1945): 175–239.

Devine, Michael J. *John W. Foster.* Athens: Ohio University Press, 1981.

Donald, David. *Charles Sumner and the Rights of Man.* New York: Alfred A. Knopf, 1970.

Dorn, Jacob H. *Washington Gladden.* Columbus: Ohio State University Press, 1967.

Dorwart, Jeffrey M. *Conflict of Duty: The U.S. Navy's Intelligence Dilemma, 1919–1945.* Annapolis: United States Naval Institute, 1983.

Dow, Tsung I. "The Impact of Chinese Students returned from America with Emphasis on the Chinese Revolution, 1911–1949." *Asian Profile* 3 (1975): 135–64.

Dower, John W. *War without Mercy: Race and Power in the Pacific War.* New York: Pantheon, 1986.

Dreisziger, N. F., ed. *Mobilization for Total War: The Canadian, American and British Experience, 1914–1918, 1939–1945.* Waterloo, Canada: Wilfred Laurier University Press, 1981.

Drinnon, Richard. *Keeper of Concentration Camps: Dillon S. Myer and American Racism.* Berkeley and Los Angeles: University of California Press, 1987.

Duus, Masayo. *Tokyo Rose: Orphan of the Pacific.* New York: Kodansha International, 1979.

Duveneck, Josephine W. *Life on Two Levels: An Autobiography.* Los Altos, CA: William Kaufmann, 1978.

Dyer, Thomas G. *Theodore Roosevelt and the Politics of Race.* Baton Rouge: Louisiana State University Press, 1980.

Eaves, Lucille. *A History of California Labor Legislation.* Berkeley: University of California Press, 1910.

Edson, Christopher Howard. *The Chinese in Eastern Oregon, 1860–1890.* San Francisco: R & E Research, 1974.

Eisenhower, Milton S. *The President Is Calling.* New York: Doubleday & Co., 1974.

Elkins, Stanley. *Slavery: A Problem in American Institutional and Intellectual Life.* 2d ed. Chicago: University of Chicago Press, 1968.

Embrey, Sue K., ed. *The Lost Years, 1942–1946,* Los Angeles: Sue K. Embrey, 1972.

Embrey, Sue K., Hansen, Arthur A., and Mitson, Betty K., eds., *Manzanar Martyr: An Interview with Harry K. Ueno,* Fullerton, CA: California State University, 1986.

Evans, James Leroy. "The Indian Savage, the Mexican Bandit, the Chinese Heathen—Three Popular Stereotypes." Ph.D. dissertation, University of Texas, 1967.

Everett, Miles C. "Chester Harvey Rowell, Pragmatic Humanist and California Progressive." Ph.D. dissertation, University of California at Berkeley, 1966.

Fan, Ting C. *Chinese Residents in Chicago.* San Francisco: R & E Research, 1974.

Farley, M. Foster. "The Chinese Coolie Trade, 1845–1875." *Journal of Asian and African Studies* 3 (1968): 257–70.

Farrar, Nancy. *The Chinese in El Paso.* El Paso: Texas Western University Press, 1972.

Farwell, Willard B. *The Chinese at Home and Abroad.* San Francisco: Bancroft, 1885.

[Federal Reserve Bank, San Francisco.] "Report of the Federal Reserve Bank of San Francisco as Fiscal Agent of the United States on Its Operations in Connection with Evacuation Operations in Military Areas No. 1 and No. 2 during 1942." San Francisco, 1942.

Federal Reserve Bulletin. Washington, D.C., April 1943.

Feichter, Nancy Koehler. "The Chinese in the Inland Empire during the Nineteenth Century." M.A. thesis, State College of Washington, 1959.

Fine, Sidney. *Frank Murphy: The Washington Years.* Ann Arbor: University of Michigan Press, 1984.

_____. "Mr. Justice Murphy and the Hirabayashi Case." *Pacific Historical Review* 33 (1964): 195–209.

Fishman, Joshua. *Language Loyalty in the United States: The Maintenance and Perpetuation of Non-English Mother Tongues by American Ethnic and Religious Groups.* The Hague: Mouton, 1966.

Fitzgerald, Stephen. *China and Overseas Chinese, 1949–1970.* Cambridge: Cambridge University Press, 1972.

Fogel, Robert W., and Engerman, Stanley. *Time on the Cross.* Boston: Little, Brown and Co., 1974.

Fong, Diana. "America's 'Invisible' Chinese." New York *Times,* May 1, 1982.

Fong, Lawrence M. "Sojourners and Settlers: The Chinese Experience in Arizona." *Journal of Arizona History* 21 (1980): 227–56.

Foster, John W. "The Chinese Boycott." *Atlantic Monthly* 97 (1906): 118–27.

Foulke, William D. *The Life of Oliver P. Morton.* 2 vols. Indianapolis: Bowen-Merrill, 1899.

Francis, Lura. "This Historic Delta." *Pacific Historian* 23 (1979): 45–57.

Freeman, Miller. "Chinese Exclusion Repeal." Seattle *Post-Intelligencer,* October 16, 1943.

Fritz, Christian. "Bitter Strength *(k'u-li)* and the Constitution: The Chinese before the Federal Courts in California." *Historical Reporter* 1 (1980): 2–15.

Fujita, M. "The Japanese Associations of America." *Sociology and Social Research* 14 (1929): 211–17.

Fukuoka, Fumiko. "Mutual Life and Aid Among the Japanese in Southern California with Special Reference to Los Angeles." M.A. thesis, University of Southern California, 1939.

Fuller, Levi Varden. "The Supply of Agricultural Labor as a Factor in the Evolution of Farm Organization in California." Part 54. *Hearings before* a Subcommittee of the Committee on Education and Labor. . . . pursuant to S. res. 266 (74th Cong.). 76th Congress, 1st session, 1940.

Gardner, John Berdan. "The Image of the Chinese in the United States, 1885–1915." Ph.D. dissertation, University of Pennsylvania, 1961.

Garner, J. Anthony. *Hawaii Under Military Rule.* Stanford: Stanford University Press, 1955.

Gibson, Otis. *The Chinese in America.* Cincinnati: Hitchcock and Walden, 1877.

Girdner, Audrie and Loftis, Anne. *The Great Betrayal: The Evacuation of the Japanese-Americans during World War II.* New York: Macmillan Co., 1969.

Gladden, Washington. *Recollections.* Boston: Houghton Mifflin Co., 1909.

Glazer, Nathan. *Affirmative Discrimination.* New York: Basic Books, 1975.

Gleason, Philip. "Americans All: World War II and the Shaping of American Identity." *The Review of Politics* 43 (1981): 483–518.

Glenn, Evelyn Nakano. "The Dialectics of Wage Work: Japanese-American Women and Domestic Service, 1905–1940." *Feminist Studies* 6 (1980): 432–71.

_____. *Issei, Nisei, War Bride: Three Generations of Japanese American Women in Domestic Service.* Philadelphia: Temple University Press, 1986.

Glick, Clarence E. *Sojourners and Settlers: Chinese Migrants in Hawaii.* Honolulu: University of Hawaii Press, 1980.

Goldstein, Jonathan. *Philadelphia and the China Trade.* University Park: Pennsylvania State University Press, 1978.

Greeley, Andrew M. *Ethnicity in the United States: A Preliminary Reconnaissance.* New York: John Wiley & Sons, 1974.

Greenwood, Roberta S. "The Overseas Chinese at Home: Life in a 19th Century Chinatown in California." *Archaeology* 31, no. 4 (1979): 42–49.

Griffin, Eldon. *Clippers and Consuls: American Consular and Commercial Relations with Eastern Asia, 1845–1869.* Ann Arbor, MI: Edwards Brothers, 1938.

Grodzins, Morton. *Americans Betrayed: Politics and the Japanese Evacuation.* Chicago: University of Chicago Press, 1949.

Gruening, Ernest. *Many Battles: The Autobiography of Ernest Gruening.* New York: Liveright, 1973.

Gulick, Sidney L. *Hawaii's American-Japanese Problem.* Honolulu: Star Bulletin, 1915.

Hada, John Juji. "The Indictment and Trial of Iva Ikuko Toguri d'Aquino." M.A. thesis, University of San Francisco, 1973.

Halseth, James A., and Glasrud, Bruce A., eds. *The Northwest Mosaic: Minority Conficts in the Pacific Northwest.* Boulder, CO: Pruett, 1977.

Handlin, Oscar. *Race and Nationality in American Life.* Boston: Little, Brown and Co., 1957.

Hane, Mikiso. *Peasants, Rebels and Outcasts: The Underside of Modern Japan.* New York: Pantheon Books, 1982.

Hansen, Arthur A. "Cultural Politics in the Gila River Relocation Center, 1942–1943." *Arizona and the West* 27 (1986): 327–362.

Hansen, Arthur A., and Hacker, David A. "The Manzanar 'Riot': An Ethnic Perspective." In *Voices Long Silent: An Oral Inquiry into the Japanese American Evacuation*, edited by Arthur A. Hansen and Betty E. Mitson, pp. 47–79. Fullerton: California State University, 1974.

Hansen, Arthur A., and Mitson, Betty E., eds. *Voices Long Silent: An Oral Inquiry into the Japanese American Evacuation*. Fullerton: California State University, 1974.

Hansen, Marcus Lee. *The Problem of the Third Generation Immigrant*. Rock Island, IL: Augustana College, 1938.

Harrington, Joseph D. *Yankee Samurai*. Detroit: Pettigrew Enterprises, 1979.

Hata, Donald T., Jr. *"Undesirables": Early Immigrants and the Anti-Japanese Movement in San Francisco, 1892–1893*. New York: Arno Press, 1978.

Hayakawa, S. I. *Through the Communication Barrier*. New York: Harper & Row, 1979.

Heidhues, Mary F. Somers. *Southeast Asia's Chinese Minorities*. Melbourne, Aust.: Longman, 1974.

Heintz, William F. "The Role of Chinese Labor in Viticulture and Wine Making in Nineteenth Century California." M.S. thesis, Sonoma State College, 1977.

Heiser, Robert F., and Whipple, M. A., eds. *The California Indians: A Source Book*. Berkeley and Los Angeles: University of California Press, 1951.

Helwig, David John. "The Afro-American and the Immigrant, 1880–1930: A Study of Black Social Thought." Ph.D. dissertation, Syracuse University, 1973.

Hendrick, Irving G. *Public Policy Toward the Education of Non-White Minority Group Children in California, 1849–1970*. Riverside: University of California, Riverside, 1975.

Hennings, Robert. *James D. Phelan and the Wilson Progressives of California*. New York: Garland, 1985.

Herberg, Will. *Protestant-Catholic-Jew*. New York: Doubleday & Co., 1955.

Herzig, Jack. "Japanese Americans and Magic." *Amerasia Journal* 11, no. 2 (1984): 47–65.

Higgs, Robert. *Competition and Coercion*. Cambridge: Cambridge University Press, 1977.

Higham, John. *Strangers in the Land*. New Brunswick: Rutgers University Press, 1955.

Higham, John, ed. *Ethnic Leadership in America*. Baltimore: Johns Hopkins University Press, 1978.

Higman, B. W. "The Chinese in Trinidad, 1806–1838," *Caribbean Studies* 12, no. 3 (1972): 21–44.

Hinckley, Ted C. "The Politics of Sinophobia: Garfield, the Morey Letter and the Presidential Election of 1880." *Ohio History* 89 (1980): 381–99.

_____. "Prospectors, Profits and Prejudice." *The American West* 2, no. 2 (1965): 59–65.

Hirabayashi, Gordon. *Good Times, Bad Times: Idealism is Realism*. Argenta, British Columbia: Argenta Friends Press, 1985.

Hirata, Lucie C. "Free, Indentured, Enslaved: Chinese Prostitutes in 19th Century America." *Signs* 5 (1979): 3–29.

Ho, Nelson C. *Portland's Chinatown*. Portland, OR: Bureau of Planning, 1978.

Hollon, W. Eugene. *Frontier Violence: Another Look*. New York: Oxford University Press, 1974.

Hong, Y. C. *A Brief History of the Chinese American Citizens Alliance*. San Francisco: Chinese American Citizens Alliance, 1955.

Hosokawa, Bill. *JACL: In Quest of Justice*. New York: William Morrow and Co., 1982.

_____. *Nisei: The Quiet Americans*. New York: William Morrow and Co., 1969.

_____. "Our Own Japanese in the Pacific War." *American Legion Magazine* (July 1964): 15–17, 44–47.

Hosokawa, [William K.] *"Better Americans in a Greater America"*. n.p., n.d. [San Francisco, Japanese American Citizens League, ca. 1968.]

Hoy, William. *The Chinese Six Companies*. San Francisco: Chinese Consolidated Benevolent Association, 1942.

Hundley, Norris, ed. *The Asian American*. Santa Barbara: Clio Press, 1976.

Hung, William. "Huang Tsun-hsien's Poem 'The Closure of the Educational Mission in America'." *Harvard Journal of Asiatic Studies* 18 (1955): 50–73.

Hunter, Louise H. *Buddhism in Hawaii*. Honolulu: University of Hawaii Press, 1971.

Huttenback, Robert A. *Racism and Empire: White Settlers and Colored Immigrants in the British Self-Governing Colonies, 1830–1910*. Ithaca: Cornell University Press, 1976.

Ichihashi, Yamoto. *Japanese in the United States*. Stanford: Stanford University Press, 1932.

Ichioka, Yuji. *"Amerika Nadeshiko:* Japanese Immigrant Women in the United States." *Pacific Historical Review* 49 (1980): 339–57.

_____. *"Ameyuki-san:* Japanese Prostitutes in Nineteenth Century America." *Amerasia Journal* 4, no. 1 (1977): 1–22.

_____. "Asian Immigrant Coal Miners and the United Mine Workers of America: Race and Class at Rock Springs, Wyoming, 1907." *Amerasia Journal* 6, no. 2 (1979): 1–23.

_____. "A Buried Past: Early Issei Socialists and the Japanese Community." *Amerasia Journal* 1, no. 2 (1971): 1–25.

_____. "Early Issei Socialists and the Japanese Community." In *Counterpoint: Perspectives on Asian America,* edited by Emma Gee, pp. 47–62. Los Angeles: Asian American Studies Program, UCLA, 1976.

_____. "The Early Japanese Immigrant Quest for Citizenship: The Background of the 1922 Ozawa Case." *Amerasia Journal* 4, no. 2 (1977): 1–22.

_____. "An Instance of Private Japanese Diplomacy: Suzuki Bunji, Organized American Labor, and Japanese Immigrant Workers, 1915–1916." *Amerasia Journal* 10, no. 1 (1983): 1–22.

_____. "Japanese Associations and the Japanese Government: A Special Relationship, 1909–1926." *Pacific Historical Review* 46 (1977): 409–37.

_____. "Japanese Immigrant Labor Contractors and the Great Northern Railroad Companies, 1898–1907." *Labor History* 21 (1980): 325–50.

_____. "Japanese Immigrant Response to the 1920 California Alien Land Law." *Agricultural History* 58 (1984): 157–78.

_____. "The 1921 Turlock Incident: Forceful Expulsion of Japanese Laborers." In *Counterpoint: Perspectives on Asian America*, edited by Emma Gee, pp 195–99. Los Angeles: Asian American Studies Program, UCLA, 1976.

_____. "Recent Japanese Scholarship on the Origins of Japanese Immigration." *Immigration History Newsletter* 15, no. 2 (1983): 2–7.

Ichioka, Yuji; Sakata, Yasuo; Tsuchida, Nobuya; and Yasuhara, Eri. *A Buried Past: An Annotated Bibliography of the Japanese American Research Project Collection*. Berkeley and Los Angeles: University of California Press, 1974.

Integrated Education Associates. *Chinese-Americans: School and Community Problems*. Chicago: Integrated Education, 1972.

Irick, Robert L. *Ch'ing Policy toward the Coolie Trade, 1847–1878*. San Francisco: Chinese Materials Center, 1977.

Irons, Peter. *Justice at War: The Story of the Japanese Internment Cases*. New York: Oxford University Press, 1983.

Isaacs, Harold. *Images of Asia: American Views of China and India*. New York: Harper and Row, 1972.

Iyenaga, T., and Sato, K. *Japan and the California Problem*. New York: Putnam, 1921.

James, Thomas. "Exile Within: The Schooling of Japanese Americans, 1942–1945." Ph.D. dissertation, Stanford University, 1984.

_____. "Life Begins with Freedom: The College Nisei, 1942–1945." *History of Education Quarterly* 25 (1985): 155–74.

Janisch, Hudson N. "The Chinese, the Courts, and the Constitution: A Study of the Legal Issues Raised by Chinese Immigration to the United States, 1850–1902." J.S.D. dissertation, University of Chicago, 1971.

Japanese American Citizens League. National Committee for Iva Toguri. *Iva Toguri (d'Aquino): Victim of a Legend*. San Francisco: JACL, 1975.

Jiménez Pastrana, Juan. *Los Chinos en la Historia de Cuba, 1847–1930*. La Habana: Editorial de Ciencias Sociales, 1983.

Johnson, Donald B., comp. *National Party Platforms*. Urbana: University of Illinois Press, 1978.

Jones, Dorothy Knee. *A Century of Servitude: Pribilof Aleuts under U.S. Rule*. Lanham, MD: University Press of America, 1980.

Kachi, Teruko Okada. *The Treaty of 1911 and the Immigration and Alien Land Law Issue between the United States and Japan, 1911–1913*. New York: Arno Press, 1978.

Kahn, Judd. *Imperial San Francisco: Politics and Planning in an American City, 1897–1906*. Lincoln: University of Nebraska Press, 1979.

Kao, Timothy T. "An American Sojourn: Young Chinese Scholars in the United States, 1872–1881." *Connecticut Historical Society Bulletin* 46 (1981): 65–77.

Karlin, Jules Alexander. "The Anti-Chinese Outbreak in Tacoma, 1885." *Pacific Historical Review* 23 (1964): 271–83.

_____. "The Anti-Chinese Outbreaks in Seattle, 1885–1886." *Pacific Northwest Quarterly* 39 (1948): 103–29.

Kashima, Tetsuden. *Buddhism in America*. Westport, CT: Greenwood Press, 1977.

Kasindorf, Martin. "Asian-Americans: A 'Model Minority'." *Newsweek*, December 6, 1982.

Kawabe, Nobuo. "Japanese Businesses in the United States before World War II: The Case of Mitsubishi Shoji Kaisha, the San Francisco and Seattle Branches." Ph.D. dissertation, Ohio State University, 1980.

Kawakami, K. K. *The Real Japanese Question*. New York: Macmillan Co., 1921.

Kawasaki, Kanichi. "The Japanese Community of East San Pedro, Terminal Island, California." M.A. thesis, University of Southern California, 1931.

Ken, Sally. "The Chinese Community of Augusta, Georgia, from 1873 to 1971." *Richmond County History* 4 (1972): 51–60.

Kennan, George F. *American Diplomacy 1900–1950*. Chicago: University of Chicago Press, 1951.

Kennedy, Ruby Jo Reeves. "Single or Triple Melting Pot? Intermarriage Trends in New Haven, 1870–1940." *American Journal of Sociology* 49 (1944): 331–39.

_____. "Single or Triple Melting Pot? Intermarriage Trends in New Haven, 1870–1950." *American Journal of Sociology* 58 (1952): 56–59.

Kim, Hyung-chan. *Dictionary of Asian American History*. Westport, Conn.: Greenwood, 1986.

Kingston, Maxine Hong. *China Men*. New York: Alfred A. Knopf, 1980.

_____. *The Woman Warrior*. New York: Alfred A. Knopf, 1976.

Kitano, Harry H. L. *Japanese Americans: The Evolution of a Subculture*. Englewood, NJ: Prentice-Hall, 1969.

Kitano, Harry H. L., and Sue, Stanley. "The Model Minorities." *Journal of Social Issues* 29, no. 2 (1973): 1–9.

Klosterboer, W. *Involuntary Labour since the Abolition of Slavery: A Survey of Compulsory Labour throughout the World*. The Hague: Mouton, 1960.

Kojima, Masamori. "Judge John F. Aiso." Chicago *Scene*, August 1954, pp. 11–12.

Konvitz, Milton R. *The Alien and the Asiatic in American Law*. Ithaca: Cornell University Press, 1946.

Kranzler, David. *Japanese, Nazis and Jews*. New York: Yeshiva University Press, 1976.

Krebs, Sylvia. "The Chinese Labor Question: A Note on the Attitudes of Two Alabama Republicans." *Alabama Historical Quarterly* 38 (1976): 214–17.

_____. "John Chinaman and Reconstruction Alabama: The Debate and the Experience." *Southern Studies* 21 (1982): 369–83.

Kroeber, Theodore. *Ishi in Two Worlds*. Berkeley and Los Angeles: University of California Press, 1962.

Kublin, Hyman. *Asian Revolutionary: The Life of Sen Katayama*. Princeton: Princeton University Press, 1966.

Kutler, Stanley I. *The American Inquisition: Justice and Injustice in the Cold War*. New York: Hill and Wang, 1982.

———. "At the Bar of History: Japanese Americans versus the United States." *American Bar Foundation Research Journal*. 1985, no.2: 361–73.

———. "Forging a Legend: The Treason of 'Tokyo Rose'." *Wisconsin Law Review* 6 (1980): 1341–82.

Kuo Wen H. "Colonized Status of Asian-Americans." *Ethnic Groups* 5 (1981): 227–51.

Lach, Donald D. *Asia in the Making of Europe*. Chicago: University of Chicago Press, 1965.

LaFargue, Thomas E. *China's First Hundred*. Pullman: Washington State University Press, 1942.

———. "Yung Wing." In *Eminent Chinese of the Ching Period*, edited by Arthur W. Hummel, pp. 402–05. Washington: GPO, 1943.

Lai, Him Mark. "Island of Immortals: Chinese Immigrants and the Angel Island Immigration Station." *California History* 57 (1978): 88–103.

Lai, Him Mark; Lim, Genny; and Yung, Judy. *Island: Poetry and History of Chinese Immigrants on Angel Island, 1910–1940*. San Francisco: San Francisco Study Center, 1981.

Lapp, Rudolph M. *Blacks in Gold Rush California*. New Haven: Yale University Press, 1977.

Larsen, Lawrence H. *The Urban West at the End of the Frontier*. Lawrence: University of Kansas Press, 1978.

Latourette, Kenneth S. "Yung Wing." *Dictionary of American Biography* 20: 638–39. New York: Charles Scribner's Sons, 1936.

Lee, Elizabeth, and Abbott, Kenneth A. "Chinese Pilgrims and Presbyterians in the United States, 1851–1977." *Journal of Presbyterian History* 55 (1977): 125–44.

Lee, Everett S. "A Theory of Migration." *Demography* 3 (1966): 47–57.

Lee, Rose Hum. "Chinese in the United States Today." *Survey Graphic* 31 (1942): 419.

———. *The Growth and Decline of Chinese Communities in the Rocky Mountain Region*. New York: Arno Press, 1978.

Leighton, Alexander. *The Governing of Men: General Principles and Recommendations Based on Experiences at a Japanese Relocation Camp*. Princeton: Princeton University Press, 1945.

Leonetti, Donna L. "Fertility in Transition: An Analysis of the Reproductive Experience of an Urban Japanese-American Population." Ph.D. dissertation, University of Washington, 1976.

———. *Nisei Aging Project Report*. Seattle: The Project, 1983.

Lewytzkyj, Borys, and Stroynowski, Juliusz. *Who's Who in the Socialist Countries*. New York: K. G. Saur, 1977.

Li, Peter S. "Immigration Laws and Family Patterns: Demographic Changes Among Chinese Families in Canada, 1885–1971." *Canadian Ethnic Studies* 12, no. 1 (1980): 58–73.

Light, Ivan H. *Ethnic Enterprise in America: Business and Welfare among*

Chinese, Japanese, and Blacks. Berkeley and Los Angeles: University of California Press, 1972.

——. "The Ethnic Vice Industry, 1880–1944." *American Sociological Review* 42 (1977): 464–79.

——. "From Vice District to Tourist Attraction: The Moral Career of American Chinatowns." *Pacific Historical Review* 43 (1974): 367–94.

Lindsay, Robert. "The New Asian Immigrants." *New York Times Magazine,* September 10, 1983, pp. 22 ff.

Locklear, William R. "The Celestials and the Angels: A Study of the Anti-Chinese Movement in Los Angeles to 1882." *Historical Society of Southern California Quarterly* 42 (1960): 239–56.

Loh, Homer C. "Americans of Chinese Ancestry in Philadelphia." Ph.D. dissertation, University of Pennsylvania, 1944.

Loomis, Augustus Ward. "The Chinese as Agriculturists." *Overland Monthly* 3 (1870): 526–32.

——. "Chinese Women in California." *Overland Monthly* 2 (1869): 344–51.

Lou Raymond. "The Chinese American Community of Los Angeles, 1870–1900: A Case of Resistance, Organization, and Participation." Ph.D. dissertation, University of California, Irvine, 1982.

Low, Victor. *The Unimpressible Race: A Century of Educational Struggle by the Chinese in San Francisco.* San Francisco: East/West, 1982.

Lowe, Pardee. *Father and Glorious Descendant.* Boston: Little, Brown and Co., 1943.

Luebke, Frederick C. "Ethnic Minorities in the American West." In *Historians and the American West,* edited by Michael P. Malone, pp. 387–413. Lincoln: University of Nebraska Press, 1983.

Lyman, Stanford L. *The Asian in North America.* Santa Barbara: Clio Press, 1977.

——. *The Asian in the West.* Reno: Desert Research Institute, 1970.

——. *Chinese Americans.* New York: Random House, 1974.

——. "The Structure of Chinese Society in Nineteenth Century America." Ph.D. dissertation, University of California at Berkeley, 1961.

McClain, Charles J., Jr. "The Chinese Struggle for Civil Rights in Nineteenth Century America: The First Phase, 1850–1870." *California Law Review* 72 (1984): 529–68.

——. "The Chinese Struggle for Civil Rights in Nineteenth Century America: The Unusual Case of *Baldwin* v. *Franks.*" *Law and History Review* 3 (1985): 349–73.

McClatchy, V[alentine] S[tuart]. *America and Japan.* San Francisco, 1925.

——. *California's Language Schools.* Sacramento, 1922.

——. *The Germany of Asia.* Sacramento, 1919.

——, ed. *Four Anti-Japanese Pamphlets.* New York: Arno Press, 1978.

McCloy, John J. "Repay U.S. Japanese?" New York *Times,* April 10, 1983.

McGloin, John B. *Eloquent Indian.* Stanford: Stanford University Press, 1949.

McGrath, Roger D. *Gunfighters, Highwaymen, and Vigilantes.* Berkeley and Los Angeles: University of California Press, 1984.

McKee, Delber L. *Chinese Exclusion versus the Open Door Policy, 1900–1906.* Detroit: Wayne State University Press, 1977.

_____. "The Chinese Must Go! Commissioner General Powderly and Chinese Immigration, 1897–1902." *Pennsylvania History* 44 (1977): 37–51.

McLeod, Alexander. *Pigtails and Golddust.* Caldwell, ID: Caxton Press, 1947.

Malloy, William M., comp. 4 vols. *Treaties, Conventions . . . 1776–1909.* Washington, D.C., 1910.

Malone, Michael P., ed. *Historians in the American West.* Lincoln: University of Nebraska Press, 1983.

Man, Bryan Dai Yung. "Chinese Occupational Achievement Patterns: The Case of a 'Model Minority'." Ph.D. dissertation, University of California, Los Angeles, 1978.

Managhi, Russell M. "Virginia City's Chinese Community, 1860–1880." *Nevada Historical Society Quarterly* 24 (1981): 130–57.

Mann, Ralph. *After the Gold Rush: Society in Grass Valley and Nevada City, California, 1849–1870.* Stanford: Stanford University Press, 1982.

_____. "Community Change and Caucasian Attitudes toward the Chinese: The Case of Two California Mining Towns, 1850–1870." In *American Working Class Culture,* edited by Milton Cantor, pp. 397–422. Westport, CT: Greenwood Press, 1979.

Mark, Diane Mei Lin, and Chih, Ginger. *A Place Called Chinese America.* Dubuque, IA: Kendall/Hunt, 1982.

Markus, Andrew. *Fear & Hatred: Purifying Australia and California, 1850–1901.* Sydney: Hale and Iremonger, 1979.

Marwick, Arthur. "Problems and Consequences of Organizing Society for Total War." In *Mobilization for Total War: The Canadian, American and British Experience, 1914–1918, 1939–1945,* edited by N. F. Dreisziger, pp. 3–21. Waterloo, Canada: Wilfred Laurier University Press, 1981.

Mason, William M., and McKinstry, John A. *The Japanese of Los Angeles.* Los Angeles: Los Angeles County Museum, 1969.

Massachusetts Bureau of Labor Statistics. *Report, 1871.* Boston: Commonwealth of Massachusetts, 1872.

Matsumoto, Valerie. "Japanese American Women during World War II." *Frontiers* 8 (1984): 6–14.

May, Ernest R., and Thompson, James C., eds. *American-East Asian Relations: A Survey.* Cambridge: Harvard University Press, 1972.

Meagher, Arnold Joseph. *The Introduction of Chinese Laborers to Latin America: The "Coolie Trade," 1847–1874.* San Francisco: Chinese Materials Center, 1978.

Mei, June. "Socioeconomic Origins of Emigration: Guangdong to California, 1850–1882." *Modern China* 5 (1979): 463–501.

Miller, Stuart Creighton. *The Unwelcome Immigrant: The American Image of the Chinese, 1785–1882.* Berkeley and Los Angeles: University of California Press, 1969.

Millis, H. A. *The Japanese Problem in the United States.* New York: Macmillan Co., 1915.

Miyamoto, S. Frank. "An Immigrant Community in America." In *East Across the Pacific: Historical and Sociological Studies of Japanese Immigration and Assimilation,* edited by Hilary Conroy and T. Scott Miyakawa, pp. 217–43. Santa Barbara: Clio Press, 1972.

———. *Social Solidarity Among the Japanese in Seattle.* 1939. 3d ed. Seattle: University of Washington Press, 1984.

Miyamoto, S. Frank, and O'Brien, Robert W. "A Survey of Some Changes in the Seattle Japanese Community Since Evacuation." *Research Studies of the State College of Washington* 15 (1947): 147–54.

Modell, John. "Class or Ethnic Solidarity: The Japanese American Company Union." *Pacific Historical Review* 38 (1969): 192–206.

———. *The Economics and Politics of Racial Accommodation: The Japanese of Los Angeles, 1900–1942.* Urbana: University of Illinois Press, 1977.

Morison, Elting E., ed. *The Letters of Theodore Roosevelt.* 8 vols. Cambridge: Harvard University Press, 1951–54.

Moriyama, Alan Takeo. "The Causes of Emigration: The Background of Japanese Emigration to Hawaii, 1885–1894." In *Labor Immigration under Capitalism,* edited by Lucie Cheng and Edna Bonacich, pp. 248–76. Berkeley and Los Angeles: University of California Press, 1983.

———. *Imingaisha: Japanese Emigration Companies and Hawaii.* Honolulu: University of Hawaii Press, 1985.

Murayama, Yuzo. "The Economic History of Japanese Immigration to the Pacific Northwest, 1890–1920." Ph.D. dissertation, University of Washington, 1982.

Murphey, Rhoads. "Boston's Chinatown." *Economic Geography* 28 (1952): 245–55.

Murphy, Thomas D. *Ambassadors in Arms.* Honolulu: University of Hawaii Press, 1946.

Myer, Dillon S. *Uprooted Americans.* Tucson: University of Arizona Press, 1971.

Myrdal, Gunnar. *An American Dilemma.* 2 vols. New York: Harper & Brothers, 1944.

Naka, Kaizo. "Social and Economic Conditions Among Japanese Farmers in California." M.A. thesis, University of California, 1913.

National Committee for Redress. Japanese American Citizens League. *The Japanese American Incarceration: A Case for Redress.* San Francisco: JACL, 1978.

Nee, Victor G., and Nee, Brett de Bary. *Longtime Californ': A Documentary Study of an American Chinatown.* New York: Pantheon Books, 1973.

Nelson, Bruce. "Asians Come on Strong." Los Angeles *Times,* October 10, 1982.

Nelson, Douglas W. "The Alien Land Law Movement of the Late Nineteenth Century." *Journal of the West* 9 (1970): 46–59.

———. *Heart Mountain: The Story of an American Concentration Camp.* Madison: State Historical Society of Wisconsin, 1976.

Nitobe, Inazo. *The Intercourse between the United States and Japan.* Baltimore: Johns Hopkins University Press, 1891.

Nordhoff, Charles. *California, for Health, Pleasure and Residence.* New York: Harper & Brothers, 1873.

Norton, Frank. H. "Our Labor System and the Chinese." *Scribner's Monthly Magazine* 2 (1871): 61–70.

O'Brien, Robert W. *The College Nisei*. Palo Alto: Pacific Books, 1949.

Ogawa, Dennis, ed. *Jen Ken Po: The World of Hawaii's Japanese*. Honolulu: University of Hawaii Press, 1973.

_____, ed. *Kodomo No Tame Ni: For the Sake of the Children*. Honolulu: University of Hawaii Press, 1978.

Oishi, Gene. "The Anxiety of Being a Japanese-American." *New York Times Magazine*, April 28, 1985, pp. 54, 58–60, 65.

Ong, Paul. "Chinese Laundries as an Urban Occupation." In *Chinese Historical Society of the Pacific Coast, Annals*, edited by Douglas Lee, pp. 68–85. Seattle: 1983.

_____. "An Ethnic Trade: The Chinese Laundries in Early California." *Journal of Ethnic Studies* 8 (1981): 95–113.

Osako, Masako K. "Japanese-Americans: Melting into the All-American Pot." In *Ethnic Chicago*, edited by Peter d'A. Jones and Melvin G. Holli, pp. 313–44, 377–80. Grand Rapids: Eerdmans, 1981.

Ourada, Patricia. "The Chinese in Colorado." *Colorado Magazine* 29 (1952): 273–84.

Owens, Kenneth. "Pierce City Incident." *Idaho Yesterdays* 3 (1959): 8–13.

Palmer, Howard. *Patterns of Prejudice: A History of Nativism in Alberta*. Toronto: McClelland and Stewart, 1982.

Park, Robert E. *The Immigrant Press and Its Control*. New York: Harper & Brothers, 1922.

Paulsen, George E. "The Yellow Peril at Nogales: The Ordeal of Collector William H. Hoey." *Arizona and the West* 13 (1971): 113–28.

Peabody, Etta B. "The Effort of the South to Import Coolies, 1865–1870." M.A. thesis, Baylor University, 1967.

Pérez de la Riva, Juan. *El barracón: esclavitud y capitalismo en Cuba*. Barcelona: Editorial Critica, 1978 (1st ed., Havana: Editorial de Ciencas Sociales, 1975).

Perkins, Clifford A. "Reminiscences of a Chinese Inspector." *Journal of Arizona History* 17 (1976): 181–200.

Petersen, William. *Japanese Americans: Oppression and Success*. New York: Random House, 1971.

_____. "Success Story, Japanese American Style." *New York Times Magazine*, January 6, 1966, pp. 20 ff.

Peterson, F. Ross. *Idaho*. New York: W. W. Norton & Co., 1976.

Pitt, Leonard. *The Decline of the Californios*. Berkeley and Los Angeles: University of California Press, 1969.

Powers, Marshall K. "Chinese Coolie Migration to Cuba." Ph.D. dissertation, University of Florida, 1953.

Pozzetta, George E. and Kersey, Harry A. "Yamato Colony: A Japanese Presence in South Florida." *Tequesta* 36 (1976): 66–77.

President's Commission on Immigration and Naturalization. *Whom We Shall Welcome*. Washington, D.C., 1959.

Price, Charles A. *The Great White Walls Are Built: Restrictive Immigration to*

North America and Australia, 1836–1888. Canberra: Australian National University Press, 1974.

Pritchett, C. Herman. *Civil Liberties and the Vinson Court.* Chicago: University of Chicago Press, 1956.

Quan, Robert Seto. *Lotus Among the Magnolias.* Jackson: University of Mississippi Press, 1982.

Quarles, Benjamin. *Frederick Douglass.* New York: Associated Publishers, 1948.

Quinn, Larry D. "Chink, Chink, Chinaman: The Beginnings of Nativism in Montana." *Pacific Northwest Quarterly* 58 (1967): 82–89.

Reinecke, John E. *Feigned Necessity: Hawaii's Attempt to Obtain Chinese Contract Labor, 1921–23.* San Francisco: Chinese Materials Center, 1979.

Rhoades, Edward J. M. "The Chinese in Texas." *Southwestern Historical Quarterly* 81 (1977): 1–36.

Richardson, James D., comp. *Messages and Papers of the Presidents.* 11 vols. Washington, D.C., 1907.

Riddle, Ronald. *Flying Dragons, Flowing Streams: Music in the Life of San Francisco's Chinese.* Westport, CT: Greenwood Press, 1983.

Riggs, Fred. *Pressures on Congress: A Study of the Repeal of Chinese Exclusion.* New York: King's Crown, 1950.

Ringle, Kenneth D. [pseud., An Intelligence Officer]. "The Japanese in America: The Problem and the Solution." *Harper's Magazine* 185 (1942): 489–97.

Rodecape, Lois. "Celestial Drama in the Golden Hills: The Chinese Theater in California, 1849–1869." *California Historical Society Quarterly* 23 (1944): 97–116.

Rohe, Randall E. "After the Gold Rush: Chinese Mining in the Far West, 1850–1890." *Montana* 32 (1982): 2–19.

Rosenman, Samuel I., comp., *The Public Papers and Addresses of Franklin D. Roosevelt, 1928–1945.* 13 vols. New York: Macmillan Co. and Random House, 1938–1950.

Rostow, Eugene V. "The Japanese American Cases—A Disaster." *Yale Law Journal* 54 (1945): 489–533.

_____. "Our Worst Wartime Mistake." *Harper's Magazine* 191 (1945): 193–201.

_____. *The Sovereign Prerogative.* New Haven: Yale University Press, 1962.

Rudolph, Frederick. "Chinamen in Yankeedom: Anti-Unionism in Massachusetts in 1870." *American Historical Review* 53 (1947): 1–29.

Rudolph, Gerald E. "The Chinese in Colorado, 1869–1911." M.A. thesis, University of Denver, 1964.

Rummel, George A. "The Delta Chinese: An Exploratory Study in Assimilation." M.A. thesis, University of Mississippi, 1966.

Rusco, Mary. "Chinese in Lovelock, Nevada: History and Archaeology." *Halcyon* (1981): 141–51.

Saloutos, Theodore. *They Remember America.* Berkeley and Los Angeles: University of California Press, 1956.

Sandmeyer, Elmer C. *The Anti-Chinese Movement in California*. 1939. 2d ed. Urbana: University of Illinois Press, 1973.

Saxton, Alexander. "The Army of Canton in the High Sierra." *Pacific Historical Review* 35 (1966): 114–52.

_____. *The Indispensable Enemy: Labor and the Anti-Chinese Movement in California*. Berkeley and Los Angeles: University of California Press, 1971.

Schwantes, Carlos A. *Radical Heritage: Labor, Socialism, and Reform in Washington and British Columbia, 1885–1917*. Seattle: University of Washington Press, 1979.

Schwartz, Harvey. "A Union Combats Racism: The ILWU's Japanese American 'Stockton Incident' of 1945." *Southern California Quarterly* 62 (1980): 161–76.

Schweitzer, John L. "The Social Unity of Tucson's Chinese Community." M.A. thesis, University of Arizona, 1952.

Schwendinger, Robert J. "Chinese Sailors: America's Invisible Merchant Marine." *California History* 57 (1978): 58–69.

Seager, Robert. "Some Denominational Reactions to Chinese Immigration to California, 1856–1892." *Pacific Historical Review* 28 (1959): 49–66.

Shankman, Arnold. "Black on Yellow: Afro-Americans View Chinese Americans, 1850–1935." *Phylon* 39 (1978): 1–17.

Shanks, W. F. G. "Chinese Skilled Labor." *Scribner's Monthly Magazine* 2 (1871): 494–99.

Shibutani, Tamotsu. *The Derelicts of Company K*. Berkeley and Los Angeles: University of California Press, 1978.

Shima, George. *An Appeal to Justice*. Stockton, CA, 1920.

Shin, Linda P. "China in Transition: The Role of Wu T'ing-fang (1842–1922)." Ph.D. dissertation, University of California, Los Angeles, 1970.

Shinn, Charles Howard. "Cooperation on the Pacific Coast." *Johns Hopkins Studies in History and Political Science* 6 (1888): 447–86.

Shirey, Orville C. *Americans: The Story of the 442nd Combat Team*. Washington, D.C.: Infantry Journal, 1946.

Shumsky, N. L., and Springer, L. M. "San Francisco's Zone of Prostitution, 1880–1934." *Journal of Historical Geography* 7 (1981): 71–94.

Sissons, D. C. S. "*Karayuki-san*: Japanese Prostitutes in Australia, 1887–1916." *Historical Studies* 17 (1977): 323–41, 474–88.

Siu, Paul C. P. "The Chinese Laundryman: A Study in Social Isolation." Ph.D. dissertation, University of Chicago, 1954.

_____. "The Isolation of the Chinese Laundryman." In *Contributions to Urban Sociology*, edited by E. W. Burgess and D. J. Bogue, pp. 429–42. Chicago: University of Chicago Press, 1964.

Skinner, G. William. *Chinese Society in Thailand*. Ithaca: Cornell University Press, 1957.

_____. "Overseas Chinese in Southeast Asia." *The Annals of the American Academy of Political and Social Science* 321 (1959): 136–47.

Smith, Bradley F. *The Shadow Warriors: O.S.S. and the Origins of the C.I.A.* New York: Basic Books, 1983.

Smollar, David. "Violence, Slurs—U.S. Asians Feel Trade Backlash." Los Angeles *Times,* September 14, 1983.

Solomon, Barbara Miller. *Ancestors and Immigrants.* Cambridge: Harvard University Press, 1956.

Somma, Nicholas A. "The Knights of Labor and Chinese Immigration." M.A. thesis, Catholic University of America, 1952.

Soule, Frank, Gihon, John H., and Nisbet, James. *The Annals of San Francisco.* New York: D. Appleton, 1855.

Sowell, Thomas. *Race and Economics.* New York: D. McKay, 1975.

Sowell, Thomas, ed. *Essays and Data on American Ethnic Groups.* Washington, D.C.: Urban Institute, 1978.

Special Committee on Chinese Immigration. *Chinese Immigration: Its Social, Moral and Political Effect.* Sacramento: State Printer, 1875.

Spencer, Robert. "Japanese Buddhism in the United States, 1940–1946: A Study in Acculturation." Ph.D. dissertation, University of California at Berkeley, 1947.

Spicer, Edward H., Hansen, Asael T., Luomala, Katherine, and Opler, Marvin K. *Impounded People: Japanese-Americans in the Relocation Centers.* Tucson: University of Arizona Press, 1969.

Spickard, Paul R. "The Nisei Assume Power: The Japanese Citizens League [sic], 1941–1942." *Pacific Historical Review* 52 (1983): 147–74.

Spier, Robert F. G. "Food Habits of Nineteenth-Century Chinese." *California Historical Society Quarterly* 37 (1958): 79–84, 129–36.

————. "Tool Acculturation among 19th Century California Chinese." *Ethnohistory* 5 (1958): 97–117.

Stanley, Gerald. "Frank Pixley and the Heathen Chinee: A Phylon Document." *Phylon* 40 (1979): 224–28.

Steel, Ronald. *Walter Lippmann and the American Century.* Boston: Little, Brown and Co., 1980.

Steelman, Joseph F. "The Immigration Movement in North Carolina, 1865–1890." M.A. thesis, University of North Carolina, 1941.

Stratton, David H. "The Snake River Massacre of Chinese Miners, 1887." In *A Taste of the West: Essays in Honor of Robert G. Athearn,* edited by Duane A. Smith, pp. 109–29. Boulder, CO: Pruett, 1983.

Sumner, Charles. *The Works of Charles Sumner.* 15 vols. Boston: Lee and Shepard, 1870–1883.

Svensrud, Marian. "Attitudes of the Japanese toward Their Language Schools." *Sociology and Social Research* 17 (1933): 259–64.

Swartout, Robert R., Jr. "In Defense of the West's Chinese: Denny's Brief for Li Hung-chung." *Oregon Historical Quarterly* 83 (1982): 25–36.

Swisher, Carl B. *Stephen J. Field.* Washington, D.C.: Brookings Institution, 1930.

Tabrah, Ruth. *Hawaii: A Bicentennial History.* New York: W. W. Norton & Co., 1980.

Taft, Philip. "Labor History and the Labor Movement Today." *Labor History* 7 (1966): 70–77.

Tanimoto, Cathy Lynn. "Changing Japanese Ethnicity: A Case Study of Gardena, California." M.A. thesis, Louisiana State University, 1975.

Tateishi, John. *And Justice for All: An Oral History of the Japanese American Detention Camps.* New York: Random House, 1984.

Taylor, Paul S. "Foundations of California's Rural Society." *California Historical Society Quarterly* 24 (1945): 193–228.

Taylor, Sandra C. *Advocate of Understanding: Sidney Gulick and the Search for Peace with Japan.* Kent, OH: Kent State University Press, 1984.

_____. "The Federal Reserve Bank and the Relocation of the Japanese in 1942." *The Public Historian* 5 (1983): 9–30.

_____. "Japanese Americans and Keetley Farms: Utah's Relocation Colony." *Utah Historical Quarterly* 54 (1986): 328–44.

Teng, Ssu-yü, and Fairbank, John K. *China's Response to the West: A Documentary Survey, 1839–1923.* Cambridge: Harvard University Press, 1965.

Thernstrom, Stephen, ed. *Harvard Encyclopedia of American Ethnic Groups.* Cambridge: Harvard University Press, 1980.

Thomas, Dorothy Swaine. *The Salvage.* Berkeley and Los Angeles: University of California Press, 1952.

_____. "Some Social Aspects of Japanese-American Demography." *Proceedings of the American Philosophical Society* 94: (1950) 459–80.

Thomas Dorothy S., and Nishimoto, Richard S. *The Spoilage.* Berkeley and Los Angeles: University of California Press, 1946.

Tigner, James. "Japanese Immigration into Latin America: A Survey." *Journal of Inter-American Studies and World Affairs* 23 (1981): 457–82.

Tinker, Hugh. *A New System of Slavery: The Export of Indian Labour Overseas, 1830–1920.* London: Oxford University Press, 1974.

Tipton, Gary P. "Men Out of China: Origins of the Chinese Colony in Phoenix." *Journal of Arizona History* 18 (1977): 341–56.

Truman, Harry S. *Public Papers, 1952–53.* Washington, D.C., 1961.

Trull, Fern Coble. "The History of the Chinese in Idaho from 1864 to 1910." M.A. thesis, University of Idaho, 1946.

Tsai, Shih-shan Henry. *China and the Overseas Chinese in the United States, 1868–1911.* Fayetteville: University of Arkansas Press, 1983.

_____. *The Chinese Experience in America.* Bloomington: Indiana University Press, 1986.

_____. *The Chinese in Arkansas.* Little Rock: Arkansas Endowment for the Humanities, 1981.

_____. "The Emergence of Early Chinese Nationalist Organizations in America." *Amerasia Journal* 8, no. 2 (1981): 121–44.

_____. "Preserving the Dragon Seeds: The Evolution of Ch'ing Emigration Policy." *Asian Profile* 7 (1979): 497–506.

_____. "Reaction to Exclusion: The Boycott of 1905 and Chinese National Awakening." *The Historian* 39 (1976): 95–110.

_____. "Reaction to Exclusion: Ch'ing Attitudes toward Overseas Chinese in the United States, 1848–1906." Ph.D. dissertation, University of Oregon, 1970.

Tule Lake Plaque Committee, Northern California-Western Nevada District Council, Japanese American Citizens League. *Tule Lake.* San Francisco, 1979.

Turner, Albert Blythe. "The Origins and Development of the War Relocation Authority." Ph.D. dissertation, Duke University, 1967.

Uchida, Naosaku. *The Overseas Chinese: A Bibliographical Essay Based on the Resources of the Hoover Library*. Stanford: The Hoover Institution, 1960.

Uchida, Yoshiko. *Desert Exile: The Uprooting of a Japanese American Family*. Seattle: University of Washington Press, 1982.

U.S. Commission on Civil Rights. *Hearings*. 1960.

U.S. Congress. House. *Coolie Trade*. 36th Congress, 1st session, 1860, House Executive Document 443 [Ser. 1069].

_____. *Japanese American Evacuation Claims*. Hearings before Subcommittee No. 5 of the Committee on the Judiciary, 83d Congress, 2d session, 1954.

_____. Committee on Immigration and Naturalization. *Japanese Immigration Hearings*. 66th Congress, 2d session, 1921.

_____. *Miscellaneous Document 81*. 42d Congress, 3d session, 1873.

_____. *Report 732*. 80th Congress, 1st session, 1947.

_____. *Report 1911*. 77th Congress, 2d session, 1942.

_____. *Report 2124*. 77th Congress, 2d session, 1942.

_____. Select Committee Investigating National Defense Migration. *Hearings*. 77th Congress, 2d session, 1942.

U.S. Congress. Senate. *Commission in Wartime Relocation and Internment of Civilians Act, Hearing before the Committee on Government Affairs*. 96th Congress, 2d session, 1980.

_____. *Japanese in the City of San Francisco, California. Document 147*. 59th Congress, 2d session, 1907.

_____. *Miscellaneous Document 20*. 45th Congress, 2d session, 1879.

_____. *Report 1531*. 80th Congress, 2d session, 1948.

_____. *Report 1740*. 80th Congress, 2d session, 1948.

_____. *Report of the Joint Special Committee to Investigate Chinese Immigration. Report 689*. 44th Congress, 2d session, 1877.

U.S. Department of Commerce. Bureau of the Census. *Census of Population*. Various volumes; various censuses.

U.S. Department of State. *Foreign Relations of the United States, 1924*. Washington, D.C., 1939.

_____. *Report of the Honorable Roland S. Morris on Japanese Immigration and Alleged Discriminatory Legislation against Japanese Residents in the United States*. Washington, D.C., 1921. [New York: Arno Press, 1978.]

U.S. Department of the Interior. War Relocation Authority. *Administrative Highlights of the WRA Program*. Washington, D.C., 1946.

_____. *Community Government in War Relocation Centers*. Washington, D.C., 1946.

_____. *The Evacuated People: A Quantitative Description*. Washington, D.C., 1946.

_____. *Impounded People*. Washington, D.C., 1946.

_____. *Legal and Constitutional Aspects of the WRA Program*. Washington, D.C., 1946.

_____. *Wartime Exile: The Exclusion of the Japanese Americans from the West Coast*. Washington, D.C., 1946.

_____. *The Wartime Handling of Evacuee Property*. Washington, D.C., 1946.

_____. *WRA: The Story of Human Conservation*. Washington, D.C., 1946.

U.S. Federal Emergency Relief Administration. *Unemployment Relief Census: October, 1933. United States Summary*. Washington, D.C., 1933.

U.S. Immigration Commission. *Reports of the Immigration Commission*. Vol. 23. Washington, D.C., 1911.

U.S. Selective Service System. Special Monograph 10. *Special Groups*. 2 vols. Washington, D.C., 1953.

U.S. War Department. *Final Report: Japanese Evacuation from the West Coast, 1942*. Washington, D.C., 1943.

Uyeda, Clifford I. *A Final Report and Review: The Japanese American Citizens League National Committee for Iva Toguri*. Seattle: Asian American Studies Program, University of Washington, 1980.

van den Berghe, Pierre L. *Race and Racism*. New York: John Wiley & Sons, 1967.

Wakatsuki, Yasuo. "Japanese Emigration to the United States, 1866–1924: A Monograph." *Perspectives in American History* 12 (1979): 387–516.

Walker, Harry T., Jr. "Gold Mountain Guests: Chinese Migration to the United States, 1848–1852." Ph.D. dissertation, Stanford University, 1976.

Walkowitz, Judith. *Prostitution and Victorian Society*. Cambridge: Cambridge University Press, 1980.

Walsh, Henry L. *Hallowed Were the Gold Dust Trails*. Santa Clara, CA: University of Santa Clara Press, 1946.

Wang, L. Ling-Chi. "The Yee Version of Poems from the Chinese Immigration Station." *Asian American Review* (1976): 117–26.

Wang, Sing-Wu. *The Organization of Chinese Emigration, 1848–1888*. San Francisco: Chinese Materials Center, 1978.

Wang, Y. C. *Chinese Intellectuals and the West, 1872–1949*. Chapel Hill: University of North Carolina Press, 1966.

Ward, David. *Cities and Immigrants: A Geography of Change in Nineteenth Century America*. New York: Oxford University Press, 1971.

Ward, David A. "The Unending War of Iva Ikuko Toguri D'Aquino." *Amerasia Journal* 1, no. 2 (1975): 26–35.

Watson, James L. *Emigration and the Chinese Lineage: The Mans in Hong Kong and London*. Berkeley and Los Angeles: University of California Press, 1975.

Waugh, Isami Arifuku. "The Trial of Tokyo Rose." *Bridge*, February 1974, pp. 5–12, 40–46.

Wax, Rosalie H. "The Destruction of a Democratic Impulse." *Human Organization* 12 (1953): 11–21.

_____. "The Development of Authoritarianism: A Comparison of the Japanese-American Relocation Centers and Germany." Ph.D. dissertation, University of Chicago, 1951.

_____. *Doing Fieldwork: Warnings and Advice*. Chicago: University of Chicago Press, 1971.

_____. "Reciprocity as a Field Technique." *Human Organization* 11 (1952): 34–37.

_____. "Twelve Years Later: An Analysis of Field Experience." *American Journal of Sociology* 63 (1957): 133–42.

Weinberg, Julius. *Edward Alsworth Ross and the Sociology of Progressivism.* Madison: State Historical Society of Wisconsin, 1972.

Welch, Richard E. *George Frisbie Hoar and the Half-Breed Republicans.* Cambridge: Harvard University Press, 1971.

White, Thomas E. "A History of Railroad Workers in the Pacific Northwest, 1883–1934." Ph.D. dissertation, University of Washington, 1981.

Wilbert, William F. "The Chinese in Whitman County, 1870–1910." *Bunchgrass Historian* 10, no. 1 (1982): 10–25.

Wilcox, B. P. "Anti-Chinese Riots in Washington." *Washington Historical Quarterly* 20 (1929): 204–12.

Willson, Margaret, and MacDonald, Jeffrey L. "Racial Tension at Port Townsend and Bellingham Bay, 1870–1886." *Annals of the Chinese Historical Society of the Pacific Northwest* 1 (1983): 1–15.

Wilson, Arlen Ray. "The Rock Springs, Wyoming, Chinese Massacre, 1885." M.A. thesis, University of Wyoming, 1967.

Wilson, Carol Green. *Chinatown Quest.* 2d ed., rev. San Francisco: California Historical Society, 1974.

Wilson, Robert A., and Hosokawa, Bill. *East to America: A History of the Japanese in the United States.* New York: William Morrow and Co., 1980.

Wittke, Carl. *We Who Built America.* New York: Prentice-Hall, 1939.

Wolf, Eric R. *Europe and the People without History.* Berkeley and Los Angeles: University of California Press, 1982,

Wollenberg, Charles M. *All Deliberate Speed: Segregation and Exclusion in California Schools, 1855–1975.* Berkeley and Los Angeles: University of California Press, 1977.

Wong, Bernard P. *A Chinese American Community.* Singapore: Chopmen Enterprises, 1979.

_____. "A Comparative Study of the Assimilation of the Chinese in New York City and Lima, Peru." *Comparative Studies in Society and History* 20 (1978): 335–58.

_____. "Elites and Ethnic Boundary Maintenance: A Study of the Roles of Elites in Chinatown, New York City." *Urban Anthropology* 6 (1977): 1–22.

_____. "Patronage, Brokerage, Entrepreneurship and the Chinese Community of New York." Ph.D. dissertation, University of Wisconsin, Madison, 1974.

_____. "Social Stratification, Adaptive Strategies and the Chinese Community of New York." *Urban Life* 5 (1976): 33–52.

Wong, Charles Choy. "Black and Chinese Grocery Stores in Los Angeles' Black Ghetto." *Urban Life* 5 (1977): 439–64.

_____. "The Continuity of Chinese Grocers in Southern California." *Journal of Ethnic Studies* 8 (1980): 63–82.

Wong, Jade Snow. *Fifth Chinese Daughter.* New York: Harper & Brothers, 1950.

_____. *No Chinese Stranger*. New York: Harper & Row, 1975.

Woon, Yuen-fong. "The Voluntary Sojourner Among the Overseas Chinese: Myth and Reality." *Pacific Affairs* 56 (1983/84): 673–90.

Worthy, Edmund H., Jr. "Yung Wing in America." *Pacific Historical Review* 39 (1965): 265–87.

Wortman, Roy T. "Denver's Anti-Chinese Riot, 1880." *The Colorado Magazine* 42 (1965): 275–91.

WPA Writers Program, Montana. *Copper Camp*. New York: Hastings House, 1943.

Wu, Ching-Chao. "Chinatowns: A Study of Symbiosis and Assimilation." Ph.D. dissertation, University of Chicago, 1928.

Wu, Ting-fang. *America Through the Spectacles of an Oriental Diplomat*. New York: Frederick A. Stokes, 1914.

Wunder, John R. "The Chinese and the Courts in the Pacific Northwest: Justice Denied." *Pacific Historical Review* 52 (1983): 191–211.

_____. "The Courts and the Chinese in Frontier Idaho." *Idaho Yesterdays* 25, no. 1 (1981): 21–32.

_____. "Law and the Chinese in Frontier Montana." *Montana* 30, no. 3 (1980): 18–31.

Wynne, Robert E. *Reaction to the Chinese in the Pacific Northwest and British Columbia, 1850–1910*. New York: Arno Press, 1978.

Yanagisako, Sylvia Junko. "Explicating Residence: A Cultural Analysis of Changing Households among Japanese-Americans." In *Households: Comparative and Historical Studies of the Domestic Group*, edited by Robert McC. Netting et al., pp. 33–52. Berkeley and Los Angeles: University of California Press, 1984.

_____. *Transforming the Past: Tradition and Kinship Among Japanese Americans*. Stanford: Stanford University Press, 1985.

Yang, Alexander Chung Yuan. "O Comercio dos 'Coolie' (1819–1920)." *Revista de História* [Brazil] 56, no. 112 (1977): 419–28.

Yarwood, A. T., and Knowling, M. J. *Race Relations in Australia: A History*. Melbourne: Methuen, 1982.

Yen, Tzu-Kuei. "Chinese Workers and the First Transcontinental Railroad of the United States of America." Ph.D. dissertation, St. Johns University, 1977.

Yoneda, Karl. *Ganbatte! Sixty-Year Struggle of a Kibei Worker*. Los Angeles: Asian American Studies Center, UCLA, 1983.

Yu, Connie Young. "The Chinese in American Courts." *Bulletin of Concerned Asian Scholars* 4 (1972): 22–30.

_____. "Rediscovered Voices: Chinese Immigrants and Angel Island." *Amerasia Journal* 4, no. 2 (1977): 123–39.

Yung, Judy. "A Bowlful of Tears: Chinese Women Immigrants on Angel Island." *Frontiers* 2 (1977): 52–55.

Yung, Wing. *My Life in China and America*. New York: Holt, 1909.

Zangwill, Israel. *The Melting Pot*. New York: Macmillan Co., 1909.

Zo, Kil Young. "Chinese Emigration: The Means of Obtaining Passage to America." *Journal of Asiatic Studies* [South Korea] 18 (1975): 215–30.

_____. *Chinese Immigration into the United States, 1850–1880.* New York: Arno Press, 1978.

_____. "Credit Ticket System for the Chinese Emigration into the United States." *Journal of Nanyang University* 8/9 (1974–75): 129–39.

Index

Chiang Kai-shek, 188–89, 301
Chiang Kai-shek, Madame, 92, 189
Chicago: Chinese Americans in, 70, 88; Japanese Americans in, 286
Chih, Ginger, 95
Chin, Irving S. K., 324
Chin, Vincent, 341–43
China, 301, 308–9; and Burlingame Treaty, 36, 38, 54; and emigration, 6, 10–15, 24, 26, 110; and regulation of overseas students, 28n; and United States, 36, 58, 189, 301, 308–9, 328; remittances to, 86; and Treaty of 1881, 55; and Treaty of 1888 (unratified), 56; and World War II, 189, 191
Chinatowns, 18–19, 324–25; in Boston, 18; in Butte, 72–76, 88–89; in San Francisco, 18–19, 22, 24, 38, 69–70, 89–95, 161, 300, 324
Chinda, Sutemi, 104–5, 109–11, 139–41
Chinese Americans: acculturation of, 26–28, 82–83, 89, 98–99, 323–28; and agriculture, 21, 48–49, 108–9; burial practices of, 88; in Butte, Mont., 72–86, 88–89; in California, 12–13, 15, 17–19, 21–22, 34–35, 38, 69–71, 89–95, 98–99; and Central Pacific railroad, 15, 19, 36–38, 46, 48; and China, 188, 304–5, 327; and communal organizations, 23–26, 81–86, 98–99, 304–5, 308–9; communities, 17–18; and "confession system," 307–8; and crime, 22–23, 85–86, 343; demography of, 16–17, 60, 67–73, 96–97, 155, 172, 190–91, 198–99, 312–13, 321–22, 343–44; and education, 26–27, 92, 111, 123, 191, 313–16, 325–26, 329; and employment, 19–21, 74, 77, 108, 160, 191–92, 313–16; as entrepreneurs, 75–79, 91, 108, 323; and ethnic economy, 22; families of, 79, 81–83, 86–87, 89, 94–98, 306–8; and Irish, 30, 47; and Japanese Americans, 109, 111, 155, 161, 184–85, 205, 302–3, 320–23; and laundries, 39, 74, 79–81; in Massachusetts, 41–43; as merchants, 25–26, 91; in military service, 299–300; as miners, 33–35, 74, 77; naturalization of, 35, 43–44, 196; and newspapers, 97, 308; and paper sons, 94–97, 307–8; and political activities, 187, 309–11; in postwar era (1945–1960), 283–99, 309; as property owners, 75–76; and prostitution, 16–17, 22–23, 51; and remittances, 85–86; and return

migration, 16, 304; in South, 40–41; as strikebreakers, 41–43; urbanization of, 68–70, 157; violence against, 58–66, 74–76, 341–43; and welfare, 88–89; and women, 16–17, 44, 78, 81–83, 96–98, 198–99, 326–28; and World War II, 186–89, 282–83, 299–300
Chinese American Citizens' Alliance, 99n
Chinese Consolidated Benevolent Association. *See* Chinese Six Companies
Chinese Educational Mission (1872–1881), 26–27
Chinese Exclusion Act, 55–58, 91–92, 107, 112, 149, 191–98, 283, 306
Chinese Exclusion Convention (1901), 113
Chinese immigrants, 9–28, 96–97, 172, 198–99, 304, 306–7, 309, 324–25, 343; in Australia, 13; Chinese attitudes toward, 11–12; and coolie trade, 10, 14, 19–22; and European immigrants, 6–8, 17–18; and Japanese, 101, 103–5, 114, 166; and Southeast Asia, 10–11
Chinese Six Companies, 24–26, 45–46, 84, 88, 90
Chiu, Ping, 21
Chong, Wa, 91
Chuck, Maurice, 308
Civilian Conservation Corps, 226
Civil Rights Bill of 1870, 34
Civil Rights Movement, 39
Cleveland, Grover, 56–57
Cleveland, Ohio: Japanese Americans in, 286
Collins, Wayne, 295
Colorado: anti-Chinese violence in, 59–61; Japanese in, 133–34
Commission on the Wartime Relocation and Internment of Civilians (CWRIC), 282, 335–41
Committee on Un-American Activities (House), 129
Communal organizations: Chinese American, 23–26, 81–86, 98–99, 304–5, 308–9; Japanese American, 114, 128–32, 164–65, 179–82
"Concentration camps," 226–28
Condit, Ira M., 92
Congressional investigation of Chinese (1876), 44–54
Connally, Tom, 310
Connecticut: Chinese in, 27
Conroy, Hilary, 100
Coolidge, Mary Roberts, 30